INSIGHT GUIDES

The world's largest collection· of visual travel guides

Jacqueline Russo

SICILY

Original edition by Lisa Gerard-Sharp
Photography by Lyle Lawson
Editorial Director: Brian Bell

Discovery CHANNEL

APA PUBLICATIONS
Part of the Langenscheidt Publishing Group

L

INSIGHT GUIDES

SICILY

CONTACTING THE EDITORS: Although every effort
is made to provide accurate information in this
publication, we live in a fast-changing world and would
appreciate it if readers would call our attention to any
errors or outdated information that may occur by
writing to us at Apa Publications,
P.O. Box 7910, London SE1 1WE, England.
Fax: (44) 171-403-0290.
e-mail: insight@apaguide.demon.co.uk.

First Edition 1993
Second Edition (updated) 1999

Distributed in the United States by
Langenscheidt Publishers Inc.
46–35 54th Road
Maspeth, NY 11378
Fax: (718) 784 0640

Distributed in the UK & Ireland by
GeoCenter International Ltd
The Viables Centre, Harrow Way
Basingstoke, Hampshire RG22 4BJ
Fax: (44) 1256-817988

Distributed in Australia & New Zealand by
Hema Maps Pty. Ltd
24 Allgas Street, Slacks Creek 4127
Brisbane, Australia
Tel: (61) 7 3290 0322
Fax: (61) 7 3290 0478

Worldwide distribution enquiries:
APA Publications GmbH & Co. Verlag KG
(Singapore branch)
38 Joo Koon Road, Singapore 628990
Tel: 65-8651600
Fax: 65-8616438

Printed in Singapore by
Insight Print Services (Pte) Ltd
38 Joo Koon Road
Singapore 628990
Fax: 65-8616438

This guidebook combines the interests
and enthusiasms of two of the
world's best known information pro-
viders: Insight Guides, whose range of titles
has set the standard for visual travel guides
since 1970, and Discovery Channel, the
world's premier source of nonfiction television programming.

The editors of Insight Guides provide both
practical advice and general understanding
about a destination's history, culture, institutions and people. Discovery Channel
and its Web site, www.discovery.com, help
millions of viewers explore their world from
the comfort of their own home and also
encourage them to explore it firsthand.

Sicily is far from being an empty
canvas. Countless films have
captured a brooding intensity, sullen
people and the shadow of the Mafia. Yet this
atmospheric island is a sunnier, more open
society than it is given credit for and, by mixing
the incisive reporting and stunning photography for which Insight Guides are renowned,
this book sets out to view it with a fresh eye.

The first edition of *Insight Guide: Sicily* was
researched during the second "Palermo
Spring", a time of hope and renewal following
the turmoil of Mafia murders in 1992. After
the massacre of Judges Falcone and Borsellino, the mood of Sicilian outrage helped
prompt the cleansing of Italian politics – a
process still underway. Contrary to popular
thinking, ordinary Sicilians were only too
eager to confide in a stranger or to speak out.

Gerard-Sharp

Lisa Gerard-Sharp, the book's project editor, is a broadcaster and journalist with a
special interest in Italy. In contributing to
Insight Guides to Tuscany, Florence and
Naples, she has beaten a steady retreat
south to Sicily, the least Italian of islands. In
putting together this book, she found herself
intrigued by the clash between the legendary
immutability of Sicily and a seeming striving
for change, at least amongst the young.

But there is no such thing as a neutral
travel writer. The experience of writing this
book was one of drowning in life stories, each

more impassioned or more improbable than the last. A shocked American from Buffalo confided that he had come in search of his grandfather's grave yet discovered that his *émigré* father, Jo Maggadino, had masterminded Sicily's Castellammare Mafia in the 1950s.

The investigative team plunged deep into Sicily to explore places on and off the beaten track. The intrepid spirit was personified by American photographer **Lyle Lawson**, an Insight Guides veteran who, despite being robbed, fell for the island's charm. She is responsible for the superb photography, accomplished with energy and determination. "For this book I made five trips to the island, logged 7,165 miles (11,465 km) and met nothing but kindness from the locals – except for the two robbers on their motorbike."

Lawson

Marks

Gattuso

Simeti

Carter

The writing team is truly international. **John Gattuso** is a second-generation American who is particularly drawn to the rural landscape of Palermo province, a way of life he sampled before settling in New Jersey. Not that he falls for a simplistic pastoral portrayal. His view of the island is tinged by an awareness of its ambivalence and complexity. Still, he is cautiously optimistic about society, agreeing with Sicilian sociologist Pino Arlacchi: "We may be at the beginning of the people's rebellion against the Mafia."

Mary Taylor Simeti is an American writer who divides her time between Palermo and her farm in Alcamo. She came to Sicily to do voluntary work for Danilo Dolci's community centre but ended up marrying a Palermitan professor and writing books on the Sicilian seasons, festivals and cuisine. As a long-term resident, she struggled to reconcile "Sicilian fatalism and an inherited American belief in civic commitment." Her perseverance is rewarded in small civic victories, an appreciation of Sicily's eclectic history, dramatic countryside and imaginative cuisine.

Rowlinson Carter is an Insight Guides stalwart with a passion for Classical history. He was fascinated by the Sicilians' early experiments with democracy but notes that "the democratic interlude soon gave way to a race of full-blooded tyrants".

Pamela Barton Sciuto, a professional guide to Sicily, uses her insider knowledge to advise on accommodation and eating out. She praises Taormina, her home and Sicily's main resort, as "sophisticated yet not intimidating, an appealing place for families, older visitors and fun-lovers". The book's Travel Tips section covers everything from festivals to further reading, shopping to security, from culture to climate and clothing requirements for climbing Mount Etna.

Gay Marks is a Palermo-based journalist and author of a light-hearted book on her experiences as a foreigner in Sicily. She is fascinated by the gulf between city and country values and "the contrast between the entrepreneurial east of the island and the more *mafioso*, lethargic west".

Alison Jones mines her experience of how Sicilian society works (or doesn't) to provide language tips (such as essential vocabulary for museums "closed for restoration"). She also guides the reader through the tricks of actually arriving at a destination rather than travelling hopefully.

The original manuscript was attended to in Apa's London editorial office by **Dorothy Stannard**, who provided invaluable editorial assistance. **Jill Anderson** managed the production, and proof-reading and indexing were completed by **Pam Barrett**.

Gabriella Ferranti interrupted her electoral campaign to mastermind the editor's research trips. **Leoluca Orlando** provided invaluable information on Sicilian politics and the Mafia. Professors **Giovanna Catinella Dara** and **Aurelio Anselmo** generously unlocked the doors to Palermitan society. **Eleanor** and **Pino Bua** embodied Sicilian hospitality and were a mine of information. **Pilar Visconti** was the perfect guide to Palermo, both the city of the living and the city of the dead. In central Sicily, **Vincenzo** and **Antonia Burrogano** and their daughter **Salvina** shared a wealth of knowledge. The current edition was updated by **Daniela Nicolosi** a native Sicilian residing in Rome.

CONTENTS

TRAVEL TIPS

"Do you really think, Chevalley, that you are the first who has hoped to channel Sicily into the flow of universal history?" The Prince's challenge in *The Leopard* hangs heavily in the torpid atmosphere. Sicily may be Italian, but the islanders are Latin only by adoption. They may look back at Magna Graecia or Moorish Sicily but tend to be bored by their exotic past. Mostly, they sleep-walk their way through history, as if it were a bad play in a long-forgotten language.

Floating not far beneath the surface is a kaleidoscope of swirling foreignness against a backdrop of Sicilian fatalism. This is the legacy of a land whose heyday was over 700 years ago. It is most visible in the diversity of architectural styles, brought together under one roof in a remarkable mongrel, Siracusa cathedral. Yet Sicilians themselves, as they often boast, are *bastardi puri* ("pure bastards"), the product of racial overdose.

The assumption that people want overt power, leadership, laws, equality, a democratically calibrated society is laughably unSicilian. The Greeks' lessons in democracy fell on stony ground: the Sicilians responded with a race of full-blooded tyrants. The Mafia, with greater superficial sophistication, have shown equal disdain for democratic niceties: their shadowy state within a state is more effective than the pale, public model. Sicilians dismiss democracy as a system only suitable for "Nordic" countries.

Until recently, most landed, educated Sicilians declined public office, preferring private gain to public good. As the Prince says in *The Leopard*: "I cannot lift a finger in politics. It would only get bitten." Poor Sicilians knuckled under or emigrated, often flourishing on foreign soil.

Millions have conquered the United States with a classic Sicilian combination: contacts, cuisine and cunning, symbolised by the Pizza Connection, the Mafia's imaginative drugs cartel. The heroin distribution and money-laundering ring operated in the guise of an international pizza chain. This is the deadly product served by Sicilian history. As the writer Leonardo Sciascia says: "History has been a wicked stepmother to us Sicilians." Yet it is this heritage of doom, drama and excess that draws visitors to an island marooned between Europe and Africa.

"Sicily is a paradise disguised as hell, a hell disguised as paradise," according to the writer Gesualdo Bufalino. "That is probably why the ferry that brings tourists across the Straits of Messina has been nicknamed *Charon*, after the boatman who ferried souls to the Underworld." Goethe too found Sicily intoxicating, from the Classical temples and Etna's eruptions to the volcanic nature of the Sicilians. "To have seen Italy without seeing Sicily is not to have seen Italy at all – for Sicily is the key to everything."

Preceding pages: a "butterfly" at Sciacca Carnival; the Trinacria, Sicily's ancient "three-cornered" symbol; four-legged friend; sailing off Panarea, Aeolian Islands; the Classical temple at Segesta; Centuripe, a traditional hill-top town; tales of Norman knights are told through stock characters in Sicilian puppetry. Left, losing one's head in a Catania park.

Paleolithic Age: First settlers make their homes in caves on Monte Pellegrino and the Egadi Islands.

15–10C BC: The Siculi (Sicels), Sicani (Sicans) and Elymni (Elymians) settle.

858 BC: Phoenicians establish trading sites.

733 BC: The Corinthians found Siracusa.

5C BC: Height of Greek civilisation in Sicily. Siracusa is the greatest city, rivalling Athens in power and prestige.

circa **570–555 BC:** Phalaris is Tyrant of Akragas (Agrigento).

485–476 BC: Gelon is Tyrant of Siracusa.

466–405 BC: Democratic interlude.

405–367 BC: Dionysius I is Tyrant of Siracusa.

254 BC: Palermo falls to the Romans.

212 BC: Siracusa falls to the Romans.

AD 276–278: Barbarians invade Sicily.

AD 324–327: Reign of Constantine the Great. The capital of the Empire is moved to Constantinople (Istanbul).

AD 395: Sicily becomes part of the Western Roman Empire.

AD 410: Rome is attacked by the Visigoths.

AD 440: The Vandals, under General Genseric, invade Sicily.

AD 493: Sicily is overrun by the Ostrogoths.

535: Belisarius, Byzantine general, conquers Sicily for Emperor Justinian of Byzantium.

651: First major Arab raid on Sicily.

726: The Byzantine emperor confiscates all Papal property in Sicily.

800: Pope Leo III proclaims Charlemagne Emperor of the Roman Empire.

831: Palermo falls to the Saracens (Arabs).

965: All of Sicily is under Arab domination. Palermo becomes second largest city in the world (after Constantinople).

1071: Norman Count Roger de Hauteville (Altavilla) takes Palermo "for Christendom".

1130: His son, Roger II, becomes King of Sicily and Palermo is one of the most magnificent cities in Europe.

1198–1250: Emperor Frederick II of Sicily (*Stupor Mundi*).

1266: Charles of Anjou is crowned King of Sicily. (Angevin rule until 1282.)

1282: The Sicilian Vespers. Popular Sicilian uprising against the French.

1302: The Aragonese begin a 200-year rule.

1442: Alfonso V, King of Aragon reunites Naples and Sicily and takes the title King of Two Sicilies.

1502: The Spanish crown assumes control of Sicily, but the Barons retain much power.

1669: Etna erupts, destroying Catania and east coast towns.

1693: Massive earthquake strikes the east.

1713: Treaty of Utrecht. Victor Amadeus II of Piedmont-Savoy becomes King of Sicily.

1720: The Duke of Savoy surrenders Sicily for Sardinia. Austrian Viceroys rule.

1734: The Spanish Bourbons rule Sicily through Viceroys.

1759: The Kingdom of Naples and Sicily passes to Ferdinand.

1798: Lord Nelson is given the Duchy of Bronte in Sicily.

1806–15: The British occupation of Sicily.

1816: The Kingdom of the Two Sicilies is created under the Bourbons when Austria reconquers Naples.

1848–49: Sicilian Revolution.

1860: Giuseppe Garibaldi and his "Mille" (1000) land at Marsala, and force the Bourbons off Sicily.

1861: Sicily joins Kingdom of Italy.

1900: Emigration is the highest in Europe.

1908: Messina destroyed by an earthquake, which leaves around 84,000 victims.

1915: Italy joins the Allies in World War I.

1922–43: Fascism in Italy. Mussolini is PM.

1943: Invasion of Sicily by the Allies.

1946: Sicily is granted regional autonomy by the Italian Parliament.

1957: Italy becomes an EEC founder.

1982: Mafia kills General dalla Chiesa.

1982: The "super-grass" (*pentito*) Tommaso Buscetta first denounces *Cosa Nostra* to Sicilian anti-Mafia pool of judges.

1986: The Mafia super-trials (*maxiprocessi*) indict hundreds.

1992: Eruption of Mount Etna.

1992: Mafia assassinations of Euro MP Salvatore Lima and two magistrates.

1995: Giulio Andreotti, seven times Prime Minister of Italy, is brought to Palermo to face charges of collaborating with the Mafia.

Sicilian history is a cavalcade of invasion. The Sicani, Siculi, Elymni, Carthaginians and Greeks were the first. The invasions continued with the second wave of Carthaginians followed by Romans, sundry Italians, mercenaries and myriad slaves, Jews, Vandals, Saracens, Normans and Spaniards. Some, like the Vandals, did little more than vandalise, but the majority remained for long periods, adding another rich layer to Sicily's extraordinary fusion of genes and culture.

The islanders may not have been great shapers of their own destiny but the powers of Sicilian subversiveness were substantial. In response to invasion, Sicily proved itself to be a ball and chain around its conquerors' necks: sullen, slothful, uncooperative, a millstone dragging its rulers into futile conflict while leaving noble Sicilians free to live in their own luxurious private theatre.

Strategic Sicily: Children spot Sicily on a map as the "ball" at the toe of the "boot" of Italy. But their grasp of Classical history would be better served by reflecting on the closeness of the island to Cap Bon, the tip of North Africa. The sea is only 100 miles (160 km) wide; from high ground, one can gaze across to ancient Carthage, where Tunis now stands, and contemplate a long-dead rival.

The straits separating Sicily from Africa are a bottleneck. The Mediterranean Sea is therefore not round but kidney-shaped. When the known world was limited to the lands lining the Mediterranean, the boundaries were Phoenicia, modern-day Lebanon, and the Straits of Gibraltar. Sicily was not only in the centre but divided "the world" into two. The ancient superpowers could settle for domination of one side of the sea or the other. To control both, they had to possess Sicily.

Size matters: Sicily's size is diminished by notions of a soccer ball. In modern terms it is not huge: a third the size of Ireland, a quarter of Cuba; but to the ancients it was almost a continent. Certainly, it was big enough for implacable enemies like the Phoenicians and Greeks to occupy separate bits without tripping over one another. There were even cases of two wholly unrelated wars being fought on the island simultaneously.

The island has always been at the mercy of larger forces swirling around its shores. Yet Sicily was never quite big enough to be a power in its own right, although Siracusa (Syracuse) was once the greatest city in Europe. Sicily has been dragged into practically every major Mediterranean war as an adjunct to one or other of the adversaries.

All nations around the Mediterranean (and others too) have shaped Sicilian history; all

languages spoken around the Mediterranean have been spoken in Sicily. Most historians agree that Sicily has been subjugated and plundered for its strategic site, fertile lands, art treasures, and endless supply of slaves, mercenaries and feudal peasants.

Yet the image of a pathetic Sicilian scapegoat should not go unchallenged. A more radical line of historical enquiry might be: did she fall or was she pushed? To most foreign historians, she was pushed, forced to cohabit with brutal foreign bed-fellows. But, as Voltaire suggested, perhaps she even jumped willingly into the conqueror's arms. Sensing a slight to macho Southern pride,

Left, Phoenician head found on Mozia. Right, anthropomorphic dancers in cave drawing.

modern Sicilian historians have fought back. They cite instances of spirited resistance: the Great Slave Revolts against the Greeks and Romans and the infamous Sicilian Vespers, the uprising against the French. More dubiously, the rise of the Mafia has also been credited to Sicilian resourcefulness.

Yet sleeping with the enemy is the classic Sicilian defence. The Phoenician temple priestesses in Erice did it literally. Later Sicilians have been more subtle. The Mafia co-operated fully with the American landings in 1943. In the same year, the Italian army, the Communists and the Mafia buried the hatchet and formed an unholy alliance against the threat of Sicilian separatism. But

this is not common prostitution: it is the arrogance of a courtesan who can retreat into the purity of her head while the sordid world flounders below.

Origins: Much like aggrieved native Americans on Columbus Day, the Sicilians do not accept that they were "discovered" by the ancient Greeks. The controversy has reverberations to this day. Depending on where Sicilians live, there is still an identification with one or other of the early racial groups. Ancestry matters in Sicily, even if larded with two millennia of intervening myth.

As a new land open to conquest, Sicily was the America of the ancient world. It was invaded in turn by Phoenicians, Greeks and Romans. But it was also a land with a disgruntled indigenous people who did not take kindly to being swamped by a refined yet more powerful culture. The native Sicilians had their own deities, it was just that the Greeks marketed their gods better.

Mythological tales have Sicily founded by Vulcan's forge, by the Promethean god Hephaestus or by the winged Daedalus from Crete. But more significant is the cultural distinction between Siculi and Sicani, Sicily's foremost native peoples. This ancestral mystique is still at the heart of the islanders' *Sicilianità*, their innate "Sicilian-ness".

Racial splits: There were three indigenous groups with separate cultures and languages. The Elymni (Elymians) held sway in the north-west; also in the west were the Sicani (Sicans); and the east was home to the Siculi (Sicels). While the Sicani were the most hostile to Greek settlers, the Siculi and even the Elymni were Hellenised by contact with the Greeks. The natives were united only in mutual dislike.

The Elymni are the most mysterious of the early Sicilians. Present from the Iron Age onwards, they were based around Segesta and Erice, where their city walls remain. According to Thucydides, the Greek chronicler, the Elymni were Trojans who escaped the Fall of Troy. They certainly claimed Trojan descent but their origins are disputed, with conflicting claims linking them to Mycenaean or Minoan civilisations and even to Asia Minor. The Elymni were clearly the most open to Phoenician culture but found it expedient to accommodate the Greeks, with the exception of the hated colony at Selinunte.

The Sicani were an ancient Semitic race, possibly immigrants from Libya and Syria. Their main colony was Sant'Angelo Muxaro in Agrigento province, where myth and history merge. Daedalus supposedly escaped Crete by making waxen wings and arrived in Sant'Angelo to a red-carpet welcome from King Kokalos of the Sicani. What is beyond doubt is that this belligerent race resisted Greek influence and fought against such Hellenised cities as Akragas (Agrigento).

The Siculi came from Liguria or Latium in the 13th century before Christ. According to Thucydides, they "defeated the Sicani in battle, drove them to the south and west of the island, and renamed it Sicily instead of

Sicania". These seafarers and farmers were gradually Hellenised by the Greek settlers on the eastern coast. However, in Dorian Greek settlements such as Siracusa, the Siculi were reduced to serfdom. Even the Ionian settlements rarely granted Greek citizenship.

Still, in exceptional cases the Greeks elevated the Siculi from the status of barbarians (non-Greeks) to persons qualified to marry Greeks, the ultimate accolade. The Siculi worshipped pan-Hellenic gods, as witnessed by a temple to Demeter at Morgantina near Enna. Sicily abounds in Siculi settlements, with the best one in Ispica.

The Phoenicians: Sicily was the exception to the rule that these seafarers, having founded

ily is dotted with Punic remains. Erice has the base of a Phoenician temple and shrine to Astarte, the goddess of fertility, while commemorative steles and stonework remain at Solunto. Lilybaeum, modern Marsala, boasts a necropolis and a sophisticated Punic ship.

On the island colony of Motya, the base for attacks against the Greeks, is a Punic harbour as well as the notorious sacrificial altar. Undoubtedly, there were sensationalist aspects of their culture, such as sacred prostitution and human sacrifice. The jars of charred infants would imply that Motya was not an ideal place to bring up a baby.

Since then, the balance of power has swung from Siculi to Sicani and back again. In black

Carthage, were keener on trading than colonising. The old Carthaginian sector occupied north-western Sicily and was closely involved with the neighbouring Sicani race. They only fortified their settlements at Solunto, Motya (Mozia) and Panormus (Palermo) when their livelihood was threatened by Greek expansion.

The Phoenicians became "Carthaginians" as their North African colony prospered and eclipsed their Levantine home. Northern Sic-

Left, stylised Greek bust. Above, the earliest Punic tomb, discovered on Mozia; winged beasts battle for supremacy in a primitive mosaic.

and white terms, it is a split between Greek Eastern Sicily and Arab Western Sicily. During Hellenisation, the Siculi, the most recent settlers, triumphed as the dominant culture. However, under Roman rule, the Sicani in the west bounced back. Under the Byzantines, the "Greek" east of the island was in the ascendant while with the advent of the Arabs, Western Sicily had its revenge.

Today, the racial split affects everything, from manners and morals to modern trade and the Mafia. Since Sicily is now named after the Hellenised Siculi race, it is clear that Greek culture ultimately triumphed, in name at least.

The Sicily of Magna Graecia had a population of over 3 million, greater than Athens and Sparta combined. The islanders, even the smouldering Sicilians and Phoenicians who monopolised cities like Panormus (Palermo), spoke Greek and practised Greek art. Agriculture flourished and the island became the granary of the Mediterranean. Athenian prosperity, then paying for the building of the magnificent Acropolis, depended on funds siphoned off from Sicily.

But none of this promise was self-evident when the Greek migrants drifted to Sicily, more as an escape from civil strife than as part of a master plan for domination of the West. Sicily's eastern flanks were settled by Ionian-speaking Greeks from the Peloponnese while Dorian colonies favoured the south coast. They were unaware that there were already Phoenician settlements on the western shore.

The first colony was Naxos (734 BC), founded by Chalcidian Greeks. After Naxos came other east coast colonies also with Ionian links: Zankle (Messina), Leontinoi (Lentini) and Katane (Catania). On the south coast were Dorian colonies settled by Greeks from Rhodes and Crete: Gela, Akragas (Agrigento), Selinunte and Heraclea Minoa. Syrakusai, the greatest colony of all (Siracusa to the Italians or Syracuse to us) was founded by Corinthians a year after Naxos. These colonies were ruled by "tyrants", a term which in its original sense simply meant men who seized power instead of inheriting it. In so far as the colonists stayed in touch with home, it was with a specific city or island. So Sicilian settlements living cheek by jowl often had conflicting loyalties, which erupted whenever Greek fought Greek at home, as they did almost continuously.

Carthage on the rampage: Sicily's first sharp taste of what the rest of its history would be occurred in 480 BC, when the Carthaginians mounted a massive attack on Greece's western flank – which included Sicily. The

Carthaginian commander Hamilcar (forerunner of the great Carthaginian general Hamilcar Barca) set sail for Sicily with an army of 300,000 mercenaries in 200 galleys and 3,000 transport ships. Hamilcar besieged Himera (Termini Imerese) by land and sea, prompting the resident tyrant Theron to appeal for help from Gelon, his counterpart in the powerful Greek city of Siracusa (Syracuse). Gelon's forced march through the mountains with 50,000 men and 5,000 cavalry is a minor military epic, and he was soon

in a position to throw a cordon around the Carthaginian siege. Hamilcar, meanwhile, had asked Selinunte, "the unfaithful (Greek) city of the west", to back up his forces.

Sicilian military history is full of trickery, and Gelon set the standard with a Trojan Horse approach: his cavalry masqueraded as Hamilcar's reinforcements from Selinunte. The Carthaginian ranks opened up, whereupon Gelon's interlopers charged the beached Carthaginian ships and torched them. The column of smoke was Gelon's signal to bring his men storming down; 150,000 Carthaginians were slain in the battle. Hamilcar died a Phoenician death at Himera: "he spread

Left, sculpture of Venus Landolina, exhibited at the Museo Archeologico, Siracusa. **Above**, the Trinacria, the symbol of Sicily, also at the Museo Archeologico.

out his arms and prayed to the setting sun, and threw himself into the flames upon the altar the last and noblest burnt-offering of his own sacrifice."

Both this astounding military victory and the equally improbable Greek naval victory at Salamis occurred on the same day in 480 BC. The Athenians celebrated by building the Parthenon; Gelon built the temples of Demeter and Persephone in Siracusa on the strength of Carthage's cash indemnity. Carthage didn't attack again for 70 years.

The victory confirmed Gelon as the most powerful figure in the Greek world. After Himera, Gelon adopted a conciliatory attitude towards Phoenician settlements on Sic-

ily, notably Panormus (Palermo) and Motya (Mozia). In return, the Carthaginians were required to build two temples to Athene and asked to sacrifice animals rather than human babies. However, babies were sacrificed for a long time to come. The archaeological evidence is found in the Tophet (sacrificial cemetery) excavated at Motya.

Fun and games: Gelon's successor, Hieron I (478–466 BC) basked in his glory and forged unity among some Greek Sicilian city states. The Sicilians, especially Siracusa, dominated the Olympiads, excelling at chariot races and mule cart racing. Officially the athletes competed for token prizes, but spon-

sorship was as lucrative then as now, so a winner could expect to enjoy free housing forever. Victory celebrations lasted a year, and the foremost poets of the day were commissioned to compose verses in the victor's honour. The poet Simonides felt his muse leave him when asked to write an ode to a victorious mule. He managed an opening line, "All hail, ye daughters of wind-swift mares", and went on to finish the poem with no further references to the beast.

The lure of quick commissions attracted the finest Greek literary talents to Sicily. Aeschylus was among them, although he probably left Greece downcast after losing the tragedy-writing competition to young Sophocles. In any case he died an extraordinary death at Gela. An eagle seized a tortoise, and looking down from a great height for a rock on which to drop and break it, mistook Aeschylus's bald pate for a polished stone. That was the end of the tragedian, who was given a moving funeral and monument by the people of Gela.

The temples of Selinunte, Segesta and Agrigento, which are the lasting monuments of this Golden Age of Tyranny, did not match the architectural subtlety of the Parthenon in Athens, but are splendid nonetheless. The ruins of Selinunte, south of Marsala, are the remains of seven temples, which fell like dominoes after an earthquake.

The dawn of democracy: The Greek tyrannies collapsed, said Aristotle, because in the absence of orderly rules of succession they fell victim to dynastic struggles. Within a few years of Hieron I's death virtually every city had sacked its tyrant, and the island moved *en bloc* into an experiment with a new form of government: democracy.

The democracy in question was hardly a multi-party system, majority rule, one-man, one-vote – still less, one-woman, one-vote. Only an elite qualified for the vote. Slaves, even freed men, were definitely out, as were the Sicilian-born descendants of immigrants. Nor did children of foreigners married to bona-fide citizens qualify.

But Greek-style democracy was present in Sicily. Public debate was lively and free, and the island produced orators of whom the mainland Greeks were envious. The ballot box existed, in that a stipulated proportion of enfranchised citizens could write down the name of someone they thought ought to be banished for a fixed term for the public good.

Great slave revolts: The Sicilian experiment with democracy lasted 70 years and stirred long dormant instincts. The Hellenised but still distinct native inhabitants felt aggrieved. They never attained citizenship so could not aspire to being second-class citizens. "Sicilian Power" was born, personifed by Ducetius in 500BC.

The native Sicilians had been pushed back into the interior by Greeks who liked living on the coast. Ducetius popped up as the self-proclaimed "King of the Sicilians". Within six years he had persuaded several Siculi towns to back him. Growing militancy led to an armed attack on Enna and Akragas. The rebels, the fear that Siracusa was involved led Akragas to declare war on the senior city.

Athenian adventures: Sicilian cities were always ready to fight at the drop of a hat. The Athenians were only too happy to intervene for their own ends, particularly as Siracusa emerged as a rival. But remoteness from Greek mainland politics meant that Sicilians avoided alignment with either the Dorian (Spartan) or Ionian (Athenian) factions.

Athens had a political stake in Sicily and, after defending its colony of Leontinoi against Siracusa in 427 BC, desired further influence. The quarrelsome Sicilian cities of Selinunte and Segesta provided a pretext. When Selinunte asked Siracusa for help,

rebels enjoyed modest success before being overwhelmed by a punitive expedition despatched by Siracusa.

Ducetius was spared on condition that he left town; the city offered him a pension to live in Corinth, "home" to most Siracusans. He cut an exotic figure in exile, and such was his appeal that Corinthians joined him in a clandestine return to Sicily, with the aim of founding a colony on Sicilian Liberation lines. But when Akragas was attacked by his

<u>Left</u>, **Athena and Perseus battle with the Medusa. <u>Above</u>, detail from Attic vase, Museo Archeologico at Gela.**

Segesta went running to Athens, offering to pay the costs of military aid, plus a handsome premium. Prudent Athens decided to look into Segesta's credit-worthiness and sent representatives on an inspection tour.

The Athenian ambassadors were received in Segesta with a show of breathtaking splendour. They were led up to the temple of Aphrodite on Mount Eryx (Erice) above Drepanon (Trapani) and shown a vast collection of sacred vessels made of gold and silver and dripping with precious stones. The treasures were too sacred, they were told, to be touched or even to be viewed except from a reverential distance. The ambassadors were then marched off to sumptuous banquets, everywhere eating off gold and silver plate.

In Athens, the ambassadors had no hesitation in recommending that 60 ships be put at the disposal of Segesta. On the question of hard payment, the city had admittedly given them only enough to cover the cost of the first month but there could be no doubt that the balance would be forthcoming. Unfortunately, the temple treasures were fakes. The gold and silver plate was a single, recycled set borrowed from the Siculi. As for the silver bullion provided as a deposit, that was also borrowed. However, the fraud was not exposed and the 250 ships which sailed from Piraeus with 25,000 men was the largest armada to have set forth from a Greek city.

But the commanders dithered, disappeared in search of booty and, only after two years at sea did they finally reach Siracusa. So many men had sickened, died or jumped ship that morale was woeful. In the meantime, Sparta had sent troops to Siracusa to organise defences. The battle for control of Siracusa's great harbour took place in 413 BC and was the greatest victory of Greeks over Greeks. The Athenians were humiliated and never returned home. The 7,000 survivors were lowered by crane into the stone quarries of Siracusa. Lush gardens now occupy the quarries, but they were then barren, a sheer drop of 100 ft (30 metres) into a hell which was stifling hot by day and freezing at night.

Carthage strikes back: It was second nature to the Sicilians that once the Athenian threat was seen off, they reverted to fighting among themselves. It was equally in character that two wars should be going on at once. One was a continuation of the wounds opened by Ionians against Dorians on the Greek mainland; more predictably, the other was between Segesta and Selinunte, implacable enemies.

Segesta turned to Carthage for help, thus triggering the second Carthaginian invasion. Hannibal, grandson of Hamilcar, had no grudge against Selinunte, but he had a score to settle with the Greeks, in particular with Himera, the Sicilian city where his grandfather died. Hannibal arrived with a mercenary force at Lilybaeum, where Carthaginian invaders landed almost as a routine. He made quick work of Selinunte. In fact, it ceased to exist as a city forever.

Then Hannibal turned his attention to personal vengeance and breached Himera's defences. "A massacre of course began," says the historian Edward Freeman. "But a mere massacre was not what he wanted." The 3,000 male survivors were taken to where Hamilcar had died, tortured, and offered as sacrifices to the memory of the dead general.

On his return in 480 BC, Hannibal attacked Akragas, second only to Siracusa among Sicilian cities but rusty in war. The ensuing siege was interrupted by Hannibal's death. In the course of digging trenches, the Carthaginians exposed corpses. A plague swept through the camp, and Hannibal was one of the casualties. Hostilities were suspended for a decent burial, and demoralised Carthaginians revived only when Hannibal's successor, Himilkon, showed that he meant business by sacrificing his own son to their beloved god Moloch.

Akragas's pampered soldiers lasted surprisingly well, and the city fell after an eight-month siege. While a huge amount of art and treasure was shipped back to Carthage, the city was not gutted like Himera. Akragas was a byword for luxury in Magna Graecia so it was reward enough to raid the temples and drain the legendary wine cellars dry.

The Siracusan generals were blamed for Akragas's defeat in speeches by a spirited demagogue, one Dionysius. Almost inevitably, in 405 BC, Dionysius was given full powers to sort out the military mess. He immediately crossed the Straits to Leontini to round up all men under 40 to serve as his bodyguards. Siracusa had another tyrant.

Dionysius I reorganised the army, but nothing could stop the Carthaginian advance on Siracusa. The city was only saved by a return of the plague among the Carthaginian forces. With over half the army dead, the vanquished force slunk home to Africa. The legacy of Dionysius was a chaos of disputed succession which brought the bewildered philosopher Plato to the Sicilian stage.

By the time Dionysius' heirs had finished, Siracusa was the sport of any adventurer who could gain the support of the soldiery. The historian Denis Mack Smith sees the rule of Dionysius as decisive. "Henceforth Sicilians were to be subjects rather than citizens; and all further political action took the form of destructive dynastic struggles, conspiracies and civil wars."

Right, gleeful Gorgon, Gela.

Sicily was, in Cato's words, "the Republic's granary, the nurse at whose breast the Roman people is fed". But the Romans did not operate a scorched-earth policy against the earlier cultures. Greek language and traditions prevailed despite Latinisation. Even old Phoenician-Carthagian traces remained in Roman Sicily, notably the cult of sacred prostitution at the temple at Eryx (Erice).

Carthage and Rome: In 264 BC the Punic Wars triggered momentous changes in Sicily. Thanks to a treaty with Carthage, Siracusa

escaped the horrors of the First Punic War but northern Sicily was not spared. With Rome's support, Messina tried to evict the local Carthaginian garrison, thus invoking the wrath of Carthage. The ensuing clash between Carthaginians and Romans was the start of the Punic Wars, which ceased only when Carthage was obliterated.

Sandwiched beween the rival powers, Sicily was the battleground. Popular images of the Punic Wars tend to be dominated by Hannibal's elephantine attack on Rome but the preliminaries to the finale in Carthage were fought in Sicily. When it was over, Sicily was firmly within the Roman Empire.

Rome's takeover during the wars was methodical. Akragas (Agrigento) fell in AD 261 and 25,000 of its inhabitants were sold into slavery. Camarina, Panormus (Palermo) and Selinunte followed over the next decade. During the 30 years that Hannibal the Great was at large in Italy with his army and his single elephant, Sicily was the vital link between Europe and North Africa.

The Carthaginians fought tooth and nail for Sicily, relying on traditional west coast sympaties to support its forces. Carthage had 40,000 troops and 200 ships on the island but ultimately Siracusa fell to Rome in AD 212. The most famous casualty of the siege of Siracusa was Archimedes (*see page 268*).

Vast quantities of art and statuary were torn from temples, public buildings and private houses in Siracusa and elsewhere and shipped back to Rome. The Greek mainland had by then been overrun by semi-barbaric Macedonians; Athens was in decline, and Sicily had the finest collection of Greek art anywhere. According to Livy, the wide-eyed excitement caused by the booty unwrapped in Rome was the beginning of Rome's infatuation with Greek civilisation.

In AD 210, by which time Akragas had fallen, the Roman commander reported that not a single Carthaginian remained on Sicily. The island became Rome's first province, as opposed to being incorporated in the republic, because it was too Hellenised.

The province was governed by a praetor answerable only to the Roman Senate. He was not allowed to buy slaves in his province except to replace those who died. (The ordinary citizen is thought to have kept about 200 slaves.) The governor was not to engage in business, and he could neither marry a local woman nor bring a wife out to join him. Administration went on much as before with many Greek features retained.

The Romans accepted that all Sicilians spoke Greek and did not attempt to force Latin down their throats. The Roman administrators used interpreters. Sicily retained the Greek calendar with its festival days, and the records of the Olympic Games show that the odd Sicilian was still winning events.

Slave revolts: In 139 BC, one of the richest

men in Sicily was Damophilus of Enna, a ruthless slave master. Whipped up by Eunus, his Syrian court jester, 400 slaves rioted, murdered their master and joined other dissident slaves. Eunus was hailed king and forced slave owners to manufacture weapons for the rebel cause or to face execution. Eunus was joined by Cleon, and the two rebels commanded more than 100,000 men. They brushed aside the Roman militia and won control of Morgantina and Tauromenium (Taormina) as well as Enna.

Cleon was declared commander-in-chief while Eunus enjoyed kingship, complete with diadem and his own coinage. Eunus's "reign" lasted seven years but Rome finally sent an army of 20,000 against him. The slaves resisted at Tauromenium (Taormina) and Enna but thousands were captured and thrown from the battlements. Yet the Romans were lenient with Eunus who was merely imprisoned. Although rebels were executed, Rome limited its revenge in order to conserve the supply of slave labour.

The second Sicilian revolt occurred in ironic circumstances. In 104 BC, the Empire was under attack by Germanic tribes and needed defending, but slave-hunting had caused a shortage of this prime resource. To help, the Senate freed slaves, and in Sicily they promptly rebelled. Although 4,000 Roman soldiers defected, the revolt failed. The captured Romans were shipped back home to fight wild animals for the entertainment of spectators at the circus. The Italian uprising attracted 90,000 rebels; their leader, a gladiator called Spartacus, was immortalised on film 20 centuries later by Kirk Douglas.

Retirement home: Veterans discharged from the victorious army of Augustus Caesar were given smallholdings in Sicily and undoubtedly added to the process of Latinisation. Moves to make Sicilians full Roman citizens were dropped when they ran into stiff (Roman) opposition. The compromise was to give certain cities a higher standing than their country cousins. Palermo, Agrigento and Catania gained influence and industry

but Segesta lost favour, despite the continued existence of its fabled sacred prostitutes.

History is silent about the next six centuries of Roman rule. In common with the rest of the Empire, Sicilians became full Roman citizens in AD 212, a sign that the island was, in Roman eyes at least, simply an extension of Italy. It acquired a reputation as a Roman tourist resort; Caligula was especially fond of it. A tantalising glimpse of Sicily as the playground of rich Romans is the Villa at Casale, Piazza Armerina. Enough survives

to give a vivid impression of a pleasure palace of 50 rooms on four levels. Mosaics show a phantasmagoria of bathing, dancing, fishing, hunting, wine-pressing, music and drama. It is a scene influenced by Greek mythology and a vision of paradise as a wealthy, contented pagan would see it while relaxing on holiday.

Whoever was occupying the Villa at Casale in the following century may well have had to leave in a hurry because the tranquillity of *Pax Romana* in Sicily, as in rebuilt Carthage, exploded under the onslaught of a people who are remembered as the unmitigated louts of Western history, the Vandals.

Left, **Roman fresco in Palermo archaeological museum. Right,** part of Roman mosaic, Marsala.

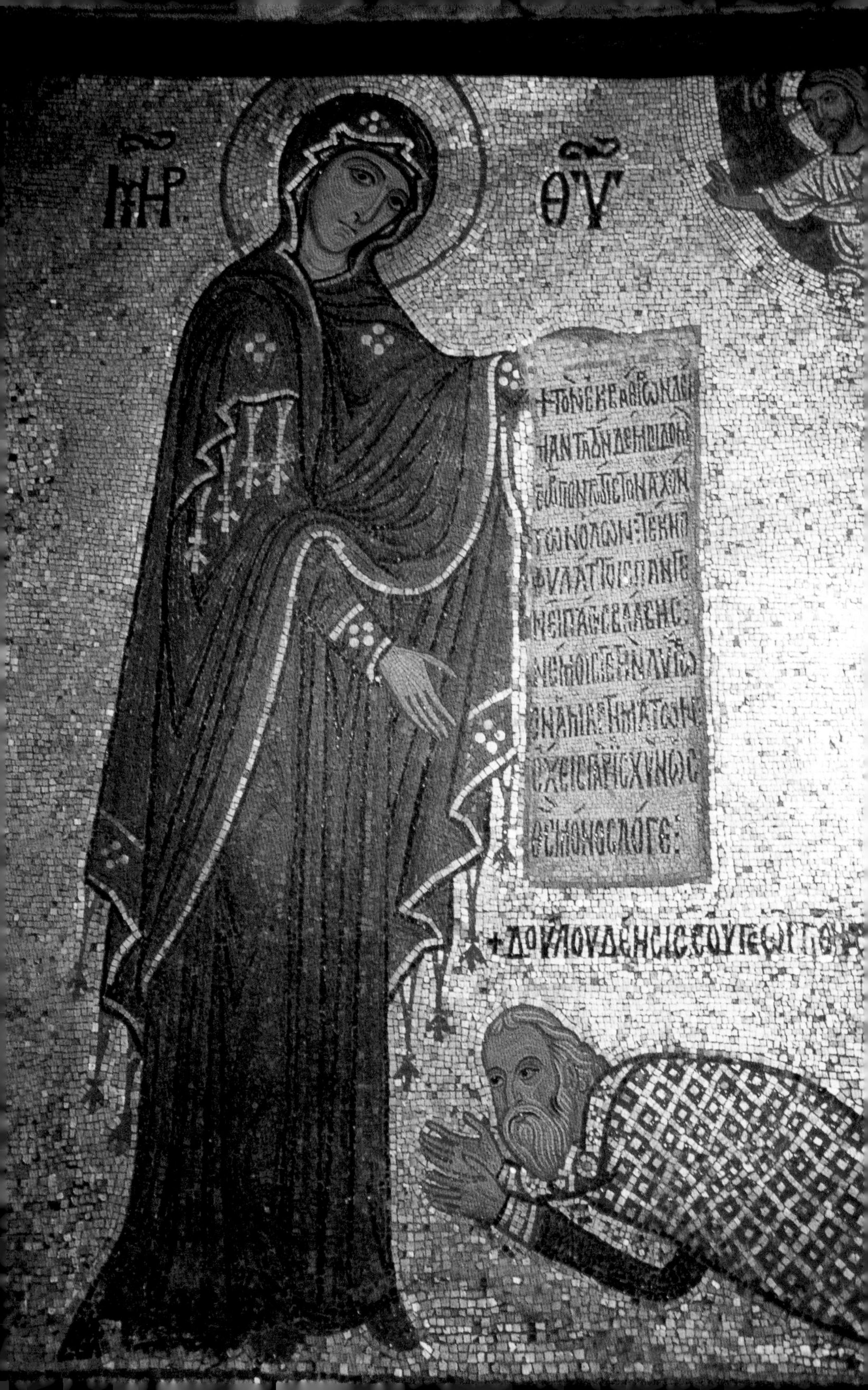
ΜΡ
ΘΥ

Christianity took root in Eastern Sicily, supposedly among Jewish communities. The first images of the faith appear on tombs in the catacombs of Siracusa. The sculpted sarcophagi found in San Giovanni catacombs suggest a clumsy striving for biblical storytelling. In AD 313, after Constantine's edict legitimising Christianity, embryonic Byzantine art emerges from the darkness of the catacombs to take its place in the churches of Eastern Sicily. St Marcianus of Siracusa and St Agata of Catania were the focus of flourishing cults.

The Vandals, an exiled Germanic tribe, provided a heathen interlude in AD 468. After conquering North Africa, they used Sicily as a springboard back to Europe. The Vandals are blamed for a common sight in museums of antiquity, statues with broken noses. Under Goth rule, Sicilians continued to clutch their noses in a century of uneasy peace, ending in a return to the Greek fold with the rise of Byzantium.

When Italy became too chaotic under the Goths to remain the seat of the Empire, the Emperor decamped to Constantinople. Byzantium, as the Eastern Empire was named, was in a real sense New Greece, and the old empire was abandoned to a long line of foreign occupiers. From here, the Greek Orthodox Church emerged as a spiritual pole to justify Sicilian antagonism to an increasingly secular and rapacious Rome.

The Byzantine general Belisarius invaded Sicily in AD 535 in the name of Emperor Justinian. The Sicilians, still Greek at heart, looked on the Byzantines both as kith and kin and as welcome relief. Only the Goth garrison in Palermo put up any resistance. Belisarius dealt with them by hoisting small boats full of archers to the mastheads of his ships so that they could fire over the city's low parapets.

In AD 651, Byzantine control was threatened by Arab raids. Pope Martin, who owned vast estates in Sicily, sent troops south to meet the Arabs, who retreated with their booty. The Byzantine Emperor Constans II,

at loggerheads with the Pope, contrived to make the Pope's intervention look like collusion with the Arabs. He had the Pope arrested, sent to Constantinople and executed.

Constans took the momentous decision to turn the clock back three centuries and return the capital of the Empire to the West. His court settled at Siracusa in 662 but Sicilians' visions of glory were soon dispelled. Constans seized property, taxed extortionately and sold debtors into slavery. It was a slave who redressed the balance in AD 668. Constans

was being soaped in his bath when the slave picked up the soap box and brought it down on the Emperor's head.

Constans's successor returned the capital to Constantinople for the next 750 years while Sicily reverted to Papal administration and produced a string of Popes. The Byzantine conquest confirmed Sicily's eastern orientation, symbolised by Greek language and liturgy. Yet, like the Romans before them, the Byzantines exploited the rich Sicilian estates and failed to stem the tide of Islamic power in North Africa.

Sicily was regularly raided by Syrians and Egyptians before the Arab conquest in 827.

Left, Byzantine mosaic in La Martorana church, Palermo. Right, Greek patriarch, La Martorana.

This was sparked off by a failed Sicilian coup against an unpopular Byzantine governor. Euphemius, a wealthy landowner, overcame the imperial garrison in Siracusa and promptly declared himself Emperor.

He fled to the Arab camp and offered to lead an expedition against Sicily. The response was a fleet of 100 ships and 10,000 troops, mainly Arabs, Berbers and Spanish Muslims. After stiff resistance at Siracusa, the Arabs gained a foothold in Mazara. Palermo fell after a long siege in 831, but Siracusa held out until 878 and pockets of resistance continued for almost a century.

Byzantine art: Visitors to Byzantine Sicily noted the women's love of ornament. Their

secrets and ciphers rather than art. More accurately, it is a mosaic, an enigmatic art form beloved by Byzantine craftsmen in Sicily. Arab and native mosaicists created a fusion of Eastern and Christian art that epitomises the rich Byzantine aesthetic.

This secret symbolism developed in the deserts of Egypt and Syria. These early Christians were inspired by mystery rather than a sense of space. Perspective, natural colours and forms were sacrificed to an iconic worship of the mysterious nature of God. The Orient brought the attachment to icons that has never left Sicily. But according to the art historian Egon Sendler, this is "not an opposition of East and West, Orthodoxy and Ca-

jewels were both a testament to the skills of Byzantine goldsmiths and a worldly counterpoint to the shimmering church mosaics. Contrary to belief, the period is well served by Sicily. It has its share of cupolas emblazoned with austere Greek bishops and inscrutable saints. In church apses, Christ Pantocrator offers his benediction in a universe of gold. Early Byzantine art is represented by sarcophagi or frescoes of wide-eyed madonnas languishing on peeling walls. The secular sphere is recalled by Byzantine baths, homes and jewellery but church art and architecture are pre-eminent.

Early Byzantine art is a maze, a question of

tholicism, more a case of complementarity". Yet, with the capital of the Empire in Constantinople, Eastern influences predominated.

Sicilian Byzantine art, however, is also a stylised variant on Roman art. As it was infused with a new spirituality, it gained in confidence and artistry. New symbolism emerges: pagan themes are erased or simply subsumed. The lyre-playing Orpheus is Jesus the good shepherd while the sacrificial lamb is the love of Christ. The vines representing rites of renewal and Bacchic sensuality symbolise the Resurrection. Imperial triumph becomes Christ in Majesty, with Christ Pantocrator resplendent in blues and golds. The golden backdrop portrays God's grandeur as a stream of light.

In essence, vigorous Classical naturalism ceded to Eastern stylisation, with realism replaced by decorative patterns and increasing abstraction. Symbolism supplanted Greek Classical beauty: three-dimensionality was an irrelevance; faces became inscrutable masks that gazed inward in contemplation. In Sicily's churches, isolated, floating figures are silhouetted against gold backgrounds.

Byzantine architecture used massive domes with square bases, spires, minarets and rounded arches. Basilica churches with a Greek cross plan were favoured only in the east of island. More characteristic are the

luminous mosaics, from serene madonnas to stony-eyed saints. There is lavish Byzantine jewellery in Siracusa and Palermo museums.

As the capital of the Byzantine Empire, Siracusa naturally boasts the greatest concentration of art and architecture. San Marziano crypt was used as a Byzantine basilica until the Temple to Athena was converted into a Christian church. In Palazzo Bellomo museum are fragments of frescoes, such as a vivid *Creation of the Birds and Fishes*, a work of swirling shapes and an impassive-faced God. There are faded frescoes of the saints in Santa Lucia, an early basilica.

During the Sack of Siracusa in 878, the Arabs captured much Byzantine booty and

cube-shaped San Salvatore in Catania and La Favorita in Noto, churches echoing models in North Africa and Sardinia. However, Sicily's rich heritage allows it to bend all the rules. In Catania, the Cathedral plunders Roman and Byzantine columns while Santa Maria della Rotonda, a frescoed basilica, incorporates the Roman baths. Whilst there is no early masterpiece to rival the mosaics in Ravenna, Sicily has a wider range of artefacts. Palermo's Palazzo Abatellis has some

Left, the splendour of La Martorana. **Above**, a tablet in La Ziza depicts the languages of Arab-Norman study: Arabic, Hebrew, Latin and Greek.

copied the rest. Nonetheless, Siracusa museum displays Byzantine-style icons dating from the 8th to the 18th centuries. Although the form often degenerated into a shallow sentimentality, these gold-framed madonnas and rich Nativity scenes are a late flowering of Byzantine art.

The style is an icon for later Sicilian painters. Antonello da Messina, the greatest of Sicilian Renaissance artists, painted a picture of San Zosimo, the first Greek bishop, which is a homage to Byzantium. Even more important is the contribution of the Byzantine style to Arab-Norman art, that glorious Sicilian marriage of East and West.

The fall of Siracusa ended its 1,500-year history as the first city of Sicily. It now took second place to Palermo, as Christianity did to Mohammedanism, and Greek to Arabic. Palermo Cathedral was converted into a mosque in 827 and resounded to Muslim prayers for nearly 250 years.

An influx of Arab settlers replaced the massacred citizens. The invaders were known as Saracens, a term encompassing Arabs, Berbers and Spanish Moors. These masters of the Mediterranean had stamped their authority on southern Spain but, after the initial slaughter, settled down to a benign and liberal regime in Sicily.

As virtually an independent emirate, Sicily played a privileged role as a bridge between Africa and Europe. Trade flourished and taxation was low. The historian Denis Mack Smith attributes its prosperity to the "immense economic commonwealth which stretched from Spain to Syria". The tolerant regime allowed subjects to abide by their own laws. Despite freedom of worship, Christians freely converted to Islam: there were hundreds of mosques in Palermo alone.

Arab enlightenment: The Arabs instigated land reforms which boosted productivity and encouraged the spread of smallholdings, a dent to the power of the landed estates. The Arabs borrowed only the best: Roman engineering skills were fine-tuned and Persian irrigation systems adopted. The Arab reverence for water meant the creation of fountains, baths, reservoirs and storage towers that are visible today. Mining techniques were improved. Sulphur, lead, silver, antimony and alum were refined, as was sea salt.

The Arabs cultivated citrus plantations and introduced sugar cane, cotton, mulberries, palms, melons, pistachio nuts, papyrus and flax. The sumac tree was used in the tanning and dyeing industries. Cotton mills and silk factories abounded, including one in the Emir's Palermo palace.

Ice from Mount Etna was stored and used to make sorbets and sherbets while sea salt

was dried on the salt flats at Trapani. The Arabs introduced coral and tuna fishing, along with the traditions and chants that survive on the Egadi Islands today. Nor did the Islamic faith deter Arabs from planting *zubbibbu* grapes.

Arabian splendour: A description of Palermo was given by Ibn Hawqual, a Baghdad merchant, who visited the city in 950. A walled suburb called the Kasr ("the citadel") is the centre of Palermo today, with the "great Friday mosque" on the site of the later Norman cathedral. A chest containing the body of Aristotle supposedly answered prayers for rain, good health, and "for every ill that causes man to offer prayers to Allah, whose name be praised".

The suburb of Khalessah (today's Kalsa) contained the Sultan's palace, baths, a modest mosque, the arsenal, government offices and the Sultan's private prison. Palermo was especially well provided with butchers; Ibn Hawqual reckoned 7,000 persons engaged in the trade in 150 shops.

The Arab hallmark was a sophisticated and cosmopolitan society. Their legacy was also a repopulation of the countryside, a process confirmed by the number of Arabic names that persist. But charges levelled at the Arabs include the abandoning of olive groves and extensive deforestation, caused by the need to supply Arab countries with timber.

Melting pot: As well as Arabs from Spain, Syria and Egypt, there were Berbers, Black Africans, Jews, Persians, Greeks, Lombards, and Slavs. In particular, Western Sicily prospered under Arab rule and acquired the character it has today. Berbers settled in the Agrigento area while Syrians and Egyptians settled in Palermo. However, Sicily was not immune to racial rivalry. In succession Sicily was run by the Sunni Aghlabid dynasty in Tunisia and by the Shia Fatimids in Egypt. The Byzantines took advantage of temporary racial discord to occupy the east of the island for several years.

The Saracen rulers of Sicily quarrelled among themselves and with their nominal superiors in North Africa and Baghdad, but their disunity was nothing compared with

Left, the palace of La Ziza at Palermo has a Moorish vestibule with a Saracenic fountain framed by distinctive honeycomb vaulting.

the Italian dilemma. Norman knights had entered Italy and were in conflict with the Lombards, and the Papacy got itself into such a pickle that in the middle of the 11th century there were simultaneously no fewer than three Popes. Against this chaotic back-cloth, backward Western Christendom struggled to respond.

Arab artistry: Ibn Hamdis, the greatest medieval Arab poet, was exiled from Siracusa and his haunting poetry exalts the loss: "Since I have been chased out of paradise, how can I bring you news of it, except in the bitterness of my tears." What he missed were lush gardens, courtyards dripping with fountains, vivid Moorish domes, Saracen fortresses,

sumptuous palaces with their interiors a shimmering universe of gold, and cool churches afloat with gauzy Byzantine mosaics.

The Arab domination of the island only served to enhance Byzantine artistry. The Emirs employed Byzantine craftsmen so earlier decorative patterns and stylisation suffused Islamic art. A thousand years of Greek-infused values could not be so easily erased. Compared with the rest of Italy, the Byzantine style lasted longest in Sicily and flowered latest, merging seamlessly into the Arab-Norman style.

Byzantine legacy: Under Arab rule, Greek craftsmen, heirs to the Byzantine tradition, created cupolas and pictorial mosaics with Cufic or Greek inscriptions. In Cefalù Cathedral, master craftsmen from Thebes and Corinth perfected the art of the mosaic, using burnished stone and marble or glittering glass and gold. The mosaics in Palermo's La Martorana church are in pure Byzantine style, being fluid, gracious, subtle and infused with spirituality.

The Arabs absorbed the central enigma of Byzantine church architecture: an aura of mystery created by screens, symbolic colours, contrasts of light and dark. Arab-Byzantine art echoed this theme to perfection, culminating in Palermo's Cappella Palatina. Also in the Royal Palace is Sala di Re Ruggero, a unique example of Byzantine secular art. Santa Maria in Mili San Pietro is reminiscent of the five-domed chapels of Byzantium, with *mihrab* (niches) of Muslim prayer halls indicating the direction of Mecca.

Sicilian conservatism made for a smooth transition from Byzantine to Islamic architecture. After the Hegira (Mohammed's flight in 622), the Arabs mainly occupied Byzantine lands and transplanted Oriental styles to Sicily. Although many churches were converted into mosques, the Arabs happily encased Byzantine art and symbolism in Islamic ornamentation. Christian and Islamic symbolism were conveniently fused. Peacocks feature often in Islamic art as symbols of the soul or eternal life, an emblem echoed by Christian imagery. The symbol is carved on columns in La Ziza and appears on mosaics in the Sala di Re Ruggero.

Islamic art rests on the negation of naturalism. In its place is fanciful geometry, exuberant embellishment and a maze of detail which offers a coded approach to the mystery of God. The Arabs were masters of decorative devices, from arabesques, zigzags and cunning mouldings to walls encrusted with niches. Other motifs are pointed arches, slender columns, double-arched lintels and stepped squinches.

But to Westerners, the most exotic effect is spun by the honeycomb ceilings. Known as *muqarnas* or stalactite work, this beehive design is created by corbelled squinches. The form is borrowed from North African *mihrab* mosques but at its finest, in the Royal Palace, rivals the splendours of Baghdad and Cordova. Iraqi artists from the school of Samarra decorated the ceiling of the Cappella

Palatina. This glorious kaleidocope of interlacing patterns represents the Arab love of abstraction. But although Koranic teaching forbids the depiction of living figures, the Cappella Palatina breaks the taboo in true Sicilian style.

The Arab imprint is also present in more humble projects, ranging from rural mosques to the delicate, arched bridge over the river Simeto. Arab urban design took root in Western Sicily, particularly in such towns as Mazara, Palermo and Sciacca. The town plan is based on a traditional "branching tree" design in which secondary roads splinter into blind alleys.

Palermo contains most surviving Islamic

commonplace name, means "enclosed fountain" in Arabic. Abd ar-Rahman, a visitor to King Roger's court, praised "regal palaces in which glory resides" in whose "superb gardens lion-headed fountains pour out the waters of paradise".

The most sophisticated Arabian baths are in Palermo province. Cefalù's baths contain a faded Cufic inscription while the walled bath-house of Cefalà Diana is still more intimate. The restored room is divided by a trio of delicate, slender arches and offered pools of different depths as well as niches for cosmetics or unguents.

Arab goldsmiths and sculptors also transformed the "minor" arts. In Palermo, the

architecture. The showcase of the arts is the Moorish palace of La Ziza, named after *aziz*, Arabic for "splendid". It is in itself a testament to Arabian craftsmanship, with stalactite vaults, latticework windows, a tiered fountain, and a wind chamber to protect the Emir's family from the enervating *scirocco*.

Such Moorish palaces are significant for their worship of water. In Sicily, fountains and fish ponds, baths and aqueducts often have symbolic Arab origins. Donnafugata, a

Left, an engraving of St John of the Hermits, a converted mosque in Palermo. **Above**, decorative Arabic script in La Ziza.

Treasury contains Egyptian coffers encrusted with gems and ivory while Palazzo Abatellis displays a Moorish vase and intricate carvings in wood and stone. But the masterpiece is a sculpted door from the Fatimid dynasty, a latticework of wood as intricate as lace.

Palermo's La Martorana church boasts a richly sculpted door resembling contemporary inlaid work in Cairo. In Palermo Cathedral, a column inscribed with a Koranic text proclaims God's glory: "He shrouds day with night; how can we owe him creation and not pay him homage as Emperor?" By contrast, the Normans worshipped art but paid lip service to God.

The Arabs called the Normans "wolves" because of their ferocity, barbarism and native cunning. Undeterred, the Emirs of Catania and Siracusa invited the Normans to invade. The Emirs were disgruntled by the concentration of Arab power in the west of the island. The Norman Hautevilles, Christian freebooters, needed no encouragement.

But this was no fully-fledged invasion, rather a campaign of attrition and conquest by political persuasion. In fact, it was the only option available to conquerors with few forces of their own. Robert Guiscard, a fortune-hunting Norman knight, was living the life of a brigand in Calabria, across the Straits of Messina, when he was joined by his younger brother, Count Roger. Robert gave him 40 men-at-arms with permission to commit unlimited depredations.

While the brothers prospered in crime, the Papacy sank into a morass: Popes were poisoned on taking office and, if they lived, were reduced to selling their vestments to survive. Ultimately, the Papacy reached an accommodation with the unruly Normans, and Robert was proclaimed "future Duke of Sicily". In exchange he swore never to endanger the Pope's "life, limb or liberty". With Papal licence, the brothers confessed their sins, vowed to live Christian lives, and attacked Sicily in 1061.

In 1068, Roger defeated the Arabs at Misilmeri but the crucial step was the siege of Palermo in 1072. Robert urged his men on to seize the city which was "hateful to God and subject to devils". The Normans laid loaves of bread out on the ground as bait. Some of the inhabitants ran the risk of dashing out to grab the bread. On succeeding days, the loaves were placed farther away, giving the Normans time to swoop in, capture the wretches, and sell them as slaves.

The great Palermo Mosque was quickly reconsecrated to Christ and a Mass of Thanksgiving held by the Normans. Robert magnanimously shared the spoils with Count

Left, the Normans vanquishing the Saracens, sculpted on the Cathedral of Mazara del Vallo. **Right**, Roger II and petitioner in Palermo's Cappella Palatina.

Roger, also known as Conte Ruggero and King Roger I. He was an autocratic ruler, buttressed by the Byzantine concept of divine rule and supported by barons, mercenaries and a strong fleet. Under Arab influence, Roger was transformed from a foolhardy crusader and rough diamond into a cultured figure.

Arab influence did not wane with the Norman conquest. Since the Normans were not an invading force, the local population was spared. The Normans recognised Saracen

superiority in culture and commerce, so welcomed Muslim courtiers and merchants. Most Arabs retained their castles, palaces and lands as well as their social prestige. Arab craftsmanship was prized in the conversion of mosques to cathedrals while their administrative skills, erudition and poetry were appreciated at court.

Norman style: The Normans were prodigious builders and went on to plant their realm with castles, churches and palaces in Romanesque and Gothic styles, inspired by Northern architecture but subverted by Moorish models. Arabian castles, based on Susa in Tunisia, the point of Arab departure, gave way to pure Norman castles stretching from Enna, in the navel of Sicily, to the majestic castle at Caccamo in the west. However, the Normans mainly built feudal castles to guard the east coast and here their references tend to be Islamic: Augusta castle resembles Al-Andarin in Syria while Catania echoes Farashbend. Like North African forts, these are severe, square castles with Moorish corner towers.

The Romanesque fortress church of San Giovanni dei Lebbrosi was built in 1071 during the Norman siege of Palermo. Cistercian and Cluniac craftsmen were imported to build churches such as San Nicola in Agrigento. But the finest Romanesque church is Palermo's La Magione, which was once a Cistercian monastery. The sobriety of its cloisters is echoed by the gravity of the interior.

Arab-Norman art: Cut off from the architectural mainstream, Norman Sicily looked East. Disentangling the racial strands is difficult since the Normans commissioned craftsmen from Byzantium, the Orient and Italy. It is an inclusive art form, reflecting Norman tolerance and their recognition of Arab artistic supremacy. Most of the Arab-Norman masterpieces lie in Moorish Palermo province.

Cefalù Cathedral is seemingly the most northern masterpiece, the one most akin to Gothic traditions. Yet even here, the mosaics are pure Byzantine and the decayed cloisters seem Moorish. Cefalù's Christ looks more Oriental than in other mosaics, a reflection of pervasive Arab influence. In such Sicilian mosaics, the depiction of God fuses Eastern and Western ideals into a hypnotic spirituality: the majesty, authority and asceticism of the Islamic ideal merge with the humanism and compassion of the Western Christ figure. Sadly, the art of mosaics died with the end of the Hauteville line: a cosseted court art could not survive in the cold.

Monreale Cathedral is a mature masterpiece of the genre. Bishop Gregorovius declared it "so luminous and bright as to appear unbecoming of a Northern god, though certainly not of a Southern god". The interior is inlaid like a jewel box. Opinion is divided as to whether the glittering mosaics were made by Byzantine, Arabian or Sicilian craftsmen. The biblical logic is certainly Byzantine while the leitmotifs of certain mosaics are Arab. An Arabian elegance of ornamentation per-vades the church and cloisters. Even the presbytery boasts polygonal floor patterns of jasper, serpentine and porphyry. The cloister's Moorish arches are decorated with mosaic inlays and arabesque carvings. An Arabian fountain and Moorish patio provide a magic carpet to the Alhambra in Granada.

Palermo's Cappella Palatina is the most sublime of Arab-Norman treasures. The magnificent walls are studded with Byzantine mosaics, while the ceiling is a starry sky with 24 small star-shaped cupolas in two lines. These octal-pointed stars in flower-petal design are part of a honeycomb ceiling. This is a pageant of Arabian scenes, the earliest datable series of Islamic paintings in existence. Musicians, dancers, hunters, royal beasts and Imperial emblems recreate the luxurious lifestyle of an Arabian Emir.

Stylistic purity is not part of the Sicilian architectural vocabulary. The cosmopolitan nature of "native" architecture makes for an exotic, heady brew. However, the style never sinks to pastiche; the fusion is organic, a result of one civilisation successfully grafted onto another. As the writer Vincent Cronin says: "In Sicily this simultaneity of time constantly bewilders, suggesting that all beauty exists in an eternal present." The Sicilians put it more succinctly: architecturally, they are "*bastardi puri*" (pure bastards).

Accession of Roger II: Count Roger died in 1101, leaving Sicily governed by his widow until the coronation of his son, Roger II, in 1130. Although this took place in the Cappella Palatina, La Martorana has a glorious mosaic of him receiving his crown from Christ in a ceremony redolent of Byzantine ritual.

As King of Sicily, Puglia and Calabria, Roger extended his empire to Malta and Africa, threatening Constantinople. He was guided by George of Antioch, his Grand Vizier or "Emir of emirs". Roger himself acted as an Oriental sultan, so much so that monks declared him a Muslim in Christian clothing. For their part, Muslim scholars adapted to the new life at court, not least to "the abundance of golden wine".

Revelling in glory, Roger spent lavishly on palaces, mosques, gardens and education. As the richest king in Christendom, he fully indulged his love of Arab art and culture. He also patronised astronomers and astrologers, Koranic scholars and Sicilian poets. This charismatic king was well-versed in three languages. His cosmopolitan court was home to French *jongleurs* and balladeers who followed the itinerant Norman knights.

As in Arab times, liberalism decreed that "Latins, Greeks, Jews and Saracens be judged according to their own laws". Norman French, Greek, Arabic, and Latin were all spoken. Even so, the Latinisation of the coastal cities led the Arabs to a gradual retreat inland. Only the Normans were granted fiefs and, with this, the Arabs' attempts to dismantle the great estates were undone.

The rise of the baronial class was the most dubious Norman legacy. However, these rugged kings also bequeathed an efficient administration and a relatively liberal re-

"more a Mohammedan than a Christian in belief, in character and in manners". He lived like an Arab Emir in a palace which contained a bodyguard of black slaves and a harem under eunuch management. His lifestyle was a matter of taste, not faith, because he had no qualms about raiding the Muslims in North Africa on behalf of the Pope.

Jealousies in Palermo erupted and the sybaritic court was sacked. A mob raided the harem, raping the women and killing the eunuchs. The King survived and a semblance of order was restored. William quietly stocked another harem, and a riot reoccurred, sparking off fighting between Christians and Muslims until the whole coun-

gime. In its day, this melting pot of racial talent made for the most culturally creative society in Christendom. Yet Latinisation under Norman rule should not be underrated. Immigration meant an influx of Pisans, Lombards and French. In time, educated Arabs emigrated, seemingly excluded from the emerging northern *mores*.

The Muslim King: On Roger's death, William the Bad reigned, followed by William the Good. William I was posthumously "the Bad" because he aroused jealousies by being

Above, the pleasure pavilions of La Cuba and La Cubola seen through romantic eyes.

try was tired of slaughter, and sank, with its sovereign, into apathy.

His son, William the Good, was only 14 when crowned in 1166, and his reign was guided by Walter of the Mill, the English Archbishop of Palermo and architect of Palermo Cathedral. The English connection was strengthened when William's successor, the bastard Tancred, was married to Joanna, King Richard the Lionheart's sister. Richard raided Messina while on his way to the Crusades but did at least present Tancred with Excalibur, King Arthur's sword, a fitting tribute to the end of a legendary line of warrior kings.

The death of William the Good in 1189 without an heir sent the succession reeling back through Tancred, Roger's bastard grandson, and thence into the House of Hohenstaufen, which produced the Prussian kings, the Aragonese and Holy Roman Emperors. The brain-numbing genealogy after Roger boils down to the fact that apart from several interludes, Norman and Spanish blood reigned over Sicily until 1860.

The Hohenstaufen: This Germanic dynasty was the next wave of invaders. In 1194, after

Roger's line petered out, Henry VI, the Holy Roman Emperor, moved in. Henry sifted through the treasures and chose which to send back home north of the Alps, and the Vienna museum thus became the repository of King Roger's cloak and William the Good's embroidered tunic and leggings.

The authoritarian Emperor built the palace of La Cuba and mopped up the House of Tancred, either murdering them or sending them to enslavement in Germany. After dying of dysentry, Henry was buried in a magnificent tomb in Palermo Cathedral, space being made for him by tossing out the bones of various Tancreds. Palermo's Muslims ei-

ther returned to Africa or moved to Mazara. By 1200 there were race riots.

Henry's son, Frederick I of Sicily, was confusingly crowned Emperor Frederick II in 1220. Born in Palermo of a Norman mother, he never considered himself Sicilian yet was known as a "baptised Sultan", thanks to his predilection for a *seraglio* and Saracen pages. Despite an Arabian lifestyle, Frederick chose a centralised, Western European policy which sealed the grim fate of Saracen Sicily.

First, he had to contend with a Muslim backlash and mobilised the barons against the Arabs. Muslims were discriminated against and transplanted to the mainland. Under his autocratic regime, rural settlements gave way to baronial estates. On Frederick's death in 1250, the empire was left in chaos, with family vendettas filling the void created by the collapse of royal authority.

Stupor Mundi: Nonetheless, Frederick's talents were enough for him to be dubbed "wonder of the world". In between empire-building, he founded a school of Sicilian poetry, wrote a book on falconry and created travelling zoos. He also studied science, pondering such arcane questions as the workings of Mount Etna and the precise location of hell. Yet while the barons found Sicily paradise, his other subjects might well have located hell in Sicily.

Frederick fortified all of eastern Sicily from Messina to Siracusa. He sacked Catania in 1232 and then built castles to control his rebellious subjects. Castello Ursino in Catania is one of the finest bastions, a lava-stone moated fort with four corner towers. Despite his reputation, Frederick loved Sicily. As an artistic memorial, he left such lovely churches as the Alemanni and Badiazza in Messina, as well as the Swabian mosaics in Monreale.

The Angevins: Successors like Charles of Anjou called themselves King of Sicily, using the title as an adornment as they pursued greater ambitions abroad. This Loire Valley dynasty had royal links and pretensions. The Angevins beat the Swabians on the Italian mainland and claimed Sicily in 1266. Backed by the Pope, Charles plundered the island and taxed so punitively that rebellion hung in the air, provoked by Charles moving the capital from Palermo to Naples.

Vespers: The Easter Monday rebellion in 1282 was the most significant in Sicily's history, both a patriotic uprising and a revolt against feudalism. The ensuing War of the Vespers between the Angevins and Aragonese lasted 21 years, mainly waged at sea, and left Sicily in Spanish hands.

Palermo's traditional Easter procession was joined by French soldiers from Charles's garrison. The festive mood turned to sullen the feet of the woman he had insulted. In the massacre, no Frenchman was safe. Any doubt about race was settled by a knife placed at the suspect's throat and the order to say *"ciceri"* ("chick peas" in dialect), a word the French supposedly could not pronounce.

The nobles of Palermo, knowing they had passed the point of no return, invited Peter of Aragon to accept Sicily on his wife's behalf. Peter agreed, attracted by the island's fabled wealth, but didn't impress Palermo. The people thought ill of these shabby knights

silence as the Sicilians suffered to be searched by the French troops for concealed weapons. The French captain drunkenly ordered his men to search the women as well. "He himself laid hands upon the fairest, and pretending to look for a knife upon her he thrust his hand out to her bosom".

She fainted in the arms of her husband, who let out the ringing cry: *"Moranu i franchiski"* (Death to the French). The church bells rang, and the French officer lay dead at dressed in blackened, threadbare armour, "and in their hearts did not believe that such men could deliver them from King Charles". Peter and Charles died within a few months of each other and, while Sicily passed down through the House of Aragon, the House of Anjou retained its mainland possessions, with the capital at Naples, also called Sicily.

As part of the Levantine world, Sicily had prospered, but from now on it was truly marginalised. The political centre of gravity shifted north, and Sicily has never thrived on the margins of Europe. The turbulent times left Sicily to sink forever: a mere province owned by absentee kings.

Left, Frederick II in the arms of his mother, the Norman Queen, Constance Hauteville. **Above**, the court of Frederick II, *Stupor Mundi*.

The struggle between the Aragonese and the Angevins ended with the Peace of Caltabellotta in 1302. Sicily was ceded to Frederick of Aragon while Charles of Anjou took Naples. In 1372 Naples agreed to Sicilian self-rule provided that the Sicilian ruler styled himself King of Trinacria ("three-cornered land"), and paid taxes to Naples.

The Aragonese: Alphonso of Aragon united the crowns of Naples and Sicily in 1442 and tried to reduce baronial power. Under his rule, Sicily clumsily crawled away from the

struction of castles. Built in the Chiaramonte style, these fortresses also acted as palaces, with lavish, painted ceilings. In Palermo, the austere beauty of Palazzo Sclafani and Palazzo Chiaramonte represent the perfection of the style. Similar tower houses exist in Enna, Randazzo and Taormina.

The 14th century saw the spread of Catalan-Gothic, a brief architectural golden age. Art was foreign-influenced, first Sienese but Catalan or Castilian by the 15th century. Spanish self-absorption and cultural isola-

Middle Ages. More significantly, his reign ushered in the foreign viceroys who were to govern over the next four centuries. The island was poetically known as "Sicily this side of the Straits" *(Sicilia di qua del faro)*.

But Sicilian independence was submission to Spain under a new guise. The island was drained to fund the *Riconquista* and wars against the Turks. The Unification of Castile and Aragon in 1479 increased Spanish power in Sicily. The Aragonese dynasty was linked to Catania and their sculpted tombs still lie in the city cathedral.

A weakening of royal authority led to the consolidation of feudal power and the con-

tion meant that Sicily sleepwalked through the Renaissance. However, exceptions are the cool Gagini sculptures and the paintings of Antonello da Messina, influenced by Flemish and Neapolitan schools.

The Inquisition: After 1487 the Inquisition was powerful in Sicily. Palermo retains the severe palace that housed the Inquisition headquarters. The Spanish spy system used a grim police force to expel all Jews. Intellectual and cultural life suffocated under the burden of fear and conformity. The system enforced the nobles' loyalty to the Spanish crown and supported baronial privileges that were being swept away elsewhere. Sicilian grandees were indulged by the Spanish and, with no freedom from feudalism, the peasants reverted to banditry. Popularly perceived as honourable lawlessness, brigandry was the breeding ground for the Mafia and was tacitly supported by the barons.

A large bronze statue in Palermo was the sublime symbol of Sicily: it was periodically removed, melted down and recast in the form of the new ruler. Sicily swiftly passed from the Spanish viceroys to the Piedmontese, the Austrians and finally to the Neapolitan Bour-

store the gold and glitter of the Spanish court. They were nonplussed when the new king appeared in clothes made of undyed wool. The King's survey of the economy underlined how far Sicily had degenerated. Why were there so many palpably unemployed people in Palermo, the King wanted to know, when agriculture was crying out for labour? Ancient Sicily had been known for its thriving agriculture yet the island had now fallen so behind that cereals had to be imported. Tax collection was put out to commercial

bons in 1734. The Bourbons ruled uninterruptedly until Italian Unification in 1860.

House of Savoy: The first switch from the Spanish to the Piedmontese occurred in 1713, after the Treaty of Utrecht awarded Sicily to Savoy. Victor Amadeus, Duke of Piedmont-Savoy, arrived in an English ship, Britain having decided that Sicily should be given to a weak Italian power rather than to the Austrian Habsburgs, who retained Naples.

The nobility hoped the Duke would re-

Left, Charles d'Anjou; Catania in 1669, before the fatal earthquake. **Above**, 18th-century engraving of the Quattro Canti, Palermo.

tender, and the highest bidder unleashed a private army of thugs to recoup the cost.

The way titled landowners ran their great estates was as unsatisfactory as tax collection. They employed *gabelloti* (bailiffs) as rent collectors and estate managers. The bailiffs offered landlords a lump sum for the right to exact whatever the estate would yield. Their aim was a quick return. The result was overcropping, slaughter of livestock, the felling of trees and a transformation of the hinterland into today's barren landscape.

In 1718 the Spanish invaded Sicily to recover their former land. The Sicilians, still smarting from austerity measures, welcomed the 20,000 troops. Anticipating a return to gold, lace and unfettered privilege, Sicilian grandees brought their Spanish finery out of mothballs. However, Austria declared war on Spain, but it was British ships which sank the Spanish fleet off Sicily and allowed Austrian troops to cross the Straits of Messina. The war between Spain and Austria climaxed in Francavilla, the biggest battle fought on Sicilian soil since Roman times.

The victorious Habsburg Emperor duly became King of Sicily. The regime was unpopular. "The Germans never became familiar with Sicilians," wrote Mongitore, "and their barbarous language was unintelligible."

than 142 princes, 788 marquesses and 1,500 dukes and barons.

The Bourbon rulers are belittled in *The Leopard*. The shabby grandeur of their palace is one of "sumptuously second-rate rooms". By contrast, Palermo boasted more palaces than the entire British Empire. Even grander were the 200 villas in Bagheria, built specifically to sort out seriously wealthy aristocrats from counterfeit title-hunters. Sicilian nobles indulged in luxury, gambling and litigation, the Prince of Villadora setting the pace with 22 simultaneous lawsuits.

British sway: After Nelson's defeat of the French in 1798, Ferdinand felt emboldened to attack French forces in Italy but was

In a replay of 1718, a Spanish fleet arrived in 1734 and took Sicily back. The conquest was bloodless, and Sicily was again joined to Naples under Charles, the Spanish infante.

House of Bourbon: When Charles succeeded to the Spanish throne in 1759 he was told he could not retain Naples and Sicily as well, so he handed them over to his son Ferdinand. His son's reign lasted 66 years but its durability owed nothing to his own skills.

The profligate Sicilian nobility abandoned their feudal castles for frivolous pursuits in Palermo, but still owned 280 of Sicily's 360 villages. This class had multiplied so that by the end of the century Sicily had no fewer

forced to flee to Palermo under Nelson's protection. The King rewarded Nelson with the Dukedom of Bronte, an estate near Mount Etna. Britain retained an interest in Sicily, if only to prevent Napoleon from moving in. In 1806, Ferdinand IV invited Britain to take over Sicily's defence. Their military presence made Sicily richer than it had been for centuries. British subsidies encouraged the mining industry and reduced unemployment.

While Ferdinand went on hunting trips, the real governor was William Bentinck, the British commander. Still, Britain could never decide what to do with Sicily. The King reluctantly accepted a constitution. "We are living with cannibals," he told Bentinck, only signing on condition that a warship was on standby to spirit him away to a safe haven.

In the event, the Austrian reconquest of Naples meant that Britain withdrew from the nightmare. In 1816, Ferdinand became King of the Two Sicilies. With that, he abolished the separate Sicilian flag and retreated to his court in Naples. In 1820, during the St Rosalia celebrations, Palermo rose against him, a rebellion only put down after the arrival of 10,000 Austrian troops. After Ferdinand's death in 1825, the government was equally inefficient, brutal and corrupt.

Garibaldi: Palermo provided the flashpoint for a revolt in 1848. In one place the riot was

That was the backdrop to rumours of revolution in 1860, centring on Garibaldi.

In May 1860, 1,000 men landed at Marsala in two small paddle steamers. Luck was on their side; normally, their chances against 25,000 regular troops would have been negligible. They were mainly middle-class idealists with no battle experience. They had sailed with no food, water or coal and voyaged 600 miles (960 km) without a chart or sextant. Their luck was compounded by the withdrawal, before they arrived, of the Marsala garrison and a Neapolitan warship.

Garibaldi proclaimed himself dictator, ruling on behalf of Victor Emmanuel of Piedmont. He combined far-sighted goals with

over the price of bread, in another against the town hall. In the aftermath, the King offered a liberal constitution but this was rejected in favour of an independent Sicily. The Bourbon flag was replaced by the tricolour. But when a Bourbon army landed at Messina, the Sicilians quickly realised that the King would be back. Only a tiny minority of Sicilians desired a federal Italy; the majority merely disliked Naples, which they knew, more than a Northern Italy they did not know except through dim memories of Piedmontese rule.

Left, Palermo harbour in 1822. **Above**, 19th-century rioters against church and state, Palermo.

advice to peasants to refrain from kissing their superiors' hands or addressing them as "Excellency". But Sicily was not ready to turn over a new leaf: as soon as the euphoria wore off, armed bands reverted to lawlessness and the English wine merchants at Marsala resorted to doling out protection money to save their crops.

In a plebiscite, Sicilians voted almost unanimously for Unification of Italy. This meant the assumption of power by Count Cavour in Turin. To many Sicilians, that sounded more like annexation than union. Even if few had heard of Victor Amadeus of Piedmont, they must have felt a twinge of *déjà vu*.

SICILIAN BAROQUE

The commentator Luigi Barzini saw baroque as a metaphor for native muddle and "a frenzied search for consolation and revenge against crude and overbearing foreign devils". If so, noble Sicilians rattled their stylish Spanish cage. The earthquake of 1693 literally wiped the architectural slate clean in many cities. The disaster gave free rein to the new tastes of the ruling class, a challenge interpreted creatively all over Sicily.

Sicilian baroque is a tantalising game of silhouettes, spectacular perspectives, and stairways to heaven. The interplay of light and shade,

jacket. As the writer Vincent Cronin says of Catania: "The capricious and highly worked interiors of Spanish baroque were superseded by more sober buildings." Catania is eternally linked to Vaccarini, who redesigned churches as well as the cathedral square and university quadrangle. Influenced by Borremans, Vaccarini opted for Roman rigour in preference to Spanish exuberance, and dignity over creativity. The result, although intellectually satisfying, fails to transport.

Southeastern Sicily is freer from the yoke of Roman restraint. The distinguished baroque cities of Ragusa and Modica indulge in spatial experimentation and flights of fancy. Rosario Gagliardi, the renowned architect from Noto,

convex and concave shapes, represents a golden age for Sicilian architecture. The style makes a feature of sculpted cornices, fanciful balustrades, and balconies as secretive as boudoirs. As Barzini said: "The age was one of display, make-believe and emotions".

The sumptuous Spanish style in Palermo is in stark contrast to the severe, more conformist Roman tradition in Catania. The pre-earthquake baroque of Acireale is quirky and rustic, a school that died out with the devastation of 1693. In Bagheria, villas acquired opulent staircases and marble-encrusted ballrooms. In Noto, baroque translated as spaciousness, symmetry and loftiness.

Catania rose from the ashes in a grey straight-

designed Ragusa Cathedral as well as much of his native town. He favoured baroque set-pieces built on sloping ground, theatrical vistas flanked by flights of steps.

Noto is a stage set of a city, sculpted in golden stone. After the earthquake, its wealthy citizens set about realising their dream of creating a model town away from the ruined masonry of Noto Antica. Like Catania, the city has a baroque coherence and unity that remains unequalled anywhere else in Sicily. Yet, unlike the grim lavastone buildings of chaotic Catania, Noto's honeyed limestone, provincial scale and theatrical vistas ravish the senses.

The severity of the grid system and perfectly proportioned architecture is softened by mellow stone and the elliptical forms of the facades. The *joie de vivre* evident in the palaces also dispels the sense of artifice. Versatile Noto is indeed the high-water mark of 18th-century Sicilian architecture.

In Palermo, the Spanish aristocracy moulded baroque architecture in its own image. *Spagnolismo*, the love of ostentation, found its natural soulmate in baroque taste. Urban planning led to grandiose squares and fancy streets. The Quattro Canti crossroads is a cynical baroque exercise in the heart of Palermo. Then, as now, these noble screens shield respectable eyes from the squalid slums behind.

Under the Jesuits' prompting, convents, churches and oratories sprang up in the historic stucco reliefs. Despite such flamboyance, sculpture showed great virtuosity and reached its apogee in Serpotta's oratories. Born in 1656, Serpotta was a master of stucco scenes.

Serpotta's chapels boast a bevy of nymphs and knights, angels and *putti*. His Oratorio di San Lorenzo has a fragile beauty bordering on the overblown. Every surface is festooned with allegorical stucco figures. His lavish Oratorio del Rosario juxtaposes frothy statues of the Virtues (such as Purity, Wisdom and Justice) beside sombre sacred paintings. As for Serpotta's Oratorio di Santa Zita, the writer Paul Duncan remarks: "You can almost hear the chortling, farting and giggling of the *putti*".

At best, baroque thrives at the centre of city

centre. The nobles commissioned private chapels where the family could pray in all decorum, aloof from the teeming mass of market life just outside.

City *palazzi* competed for attention. Balconies and cornices were adorned with angels, nymphs, gargoyles and grimacing monsters. While many mansions are mere shells, Palazzo Gangi retains a baroque decor: dappled mirrors, gilded panelling, *trompe l'oeil* devices and a majolica-encrusted floor. This insular form of baroque favoured Bourbon excess, from vivid inlaid marble and mother of pearl to riotous

Left, stories in stone, Ferla. **Above**, the frescoed finery of the church of San Sebastiano, Acireale.

life, as a place for processions or dramatic set-pieces. The exteriors provide majestic facades, effortless height, sweeping curves, tension between flight and stability, and grace on a grand scale. At worst, Sicilian baroque degenerates into cloying sentimentality, a grating sweetness of gambolling nymphs, pompous statues, and ponderous facades.

Palermo's Santa Caterina indulges in orgiastic frescoes and multi-coloured marble in ice-cream colours. It is a Christmas cake of ornamentation, appropriate since it faces a convent once famous for sweet confectionery. It's also a playful reminder that the baroque style is the strawberries and cream of Sicilian architecture, easily soured but sublime when it succeeds. ∎

"Just negotiations punctuated by a little harmless shooting, then all will be the same though all will be changed". Lampedusa's views accurately describe Garibaldi's impact on Sicily. Unification did not bring prosperity, merely a substitution of Torinese dialect for Neapolitan dialect.

Sicily remained an emblem of the benighted *Mezzogiorno*. The century began ominously with the Messina earthquake in 1908, which destroyed the city and killed up to 84,000 people. However, centuries of subservience had dented the Sicilian air of supine resignation: flight was an option. Emigration has always been a barometer of the state of Sicily. In Magna Graecia, Sicily creamed off talent from the Greek city states.

Thereafter, immigrants were conquerors and the flow was clearly in the other direction. In 1900 Sicily despatched more emigrants than anywhere else. Villages lost their male populations to the United States, Argentina, Tunisia and Brazil. In a single year, Sicily waved goodbye to 20 per cent of its population, although the economic slump was offset by remittances to relatives.

Mussolini: After 1918, feudal relationships were severely weakened. Returning *americani* came home with self-respect as well as savings. But the cloud on the horizon was Mussolini. While Sicily was not predisposed to Fascism, it was swept along by Mussolini's empty posturing. A magazine called *The Problems of Sicily* was forced to change its name since there *were* no more problems, the dictator declared. A plebiscite in 1934 confirmed his confidence. Only 116 Sicilians out of 4 million disagreed that Fascism had been good for them.

The plebiscite was a testament to Mussolini's demagoguery. Three generations after Garibaldi, little had changed. *Il Duce* talked about building dams, supposedly the panacea for Sicily's agriculture, but few materialised. Peasants still lived in one room with their animals. The railways were single track and the extraordinary level of mule-ownership was the concomitant of the lack of roads. This was at a time when highways were being cut through the Libyan desert.

Anti-Mafia campaign: In reality, Mussolini's masterplan was to industrialise the influential north and to use Sicily as the provider of raw materials. Projects suited his purposes only if they generated publicity, and Sicily offered one worthwhile cause: bringing the Mafia to heel. Initially the Mafia were all for Mussolini; not so when he despatched Inspector Mori, an expert in uprisings, to eradicate the scourge.

Mori started briskly. Various "Dons" were rounded up, walls were removed from roadsides where they facilitated ambushes; cattle brands were altered to make tampering more difficult, and the carrying of firearms forbidden. Mori made an example of the hill town of Gangi, laying siege to it and then locking up a hundred *mafiosi*, including the formidable "Queen of Gangi", a woman who dressed as a man.

Mussolini announced that the Mafia had been eliminated. The murder rate, he said, had dropped from 10 a day to only three a week. Mussolini had indeed curbed the Mafia by depriving them of official protection.

Left, Mussolini takes the stage. **Right**, rural life at the beginning of the 20th century.

As Mack Smith points out, if the Mafia had simply been a secret organisation, Mussolini may have been able to wipe it out. "But in fact its complicated social and economic causes could not be removed in this brief period or by these methods alone." Inspector Mori may have been given food for thought when he offered a prize for the best essay by a schoolboy on how to destroy the Mafia. He received not one entry.

War looms: In 1937, when World War II was just below the horizon, Mussolini visited Sicily to review his achievements. He informed his audience that Sicily was poised for "one of the happiest epochs in [its] 4,000 years' history". If Sicilians knew anything

about previous epochs, they could anticipate a grim future.

The Allies chose Sicily as the landing stage for bringing the war against Hitler back to Europe. Mussolini had always said that the Allies would never be able to invade Sicily. This was military madness: the coast was defenceless, the air cover minimal, and even if there had been good roads, most of the artillery was still horse-drawn. Gela found itself yet again playing host to an invading army. The Americans landed in July 1943 while British and Canadian forces tackled the east coast.

General Patton commanded the US 7th Army in Sicily, running a short and relatively sweet campaign. The German forces and their Italian rump scrambled across the Straits with most of their equipment, and once more Sicily was detached from the mainland and under foreign control.

The Mafia: The role of the Mafia in the Allied conquest of Sicily was open to attack, given deals struck between Allied military planners and Lucky Luciano in his American prison cell. Vito Genovese, while wanted for murder and other crimes by police in the United States, turned up as a liaison officer attached to an American army unit.

Ironically, the Allies helped restore the Mafia's authority in Sicily and so erased Mussolini's only solid achievement. In the absence of the previous Fascist administrators, the army invited Don Calogero Vizzini to do the job. The Allies, whose principal interest was to keep Sicily quiet, did not look into his background. He had been bankrupted and locked up by Mussolini as one of the most undesirable *mafiosi*.

Separatism: Influential voices in Sicily wished to formalise the division between Sicily and Italy, and there was heady talk of Sicily becoming part of the United States. When the Allies then returned the island to Italian administration, one frustrated group of extremists formed a secret army, raised their own flag, and declared war on Italy.

Autonomy was declared in 1946, in areas like agriculture, mining and industry. Separatists still insisted that Italy owed Sicily reparations for misrule since 1861, but this issue soon gave way to the new rhetoric of the Cold War, a contest between Christian Democrats on the one hand and Socialists and Communists on the other.

The balance of power between the two factions lay in the dubious hands of Don Vizzini. For the Mafia, the issue was merely one of choosing political partners in the allocation of building licences, import permits and state contracts. In 1948 the Christian Democrats doubled their number of seats and were comfortably installed as the majority party for the next 40 years. Don Vizzini had reached a decision. Subsequent demands for government action against the Mafia fell on curiously deaf ears.

In recognition that the Italian government was at last willing to make an effort to close the economic gap between Sicily and the mainland, the United States, the World Bank and later the EC chipped in with support. The most radical transformation was in the thorny business of land ownership. After the war, 1 per cent of the population still owned at least half of all agricultural land. The old absentee landownership system was now subject to controls which required that any holding of more than 500 acres (200 hectares) could be expropriated if the owners did not carry out improvements. The number of small and medium holdings rose significantly.

Industry: Dams proved as intractable as ever. Some projects had been on the drawing board for 100 years. There was nothing wrong with them except that the Mafia had a line in

industry attracted its chemical derivatives; gas was discovered at the Nelson estate at Bronte; and Sicily at last commanded the power to make industrialisation practicable.

The effect on the topography worked in opposite directions. As a port, once mighty Palermo was eclipsed by Augusta with its oil facilities, while forgotten Siracusa began to emulate the greatness it had known in Greek times. The overall pattern was the emergence of a new Sicily in the east to replace the domination of the west.

Palermo was still the largest city by far, but northern industrialists had no patience with the old mob rule which could immobilise the place. In 1956 Palermo was crippled by open

controlling the water supply and was in no hurry to have the system altered. Dams were half-built and then abandoned, with a stream of water running uselessly into the sea.

Just as it began to look as if the economy was racing to stand still, Gulf Oil struck lucky near Ragusa in 1953 and another discovery near Gela quickly followed. The cinderella island was suddenly the basis of the Italian oil industry, and by 1966 one of several refineries was alone handling eight million tons of crude a year. The petrol

Left, World War II memorial in Messina province.
Above, Palermo's port has been losing business.

gang warfare over control of the food markets. "The Mafia did not want industrialisation," says Mack Smith, "because industrial workers would be relatively concentrated, educated, self-assured."

Although conditions improved after the discovery of oil and gas, the island still had to compete with the knowledge that a job in Northern Italy paid more in a month than a Sicilian could expect to earn at home in a year. Sicily's fortunes have always depended on events overseas, and it is the island's ability to stem the flight of its best people across the Straits of Messina that will write its history for the foreseeable future.

Palermo's popular advertising slogan is "Invade Sicily, everyone else has." Sicily has never been its own master. Even now, critics call the island an occupied territory, a Roman colony (albeit a heavily subsidised one) subject to the polices of Rome and the European Community. The only homegrown institution that seems to wield any lasting power is the Mafia, an organisation that enriches itself on the island's poverty.

The Mafia is a bad thing, but at least, as *mafiosi* say, it's *la Cosa Nostra*, "our thing", which may account for the ambivalence some Sicilians feel about attempts to eradicate it. They feel it empowers them even as it saps their strength.

Sicilians express this feeling of powerlessness in no uncertain terms. In the evening, when men gather at the *piazza*, they rail against the government, political parties, the Mafia, anyone they can pin the blame on. They talk about being trapped, paralysed, immobile, frozen. One young teacher compares life in Sicily to a feeling of breathlessness. He calls the sensation *apnea*. "Do you know what *apnea* is?" he asks. "It's when a person can't breathe. That's what it's like in Sicily. We're suffocating on this island."

Consumerism: Yet relative prosperity is filtering through and *per capita* income has quadrupled since 1950. Up to 20 percent of the workforce are state employees, from lecturers to office workers and museum attendants. These used to be jobs for life.

In conversation, an elderly woman talks about the old days, *i tempi di miseria*, the "times of poverty," before World War II when her village was dominated by rich landowners and the peasants had barely enough food to survive. "We don't suffer the way we used to," she says. "We have electricity now, toilets, cars, doctors." And then she stops talking and looks around as if to size up the effect these things have had on their lives. She looks toward the cafés where unemployed men spend their days playing cards, at the broken fountain at the centre of

the *piazza*. "Listen to me," she says. "This is not what we wanted."

Sicily has a population of six million, making the island the most densely populated region in Italy. Unemployment hovers around 25 percent. Income per capita is little more than half of Northern Italy's. Yet Sicily boasts the best-qualified unemployed: more than 80 percent are graduates. Despite such problems, Sicily received 20,000 Albanian immigrants in 1991, a figure to be juggled with the incalculable numbers of illegal Tu-

nisian and Moroccan fishermen working along Trapani's African coast.

Emigration: A university student in Palermo discusses the economic conditions. She is asked what Sicilians can do to make things better: "In Sicily?" she asks. "There's nothing we can do in Sicily but leave."

And they do leave, in search of jobs and education. Often the best and brightest go first. Many send money back to their families; others eventually return. But most resettle in their adopted homes, draining Sicily of both financial and human resources.

Chi n'esce rinasce (whoever leaves, succeeds) says the proverb. A million fled to

Preceding pages: Palermo harbour. Left, Trapani province. Right, 20th-century pollution provides a backdrop to the Temple of Concord, Agrigento.

success between 1950 and 1970. Of the 25 million Italians in the United States, 18 million are of Sicilian origin and many are married to fellow Sicilians or those of Irish descent. Beyond that, stereotypes end. Sicilian waiters may run Toronto's pizzeria but *mafiosi* hitmen rarely hit New York. Sicilians from rugged Mussomeli can end up in England as gardeners in genteel Woking. Fishermen from Castellammare work as Great Barrier Reef divers. One high-flier became president of Euronews in Lyons.

There are at least 5 million Sicilians outside Italy. Of the 500,000 declared Sicilians elsewhere in the European Union, most are in Germany, France, Belgium and Britain.

Economic miracle?: Sicilian politicians regularly proclaim the sighting of an "economic miracle". In Mussolini's day it was dams; in the 1960s it was oil; in the 1970s it was greenhouses and reservoirs; in the 1980s it was a building boom; now it is tourism and a bridge across the Straits. Yet the real miracle is that Sicily has an economy at all.

An estimated 40 percent of the population works on the land, producing 20 percent of the island's GNP. Sicily also possesses a quarter of Italy's fishing fleet, mostly based on Trapani and Mazara del Vallo. But to surmise that Sicily is an agricultural economy would be wrong. It would be more accurate

to talk of an agrarian outlook marginalised by encroaching industrialisation. What the rural hinterland and industrialised coast share is a rootedness in the land.

The traditional crops of olives, grapes and cereals remain vital. The hinterland is a mix of mechanisation and sweated brow. While the vast wheatfields are intensively farmed, sights of elderly peasants laden with olives are common, as are burdens of brushwood shared between mules and masters.

In agriculture, Ragusa province is held up as a model, with cattle-breeding, market gardening and wine-growing. Farmers transformed a once malaria-infested plain into a forest of greenhouses bursting with spring vegetables and hot-house flowers.

Since this is Sicily, there is a downside. Giuseppe Fava, a journalist murdered by the Mafia, lamented the unaesthetic tracts of glass covering the coastal dunes. He also had a Sicilian nostalgia for the passing of local cottage industries, such as cheese-making. Still, the past is salvaged: *caciocavallo* cheesemakers survive, and Modica herders ride the plains like Wild West cowboys.

Elsewhere, anomalies abound. Despite the lush groves in Palermo's Conca d'Oro, bottled orange juice is imported. Oranges from Morocco and Israel are cheaper; besides, Sicilian machinery has trouble extracting the pips. But the locals can be enterprising when it suits them. In 1992 EC inspectors were outraged to find they had been fooled by "walking" olive trees. In order to gain extra subsidies, farmers planted their trees in tubs and moved them from field to field as the EC counting team advanced.

Industry: Sicily suffers from the "cathedrals in the desert" syndrome, with the siting of uneconomic plants in empty locations, devoid of infrastructure. These great white elephants have trampled the once lovely coast and polluted the seas. None of these oil refineries or chemical plants are labour intensive and the profits have been siphoned off to Milan. Heavy industry defaces the coast at Augusta, Gela, Siracusa and Milazzo. But oil, asphalt and petro-chemical plants have failed to bring dramatic prosperity.

Barzini describes the difficulties of building a notional *cassate* factory in Sicily. If created locally, it could be the best in the world but would never open.

Tourism: As a growth area in Sicily, tourism is being heavily promoted, not just to the familiar markets of Germany, France and Scandinavia. The results are as variable as the Sicilians themselves. The tourist offices for the provinces of Palermo, Siracusa and Trapani have clear brand images and a warm welcome. Trapani is particularly perceptive about the provision of cultural activities in Classical sites. By contrast, Agrigento and Caltanissetta province sleep on, oblivious to the new wave of invaders. On a local level, many museums have odd opening times and believe they exist for the benefit of staff coffee breaks.

Complaisant culture: It is easy to criticise Sicilians' lack of entrepreneurial spirit, but

North versus South: The North is resentful of Sicily, seething at real crime and imagined subsidies. "Our taxes go straight to Rome," a Lombard League member complains, "and Rome moves the money into pointless public projects in the South." Support for Bossi's separatist party, Lega Nord, is growing, along with similar parties which advocate the dismantling of Italy into self-governing states. It's not independence the Northerners want so much as freedom from the South.

Sicily is Bossi's *bête noire* and he always raises a cheer by ridiculing Italy's inefficient postal system. Letters between Milan and Turin are sorted in Sicily, thus providing Southerners with hate mail and Northerners

the whole business ethos is against risk. Private initiative is discouraged by the habit of state support and Pirandellian layers of bureaucracy. Not only are individuals often powerless to act but their projects, or even lives, are endangered if they choose not to fit into the framework. At best, obstacles take the form of incomprehension, bureaucratic delays, and expected bribes. At worst, there are threatening phone calls and *pizzo* (protection money).

Left, a good citrus crop. **Above**, bizarre roads on stilts were a cover for some futile make-work projects – and reputedly for the odd corpse.

with late mail. Such sinecures may be on their way out as the newly moral Italian government indulges in uncharacteristic cost-cutting and nudges industrial fiefdoms towards privatisation.

Young entrepreneurs are struggling to change the business culture and are having some success in Catania and Siracusa. The "Arab" west of the island is more allergic to private initiative, with the exception of the wine industry. Honest executives exist but their probity has been won at considerable cost: honesty is rarely the best policy.

Economic fears: Corporate investors have been hesitant about setting up in Sicily. They baulk at the lack of infrastructure. There's no sense developing products, investors say, if there aren't reliable highways, railroads, airports and telecommunications to get the products to market. The Messina-Palermo *autostrada* remains incomplete after more than 10 years; the Mafia's complicity is blamed.

With the end of subsidies from the Cassa del Mezzogiorno fund and with recent reforms of the abused state pension system, Sicily is now exposed to the chill winds of the market economy. After the planned switch to privatisation, politicians will no longer be able to use the bloated state sector for personal patronage.

Most importantly, however, investors fear mayhem". Government rolls are swollen with fraudulent pensions and do-nothing jobs that are doled out by local politicians in exchange for votes. Sicily and Campania compete for the title of graveyard of public works.

The passion for road construction is particularly Sicilian. Such labour-intensive projects are often diverted through fiefdoms, or unnecessarily built on stilts over flat land. Many roads are little more than sets of potholes joined by tar, so badly built – conveniently – as to be in a perpetual state of renovation. Travelling the island, one finds incomplete highways, museums *in restauro* for 20 years, and unfinished housing projects, all testimony to the bureaucratic black holes

the Mafia and the pervasiveness of crime. It's not only the drug trade, extortion rings and street crime but also the Mafia's infiltration of the political system. It is yet another vicious circle. The Mafia cannot truly be beaten until Sicily has a free-standing, vital economy. Yet the more money Rome pumps into Sicily, the stronger the Mafia becomes.

A bulging bureaucracy: Fat state contracts, one of the mainstays of Rome's strategy for stimulating development in Sicily, are soaked up by layer upon layer of graft, kick-backs, overbilling and no-show workers. Writer Frederick Raphael labels modern Sicily "a byword for corruption, mismanagement and

through which state funds fall.

Many town councils are regularly dissolved for corruption. In industrial Gela, 5,000 citizens converged on the town hall and burnt documents in protest against maladministration in 1983. The town council was again suspended in 1992 after accusations of criminal ties.

Administrator Giuseppe Vitale says: "As recently as the 1970s, we had dire poverty in Gela and a chronic housing shortage. A living area of 30 square metres was occupied by a family of eight and their farm animals."

Poverty is still endemic in Licata and Palma di Montechiaro, blackspots in the Agrigento backwoods. Palma has the highest child mortality rate in Europe, with *vedove bianche* left pregnant after each fleeting visit from their emigrant husbands in Belgium or Germany. By day, the town is merely depressed, a place partly without running water, sewers or electricity. At night the town is overrun by hungry, marauding dogs; in Palma, individuals own large packs, both for protection and as a symbol of human worth.

Derelict *palazzi* line the bombed centre of Palermo while one boarded-up Catania suburb is known as Little Beirut. Slums without services should be demolished under the laws on unauthorised building (*abusivi*) but most are not. Tucked out of sight in Messina and many other towns are the tenements or insanitary shacks of the *terremotati*, those made homeless after a series of earthquakes. The squalid living conditions and high crime rate tend to be hushed up.

Despite *miseria*, there is cause for hope, both in individual initiatives and a new political climate. Since the 1950s, when activist Danilo Dolci set up his Centre for Research in Trappeto, one of the most corrupt and squalid areas in Western Sicily, a persistent effort has been made to expose Sicily's problems. As an advocate of passive resistance, Dolci helped ordinary people reclaim political power, sparking off a wave of reform that is still being felt today.

Politics: The Christian Democrats (DC) considered they had a divine right to Sicily until the sands suddenly shifted in 1992. A political shift in post-Cold War Italy opened a window of opportunity for reformers. Traditionally considered a bulwark against Communism, the Christian Democrats lost much of their power base in Sicily. Amidst accusations of vote-rigging by their opponents, the Christian Democrats were discredited (*see pages 96–97*).

La Rete, a new reforming party committed to anti-Mafia and anti-corruption policies, moved to fill the vacuum. According to La Rete's leader, Palermo mayor Leoluca Orlando, the only requirement for party membership is honesty. His left-wing Catholic party gained ground until the 1994 national elections, won by Berlusconi's right-wing

Left, a 1960s building boom concreted Palermo's Conca d'Oro, the "golden shell" of citrus groves. Above, a cork-making factory in Castelvetrano.

alliance. In Sicily, the result was seen as a vote for the Mafia.

Attitude problem?: Some people blame Sicily's problems on the so-called Southern mentality: if nothing is done, no one can be blamed. Sicilians are castigated as backward, fatalistic, lacking in initiative and unwilling to co-operate. Anthropologists call it "amoral familism," an ethic of voracious self-interest that precludes community effort.

Yet, in a place like Sicily, where jobs are scarce, resources are limited and political connections mean just about everything, looking out for oneself and one's family isn't just a matter of attitude, it's a matter of survival.

"There is no co-operative spirit in Sicily," an unemployed electrician says. "We don't share because it's not in our nature to share. We take what we can get and to Hell with everyone else." "*Chi gioca solo gioca bene,*" a Sicilian saying goes. (The man who plays alone always wins.)

But Elvira Sellerio, a respected publisher from Palermo, is cautiously optimistic: "We Sicilians have always been subjects, never citizens. The awakening of a civic consciousness is new: give us time to learn how to become citizens." If the optimists are right, Sicily may be due for the Renaissance it missed the first time round.

Luigi Barzini calls Sicily "the schoolroom model for beginners, with every Italian quality and defect magnified, exasperated and brightly coloured." Sicilians also have a reputation for being brooding, suspicious, withdrawn and unfathomable. Closer contact reveals stoicism, stifling conservatism, escapism, spirituality and deep sensibility. This contradictory character does not match the sunny Mediterranean stereotype of *dolce far niente*. But, once over the initial hurdles, outsiders may encounter overwhelming hospitality, boundless curiosity and smothering friendship on the slimmest of pretexts.

Public stage: According to Cicero, Sicily gave the world Rhetoric. The passion for debate remains a Sicilian trait but is a substitute for public initiative. As Vincent Cronin says: "Lack of purpose in life is exalted into a kind of purpose, and lack of action into a mode of action." The writer Bufalino confirms this: "We feel no need to turn our desires into deeds." On arrival in Sicily, King Victor Emmanuel was told the nobility were "work-shy, soft and effeminate". This is more subtle than it seems: "It's best to say no, then one can't be blamed," explains a Palermitan aristocrat and university professor. This passivity springs from an individual's sense of alienation from the state.

In 1814 the British Governor of Sicily was perplexed that "Sicilians expect everything to be done for them; they have always been so accustomed to obedience". His Sicilian minister argued for absolutism: "Too much liberty is for the Sicilians, what would be a pistol or stiletto in the hands of a boy or a madman." Critics claim that Sicilians remain sluggish citizens, subsidy junkies with little sense of self-help. Sicilians reply that power and prestige lie elsewhere. History has taught them to have no faith in institutions. This historical hangover has led them into a moral morass in which the illusion of social change is confused with reality.

Preceding pages: saying it with flowers, Messina; Sicilian students let their hair down on the mystic mountain overlooking the Trapani coast; a trade unionist club in Mazzarino. Left, mending the nets. Right, widow's weeds in Naro.

According to the journalist Giuseppe Fava, "the inability to structure society is the Sicilian tragedy." In the face of this dilemma, the traditional responses are emigration, resignation, complicity or withdrawal into a private world. In Sciascia's eyes, emigration is no answer; it is merely "modern slavery, albeit voluntary, necessary and apparently inevitable". Instead, most Sicilians choose to stay but avoid confrontation with the shadow-state of patronage and the Mafia. They shrink from the public sphere, prefer-

ring to live intensely but in private. As a result, their world is circumscribed to the family, the bedrock of island life.

Society: Palermo is emblematic of the retreat from the world and also of an ambivalence about class. It goes against the grain of Sicilian sentimentality to admit that the middle classes have fled the historic centre in droves, to settle in leafy villages or in safe suburbs in the foothills of Monte Pellegrino. Yet even here, many modest homes maintain a level of security more common to a South American dictatorship, with watchmen, electronic gates and savage dogs. Optimists point to a gradual return of the middle classes to the *centro storico*, with one square held up as a shining example, a socially mixed island which could be the city's salvation or Old Palermo's *coup de grâce*. Elsewhere, gentrification looks a long way off. Arab and African immigrants occupy derelict buildings by the port while neighbouring quarters are home to the underclass (*sottoproletariato*). Pitiful hovels lurk in the shadow of splendid mansions or villas.

Partly as a result of this social imbalance, bars are scarce and the historic centre tends to be deserted at night. The Sicilian upper classes lead such a separate lifestyle that a social vacuum is inevitable. In rural Sicily, the divide is further consolidated by educa-

Sicilian temperament in aspic. "Under Arab rule, Sicily lost its sunny, balanced Classical character and acquired the ponderous, melancholic, brooding nature that still hangs over western Sicily." Even today, the Arab west is overladen with Oriental inscrutability, Spanish manners and ceremony. By contrast, the Greek east is more democratic, with closer links to the Italian mainland.

Giuseppe Fava sees Palermo as the *alter ego* of Catania: where Palermitani are noble, bureaucratic, parasitic, indolent and decadent, Catanesi are *popolare*, commercial, industrious, cunning and cynical. Citizens from Siracusa, the quintessentially Greek southern city, are perceived of as cultured,

tion, Mafia affiliation and isolation.

The story of private virtues and public vices is linked to Sicilians' hybrid past. As Bufalino says: "The Greeks shaped our sensitivity to light and harmony. The Muslims brought us a fragrance of Oriental gardens, of legendary *Thousand and One Nights*; but they also sowed in us a fanatical exaltation and an inclination to deceit and voluptuousness. The Spanish gave us hyperbole and haughtiness, the magnificence of words and rites, the magnanimity of our code of honour, but also a strong taste of ashes and death."

The historian Giuseppe Quatriglio sees the Arab period as seminal in fixing the

educated, open, honest but *babba* (naive).

Sicily's miscegenation lives on in the language. *Cristiani* (Christians) is a generic word for people, just as *turchi* (Turks) refers to heathens. Appearances matter in Sicily: the word *azzizzare* (to beautify) comes from the Arabic; *orfanità* is Spanish-Palermitan dialect for looking good; *spagnolismo* naturally means seeming better than you are, conveying the Sicilians' transparent vanity.

Culture: The hybrid Sicilian dialect has no future tense, a sign that nostalgia shapes the culture. Bufalino laments the passing of a "poorer but kinder" Sicily. "Where are the knife-grinders, the blacksmiths, the carters, the tanners, the tooth-pullers, the wandering storytellers, the singers of serenades... the match-makers, the fortune-tellers?"

Sicilian culture feels intellectually out on a limb yet is curiously smug for being so. Norman Lewis refers to the "sullen mental climate" but the culture is visceral and exotic rather than moribund. Gagini's pure white marble Madonnas contrast with the archetypal sly Sicilian in Antonello da Messina's *Portrait of an Unknown Man*. Modern art encompasses Guttuso's rural landscapes and Francesco di Grandi's morbid paintings capturing the moment of death.

Palermo is officially the noisiest city in Europe, yet even the traffic cannot drown the *tamureddu* (skin drum) and *guatrara* (terracotta wind instrument). Haunting folk songs, often composed in prison, are steeped in memories of poverty. The complex Sicilian temperament is revealed in these lilting ballads, bawdy ditties and heroic tales of banditry and vanquished law-makers.

Private theatre: Within a cocoon of personal loyalty to friends and family, individuals cultivate their patch. "Anything that slights our prestige is regarded as an outrage that sometimes not even revenge can assuage". Bufalino's view is widely shared, especially among the upper and lower classes. In a traditionally oppressed culture, one's word is one's bond; lives have depended on a

Sicilians' passion for music. Bellini, the father of *Bel Canto*, was born in Catania, where his music is celebrated in *pasta alla norma* as well as in the opera house. Eclectic home-grown music also embraces Gregorian chant, Scialpi's romantic ballads and Kunsertu's wailing Arab chants. But at its heart is music drawn from plaintive Greek or Arab laments, played on the shepherds' *scacciapensieri* ("worry chaser"), a curious mouth organ.

Equally traditional are the *ciarameddu* (goatskin bagpipes), *friscalettu* (reed flute)

Left, a hard bargain is struck over the price of squid. <u>Above</u>, volcanic emotions near Etna.

parola d'onore so promises must be kept. But in the eyes of a pessimistic or powerless individual, betrayal can happen only too easily, sparked off by a casual rebuff.

Any rejection of hospitality is seen as a betrayal. As a Palermitan lawyer says: "For us, hospitality is a joy and a duty with obligations on both sides. A refusal is not just rude but fuels our *complessi di tradimento* (betrayal complex)." According to Bufalino, "pride conducts the orchestra of our feelings" – especially sensuality and sex.

Sicilian men of all classes mythologise their virility. "We males of Catania are generally thought capable of making our wet-nurses pregnant," boasts a character in Lampedusa's *The Professor and the Siren*. On his way to a prostitute, Prince Salina says: "I'm sinning, it's true, but I'm sinning so as not to sin worse, to stop this sensual nagging." He emerges "immersed in sated ease tinged with disgust". Yet Bufalino reveals the dark side of Sicilian *machismo*: any sexual slight "causes a turmoil of depression and black rage in our blood that tilts our minds towards the tragic".

In rural Sicily, Verga's 19th-century views on the "ideal female" would not seem out of place today: "She is a short person who busies herself weaving, salting anchovies and producing children as a good housewife

should." His novels present a typically bleak view of relationships: "A woman at the window is a woman to be shunned"; "married couples and mules like to be alone." In *Sicilian Uncles*, Sciascia is more sophisticated yet equally sombre: "The more distant she was from me, the more she pretended desire. She was a good wife."

Sicilian heroes tend to be dead, ideally martyred like St Agata. However, the cult of the anti-hero and the under-dog gives prime place to the bandit Giuliano, the incarnation of rebellious bravery. By contrast, state-sanctioned heroes like Judge Falcone are honoured too late; and Leoluca Orlando, his

anti-Mafia successor, is barely respected. Any genuine hero trying to change the system is scorned with the ultimate insult: *"idu nu du è"* (he's a nobody). The *disfattista* temperament, full of destructive criticism, is also brought to bear on new initiatives.

Island between heaven and hell: Most modern Sicilian writers see the natives' sombre temperament as the product of insularity. To Sciascia, "Sicily has always symbolised a vanquished island as opposed to the victorious insularity of England." To Bufalino, Sicily is "a stone's throw from Africa... a paradise disguised as hell, a hell disguised as paradise." The island offers sweet solitude and self-sufficiency which can sour into enforced exile or solitary confinement.

Yet despite their melancholic immutability, Sicilians have a passion for the present. Thanks to a heightened sense of history, the islanders attach supreme importance to time. It is not a question of punctuality but of a commitment to the present that cannot be bartered. Sicilians play for keeps, with strong convictions and a serious view of life.

They see themselves as volatile forces of nature, as violent as Etna, but imbued with a sense of the sacred. Spirituality is expressed in spontaneous church services led by lay women. In festivals, Classical polytheism merges with Christianity. But the everyday intimacy of the relationship with God bespeaks a chatty equality and an acceptance of Him in any guise. As Sciascia says, "Sicily exists on the plane of fantasy. How can one live there without imagination?"

Superiority complex: "If we're going to be criminals, then we're the best of all," claims an honest housewife proudly. Bourbon arrogance can make a moody Sicilian feel like a god. Bufalino, the carrier of the Sicilian torch, eulogises: "In no other country is the individual so unrepeatable, so unique".

Lampedusa's *The Leopard* is illuminating in unravelling this state of being Sicilian: "Sicilians never wish to improve for the simple reason that they believe themselves perfect. Their vanity is stronger than their misery. Every invasion by outsiders... upsets their illusion of achieved perfection, and risks disturbing their self-satisfied waiting for nothing at all."

Left, a break for *bocchi* (bowls). **Right**, teenage culture vultures in Monreale cloisters.

FAMILY VALUES

In 1989 Lara Cardella, a 20-year-old Classics student, caused a sensation with her book *Volevo I Pantaloni* (I Wanted to Wear Trousers). Although unnamed, the setting is undoubtedly Licata, the backward Sicilian town in Agrigento province where the writer was born. The novel highlights the bigotry, prejudice and ostracism of a girl who longs to wear trousers but who becomes the town *buttana* (*puttana* or whore in dialect) through refusing to conform.

"Only men and prostitutes wear trousers," she is told. But a *buttana* is not so much a prostitute as a label for someone who transgresses the peasant code. The story confirms outsiders' view of Sicilian women as underdogs: "We are dogs looking for an owner to cuddle, beat and above all, protect us," the narrator laments. "But who will protect us from our owners, our parents?" The success of this mediocre novel is significant, pointing to a morbid fascination with Sicilian sentiments and *mores*.

Literary love: Sicilian literature does not present women in a good light. In Verga's *I Malavoglia*, the fisherwomen come out "like slugs after the rain"; women are "long of hair and short of judgment". "Women will be faithful to man when the Turk becomes Christian"; girls must marry "or otherwise they are left hanging around for you to trip over, like old saucepans". "Girls go where God sends them" yet a desirable single girl, "like a good horse, does not lack for a saddle". As for wedlock itself, "married couples and mules like to be alone".

Until recently, romantic relationships were a matter of strict supervision. In the 1950s, Gavin Maxwell chronicled the lives and loves of a fishing community in Castellammare. At festivals, unmarried girls could not dance for fear they would be "touched" by a man. Engagements lasted up to 10 years, with the first five years known as *ammucciuni*, or "secret bonds". After military service, the couple could become engaged formally but had to wait three years until they were al-

lowed to sit together but never kiss. Chastity was one-sided: while the girl sewed her *trousseau*, her fiancé spent his evenings in the brothel.

In *The Sicilian*, Mario Puzo writes that when sewing outside their homes, single girls had to sit in profile to the street for fear of being called wanton. "If a young man fell madly in love with the profile in the few words of respectful chatter, he had to put it in writing." Leonardo Sciascia's novella, *Sicilian Uncles*, confirms these sentiments: "I

had married for love which, in Sicilian towns, is a business of furtive glances and wordless meetings." Yet behind the scenes are tales of adultery, homosexuality, incest, *machismo* and smothering maternal love.

Public faces: Protecting the family's *figura* (image) and *roba* (property) remain fundamental to individual prestige. Above all, a man is expected to take care of his public image, and his family, not the state, acts as the final judge of behaviour. As a character in one of Sciascia's novels explains, "the only institution in the Sicilian conscience that really counts is the family. The family is the Sicilian's State. The State, as it exists for

Left, spiritual encounter at Palazzo Adriano. **Right,** crocheting and lace-making are almost a Sicilian art form.

us, is extraneous to them, merely a *de facto* entity based on force. [The Sicilian] may be carried away by the idea of the State and may even rise to being Prime Minister; but the precise and definite code of his rights and duties will remain within the family."

According to Lara Cardella, "my granny counted in as much as any woman can count in a patriarchal society." Yet in the eyes of many Sicilian women, society is matriarchal. In aristocratic Palermitan families, it was always the lady of the house who kept the keys, who literally unlocked, decided and dictated.

Pilar Visconti, a Palermitan born and bred, warns against a facile feminist reading of the

Siracusa and Messina, enjoy liberal lifestyles, at least for the *borghesia*. A relatively high proportion of women have careers and the trappings of independence.

By contrast, provincial girls are often overprotected and under-employed, especially after marriage. At Selinunte, the fishermen's wives need to supplement the family income but their husbands wouldn't dream of allowing them to go out to work. One woman accepted work as a cleaner but the presence of her possessive husband outside the house finally provoked her (female) employer once too often. Given the Arab legacy, few women work in the fields. As the writer Mary Simeti says: "The olive harvest is one of the few

medieval carapace of Sicilian society. "In private, women control everything, not just in the traditional domestic concerns. But the price for being the power behind the throne is that in public a wife should defer to her husband, avoid teasing or belittling him." At home, it's another story. A husband's mild rebuke for a late dinner is greeted with: "Be grateful for what you get – I didn't study for years to become your chef."

City versus country: A yawning gulf exists between city and country lifestyles. This is understandable if one considers that Sicily was until recently predominantly rural. Palermo, and to a lesser extent Catania,

occasions in the year when the women go out in the fields alongside the men."

Outside the cities, few women over 40 can drive. Indeed, a woman driving alone at night is likely to provoke comments from passing male motorists. In any event, by staying at home, Sicilian housewives are assured of society's blessing. As Mary Simeti says, "making the year's supply of tomato sauce is *the* most important domestic ritual in the Sicilian summer".

The model peasant girl in Caltanissetta or Agrigento province wears long pleated skirts and downcast eyes. She attends Mass but otherwise only appears in public at festivals, and then at her parents' side as a husband-hunting exercise. It is hard to reconcile this old-fashioned image with the sophistication of society in Siracusa or Palermo.

On a summer's evening at a chic Mondello boat club, Palermo's *jeunesse dorée* confirm private parties on their mobile phones. Just downmarket, at *Anni 20 gelateria*, "a cool place for a hot date", there is no sign of downcast eyes or peasant skirts among the dating teenagers.

Castes: Differences between social classes, or "castes" as the nobility calls them, were even more pronounced until recently. In a "good" family, physical work was considered shameful, yet wealth was never flaunted.

Palermitan sons could expect little freedom before marriage, and daughters none, so the wedding was a tremendous relief. Legalised marriage meant legalised sex.

Their counterparts in the village or urban working class might have been more successful in circumventing the sexual veto, with greater freedom accorded to the boy, and marriage for the girl a blessed release from crippling parental control. Things have moved on since then, but geography and class are still the deciding factors.

An amiable Mafia stonemason freely admits that his wife has never been shopping alone but adds quickly, lest one think him mean, "she has her own purse." In the lower

Children underwent an almost spartan childhood with hand-me-downs and virtually no toys. As their parents prudently taught them, *"si sapi unni si nasci e un si sapi unni si mori"* (you know where you're born, but not where you die).

This may seem a cruel parody of the true poverty on their doorstep, yet apart from wealth and breeding, some of the moral questions among the classes were surprisingly similar. One was the value put on virginity. Until World War II, well-bred

Left, traditional weddings, like this one in Caltanissetta, are *de rigueur*. **Above**, family gathering.

classes, especially in rural Sicily, shopping for meat is a male activity. The mason is relieved to have three sons and would not waste money on sending daughters to school. His non-Mafia colleague agrees that a girl is "always a terrible risk" and controls his daughter's movements, "not because I don't trust her, but because I don't trust society".

A man is expected to control his family's behaviour, including his daughter's (and his wife's) sexuality. Any breach of control is considered an affront, and a man can either accept the loss of public esteem or try to reclaim *onore* by seeking revenge or forcing the lovers to marry. This attitude is at the heart of understanding the island's character. It is not sex itself that the family fears, but the scandal.

Lovers' flight: The *fuitina* (lovers' flight) is one of Sicily's more curious phenomena, and is still a reality among the working classes. The *fuitina* takes place when a teenage couple fall in love but can't sleep together. Their flight signifies their serious intentions both to the families concerned and to society, and they will be given a room in a relative's house in which to consummate their "marriage". When they are older and self-supporting, their union will be legalised. The point of the *fuitina* is to save the girl's honour, for were she to sleep with the

of a crime of passion was sentenced to a mere two to five years' imprisonment.

Today's marital disputes and infidelities are resolved in a much lower key. The 1974 divorce law led to a succession of family rights which gave women equal status. Nowadays, the overbearing husband or father thinks twice before refusing to let his wife go out to work or his daughter study away from home as he knows that he is likely to lose both. To add to his troubles, Sicilian middle-class women no longer marry young; while this is partly due to the economic situation and dearth of accommodation, it also reflects their strong desire for independence.

The white wedding: But no matter how en-

boy without family sanction, she would be considered a *puttana* (prostitute).

Feelings have always run high where women are concerned, and the crime of passion or *delitto d'onore* is a crucial element. Murder committed to save male honour was confined to closed communities where a husband who had discovered his wife's infidelity felt compelled to kill her lover. Compelled is the key word, for if the act was not motivated by the husband's own sense of outrage it would have been by public opinion. The cuckolded husband was shunned by the village until he had "done his duty" and made his *gesto esemplare*. The perpetrator

lightened the family, a grand white wedding will normally still be a mother's greatest aspiration for her daughter. Engagements must be sanctioned *in casa* with the young man brought home and both sets of parents introduced. While many girls find this tradition irksome, they may be forced to fit in with their parents' wishes. The majority of young people in Palermo live at home well into their twenties.

In well-to-do households, it used to be common for three generations of an extended family to live under the same roof, an apparently pleasurable state of affairs. Tomasi di Lampedusa shared the *piano nobile* with his parents; his paternal grandparents and bachelor uncles occupied other wings. The few families who have been able to preserve their beautiful crumbling 18th-century *palazzi* in Palermo's historic centre still manage a potted version of this togetherness. But they are the minority: fabled Sicilian family ties may finally be slackening.

When offered a stark choice between "school or housework", Lara Cardella's narrator chose school over "long sessions in front of the loom or bottling pots of tomato paste". However, the reality is a rural exodus to university in the city. Sicily has a long tradition of girls excelling in higher education. The lure of academia is due to a desire for greater autonomy as well as to high unemployment. While nobody is under the illusion that academic qualifications automatically lead to employment, study offers many Sicilian girls a valid escape.

If asked, the parents of a girl attending Palermo or Catania University will say their daughter is staying with nuns during term time. It is common knowledge she has an apartment, but this is never referred to. "*Cosi è se vi pare*," as Pirandello said: "if it looks that way, that's how it is."

If a couple want to live together, they must move to Palermo or Milan. Not long ago, a couple brave enough to set up house together in their home town provoked a scandal and were forced to leave. You need courage to rock a boat that has been chugging steadfastly round the Mediterranean for centuries.

Sicilian proverbs define all relationships: "Honour your father and listen to him always, then even the stones will love you"; "your mother is your soul, he who loses her will never find her".

One result of such devotion is *mammismo*, an infantile dependence on one's mother, particularly prevalent among the urban upper classes. Yet the writer Vincent Cronin calls Sicily "a benevolent paedocracy; a society in which children hold the dominant power". His logic is that children are prized for their youth and beauty, and so, "being the most loved, are the most powerful".

Nonetheless, the majority of forward-looking Sicilians bring up their children with fewer distinctions and privileges between

the sexes. Yet, as one woman said when referring to the stereotypical image of modern Sicily as a violent, socially backward island: "When it's a skyscraper to demolish, it's going to take a long time."

Tradition has its charming pockets of old-world courtesy Although a woman is unlikely to be offered a seat on the bus, elderly gentlemen may kiss her hand while she is waiting. On the minus side, Sicilian women may feel exposed on Palermo's streets.

The real threat is more harmless: inborn *braggadocio* rather than sexual harassment. Sicilian men see no reason to hide their appreciation of women. This type of behaviour is in evidence on the street. Not that

propositioning is restricted to street encounters. After settling her legal bill, Pamela Sciuto was surprised when her lawyer lasciviously demanded more: "You haven't paid your dues."

Still, at best, courting is a game underpinned by chivalry. Scialpi, a Sicilian pop star, drives Italian girls wild with his ballads. Scialpi's advice to would-be Romeos is calculated to upset or amuse feminists: "Be assertive and pay for everything. Women should save their money to spend on sexy clothes". His success is also a reminder that, in romantic Sicily, some men still do serenade their lovers.

Left, on parade at Palazzo Adriano. **Above**, the very different pace of the countryside.

It is dawn in the Madonie mountains of Western Sicily. The first light of morning spills over a chink in the mountains as two young shepherds coax a flock of sheep down a rocky slope towards a tiny stone hut. Even before they come into view, the clanking of cowbells and high-pitched whistles echo across the valley.

The sheep are guided into an open pen and while the boys start to milk, an old man comes out of the hut. He is a bit bow-legged, with a dark and deeply lined face framed by a shock of downy white hair. He stokes an already blazing fire, feeding four broad logs into the flames and setting a blackened cauldron on the grate above. The boys pour pails of milk into the cauldron, and the old man stirs it with a whisk made of bunched-up twigs. He throws a handful of salt into the pot, making the sign of the cross as he sprinkles it on the surface.

Twenty minutes pass before the milk finally bubbles. He pulls out the whisk, crosses the pot a second time, and then skims off the whey – sweet, steaming *ricotta* cheese. Later, when the cheese is packed in baskets and loaded in the car for the long ride to Palermo, he sits with a bowl of hot *ricotta* and day-old bread, and talks about his life.

"We do everything the old way," he says. "Everything by hand." He spreads his fingers and shows his hands. They're thick with calluses and slightly bent. "Not like they do it in the city," he says. "They do everything with machines over there." His son has gone north, to Turin, to find factory work. "But that's the way it is around here," he says, referring to more than just his remote corner of the island. "Everything stays the same."

Natural ties: Little wonder that the ancient Greeks regarded Sicily as the domain of Persephone, goddess of fertility, whose yearly return to the island marked the onset of spring. The elements still rule here. The rumblings of Mount Etna, the scorching African wind known as *scirocco*, the drenching rains of summer, the explosive fertility of Sicilian soil, all this testifies to the supremacy

of the natural world. For countless generations, villagers have been bound by their connection to the land, and by a profound sense of humility in the face of nature.

Alien island: A wild mountain road leads to Novara di Sicilia. The views span streams, derelict farms, deserted countryside, and poor pastureland. Set on a rocky outcrop overlooking Etna, Novara could be anywhere in Sicily, with its humble grey-tiled homes and oversized churches. In such defiantly rotting towns near Etna, brown-suited pensioners

mill around outside their veterans' associations and mutter through their felt hats.

In *The Leopard*, the Prince speculates on one of the enigmas of Sicily: "In this secret island, where houses are barred, peasants refuse to admit they know the way to their own village in clear view on a hillock within a few minutes' walk." Secrecy and melancholy are palpable in rural Sicily. Sepia snapshots suggest that little has changed the battered charm of the landscape. The composite town is crumbling around the ears of its elderly inhabitants yet has an other-worldly, almost squalid, mustiness.

Cesarò is a scruffy one-horse town with a

Preceding pages: woolly encounter. **Left,** rural transport. **Right,** stirring ricotta.

suspicion of outsiders. A lone woman traveller can expect to be welcomed as if she were a creature out of *Alien*; all rooms in the one deserted inn are inexplicably declared full. Luckily, apart from a puncture, there is no reason to stay in this forgotten spot in the Nebrodi mountains. As a holiday experience, Cesarò lacks fun; but, as an insight into village life, it is illuminating. The air smells of woodsmoke and incense, inside and out. While wizened men crowd the malodorous bars, widows in black fill the churches with spontaneous services.

As the writer Paul Duncan points out, it is tempting, when driving through these battered villages, to make scathing comments

about the shabby bars, locked churches, loutish youths, and witch-like crones half-buried under brushwood bundles. "If there is no specific monument, no great painting, and the people in the bar fall silent when you enter, it is very easy to drive on cursing. Sicily is an exclusive place; it can alienate you and shut you out." But persevere.

Appearances are deceptive: Despite the old man's assurance that "nothing changes," time has hardly stood still. Even the most secluded villages are building bridges to the future. Travellers may notice certain technological incongruities: fancy sports cars racing past donkeys laden with bushels of firewood; apartment buildings towering over the clay-tile roofs of ancient cottages.

Most villages are neither wholly traditional nor wholly modern. They are caught in the middle, in a never-never land between the feudal past and high-tech future. Forty years of government aid have raised the standard of living in the villages, but have done little to encourage lasting economic change. A generation ago, basic services like electricity, indoor plumbing, medical care and education were considered a luxury. Today, these are often taken for granted, as is the spread of consumerism. The traditional peasant dream of buying land and farming for oneself is being supplanted by the desire for consumer goods, a colour television, a new car, or luxury apartment.

But, while consumerism is on the rise, there is little evidence that any deep-seated changes have taken root in the villages. A team of anthropologists described the situation in the provinces as "modernisation without development": villages are being subsidised (both by government funds and immigrant remittances) just enough to give them a taste of the North's wealth, without fostering economic self-sufficiency.

Underemployed and undercapitalised, many people have to piece together a livelihood from a variety of jobs. It is not unusual for a family to farm one or more tiny parcels of land, share-crop another, own a stake in an olive press or harvesting machine, and take occasional construction work or other state-funded jobs. Needless to say, competition is stiff, and shrewdness, or *furberia*, is considered an asset, especially in business. "Better to be a devil with a pocketful of money," the saying goes, "than a fool with a few lire." A man is expected to take care of his family, to take advantage of opportunities and, if necessary, other people, without worrying too much about ethics or the law.

Charity begins at home: Generosity and kindness are only considered virtues to a point. Villagers generally agree that a person can be too kind-hearted for his own good. They call this type of person *fesso* (simple), an easy target. Again, the proverb says it all: "The man who makes himself a sheep will be eaten by the wolf."

The success of the family is not measured solely by wealth, but by the accumulation of influence and prestige. As Luigi Barzini points out in *The Italians*: "Southerners tend to make money in order to rule, Northerners to rule in order to make money." In a land where government is historically weak, personal power is highly valued. The man who is able to take care of his own affairs is someone who commands respect, a man of honour. And this "man of honour" is not only in a position to help his family, but his friends as well. *Clientelismo* (patronage) is the only sure way of getting ahead. "A man needs friends," says a day-labourer in a small town in the west of the island. He's digging post-holes outside a new villa, a merchant's country house. His two young sons work with him. "Look at these boys," he says. "They

Sicilians or, less commonly, Italians. Such feelings of identification are natural enough. Small villages tend to be dominated by three or four surnames and, after years of inter-marriage, the entire village may seem like an extended family.

As in an extended family, everybody knows everybody else's business, and keeping up appearances is absolutely essential to family pride. This involves dressing and behaving well, performing religious duties, maintaining the appearance of modest wealth and fulfilling family obligations. In short, it means making a *bella figura*, a good impression.

Gossip is a great leveller. God help the widow who doesn't weep with sufficient

ought to be on holiday, playing in the fields. Instead they have to work with me. How come? Maybe I don't know the right people. You see all these houses, they're *abusivi* (illegal). But the owners know somebody, and so the houses go up."

Tutti cugini: Family loyalty extends to the village as a whole, too, especially when villagers are confronted by outsiders. It's not unusual to hear people refer to themselves first as members of a village, *Stefanesi, Sciaccatani, Caltabellotesi*, and only then as

<u>Left</u>, crushing nuts in Montalbano. <u>Above</u>, a meal on the move in Agrigento province.

gusto at her husband's funeral (is she already thinking of another man?); the man who shows off a fancy new car ("*pezzo da novanta!*"); or the woman who seems too familiar with the opposite sex ("*disgraziata!*").

Although vengeance killings and forced marriages are now considered archaic, the attitudes behind them are still very much in place. As a nervous young man who just jilted his fiancée says, "I keep my eyes open, just in case."

And that "just in case" attitude is what one finds in villages. Perched on the verge of modernisation, people cling to the old ways "just in case" the new ways don't work out.

Giulio Andreotti, 76, seven times Prime Minister and one of the country's most respected elder statesmen, shuffled into the courtroom of the Ucciardone prison in Palermo. It was September 26, 1995, and the charge against him was that he was a member of the Mafia. The arms of the peculiarly Sicilian organisation had, it seemed, reached right to the top.

"The Mafia is not just an octopus. It is a vicious panther with the memory of an elephant," said the Mafia fighter Judge Falcone

The Honoured Society *(società onorata)* is a debased form of the family with a caste-like mentality. The clans are *cosche*, named after the dialect word for artichoke leaves. The pathology of power is entrenched in secret rites, from the initiation ceremony onwards. The rules include not profiting from prostitution; not to kidnap; not to desire the wife of another Man of Honour. If a Man of Honour breaks the code, he is *morto nel cuore degli amici* (dead to his friends). Still, when the chips are down, *"meglio comandare*

shortly before his assassination three years earlier.

A distinction must be made between the Mafia, the criminal organisation of *Cosa Nostra*, and *mafia*, a frame of mind. *Tutto il mondo è un paese* (all the world's the same) is the common cry in Sicily, at once an excuse for the Mafia and an attack. Behind it lies a denial of the lower-case *mafia* and the public acquiescence it rests on: in such a way are the lines between a healthy society and the Mafia blurred. Fatalists see the Mafia as a Sicilian genetic flaw but Falcone disagreed: "It is a human phenomenon and has a beginning, an evolution and an end."

che fottere" (better to command than to fuck). Antonino Calderone, a high-ranking Mafia turncoat from Catania, reveals that, while the code survives, it has taken a battering during the reign of the Corleonese clan.

Sowing the seeds: The origins of the Mafia are shrouded in mystery, although the island has abounded in secret sects since the Sicilian Vespers uprising in 1282. "Mafia" is a corruption of the Arabic words for courage and protection. The sect is the product of a poisoned history: poverty, neglect, misrule, servitude and desperation.

Before Unification in 1861, the great landed estates of western Sicily came to be run by *gabelloti*, bailiffs and power-brokers who mediated between absentee landlords and the peasants. They settled disputes and created a network of shadowy allegiances which filled the power vacuum where the state should have been.

The state represented a threat to fierce individualism, an Italian trait writ large in Sicily. Here, a mistrust of public institutions hardened into alienation and withdrawal: behind the pale screen of the Italian republic arose a shadowy island state. As the prototypical Don Mafioso, the *gabelloto* dispensed feudal rights and favours but the price of his subjects' survival was complicity. According to Mafia expert Clare Sterling: "Not a single Sicilian politician was elected to the Italian Parliament without the Mafia's stamp of approval from 1860 to 1924." Not too many are even now.

The moral gap between state and society meant that law-makers were often derided while law-breakers were shielded, even honoured. Judge Falcone called himself "simply a servant of the state *in terra infedelium*" (the land of disbelievers). The tradition fostered *omertà*, the code of silence, and cloaked common Mafia crime in an aura of legitimacy. As the Sicilian proverb says: "The man who speaks much says nothing; he who says little is wise." A predisposition to private justice until recently interpreted recourse to the law as a sign of cowardice.

First Godfather: Don Vito Cascio Ferro is seen as the father of the modern Mafia and is the source of misconceptions about the good "old Mafia" and the degenerate "new Mafia". After being accused of committing 20 murders, he fled to New York in 1901 and founded the American Mafia. Nonetheless, he is romanticised as the personification of "beauty, grandeur, perfection, excellence" by Pitré, the respected Sicilian folklorist.

The legend of the *mafioso* as a valiant outlaw is wholly false. Until the 1950s, the Mafia is fondly portrayed as a charitable society rather than a criminal organisation.

Left, Don Genco Russo surveys his fiefdom of Mussomeli. **Above**, the arrest of Luciano Liggio, the first of the Mafia's smooth operators.

Insofar as the Mafia *di vecchio stampo* (old school Mafia) ever existed, it confined its morality to members. The Mafia refrained from murdering women, children and distant relatives; it rarely murdered judges or the police; it went to church regularly; and it supported the Christian Democrats.

Even today, each new *pentito* (Mafia turncoat), claims to be disgusted by the Mafia's decline in moral standards. In denouncing the abominations of the latest drugs deals, he singles himself out as the sole remaining

"true *mafioso*". His change of heart is presented not as repentance for personal errors but as the Mafia's betrayal of its ancient values. Self-delusion or sophistry, both are Sicilian drugs.

During Mussolini's anti-Mafia purges, the Mafia were almost crushed but were inadvertently restored by the Americans during the Allied invasion of Sicily (*see page 58*). The leaders were Calogero Vizzini (*see page 197*) and Lucky Luciano, a mobster released from an American jail to supply the Allies with intelligence material. Luciano described *Cosa Nostra* in terms still valid today: "The Mafia is first, then your own family, then your business, then the Mafia again. You might say it's like a private club that a lotta people belong to."

Gangland massacres: In the 1950s a war of attrition was fought between Don Genco Russo's "country" Mafia dei Giardini who dominated Palermo province, and the "city" Mafia dei Cantieri. The former were old-school spivs who controlled the citrus groves, markets, construction industry, water supplies and public appointments. The latter were modern-day gangsters who ran the docks, distribution, contraband cigarettes and most industries. Don Genco Russo represented the losing side, with the La Barbera Brothers and Luciano Liggio in the ascend-

firming the shift of the Mafia's economic centre of gravity from the country to the city.

Luciano Liggio, a pitiless peasant and undisputed *padrone* of Corleone, was confirmed as the leader of the new Mafia. He was a fast learner: when arrested, he was found reading Kant's *Critique of Pure Reason*. On his capture he announced: "If you want me to survive, I'll need a soft bed, a meat diet, and summer holidays by the sea." From 1974, the semi-invalid ran the Mafia from a prison cell equipped with a personal bar and an entourage of lawyer, barber and doctor. At the 1987 Maxi-Trials no one could prove he was the Godfather and so Liggio was the only member of the *Cupola* not to be convicted.

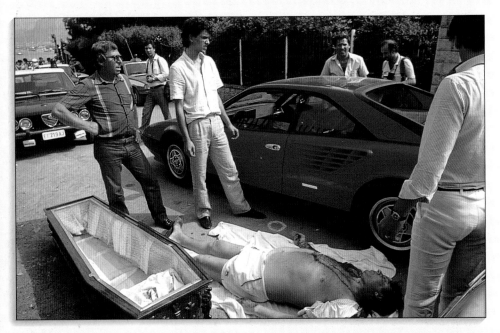

ancy. When Lucky Luciano died in 1962, Liggio became the new Godfather.

In 1957 the American and Sicilian Mafias met in Palermo's Hotel des Palmes, a summit called to create the *Cupola* or Commission and to establish the Sicilians' heroin franchise. The result was a criminal organisation with a clear pyramid structure. The island's *mammasantissima* also had the satisfaction of securing the import and distribution of all heroin in the United States. It was known as the Pizza Connection since pizza parlours were a cover for the money laundering. Sicily emerged as a strategic centre for drugs, arms and international crime, con-

Great Mafia War: From his cell, Liggio masterminded the wars over the drug spoils. Between 1981 and 1983, the clans settled old scores and the Corleonesi emerged as the victors. Corleone had the highest murder rate in Europe in the early 1980s, even allowing for disappearing corpses in the traditional *lupara bianca* ("white deaths"). No wonder Corleone became known as "tombstone" to returning Italo-Americans. Buscetta presented himself as the sole significant survivor of the Great Mafia War: "The winning and losing clans don't exist, because the losers don't exist; they killed them all."

General dalla Chiesa, the new anti-Mafia

commissioner, was assassinated in 1982. Dalla Chiesa predicted his end: "In Sicily, the powerful man is killed when a fatal combination comes about, when he has become too dangerous but can be killed because he is isolated." After his murder, a public backlash led to a Mafia crackdown and the round-up of thousands of suspects.

However, after winning the trust of witnesses, judges of the calibre of Falcone and Borsellino built up cases which culminated in the 1986 Mafia Maxi-Trials. Even so, one defendant entered court with his lips stapled together, proof he was not a *pentito*. Tommaso Buscetta, a *mafioso* boss arrested in 1983, proved to be Judge Falcone's star witness. Now living a new life in America, the supergrass has been an oracle ever since, warning Falcone of his fate.

Life sentences: Falcone feared the state would wash its hands of him; his Sicilian pessimism proved correct: "First they said, 'Go to war, we're all with you'. Now they say, 'Go to war, but don't bother us'." Most of the verdicts were later quashed by Carnevale, a Supreme Court judge known as the "sentence-killer". In a subsequent purge, Carnevale was transferred and the verdicts confirmed by new judges. As a result, 365 *mafiosi* bosses should remain behind bars, many for life.

Borsellino and Falcone were founder members of the anti-Mafia Pool which scored great successes until it was suspiciously disbanded in 1988. After his investigations were thwarted by superiors, Falcone moved to Rome as Director of Penal Affairs and lobbied for a force with powers similar to the American FBI. He was on the point of being nominated *super-procuratore*, its head, when he was assassinated by the Mafia.

Borsellino, Falcone's boyhood friend and obvious successor, became another "illustrious corpse" several months later. His family refused a state funeral, implicitly accusing the government of failing to protect a state servant. "Better one day as Borsellino than a hundred as *mafiosi*," screamed the Palermitan crowds at his funeral. Amidst the despair, Buscetta offered a note of optimism: "The Mafia is on its last legs." He viewed the spate of public killings as an aberration, a rashly

confrontational course of action inimical to the smooth progress of Mafia power.

In recessionary times, the Mafia is the only multinational with supreme liquidity. "Sicily does not have a market economy," says banker Salvatore Butera. "In a normal market economy, supply and demand meet one another at the moment of exchange; here, everyone knows everyone else and knows whom he can sell to and whom he can't." A Palermitan lawyer puts it more personally: "The Mafia has changed normality into utopia: a job should not be a gift; it is a necessity. By refusing to accept this upside-down world, we normal people are turned into heroes."

Until the corruption scandals in 1992–93,

Northern Italians tended to blame the Sicilians for impoverishing the North. Instead, Falcone claimed that the Mafia enriched the North, investing huge sums in the Milanese stock exchange, financial services, construction and recycling operations. Since the state is the motor of the Sicilian economy, the Mafia's profits traditionally come from public contracts. However, extortion, drugs and the opening of European borders also provide great spoils. Ironically, Falcone was informed by his superiors that his investigations were "ruining the Sicilian economy."

In the late 1980s, at the height of the Mafia's control of the drug trade, heroin

Left, victim of the Mafia feuding. <u>Above</u>, Mafia round-ups increased in the early 1990s.

distilleries were discovered near Palermo and Alcamo. Today, the drug market is disputed with myriad newcomers. Still, in towns like Gela and Catania, where juvenile crime is skyrocketing, *mafiosi* recruit teenage thieves, bagmen, drug couriers, even hitmen, to do their dirty work. However, the 7,000 troops despatched to Sicily in 1992–93 halved street crime; they remain a deterrent and theoretically allow the police to concentrate on catching *latitanti* (*mafiosi* on the run). Yet politicians condemn the operation as mere shadow-boxing and Sicilians continue to regard the army as an occupying force.

Mafia experts paint bleak scenarios for Sicily's future. Already, public works have

pean parliament and Andreotti's viceroy. But as one of the *intoccabili* (untouchables), Lima survived the state but fell foul of the Mafia. He was killed in 1992, supposedly as punishment for failing to fix the quashing of the Mafia Maxi-Trial convictions.

According to such outspoken critics as Leoluca Orlando, Mafia tentacles stretch to the heart of the government in Rome. Lima, and many other Sicilian deputies, were alleged to have been involved in wholesale vote-rigging, on behalf of the Mafia and the DC, the Christian Democrats. A quarter of all members of the Sicilian Regional Assembly have been under criminal investigation, rivalling the number of Italian *deputati* (par-

come to a standstill since politicians are too afraid of prosecution to sign contracts. Mafia hostility to the crime crackdown, the political purges and the privatisation of state industries is likely to express itself in retrenchment or a crime backlash.

Partners in crime: The Parliamentary Anti-Mafia Commission, set up in 1962, had some impact but lacks the legal support in Sicily. Exhausted prosecutors kept resigning and their proposed replacements refused to be transferred to Sicily. The result is an understaffed judiciary. The Commission established a case against the most powerful man in Sicily, Salvo Lima, a member of the Euro-

liamentarians) in the same corrupt boat.

Such allegations cost the careers of Italy's two most senior politicians in 1993. In particular, former Prime Minister Giulio Andreotti was not only denied another chance, he was also brought before the courts in Palermo two years later. The 1992 and 1994 elections rewarded Leoluca Orlando, known as "the walking corpse", whose mission is to rout the Mafia and whose dream is "to live a normal life in a normal country." He became a politician after his best friend was killed by the Mafia and, as Mayor of Palermo, defied the Mafia and refused to pay the *pizzo*.

The achievement of the anti-Mafia front

was to shatter the code of *omertà*. Sicilians' complicity with the Mafia is shaped by past insecurity, conservatism and political disillusion. Silence is a race memory in Sicily but even hardened observers notice a change in attitude. The Church, often accused of turning a blind eye to alleged links between the Mafia and the Christian Democrat political machine, now takes a stand, from the Pope downwards. Cardinal Pappalardo, known as Palermo's anti-Mafia cardinal, has denounced the *malavita* (underworld).

The programme of *pentiti*, modelled on the American Federal Witness Protection Program, provides the state with a tool to dismantle the "wall of silence". These "turn-

Godfather himself, captured in Palermo in 1993 after 23 years on the run – not that Totò Riina ever strayed far. Known as *la belva* (the beast), he was convicted *in absentia* of 150 murders and sentenced to three life terms. Riina's philosophy shows his shrewd peasant origins: "If someone's finger is hurt, it's better to be safe and cut off his arm." But instead of a monster, Italians were shocked to see a podgy 62-year-old diabetic oozing false humility. At his trial for ordering political murders, Riina claimed never to have heard of *Cosa Nostra*, except on television: "I was all house, work, family and church."

The Corleonesi clan apparently passed into the hands of Bernardo Provenzano, but

coats" or "super-grasses" embrace both the genuinely repentant and those who find it expedient to turn state's evidence. Several hundred have accepted state protection, new identities and immunity from prosecution.

The Godfather: Francesco Madonia, the second most feared Mafia boss, was arrested in 1992; the courts confiscated his 62 legitimate businesses and property worth $400 million. However, the ultimate prize was the

Francis Ford Coppola's *Godfather* movies were well-liked by the Mafia because they emphasised the family values of the Dons, played by Marlon Brando (left) and Al Pacino (above).

he, too, was old and in ill health. Any Pax Mafiosa that might have existed after Riina's imprisonment was rocked by the arrest of further suspected Mafia accomplices, including Andreotti, and the continued campaigns of Mayor Orlando. In spite of this, and in spite of increased public outcry, the killings have not stopped.

"The city is standing at the window to see who wins the bullfight," Falcone said. The press had seen the imprisonment of Riina as an end of the old Italy, but a Sicilian proverb makes a mockery of any perceived progress: *Finchè c'è morte, c'è speranza* (Where there's death, there's hope).

One of Sicily's best kept secrets is its ancient and distinguished gastronomic tradition. Only a few Sicilian dishes, such as the eggplant pickle known as *caponata* or the sweet ricotta-filled *cannoli*, have crossed the Straits of Messina to find fame and fortune abroad. Even Sicilians are often unaware of how history seasons their favourite foods.

The Greek colonists who arrived in the 8th century BC were astonished at the fertility of Sicily's volcanic soil. The parsimonious, Spartan dietary habits of their homeland could not withstand the challenge of such abundance, and Siracusa soon became the gastronomic capital of the Classical world.

In the 5th century BC the city gave birth to the first cookbook written in the West, Mithaecus's *Lost Art of Cooking*, and to the first school for chefs. It was apparently a rich and elaborate cuisine: in the 4th century BC, a Sicilian poet, Archestratus, author of a cookery book in rhyming verse, complained of an excessive use of fancy sauces, and Plato condemned the court of the Siracusan tyrant Dionysius for the same culinary crime.

Cosmopolitan cuisine: We know too little of the Classical dishes to trace direct descendants in modern Sicilian cuisine, but many sweet-and-sour dishes, such as *caponata*, have a vinegar-based sauce similar to ones described by Archestratus. Classical authors describe cakes that sound like *mustazzoli* (biscuits sweetened with a syrup made from grape must) or *regina* biscuits rolled in sesame seeds and sold in Sicilian bakeries today. *Cuccia*, a sweet pudding made from wheat berries which western Sicilians eat on St Lucy's Day, has echoes of the ritual dish of boiled seeds with which the ancient Greeks marked the onset of winter.

The Arabs brought innovative agricultural and culinary techniques and introduced crops which enriched Sicilian cooking: citrus fruits, rice and aubergines became staples. They also made Sicilian cuisine sweet and spicy. Cane sugar was introduced, accompanied by an Oriental taste for sumptuous sweets which

is still a Sicilian trademark. The most famous dish of the Arab legacy is *cassata siciliana*, the spectacular and overpoweringly sweet sponge filled with ricotta cream and decorated with almond paste and candied fruit.

By the end of the Saracen occupation, the mould of Sicilian cooking had been set. The Normans employed Arab chefs and, until the Renaissance, Sicily exported luxury foods (pasta, sugar, confectionery and citrus fruits) to Northern Italy. Although the Spanish brought chocolate and tomatoes from the

New World and French chefs were fashionable in the 19th century, significant developments in Sicilian cuisine followed class lines.

Kitchen class struggle: The poor survived on bread and wild greens; the aristocracy enjoyed the costly and conspicuous dishes of the *cucina baronale*. As for the emerging *borghesia,* it borrowed from both classes to create what is essentially contemporary Sicilian cooking. In essence, it is a flexible cuisine: extravagant in its festive dishes, straightforward in its daily fare, but always dedicated to exalting the extraordinary flavours of the island.

This class-ridden culinary tradition has

Preceding pages: Palermo's Vucciria Market. **Left**, a *formaggeria* (cheese shop) in Siracusa. **Right**, *pasta reale*, traditional marzipan fruits.

been put to clever use in many Sicilian restaurants to overcome the lack of a traditional *antipasti*. Menus draw on popular street snacks, as well as on the spicy cold dishes that once graced elegant tables as a *torna-gusto*, or a palate cleanser between courses.

For starters: Trays of *caponata* vie with *sarde a beccafico*, sardines rolled in breadcrumbs, with a pinenut and currant filling and baked with bay leaves and orange juice, or *involtini di melanzane*, stuffed aubergines (eggplant) in tomato sauce.

These *antipasti* stars share the high table with humbler but equally delicious snacks beloved of Sicilian students and workers: chick pea fritters (*panelle*), potato croquettes

sharpen the taste of seafood. The harsh sun intensifies the flavours of the fruits and vegetables and produces pungent oregano, mint and garlic, fruity olive oil, and nutty durum wheat for loaves of country bread baked in a wood-fired oven (*forno a legno*). Recently, Sicily has produced good smoked swordfish.

Pasta please: Rice, introduced by the Arabs and cultivated until the 18th century in the Lentini area, survives in *arancine* snacks. In Catania, rice features in a cheese and meat timbale or in *crespelle*, sweet, honey-dipped fritters.

However, most Sicilians feel pasta to be the proper first course. Under Arab rule, Sicily was arguably the first place to produce

(*crocche di patate*); fried rice balls filled with chopped meat and peas (*arancine*); even miniature versions of *pani cu la meuza*, breadrolls stuffed with sautéd beef spleen.

In the mountain towns of the Madonie and Nebrodi, rustic products are served as *antipasti*. These include salami, cow's milk cheeses (*caciotta* and *caciocavallo*), sheep's milk cheeses (*tuma, primosale* or *primiticcio*), sun-dried tomatoes and wild mushrooms *sott'olio*. On the coast, the sea provides the inspiration. It may be a classic *insalata di mare* or a fry of tiny cuttlefish, each no bigger than a thumbnail.

The salty waters of the Mediterranean

dried pasta on a commercial scale. Today's best pasta dish is the simple but sublime *pasta con le melanzane*, known in eastern Sicily as *pasta alla norma*. Here, sun-ripened fresh tomatoes, basil, fried aubergines and a sprinkling of salted ricotta melt into a magical blend.

Tomatoes are an essential ingredient in dishes such as the *pasta alla carrettiera* ("carter-style") in which raw, ripe tomatoes are pounded in a mortar with garlic, red pepper and olive oil, then poured raw over hot pasta. The celebratory *pasta al ragù* also uses a tomato sauce, this time made with *'strattu*, tomato paste dried in the sun to the consistency of clay, in which pieces of pork or beef have been simmered.

Saucy Sicily: A fancy *ragù* might have sausage, meat balls and a stuffed beef roll. In Enna at Christmas, it is spiced with cinnamon, cloves and bitter cocoa powder. At weddings in the area between Syracuse and Ragusa, *ragù* is served *'ncaciata*, baked with layers of cheese and hard-boiled eggs in a casserole lined with fried aubergine.

A host of vegetables are served with pasta, ranging from fancy preparations like *fritella*, a spring sauté of new peas, baby fava beans and tiny artichokes, to simpler combinations of pasta garnished with sautéed courgettes or boiled with wild borage or mustard greens. A

dines, saffron, pinenuts, dried currants and sprigs of wild fennel. In the east, a potent sauce of anchovies and breadcrumbs is still popular (*anclova e muddica*). In spring, when tuna and swordfish are available, small pieces are stewed with tomatoes and mint and served with pasta. In another dish, smoked tuna roe is grated over spaghetti mixed with olive oil and parsley.

In the Trapani area, where the Arab influence is strongest, a local version of *couscous*, steamed in a fish broth, is a substitute for pasta. The interior boasts a survivor from Classical times: *maccu*, a thick purée made from dried fava or broad beans flavoured with oil and wild fennel seeds.

typical summer dish in Western Sicily is *pasta cui tenerumi*, spaghetti broken up into short lengths and cooked with tender sprouts of the vines on which the long thin, pale green *cucuzza* marrow grows. It is topped with raw tomatoes, chopped up with garlic and basil, then doused with olive oil.

Western Sicily's most famous pasta dish is made with fish. Legend has it that the exotic *pasta con sarde* was invented in the 9th century by the cooks of the invading Arab army who used whatever was at hand: sar-

Fishy meat: Often meat as a main course is disappointing. Beef can be tough and tasteless, except when stuffed and braised in tomato sauce (*bracialone* or *farsumagru*) or skewered and grilled (*involtini alla siciliana*). An exception is the excellent lamb and pork raised in the mountain pastures and oak forests of the Madonie and Nebrodi. Pork sausage, often sprinkled with wild fennel seeds, is uniformly good. However, to the *contadini* (peasants and farmers), the daily *bistecca* is a sign of their new prosperity.

Poor meat is compensated for by exceptionally good seafood. Fish, whether fried, grilled or simmered *alla ghiotta* with tomatoes, capers and olives, is popular in the Messina area. Siracusa favours a sweet and sour *stemperata* made of Sicilian fish which, although expensive, is usually fresh and tasty.

Given the superb quality of the vegetables, it is hard to forgive restaurants for relying on an undistinguished *insalata mista* to accompany the main course. *Melanzane alla parmigiana* was a Sicilian invention, after all, and there are myriad ways of preparing this delicious vegetable. Artichokes may be fried, stuffed, roasted on coals, or braised with oil, parsley and garlic *alla viddana*. Bright green cauliflower is boiled and served with oil and lemon, or cooked with anchovies, cheese, olives and red wine.

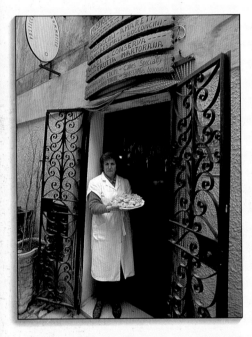

Street snacks: Markets are the place to admire Sicilian vegetables. Palermo's Vucciria and Ballarò are famous for brilliantly coloured and beautifully displayed abundance. Sicily's street food is also worth investigating, although the timid may prefer to seek it out in *tavola calda* bars rather than try it on the street. In western Sicily, fritters and croquettes are popular, along with squares of an oily, spongy pizza called *sfincione*. The east favours a bread dough wrapped around a meat, cheese or vegetable filling, then baked or fried. The names and shapes vary, but requesting an *impanata* ("in breadcrumbs") produces something good.

Sweets: Choice becomes hardest towards the end of a meal. The Arabs introduced sorbets, to the Sicilians' eternal gratitude. Etna provided snow throughout the summer and its preservation and sale was the lucrative monopoly of the Bishop of Catania.

The habit of mixing sugar and jasmine essence in a glassful of snow also dates from Arab times. Sicilians, rich and poor alike, have had a passion for ice cream since the 18th century. Homemade ice cream, in a bewildering and tantalising variety of flavours and shapes, is available in bars and restaurants everywhere.

Convent cooks: Then there is the gamut of Sicilian pastry, from the chewy *mustazzoli* biscuits or the nut-and-fig-flavoured *buccellato* or *cuddureddu* of classical origins, to the opulent Arab tradition of *cassata* and *cannoli*. For centuries, the chief pastry producers were nuns: Palermo alone boasted more than a score of convents, each famous for a particular sweet. A few convents, in Agrigento, Sciacca or Palma di Montechiaro, still sell their pastries. Elsewhere, as in Erice, the tradition is carried on by women who learned their trade in convent orphanages.

On All Souls' Day, Sicilian children traditionally awake to find sugar dolls and baskets of fruit at the foot of their beds, left there by "the souls of their forefathers". The fruit is made of marzipan, known as *pasta reale* or *martorana*, one of Sicily's most delightful culinary traditions. Nowadays, *pasta reale* is readily available all year round in the standard forms of fruits and vegetables, or in the Paschal lambs and flowered hearts that Maria Grammatico of Erice learned to make from the nuns.

Marzipan aspires to an art form in the fanciful creations of Luigi Marciante of Siracusa, Giuseppe Chemi of Taormina and Corrado Costanzo of Noto. Delicious, decorative and durable, marzipan is a lingering taste of Sicily, one you can take home with you. Visitors with more linguistically salacious tastes can be transported by the nuns' sweet triumphs: virgins' breasts (*minni di vergini*) or chancellors' buttocks (*fedde del cancelliere*) could only be Sicilian.

Left, Maria Grammatico in her *pasticceria* in Erice: she learned her sweet secrets from the nuns. **Right**, roasting artichokes over the fire is a popular part of a Sicilian picnic.

To Goethe, Sicily was a unique place, "clear, authentic and complete". The landscape mythologised by Homer and Virgil is still there for the taking, but its context is confused. Modern Sicily has its share of scruffy, one-horse towns, inscrutable hill-top villages and industrial sprawl. As a touchstone, Tomasi di Lampedusa's vision of his homeland is more perceptive: "a landscape which knows no mean between sensuous sag and hellish drought; which is never petty, never ordinary, never relaxed".

Sicilian scenery is gruff but seldom graceless. The granary of the ancient world boasts citrus groves, pastureland and vineyards as well as endless wheatfields. Trapani's weird lagoons and salt pans seemingly float in the unrelenting heat. Away from the accessible coast, an intriguing volcanic hinterland unfolds in mountains, gorges and the scars of abandoned sulphur mines. Like a dragon in its lair, Etna's smoking breath threatens vineyards and lava-stone castles.

Still, first impressions are safer. After breakfasting in Taormina, Cardinal Newman found it "the nearest thing to paradise". To most tourists, Taormina is still the acceptable face of Sicily, a place of undiluted pleasure where culture shock is absent.

Outside this cosmopolitan pocket, the adventure begins. Sicily is not what it seems. The souks and inlaid street patterns of Mazara and Sciacca would not be out of place in Morocco. The perfect medieval town of Erice is a shrine to pagan goddesses, Astarte and Venus. In Sicily, all periods are petrified for posterity. The jewel box of Palermo's Cappella Palatina is a fusion of Arab and Christian. The Arab west of the island is overladen with Spanish finery while the Greek east is truest to the pure Classical spirit.

Despite a patina of neglect, Sicily's architectural riches gleam. The island of Mozia retains its Phoenician port and sacrificial burial grounds. Built to "intimidate the gods or scare human beings", the Greek temples of Agrigento, Segesta and Selinunte are a divine reflection of *Magna Graecia*. The Romans may not have matched these lovely sites but left the vivid mosaics of Piazza Armerina as an imprint of a sated but sophisticated culture.

Cefalù and Monreale Cathedrals are a tribute to Byzantine craftsmanship, Arab imagery and Norman scale. Elsewhere, Moorish palaces, Swabian castles and domed churches are interpretations of this inspired Sicilian hybrid. Baroque, the island's last great gasp, explodes in the theatrical fireworks of Noto and Catania. As the cultural capital of the ancient world, Siracusa presides over Greek ruins and Christian catacombs with a luminous grace all its own. Palermo, its psychic opposite, radiates sultry splendour.

Preceding pages: the cloud-capped Nebrodi Mountains; almond trees in bloom, Agrigento province; Palermo's ornate Politeama theatre. **Left,** Caltabellotta, the loveliest village in Agrigento province.

Sicily

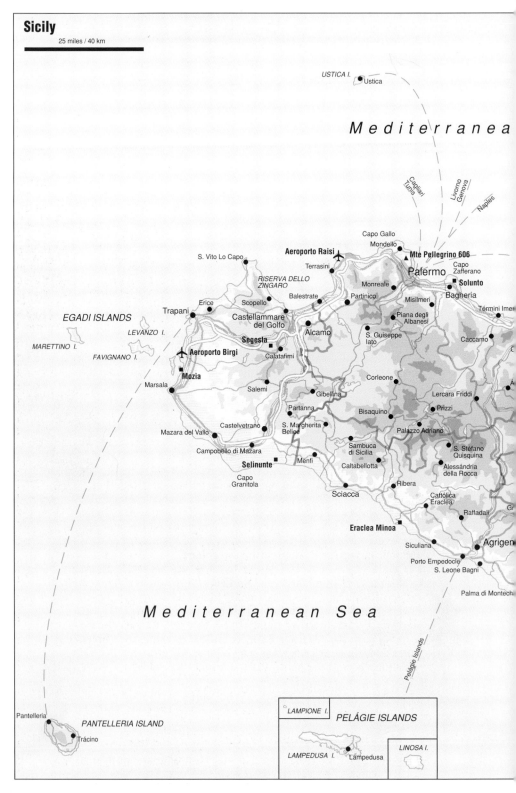

25 miles / 40 km

USTICA I. • Ustica

Mediterranea

Cagliari
Tunis

Livorno
Genova

Naples

Capo Gallo
Mondello

S. Vito Lo Capo

Aeroporto Raisi

Terrasini

Capo Gallo

Mte Pellegrino 606

Capo
Zafferano

Palermo

Monreale

Solunto

RISERVA DELLO
ZINGARO

Scopello

Balestrate

Partinico

Misilmeri

Bagheria

Erice

Trapani

Castellammare
del Golfo

Alcamo

Piana degli
Albanesi

Términi Imer

EGADI ISLANDS

LEVANZO I.

Segesta

S. Guiseppe
Iato

Cáccamo

MARETTINO I.

FAVIGNANO I.

Aeroporto Birgi

Calatafimi

C

Mozia

Marsala

Salemi

Gibellina

Corleone

Lercara Friddi

Á

Partanna

Bisaquino

Prizzi

Mazara del Vallo

Castelvetrano

S. Margherita
Belice

Palazzo Adriano

Campobello di Mazara

Menfi

Sambuca
di Sicilia

S. Stéfano
Quisquina

Selinunte

Caltabellotta

Alessándria
della Rocca

Capo
Granitola

Ribera

Cattólica
Eraclea

Sciacca

Raffadali

Gr

Eraclea Minoa

Siciliana

Agrigen

Porto Empedocle

S. Leone Bagni

Palma di Montechi

Mediterranean   Sea

Pelágie Islands

Pantelleria

PANTELLERIA ISLAND

Trácino

LAMPIONE I.

PELÁGIE ISLANDS

LAMPEDUSA I.   Lámpedusa

LINOSA I.

114

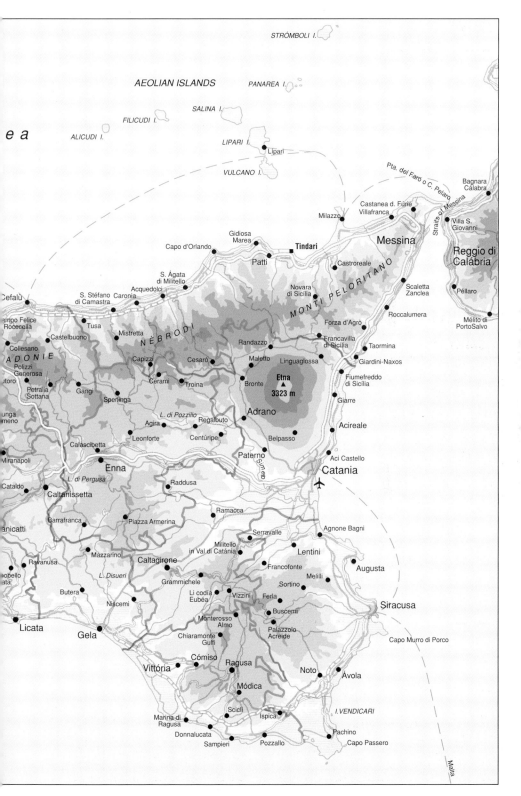

STRÓMBOLI I.

AEOLIAN ISLANDS   PANAREA I.

SALINA I.

FILICUDI I.

e a   ALICUDI I.

LIPARI I.
Lípari

VULCANO I.

Pta. del Faro o C. Peloro

Bagnara
Cálabra

Castanea d. Fúrie
Villafranca
Milazzo

Villa S.
Giovanni

Straits of Messina

Gidiosa
Marea   Tindari

Messina

Capo d'Orlando

Patti   Castroreale   Reggio di
Calábria

S. Ágata
di Militello
Acquedolci   Novara
di Sicília   Scaletta
Zanclea   Péllaro

Cefalù   S. Stéfano   Caronia
di Camastra

MONTI PELORITANO

ampo Felice
Rocecella   Tusa   Roccalumera   Mélito di
PortoSalvo

Collesano   Castelbuono   Mistretta   N È B R O D I   Randazzo   Forza d'Agrò

A D O N I E   Capizzi   Cesarò   Maletto   Francavilla
di Sicília   Taormina

Polizzi
Generosa
utoro   Petralia   Cerami   Troina   Bronte   Linguaglossa   Giardini-Naxos
Sottana   Gangi   Sperlinga   Etna   Fiumefreddo
di Sicília

unga
meno   L. di Pozzillo   ▲   Giarre
Agira   Regalbuto   3323 m

Calascibetta   Leonforte   Centúripe   Adrano   Acireale

Miranapoli   Enna   Belpasso

L. di Pergusa   Raddusa   Aci Castello

Cataldo   Paternó   Catania

Caltanissetta   Ramacca

anicatti   Barrafranca   Piazza Armerina   Serravalle   Agnone Bagni

Mázzarino   Militello
in Val di Catánia   Lentini   Augusta

Ravanusa   Caltagirone   Francofonte   Melilli

obello
ata   Butera   L. Disueri   Grammichele   Sortino   Siracusa

Niscemi   Li codía
Eubéa   Vizzíni   Ferla

Licata   Monterosso
Almo   Buscemi

Gela   Chiaramonte
Gulfi   Palazzolo
Acreide   Capo Murro di Porco

Cómiso   Ragusa

Vittória   Noto   Ávola

Módica   I. VENDICARI

Marina di   Scicli
Ragusa   Ispica

Donnalucata   Pachino

Sampieri   Pozzallo   Capo Passero

Malta

PALERMO CITY

Palermo is both an essay in chaos and a sensuous spice box of a city. In Tomasi di Lampedusa's *The Leopard*, the Prince breathes in the orange blossom on a sultry night in Palermo, and is flooded with "the Islamic perfume evoking houris and fleshly joys beyond the grave". Palermo luxuriates in a sultry decadence. In *Persephone's Island*, the writer Mary Simeti, born in America but long based in Sicily, describes her regular return to Palermo city-living in the autumn: "The city awaits us... early persimmons glowing orange amidst pyramids of bright green cauliflowers, smoking tripods of chestnuts roasting at the curbstones, bloodshed and decaying beauty." Like the persimmon, Palermo is tropical, ripe, decadent, the soul of brooding Sicily.

Melting pot: A Phoenician colony existed from the 8th century BC but not a stone of Punic Palermo remains, nor its original name. The Greeks named the city *Panormos* (all-haven) for its harbours stretching along a bay known as the Conca d'Oro (the golden shell), thanks to the glittering citrus groves. As a Roman province, Palermo has revealed scant Classical remains compared with its cultured east coast rivals. The only traces of Classical Palermo are in the grid-like urban plan around La Cala, the original harbour.

Elsewhere in the historic centre, Palermo is a maze of Moorish alleys, confirming the city's deeper affinities. Under Byzantine rule, the city developed its principal poles of power: a Byzantine church on the site of the future cathedral; and the Palazzo dei Normanni, the later royal palace and seat of the current Regional Government.

However, it was only with the Arab colonisation that Palermo prospered and came into its own. The city was home to Jewish and Lombard merchants, Greek craftsmen and builders, Turkish and Syrian artisans, Persian artists, Berber and Negro slaves. It was the most multiracial population in Europe, and out of such diversity was born the complex city culture that knows many masters.

Arab rule: The city welcomed 300 mosques and was ringed by pleasure palaces such as La Ziza and hunting lodges like La Cuba. Norman rule coincided with Palermo's golden age, one of expansion, enlightenment, prosperity and cultural riches. Citizens acquired a love for Arab ornamentation that has never left them. The city outskirts were ringed by palms, vineyards, citrus groves, silk farms and rice paddies.

Under Spanish rule, the Moorish city was remodelled along grand baroque arteries. This attempt to impose order on the chaotic Arab maze provided a misleading semblance of control. Streets such as Via Maqueda and Via Toledo were extended, formalised and opened up to the sea. But behind the grand new crossroads of **Quattro Canti**, the old Moorish city swirled in crooked alleys, lively markets, and poor housing. The urban design formalised the separation of nobles and artisans, rich and poor.

Urban decay: In a sense, little has

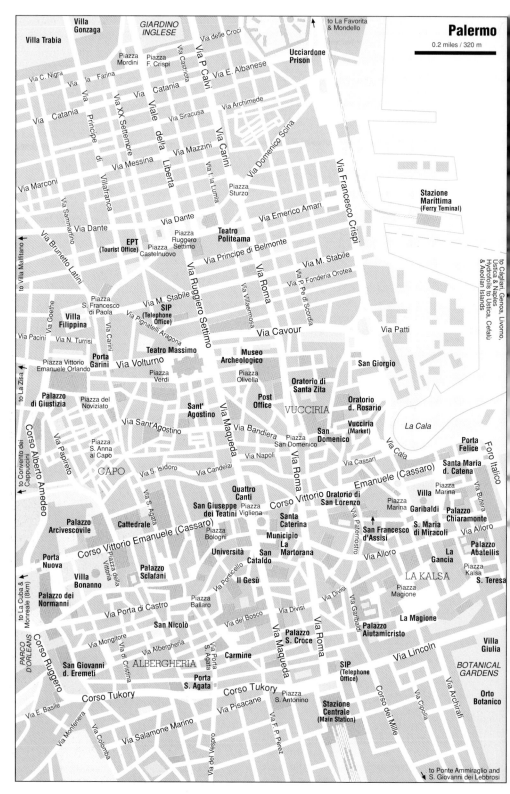

Palermo

0.2 miles / 320 m

changed since then, except that the middle classes have largely deserted the city centre. In 1943, Allied bombs destroyed the port and much of the historic centre, leaving it with gaping holes half-filled with crumbling baroque *palazzi*. The Mafia stepped into the hole, accepting funds from Rome and the EC to rebuild the devastated centre. Instead, corrupt politicians in league with *mafiosi* building contractors siphoned off the funds for their own illicit ends.

One key culprit was Salvo Lima, the political power-broker for the Mafia in Rome. When he was gunned down in Palermo in 1992, the balance of power shifted (*see page 96*). Following the Mafia murders of Falcone and Borsellino, high-profile public prosecutors, Palermitans experienced a wave of revulsion, rare in its ability to provoke citizens to public protest. After a period of political instability, a rare feeling of hope permeates the air, personified by local boy Leoluca Orlando and his anti-Mafia party, La Rete. Still more significant is the sense of civic responsibility felt by citizens, especially the young.

Sights: Palermo is an incredible jumble of periods and styles. No map does justice to the city's confusion. Given that the Spanish grid system is subverted by Moorish blind alleys, squalid bomb sites and rampant urbanisation on the outskirts, it is surprising that the city is so legible. North of Via Cavour lies the bland **Viale della Libertà** quarter and chic hotels. Divided by Quattro Canti crossroads, the historic city forms four traditional quarters with its off-centre heart in the **Kasr**, the great Arab-Norman nucleus. Each quarter reveals a picturesque clutter of mansions, markets and dark baroque churches with luminous interiors.

The Kasr contains both the city seats of power, temporal and spiritual. North of Corso Emanuele is the **Capo** quarter, the medieval working-class district behind the Cathedral. West of Via Maqueda and south of Corso Emanuele lies the poor quarter of the **Albergheria**. East of Via Roma lies the **Vucciria**, the dilapidated market district crammed between La Cala harbour and San Domenico.

South of the Corso and east of Via Roma is the **Kalsa**, a bomb-damaged quarter with a fine museum and austere Catalan-Gothic *palazzi*.

The Kasr quarter, named after the Arabic for castle, contains the cathedral and the royal palace, once the upper castle. The **Duomo** is a Sicilian hybrid: mentally erase the incongruous dome and focus on the desert-coloured stone, sculpted doorway and Arab decoration of the facade. The peppermint and grey baroque interior is a cool shell, a wanly neutered setting for the royal **Norman tombs**. Borne by crouching lions, the tombs are made of rare pink porphyry and sculpted by Arabs masters, the only craftsmen who knew the technique in Norman times. The **treasury** contains royal mantles and a Norman crown resembling a bejewelled skull cap, bedecked with gold, pearls and gems.

Behind the Duomo emerges the geometric design of the Arab-Norman apses, with black-and-white inlays and blind arches. In alleys encircling the Cathedral, high stone buildings are hung with

Monument to Philip II of Spain in Piazza Vigliena at Quattro Canti.

washing. A stone's throw from the grand Duomo, is **Vicolo Brugno**, a mean alley where families fuel open fires, roasting wild birds and chestnuts or simply keeping warm. These sombre *vicoli* are the underbelly of opulent Palermo.

Palazzo dei Normanni, in the south, is the eclectic royal palace and centre of power since Byzantine times. Now the seat of the Sicilian Parliament, this cube-shaped palace has walled gardens overgrown with royal orchids, papyrus, hanging banyan trees, *ficus belgamine* and kapoks. The African kapoks store water in barrel-like trunks and are a favourite with monkeys, a reminder that the Arab Emirs bred an exotic menagerie here. The most precious trees are the *cicas*, dwarf palms whose leaves take 50 years to grow. An 18th-century carriage drive leads to the Arab-Norman palace that rivalled Cairo and Córdova.

Leading off a lovely loggia is the **Cappella Palatina**, the royal chapel designed by Roger II in 1130 and representing the fusion of Byzantine, Arab, Norman and Sicilian civilisations. The gold mosaics recall the Crusades; Palermo was the port of departure for the Holy Land. In the penumbra, the mystic **Byzantine mosaics** slowly emerge. Christ Pantocrator occupies the cupola, surrounded by archangels and saints. On the walls are sumptuous Biblical scenes framed by Islamic decorative devices with the texture of tapestry.

Individual masterpieces include the delicate marble paschal candlestick, Corinthian capitals, an inlaid Cosmati marble pulpit, marble and porphyry paving underfoot and a **treasury** containing Islamic caskets. The gold and porphyry **throne** occupies a dais below a mosaic pointedly entrusting the Norman kings with the Holy Law. No wonder Guy de Maupassant praised the chapel as "the most perfect sacred work ever conceived by mankind".

The **ceiling** is unique in a Christian church, a composition of ineffable Oriental splendour. The Normans asked Arab craftsmen to portray paradise and they maliciously obliged with naked maidens which the Normans prudishly

Arab-Norman detail on the Duomo.

clothed and crowned with haloes. Still, the roof remains a paradise of the senses: Persian octagonal stars meet Islamic stalactites. Amidst palm trees and peacocks, men play chess, hunt or drink; entwined dancers and female musicians belong to *Arabian Nights* fantasies.

On the floor above is the gilded **Parliamentary Chamber** (1350). From the balconies stretch views of the Conca d'Oro, the scenic shell surrounded by lemon groves, the port and hills.

The **Royal Apartments** reflect the tastes of past viceroys. The suites include a gold chamber in faded *Gattopardo* style and a pink Bourbon salon used for anti-Mafia committee meetings. However, the loveliest rooms are the Arab Sala dei Venti, open to the winds; and the Sala di Re Ruggero, frescoed with hunting scenes including lions, deer and limpid peacocks. The lowest courtyard boasts a Norman fountain, Islamic star-shaped windows and stalactite ceilings.

Parco d'Orleans, the lush gardens behind the palace, belong to the Sicilian President but are open to the public. A sign specifies that only adults accompanied by children can enter. Shrewd ragamuffins offer their services as "borrowed" kids for the duration of the walk. Arabs play cards and chat; mothers play with genuine children; office-workers eat ice creams sandwiched into buns, a Palermitan speciality. Like an island in the shark-infested sea of the *centro storico,* the park is a rare image of Palermo at ease with itself.

The battered **Capo quarter** lies north of the Kasr, sandwiched between the Cathedral and Teatro Massimo. Since its origins as the slave-traders' quarter, the Capo has been isolated and slightly menacing. Despite slum clearance, this shack-infested quarter was used as backdrop for Beirut in a recent film. Plans to build a city metro were scuppered by fears of subsidence, given the covered rivers and underground passages.

The quarter's centrepiece is still **Sant' Agostino**, the imposing monastery that ran the region in medieval times. Although built in 1275, the sober church

Below, ceiling of the Cappella Palatina. Right, Moorish figures on the Porta Nuova.

was enlarged by the powerful Chiaramonte and Sclàfani dynasties. Their crests decorate a delicate portal which is surmounted by a rose window. Inside are Serpotta frescoes and charming cloisters which were originally polychrome like those at Monreale.

South is **Piazza Beati Paoli**, supposedly the site of a secret masonic society Palermitans believe spawned the Mafia. Nearby are the modern criminal courts at **Palazzo di Giustizia**, whose Mafia cases are an inviting target for the television cameras. This odd quarter is at its most cheerful during the daily flea market. Within the market, at number 6 Via Cappuccinelle, is an enchanting **Art Nouveau bakery**, a vestige of elegance in the poverty-stricken Capo.

South of the Corso is the ramshackle **Albergheria** quarter, once inhabited by Norman court officials and rich merchants from Pisa and Amalfi. Depending on taste, it is a squalid slum or the old hugger-mugger of backstreet life.

The romantic red-domed **San Giovanni degli Eremiti** lies just south of the royal palace. This Byzantine basilica was converted into a Benedictine abbey and a mosque. Byzantine foundations cede to Arab squinches, filigree windows and Norman cloisters overgrown with jasmine. The shape of the early mosque is still visible, as are stiff frescoes and Muslim arches. The garden is enchanting.

Arab architectural motifs haunt **Palazzo Sclàfani**, a Catalan-Gothic *palazzo* north of San Giovanni. The mansion, adorned with a sculpted portal and decorative facade, belonged to one of the most powerful feudal families. Like most of Palermo's fortified mansions, this square hulk was built on a mole yet given a patrician charm through Arab arches and a private inner loggia.

Further east is the Carmine, a Carmelite convent in the heart of the **Ballarò market**. It meets second-hand clothes stalls by **Casa Professa**, also known as Il Gesù. This Jesuitical church boasts a baroque marble interior that teems with tritons and cherubs. The market spills over into **Corso Turkory**, a poor immi-

The exotic gardens and cloisters of San Giovanni degli Eremiti.

124

grant district lining the former city bastions. Traders, covered in anything from shawls to sawdust and blood, joke about the layer of *grascia* (grease) that coats the grimy quarter.

Quattro Canti: Known as "*il teatro*" (the city theatre), this central spot offers a cross-section of Palermitan baroque, Arab-Norman splendour and medieval muddle. The four screens of the city conceal chaotic or conflicting districts behind their neat Spanish facades. Close to this notional quarter, tracks lead into the warren of old Palermo. West of pollution-blackened Via Maqueda, alleys lead back to the battered Capo and Albergheria quarters.

Alternatively, the city shows its best public face in **Piazza Pretoria**. The baroque square was originally nicknamed Piazza Vergogna (Square of Shame) after its riot of saucy nude statues cavorting in the fountain. Amidst uproar, this Florentine Mannerist fountain was reassembled in Palermo. The vast circular basin is peopled by tritons, nymphs and river gods. Reputedly, the local nuns chopped off the noses of the nude gods but stopped short of castration. Adjoining the square is the **Senatorio**, the over-restored Gothic city hall and the towering presence of **San Giuseppe Teatini**, a theatrical baroque church. The interior is covered in multicoloured marble and is crowned by a cupola with a restored frescoe.

Piazza Bologni, the site of **Palermo University**, was the city's finest baroque square until 1943. One *palazzo* housed Nazi headquarters and so the site was destroyed in Allied raids. Even so, a statue and several sculpted facades give a sense of the past. Local journalist Rosario La Duca laments the neglect of this classic square, but the busy law students seem more intent on buying second-hand books.

On the far side of Via Maqueda lies the Jewish quarter centred on **San Nicolo'**, the erstwhile synagogue. It was called *mesquita* since it resembled a mosque but is now less Moorish than the two delightful domed Arab-Norman churches nearby. **La Martorana** was

The Byzantine glitter of La Martorana church.

founded in 1143 by George of Antioch, King Roger's Syrian emir and admiral. Although raised in the Orthodox faith, the Emir planned La Martorana as a mosque. To complicate matters, he chose Greek Byzantine craftsmen to make the splendid mosaics. Baroque additions confirm this as a coded church within a church. The space interweaves Byzantine and Moslem iconography: the Pantocrator is present but so is the figure 8, the Arabic number of perfection.

At **San Cataldo**, a queue for wedding dates forms at the sacristan's desk but a lavish tip ensures the keys. The triple-domed church is one of the last sacred buildings built in the Arab-Norman style. The Oriental impression is confirmed by the brooding Syrian interior. If this exquisite space at first appears sparse, it is only as a reaction to the gilded La Martorana. The subdued light reveals three domes supported by squinches and piers; the Fatimid capitals are so delicate they appear to float. In the crypt are sections of Palermo's Roman walls.

La Kalsa quarter: Meaning "pure" or "chosen" in Arabic, **La Kalsa** is no longer ironic now that Mother Teresa's mission has settled in bomb-struck **Piazza Magione**. Well-heeled Palermitani were horrified to be lectured at by an Albanian nun, even one incarnating sainthood. Her message was that since Palermo was as poor as the Third World, charity should begin at home.

However, this decrepit square houses a wonderful Norman church as well as Mother Teresa's nuns. Moorish filigree windows and blind arcading announce the ancestry of **La Magione**. This Cistercian church was founded in 1191 and given to the Imperial Teutonic Order by Henry VI. The Arab-Norman interior is plain without being austere. After Sunday Mass, the *borghese* congregation is met by beggars who threaten to increase the car graveyard outside unless drivers contribute "alms".

Palazzo Aiutamicristo, on the next square west, is a Catalan-Gothic mansion containing the remains of a loggia and porticoed courtyard. Just east, **Via Alloro**, the city's patrician centre in the

Antica Focacceria, the traditional place to devour innards.

Middle Ages, leads to Sicily's most endearing art collection. Housed in **Palazzo Abatellis**, a Catalan-Gothic mansion, the treasures are matched in scale and quality by a charming setting.

Off a Renaissance courtyard and loggia are rich Byzantine mosaics, Neapolitan Madonnas, painted medieval crucifixes, sweet Gagini sculptures and soft-hued Renaissance portraits. Other highlights are a serene bust of Eleanor of Aragon; a haunting da Messina Annunciation; and a geometric Moorish door. The undoubted masterpiece is the powerful *Triumph of Death*, a 15th-century *danse macabre*. The fresco shows the vanity of human wishes: a skeletal grim reaper cuts a swathe through the nobles' earthly pleasures.

Piazza Marina was a swamp until drained by the Arabs and used as their first citadel. Since then, the square has witnessed the shame and glory of city history. **Palazzo Chiaramonte**, a Catalan-Gothic fortress, was a feudal stronghold before becoming the seat of the Inquisition in 1598. Carved on the grim prison walls inside is a poignant plea for *pane, pazienza e tempo* (bread, patience and time). Outside, heretics and dissenters were burned. Commonly known as the Steri, the mansion belonged to the Spanish viceroys and the law courts before falling into the hands of the Chancellor of Palermo University. It is worth concocting an academic pretext to see the gorgeous inner courtyard and the salon with a coffered Moorish ceiling. As the only gentrified square in the old quarter, Piazza Marina is self-consciously proud of its **shady park** and well-tended banyan trees.

In Via Merlo is **Palazzo Mirto**, an unprepossessing *palazzo* with a delightful period interior. Now a museum, the mansion is a testament to the eclectic tastes of Palermitan nobles in the 18th century. Chinoiserie and Empire style clash with neo-Gothic and baroque. Below *trompe l'oeil* ceilings are Louis XVI chairs, rustic panelling, heroic tapestries or crib figures. Best is a chinoiserie salon with lacquered Oriental cabinets, porcelain and pagoda-style seats.

A tip and a smile gain access to **Oratorio di San Lorenzo** in Via Immacolatella. This whimsical yet overwrought oratory is a Serpotta gem, with every surface awash with cheeky cherubs waving impish bottoms.

Close by is **San Francesco d'Assisi**, arguably Palermo's loveliest Gothic church, its austerity softened by a delicate rose window. This northern church once served the Pisan merchants who traded nearby but the abstraction of the portal reveals an Arab-Norman influence. Opposite the church is **Antica Focacceria**, a legendary Palermitan inn, its battered bow windows matched by marble slabs and a gleaming brass stove. This period piece has a reputation for rustic snacks: *panini di panelle*, fried chick pea squares and *pani cu' la meusa*, greasy beef spleen served in a bun.

The **Marina** was Palermo's grand seafront until the *Belle Epoque*. It was both a grand parade and a chance for louche encounters. Patrick Brydone, an 18th-century traveller, records that unfaithful husbands and wives extinguished *flambeaux* and donned masks

Grotesque detail in San Giuseppe Teatini.

to enjoy sexual favours in darkened carriages. Coupling was disturbed only by "the intruding moon, with her horns and chastity".

Now known as **Foro Italico**, the waterfront is home to a scruffy fun fair, with Arab and African children riding ponies. The view is overlooked by the crumbling **Palazzo Butera**, eulogised by Goethe but bombed by the Allies. Once Sicily's grandest palace, it is still used for receptions. To improve the tone of the area, the council have created a park and re-opened the **Cattive**, a terrace named after the bad-tempered widows and spinsters who glowered at lovers entwined below. American bombing and Sicilian neglect may have blighted the waterfront but illicit assignations have merely moved to **Villa Giulia**. These formal gardens border the grey Kalsa area and are picturesquely run-down, with Classical pavilions and a baroque fountain with a sundial.

Next-door are the **Botanical Gardens**, dotted with pavilions, sphinx statues and a lily pond. There are clumps of bamboo and bougainvillaea, plus magnolia, kapoks, pineapples and petticoat palms. Most Sicilian is the banyan tree, trailing its cumbersome roots like a weary aristocrat waiting for an iced tea.

Vucciria quarter: The name is a corruption of the French *boucherie*, thanks to the quantity of flesh on sale in the traditional **Vucciria market**. The stalls straggle along alleys behind San Domenico and Via Roma. In the 18th century, the Spanish viceroys tried to impose order on Palermo's most chaotic market but failed dismally. The names of the surrounding streets echo their old trades: silversmiths, ironmongers, pasta-makers, shoe-makers. These colourful alleys are the noisy haunt of artisans and students, housewives and bootleggers.

If the frenzy of the Vucciria palls, consider a drink in the faded grandeur of **Hotel des Palmes** in Via Roma. Wagner composed part of *Parsifal* in one gilded salon. The wartime Mafia boss Lucky Luciano held court in the dining room.

Sustenance is necessary since between **San Domenico**, a vapid 17th-century

The battered old fishing port of La Cala.

church, and the port is devastation. However, Via Bambinai, a former doll-makers' street, has stayed close to its roots: shops sell votive offerings and Christmas crib figures. The street boasts a baroque jewel in **Oratorio del Rosario**, a theatrical Serpotta chapel, where *putti* play cellos amidst sea-shells, eagles and allegorical exotica.

In Via Valverde lies **Oratorio di Santa Zita**, reached through lush gardens. Serpotta's ravishing stucco-work depicts the intercession of the Virgin during the Battle of Lepanto, with all boats exquisitely differentiated.

Beyond the chapel is **La Cala**, the scruffy portside. Fishing boats bob against a backdrop of bombed *palazzi* whose cellars house immigrant families. **SM della Catena**, named after the medieval chain that once shut off the port, is a dilapidated Renaissance church with a fine portico. The skeletal interior is enlivened by sculpted columns. On neighbouring Piazza Tarzana are ruined *palazzi* occupied by squatters: Singhalese beggars and Filipino hawkers.

From Via Maqueda, Via Orologio leads to Piazza Olivella via a charming artisans' quarter of puppet-makers, *pasticcerie* and *trattorie*. The baroque **Olivella** church adjoins the **Museo Archeologico**, the essence of Classical Sicily encased in a late Renaissance monastery. The inner courtyard is a tangle of lush vegetation and a lily pond. Nearby are inscrutable Egyptian priestly figures found near Mozia. Anthropomorphic Phoenician sarcophagi stare out of Semitic faces and square bodies. A tablet carved with hieroglyphics, animals and birds vies with an ancient Greek bronze decree from Segesta.

The fabulous **Sala di Selinunte** displays the main frieze from Temple C: Athena protecting Perseus as he battles with the Medusa; and Hercules slaying dwarves. Other stylised friezes portray Hercules tackling a muscular Amazon; Zeus marrying a frosty Hera; and Actaeon attacked by savage dogs. Almost as compelling are the majestic lion-head water spouts and the graceful bronze Ephebus of Selinunte (470 BC).

By comparison, the Etruscan friezes look stilted: a mere procession of sleeping warriors, chariots and carved beasts.

Modern quarter: From here, Via Cavour leads north to Teatro Massimo. This neo-Classical district contains remnants of Palermo's *Belle Epoque* late flowering. The imposing **Teatro Massimo** is now open after being closed for 20 years due to civic lethargy and political wrangles. As cynics say, Palermitans would rather do nothing than be blamed for taking action. Ironically, the theatre was opened briefly to stage a scene in Coppola's *The Godfather, Part III*.

Viale della Libertà, considered one of the most chic streets, disappoints. It was once studded with Art Nouveau villas designed for the *haute bourgeoisie*, but most have been demolished or disappeared in fires linked to fraudulent insurance claims. The northern end leads to attractive gardens but smart bars and the sophistication of the evening *passeggiata* cannot conceal the fact that style has deserted the quarter.

Villa Malfitana is one of the few

stylish villas to have survived near the city centre. It is now a concert hall and charitable foundation set among yuccas, bamboos and palms. The interior is given over to polished mahogany, Sicilian coral and Louis XV furniture.

Society: The popular view is that Viale della Libertà is for rich residents but that all other areas are socially mixed. Certainly, at least 20 noble families retain their city *palazzi* and live cheek by jowl with all classes. Near the Politeama, a baron's *palazzo* overlooks a street of child beggars. Cynics might add that the upper classes also maintain country estates or villas on the coast. Yet in some baroque mansions, *nobili* inhabit the upper floors while artisans and tradesmen occupy tiny flats below.

The suburbs: San Giovanni dei Lebbrosi lies off Corso dei Mille, one of the main Mafia quarters to the south-east. Built as a castle chapel, this is one of the city's earliest Norman monuments. Made of warm limestone and brickwork, this red-domed chapel became a leper hospital. Nearby is **Ponte dell'Ammiraglio**, a genuine Norman bridge over a now-diverted river.

Further west, in Brancaccio, the South Bronx of Palermo, lies **La Favara**, the legendary Arab-Norman palace now sunk under Mafia-encrusted slums. Poverty-stricken families and farm animals have burrowed into the domes, geometrical walls and blind arcading. Before industry intervened, La Favara viewed the glistening groves of the Conca d'Oro to La Ziza, another of the palaces that encircled the city "like gold coins around the neck of a bosomy girl" in Norman times.

The vivid description given by the Arab poet, Ibn Jubayr, better conjures up the pleasure dome of **La Ziza**. An Arab arch leads to a palace built on the site of a Roman villa, to exploit the existing aqueduct. Fed by canals, the lake was paved with marine-inspired mosaics. La Ziza's most charming spot is the vestibule, adorned by honeycomb vaults, a Saracenic fountain and a glorious mosaic frieze of peacocks and huntsmen. In this breezy chamber, the Emir and his court listened to the lapping of

Ghoulish mummy of 18th-century priest in the catacombs of the Convento dei Cappuccini.

water. The interior, now a **museum of Arab culture**, is a mixed success. Critics claim that clumsy restoration has ruined the Arab lines and replaced filigree windows with heavy-framed versions. However, some Islamic features remain; the highlights are the mosaics and Cufic script.

Beyond the walls is the **palace chapel**, a domed Oriental affair whose stalactites, squinches and rib vaulting form part of a baroque church. A Palermitan teacher who lives beside La Ziza says that an orange full moon over the palms and fountain is enough to transport her to Tunisia.

La Cuba lies along Corso Calatafimi, opposite Via Quarto dei Mille. In Arab times, this quaint pavilion was marooned on a lovely artificial lake within the grounds of La Ziza. Boccaccio set a story from *The Decameron* in this "sumptuous villa" which is now a windowless, roofless ruin, marooned in an army barracks. **La Cubola**, the last link in the Arab chain, lies at the end of Via Aurelio Zancla. Sadly, this tiny domed

folly is ringed by modern apartment blocks. The return to Palermo is via **Porta Nuova**, a Spanish gateway decorated with turbaned Moorish giants.

Convento dei Cappuccini, the grim catacombs, lie just south of La Ziza. In macabre Sicilian style, superior corpses were mumified here from the 16th century to 1920. In death, the clergy, nobles and bourgeoisie opted for posterity rather than the communal trench. In these galleries, embalmers have stored over 8,000 moth-eaten mummies.

Conca d'Oro: Mary Simeti looks for "proof that not all Palermo's decay is irreversible" but it is not to be found in the Conca d'Oro. The city outskirts should be carpeted with marigolds and lemon groves but land speculation and Mafia funding have ensured that Palermo's countryside is being encased in concrete. Laws protecting green sites are flouted by unscrupulous builders.

Yet **Villa Igiea**, Palermo's *de luxe* hotel, is a swan song to the city's last flicker of greatness. It was designed for the Florio family, possibly Sicily's great-

Art Deco nymphs frolic in the Hotel-Villa Igiea.

est entrepreneurs. While the Whitakers invested their fortune in the grand Villa Malfitano, the Florio chose an exotic terraced setting overlooking the sea. The glorious Art Nouveau dining room is a harmonious composition of elegant cabinets, functional furnishings and ethereal frescoes.

On the northern outskirts lies the **Parco della Favorita**, a Bourbon park designed by the exiled Ferdinand III. His domineering consort, Maria Carolina, conceived of the **Palazzina Cinese** as a Petit Trianon to rival the creation of her sister, Marie Antoinette. This *chinoiserie* pavilion remains an inspired folly, with its original 18th-century furnishings. By billeting Allied troops there during World War II, the villa was spared but now seems destined for ruination by Palermitan officialdom and neglect. The **Piana dei Colli** villas, once patrician summer retreats, are sinking under bougainvillaea, oleander and neglect.

Next-door is **Villa Niscemi**, whose interior is also *"chiuso per restauro"* but whose fate seems assured. The villa

was used as Lampedusa's model for Tancredi's home in *The Leopard* and is a *recherché* film set. Owned by a noble family who came to Sicily with the Normans, the villa combines elegance with rustic charm.

A scenic road climbs **Monte Pellegrino**, passing citrus groves and shrubland. In these sandstone slopes, the **Addaura caves** have revealed prehistoric drawings. From the terraced slopes, sweeping views span the glinting bay of the Conca d'Oro.

Santuario di Santa Rosalia, a shrine to Palermo's revered patron saint, lies in a mountain grotto on San Pellegrino. Her origins are mysterious but in 1624, while Palermo was in the throes of the plague, her vision instructed a dreamer to hunt for her relics and wave them three times round the city walls. Thus Palermo was saved and devotedly built a sanctuary in Rosalia's honour. Patrick Brydone believed that the bones belonged to "some poor wretch that was probably murdered". His suspicions were not too far off the mark: recently the bones have been proved to be those of a goat. Mountain views and an insight into Palermitan sentimentality are the main rewards for trailing up to this kitsch spectacle in a damp cave.

On the coast lies the fashionable resort of **Mondello**, pioneered by the Bourbons. The striking Art Nouveau pier was created by a Belgian entrepreneur. Like the city catacombs, the Mondello resort reflects one's social status. Beaches range from modest pocket-handkerchief class to smart boat-club exclusive.

Sleeping beauty: The last child to be entombed in the catacombs was a tiny girl nicknamed Sleeping Beauty. She personifies the city's *disfattista* temperament whereby lethargy, criticism, pessimism and fear of action make Palermo a graveyard for private and public initiatives. As Anatole France said: "Palermo is a splendid slavegirl whom her masters have adored one after another. Weighed down by all her jewels, she sleeps in the sun." Many a bronzed Mondello beauty would accept this as a compliment before dozing off.

<u>Left</u>, Mondello's stratified beaches cater for every class. <u>Right</u>, the Art Nouveau pier at Mondello's main beach.

PALERMO PROVINCE

Outside Palermo, the centuries unfurl in a clannish yet sparsely populated countryside. It is a province of extreme light and shade, of esoteric cults and exuberant festivals. This is the brooding Mafia heartland of gulleys and mountain lairs. Nurtured by the mythology of banditry, the region falls back on ancient suspicion and insularity. Small-town battles and spiritual isolation pervade a wild province. Yet these rural pockets feels far away from the Moorish voluptuousness and sophistication of Monreale.

In the words of a Sicilian proverb, "He who goes to Palermo without seeing **Monreale** leaves a donkey and comes back an ass." Certainly, this sumptuous Cathedral is the apogee of Arab-Norman art. The **cathedral** and Benedictine monastery were built by William II, allegedly inspired by a vision. In truth, his political rivalry with Walter of the Mill, the Palermitan archbishop, fuelled his desire to build a cathedral greater than Palermo's. Ultimately, William triumphed and his white marble sarcophagus lies in Monreale.

Flanked by severe belltowers, the cathedral is not instantly awe-inspiring yet the details are exquisite. An arched **Romanesque portal**, made by a Pisan master, is framed by a greenish bronze door. The portal displays sculpted bands of garlands, figures and beasts alternated with multi-coloured mosaics. To the left, a Gagini portico shelters another Romanesque **bronze door**, inspired by the delicacy of Byzantine inlaid ivory. The **apses** are the most opulent in Sicily: a poetic abstraction of interlacing limestone and lava arches, sculpted as delicately as wood.

Monreale drew craftsmen from Persia, Africa, Asia, Greece, Venice, Pisa and Provence. The shimmering **gold interior** fuses Arab purity of volume with Byzantine majesty. The date of the **mosaics** is disputed: some scholars believe they were finished by 1100; others maintain that while the Byzantines began before then, the Venetians only completed the work by 1250. But certainly their shimmering tapestry is unequalled in Europe. It is worth investing in binoculars to admire the **Creation series** on the upper walls in the right of the nave. The delicacy of the flowers, fruit trees and exotic birds singles out these scenes from Genesis. However, the whole series is a *Biblia pauperum*, a poor man's Bible. The **Pantocrator** in the apse is an authoritarian God, unlike the softer Christ in Cefalù. Above the royal throne is a mosaic of Christ crowning William the Good, a tribute to the king whose world view embraced concubines, eunuchs and negro slaves.

Other delights include Cosmati paving; **Roman capitals** incorporating busts of Ceres and Proserpine; and a gilded **ceiling** whose rafters resemble the spines of beautifully bound books. A supply of coins ensures that the mosaics are not plunged into darkness.

The **cloisters** express William's love of Islamic art and are the most sumptuous Romanesque cloisters in the world. Every second pair of white marble col-

umns has a vivid zigzag mosaic pattern spiralling up the shaft. The sophistication of these columns suggests a Provençal influence while the Moorish mood, evoked by mosaic inlays or arabesque carvings, conjures up the Alhambra.

Many sculptures echo the mosaics but add a personal note, including the name of a mason or musicians playing Sicilian instruments. The *Allegory of the Seasons*, an enchanting marble composition, depicts tree-planting and pig-killing. In one corner, a loggia creates a *chiaroscuro* effect with a glorious, if slightly phallic **fountain**. Shaped like a palm tree trunk, the shaft is crowned by lions' heads, as at the Alhambra.

Town: The **monastery** has been under restoration after a plague of weevils munched their way into the dormitory and chapter house. However, a terrace affords sweeping views of the former royal estates, with citrus groves slightly marred by new building. While Monreale is an anticlimax after the mosaics, a horse and cart ride from the Duomo is a chance to enjoy crumbling baroque churches and old-fashioned shops. After raucous Palermo, Monreale exudes provincial calm. Yet Sicily's largest Carabinieri barracks was built here after the Mafia murdered local officers in 1983–84. Local *trattorie* offer *pasta con broccoli; pasta con le sarde,* a sardine speciality; or dry *biscotti di monreale*. **Madonna delle Croci**, set on a hill, offers a last lingering view from the cathedral to the coast. Despite the dry biscuits, Monreale's afterglow takes a while to fade.

In the lushly mountainous landscape of Boccadifalco is the Benedictine abbey of **San Martino**. The abbey is known for charitable works amongst the lay community and for its monumental staircase, rich monastic library and 18th-century paintings. Beyond is the village of **Baida** (Arabic for white), boasting a Gothic church. The surrounding pine forests are a cool escape in summer.

In 1873 John Addington Symonds wrote of **Montelepre**: "The talk was brigands and nothing but brigands." This was especially true on the eve of World

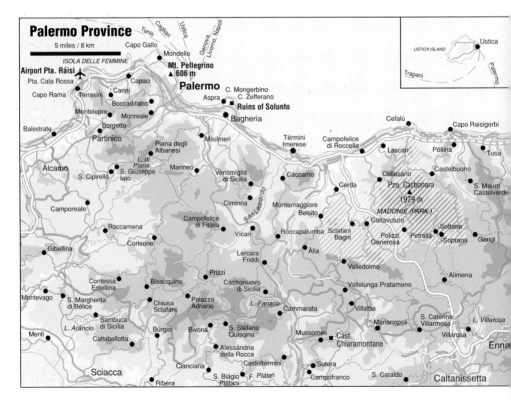

War II, when the bandit Salvatore Giuliano reigned over these desolate crags. He became both an unwitting stooge for the Separatist cause and a Mafia pawn. If today's Mafiologists are correct, this is still bandit country. Certainly, local graffiti mention Giuliano's name. Little appears to have changed since Giuliano's mysterious murder in Castelvetrano in 1950. The medieval heart of Montelepre is enclosed by scruffy alleys and compact courtyards coiled around the Chiesa Madre.

On the edge of town are boulders and cacti. Views of deserted farms and fields dotted with boulders indicate that although the feudal estates have gone, little has replaced them on the land. Neighbouring **Partinico** is a byword for urban poverty. In the 1950s Danilo Dolci, Sicily's Gandhi, chose benighted western Sicily to set up his centre.

Piana degli Albanesi appears suspended above a lake. Lush pastures are encircled by hills, home to 15th-century Greek-speaking immigrants, confusingly designated Albanians. The community settled here in 1488 after Turkish troops invaded their homeland. Since then, generations have kept their customs and their Orthodox faith in this cheerful town. Marriages and funerals, Epiphany and Easter are times for traditional Byzantine ceremony and folk costumes. The community speaks Greek at home; signs are in Greek as well as Italian. Local cuisine is a cultural stew: *stranghuie* (gnocchi), *brumie me bathé e thieré*, a filling bean casserole or *dash*, castrated ram, Albanian-Greek style

Corleone is enfolded in desolate, scorched hills and high verdant plains. The town lies clamped between two rocks, below a weather-beaten escarpment called "Montagna Vecchia". At first sight, Corleone fails to live up to its infamous reputation. But on closer inspection, an air of watchfulness hangs over the town. At times, it passes for a topsy-turvy world with mysterious undercurrents bordering on lawlessness. Madonnas with snapped heads dangle from car dashboards; teenagers toss olive trees over the cliff; grizzled crones

Monreale Cathedral.

carry piles of brushwood for their able-bodied sons; and 12-year-old children in three-wheeled cars speed along cobbled alleys.

In the town centre is the **Castello**, a rocky outcrop topped by a Saracen tower. It was a prison until 1976 but is now home to Franciscan friars who take their vow of poverty seriously. Below, the rooftops are stacked in a chromatic range of greys. Corleone's baroque convents and *palazzi* are crumbling; the churches are padlocked; the once dignified 18th-century town is falling apart while the citizens watch with mild curiosity. Only the **Chiesa Madre** retains a semblance of standards, with its white baroque interior and garish, frescoed ceiling.

Unlike neighbouring towns, Corleone's shops and businesses pay no *pizzo* (protection money) because the town is the stronghold of the most powerful Mafia clan. However, the arrest in 1993 of Totò Riina, the Corleonese *capo di tutti capi*, promised to spell turmoil. When news of his arrest spread, local school-children burst into applause, but the men in battered fedoras stood motionless on the *piazza*.

Prizzi, a sloping checkerboard of rust-tiled roofs, is celebrated for its bizarre **Easter festival**. Known as the *ballo dei diavoli* (dance of the devils), the festival dates back to Sicani times. The dance depicts the eternal struggle between Good and Evil, darkness and light, winter and spring, Christianity and paganism. The gap-toothed devil masks are primitive but menacing while the atmosphere of ritualised violence is echoed by Mafia lore. In this fleeting escape from *miseria*, citizens fall upon Prizzi's cheeses, pastries and wines.

The neighbouring village of **Palazzo Adriano** encapsulates the festering rivalries of these provincial backwaters. Two sombre churches share the main square in mutual antipathy: the Orthodox Santa Maria dell'Assunta scorns the Catholic Santa Maria del Lume. Ironically, the square starred in the warmly evocative *Cinema Paradiso*.

From here, the route back to the coast passes the hilltop village of **Mezzojuso**,

Courtyard in Prizzi.

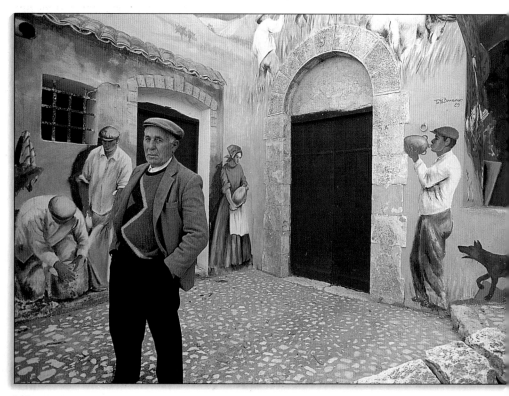

snug in the Ficuzza woods. Like many others, the village has mixed Albanian and Arab ancestry and religious frictions. **Dell'Annunziata**, the Catholic church, is literally overshadowed by the Orthodox **San Nicola**, home to lovely Byzantine icons. Nearby, the Albanian **Santa Maria delle Grazie** houses frescoes and the finest *iconostasis* in Sicily. The adjoining monastery restores and displays precious Greek manuscripts and miniatures.

Cefalà Diana, just north, is firmly in the Arab camp, with a tumbledown castle and the island's best-preserved Moorish bath-house. Lying on the old road to Agrigento, these warm, vaulted baths were a tempting stop for travel-weary pilgrims. Then as now, travellers were also drawn to the strong white *passito* wine from **Misilmeri**.

West coast: By boat, leave behind the looming hulk of Monte Pellegrino to sail along the west coast. Beyond Mondello is the headland and lighthouse of **Capo Gallo**, the site of weird rock ledges and deep coves. From the prettified harbour of **Sferracavallo** are picturesque views of Palermo and seagulls circling a Saracen watchtower at **Isole delle Femmine**.

Beyond the cement works and airport on Golfo di Carini, the jagged *faraglioni* rocks come into view. The sheltered port of **Terrasini** may be a tourist trap yet is ideal for drinks or a seafood lunch. Secluded beaches alternate between sandy and rocky, leaving the province at San Cataldo and Trappeto.

East coast: From Palermo to Cefalù, the coast curves past fishing villages and coves to Capo Zafferano and **Solunto.** Set on majestic cliffs, the ruins are less impressive than the wild location. The Phoenician colony of Solus was one of the earliest trading posts on the island and survived until destruction by Siracusa in 398 BC. It was later Hellenised and taken by Rome, with the result that traces of the three civilisations remain. The highlights are the floor mosaics and a luxurious villa dwelling with a colonnaded peristyle. From the agora are stunning views of vineyards, a castle and Cefalù. Beyond the wizened olive

trees and battered boulders are charming swimming spots near the lighthouse on the cape.

Beyond is **Bagheria**, which developed during the *Ottocento* vogue for ostentatious country villas. The 17th-century pioneers were the Branciforte family, the Princes of Butera, Sicily's most powerful dynasty. The summer villas are mostly in late Renaissance style, with grand staircases and a central body flanked by sweeping concave wings. The U-shaped lower wings were reserved for servants. Most villas were encircled by French formal gardens, with *roseraies* and *parterres* interspersed with statues and summer houses.

Bagheria was a mere servant to its feudal masters and the town would never have come to prominence were it not for its entrenched *mafioso* culture. While some villas are pitiful wrecks inhabited by artisans, others like **Villa Trabia** and the glorious **Villa Valguarnera** remain in noble hands, albeit with reduced parkland. *Bagheria*, Dacia Maraini's latest novel, describes her childhood in this

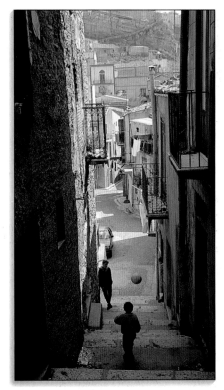

Corleone, where the Mafia casts a dark shadow.

ARISTOCRATIC LIVES

U nder Spanish rule, the aristocracy acquired a taste for *spagnolismo*, the pomp and circumstance. Prince Lampedusa's vision of this splendour was one Sicilians would die for: "The ballroom was all golden; smoothed on cornices, stippled on door-frames, damascened pale, almost silvery, over darker gold on door panels and on the shutters which covered and annulled the windows, conferring on the room the look of some superb jewel-case shut off from the unworthy world."

The grandeur intensified under the Bourbons when status-seeking required the purchase of illustrious titles, no matter how undeserved. The puritanical House of Savoy had little effect on patrician tastes in 18th-century Sicily.

A palace in Palermo and a villa in Bagheria were the minimum required to keep up appearances. Lampedusa described his villa at Santa Margherita as "an eighteenth-century Pompeii". Palermo's Gangi palace and Villa Palagonia at Bagheria are equally lavish. Palazzo Gangi-Valguernera's sump-

tuous interior caused a contemporary English visitor to remark of the Palermitan aristocracy: "Their time is wasted in balls, masquerades and dissipation."

So competitive was the race for status that the nobility pleaded with the King to outlaw the extravagance. They complained that the lower classes were aping them in dowries, funerals and retinues. The government dutifully put a ceiling on such expenditure, but all that achieved was social *kudos* for those who could afford to buy exemptions.

Victor Amadeus's attempt to limit carriage ownership was no more successful, and Palermo had bad traffic jams. Nobles were urged to come into town by horse instead of carriage. The afternoon carriage drive remained *de rigueur*. However, the Bourbons banned Prince Lampedusa's grandfather from the seafront after he drove his carriage stark naked. On asking why dung was never swept up, Goethe was told that the gentry preferred the soft ride for their carriages.

When the hare-brained King Ferdinand II, a hunting fanatic, fled from Naples to Sicily, his first action was to proclaim draconian penalties for poaching on the royal estates. Following his example, the nobility walled off common land near Palermo for their private hunting.

The consumption of ice-cream, snow-cooled sorbets and iced drinks was colossal. The snow was collected in March, pounded into balls, and rolled into cool caves. It was then wrapped in straw and salt and brought down on donkeys.

During the 18th century, Palermo's population doubled to about 200,000. The city spent lavishly on public entertainment, with 100 parades a year, including floats, fireworks and masquerades. The grandest one was the festival of Santa Rosalia, Palermo's patron, which lasted five days. A 70-ft (21-metre) *carrozza* resembling a Roman galley was pulled by elephants, bears and mules; on top of the contraption sat a tiered orchestra.

In 1783, the Viceroy attempted to shorten the festivities and ordered the savings to be given to poor girls as dowries. No act could have united rich and poor in such outrage and, fearing revolution, the King had to intervene and countermand the curtailment. Be ginning on 15 July every year, the celebrations today are conducted as zealously as ever. ■

Mandolin player at the weird Villa Palagonia, Bagheria.

splendid villa. The dilapidated but still florid **Villa Butera** commands the slopes of Corso Butera. **Villa Cattolica** houses the bizarre tomb of Renato Guttuso, Sicily's best-known modern painter, who died in 1987. A sculptor friend made him a surreal blue capsule tomb to match the sky, a harmonious sight among the scrubby cacti and lemons.

Villa Palagonia, the strangest of the villas, was built in 1715 by the Prince of Palagonia and is owned by an absentee professor. Arranged around a curved axis, the villa is celebrated for the eccentricity of its grotesque sculptures. A concave wing curves back towards the main *corps* and is topped by a variety of weird Mannerist sculptures: dwarfs, hunchbacks, monsters, dragons, a two-headed dog, and a horse with human hands. Most were created by the surreal imagination of the iconoclastic Prince and are thought to represent his faithless wife's lovers.

Sadly, the octagonal entrance is ruined and one approaches from the back. Beside the main entrance, two gargoyles with gaping mouths were used to extinguish the footmen's torches. A flamboyant double staircase ascends to the *piano nobile*, with the salon's mirrored ceiling representing the sky. At balls, the eccentric Prince dressed monkeys as musicians. Goethe was astonished by trick chairs with sawn-off legs and nails in the seats. The Prince had the following message engraved over the door: "Mirror yourself in these crystals and contemplate the image of human frailty."

San Nicola l'Arena is a picturesque fishing village with a 15th-century crenellated castle overlooking the harbour. Now converted into a nightclub, the castle belongs to Palermitan aristocrats. Beside it is a solid brick *tonnara*, a reminder that the coast was devoted to tuna fishing until recently.

Termini Imerese is an unfortunate jumble of industry, resort and Classical ruins. However, the upper town remains fairly unspoilt, with clumps of Roman remains, from an amphitheatre to city walls, as well as a Greek temple to Zeus. Founded by Zankle (Messina), the city

Capo Zafferano.

was known as **Therma Himera** to the Romans, and famed for its mineral waters and baths. The baroque **cathedral** lies near the ruins of ancient Himera and fittingly incorporates a Roman cornice below the tower. Just east of town is an impressive Roman aqueduct set in a wild olive grove. Inland is **Caccamo**, a dramatic 12th-century hill fort redesigned during the baroque period.

A return to the coast at **Cefalù** is a chance to visit the province's great counterpoint to Monreale Cathedral. Sitting snugly below a headland, Cefalù is Taormina's west coast rival. The consensus is that Taormina has better nightlife but Cefalù is more compact and family-oriented.

Built in 1130 by Roger II, the **cathedral** has a bold twin-towered facade and a triple apse with blind arcading. Roger used the See of Cefalù as a counterweight to Monreale and favoured Cefalù as the official mouthpiece of the state church. The King confidently had porphyry sarcophagi made for posterity but these are now in Palermo Cathedral.

Inside, a severe nave is flanked by Roman columns surmounted by Romanesque arches, a reminder that a temple lies below. A sense of space and majesty is created by the concentration of otherworldly mosaics in the distant dome. These luminous **Byzantine mosaics** are among the earliest created by the Normans yet are also praised as the purest extant depiction of Christ.

The rest of the interior is imbued with majesty. The raised choir represents an Oriental element whereas the gold firmament behind Christ is Byzantine. The open-timber roof has traces of the original Arab-Norman paintings. Below is a Norman font guarded by leopards, the symbol of King Roger's Hauteville dynasty. Birds often circle the nave, adding a note of life to this pristine temple.

Out of season, **Piazza del Duomo** is a delightful sun trap, with a view of the cathedral at the foot of steep cliffs running up to the fortifications. The square is also framed by the Corso, a Renaissance seminary and a porticoed *palazzo*. In the good *Osteria*, one can dine *al*

Baroque facade in Termini Imerese.

fresco, served by a London-trained chef or a much-travelled folk singer: such is Cefalù's quirky internationalism.

Town: The **old port** is tangibly Moorish and North African fishermen are in evidence. A warren of alleys leads west from **Corso Ruggero** and reveals Renaissance facades, Gothic parapets and mullioned windows overlooking tiny courtyards. An underground spring bubbles up in the arcaded **Arab baths**, sited at the bottom of curved steps.

Via Porto Salvo passes battered churches and flourishing craft shops. In summer, the town is a delightful tourist trap with quaint craft boutiques selling ceramics and gold jewellery, matched by sophisticated restaurants catering to fastidious French palates. **Porta Pescare**, one of the surviving medieval gates, opens onto a creek, beach and boatyard. In the evening, the seafront, bastion and Corso become a cavalcade devoted to *passeggiate* and *gelati*.

From Piazza Duomo, a steepish hill leads down to **Museo Mandralisca**. Apart from several Madonnas, this is a dusty collection, with the shining exception of Antonello da Messina's *Portrait of an Unknown Man*. The painting served as a back door to a pharmacy cabinet on Lipari island until an assistant was unnerved by the sneering face and scratched out the portrait's eyes.

A jagged outcrop overhangs the medieval town and is the site of the **Citadel**, the original Arab town. After the Norman conquest in 1063, the populace left the loomimg crags for the port below.

Salita Saraceno leads up through three tiers of city walls. Two marked walks climb through pine groves to the rocky cliffs and views over rust-coloured roofs. The path leads past foxgloves and wild fennel, acanthus and mandrake. Below are rocky inlets, an azure sea and sandy beaches, one of which belongs to Club Med.

The stone citadel, restored in 1991, occupies a megalithic mound. The climb to the top passes ruined water mills, the remains of a Byzantine chapel, a Roman well, water course, battered terracotta pavement and rooms hewn into the rock.

Caccamo Castle, set in rugged terrain.

Above are traces of a pool, fountain, cistern and prison.

Set among olive and cypress groves, the muddled ruins are overgrown with euphorbia. Nearby is **Tempio di Diana**, a 4th-century temple to Diana built over a megalithic shrine to a water deity.

Madonie mountains: A gentle circuit from Cefalù visits accessible mountain enclaves. Thanks to low-key tourism, based on outdoor pursuits such as trekking, horse-riding and winter sports, these Madonie villages escape grinding poverty. *Agriturismo* (farm stays) makes an appealing way of exploring the area. Colourful festivals, hearty cuisine and a cultural confidence ensure that the Madonie lack the usual harshness of the mountainous interior.

After Cefalù, coastal olive groves give way to pine woods and the rugged valley town of **Isnello**. Its ruined Byzantine castle overlooks majolica-encrusted spires and limestone cliffs. A vastly superior feudal castle towers over **Castelbuono**. Once a fief of the Ventimiglia dynasty, the scenic village is rich in chapels, cloisters and frescoes. The Matrice Vecchia has a Catalan-Gothic portal, quaint portico and, in the crypt, fine Gothic frescoes.

Further south is **Gangi**, a tortoise-shaped town with a crumbling watch-tower. The castle chapel has an unusual barrel-vaulted ceiling. The grey-green slopes of the Madonie rise to the snow-capped Madonna dell'Alto, the highest peak. In the foreground are farms selling wine, oil and salami.

Beyond is the jagged skyline of **Petralia Soprana**, a seemingly prosperous town set on a spur. On the stone-flagged Piazza del Popolo is **Maria di Loreto**, a delicate, tiny church built over a mosque. Covered passageways lead to a belvedere and bracing views, marred by the vast car park on stilts that every up-and-coming hamlet feels obliged to build. Half-hidden in alleys are striking mansions with baroque or rococo balconies as well as two watchtowers.

Petralia Sottana, nestling in a wooded hillside, also exudes a quiet ease. Now a mountain resort, this former Norman citadel boasts a trio of Romanesque, Gothic and baroque churches. **Chiesa Matrice** is perched on a belvedere and swathed in mist; inside is a precious Arabian candelabra.

The road north to **Polizzi Generoso** passes *masserie*, feudal farmsteads that were as self-sufficient as most villages. Chiesa Matrice has a medieval triptych of the Madonna and Child, a flower-ringed work that glows with Flemish mastery. The village is a trekking centre which sustains walkers with pasta and asparagus (*pasta cu l'asparaci*).

The Madonie: Unlike most of Sicily, the Madonie has not been scarred by deforestation. At the lower levels are almonds, olives and hazelnuts. On the higher slopes are beech, holm oak, chestnut and maple, as well as broom, lentisk and starflower. Piano Cervi and Monte San Salvatore are riddled with aqueducts and streams. Majestic Nebrodi firs have grown on these rugged ridges since the Ice Age and were used to create the roof of Monreale Cathedral. In the remoter regions, wolves, wild cats and eagles still thrive.

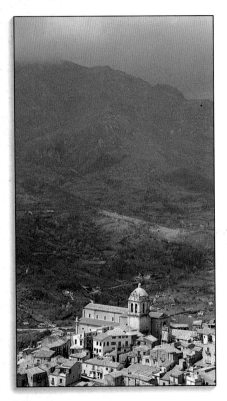

Left, Petralia Sottana rises out of the misty Madonie mountains. **Right**, the towers of Cefalù Cathedral are just visible across the rocky bay.

TRAPANI PROVINCE

As the least definable yet most varied province, Trapani is a puzzle. This seafaring region represents a swathe of ancient Sicily, from Phoenician Mozia to Greek Selinunte, medieval Erice and Arab Mazzaro. The landscape spans salt pans, vineyards, woods and coastal nature reserves. The province is the most African and Phoenician yet this heart of Muslim Sicily produces alcoholic Marsala.

Trapani has the most dynamic provincial tourist board: advice is fulsome and readily available; sites are well-organised. Far from conforming to Sicilian lethargy, the board is continually opening new museums or fostering music and drama festivals in Classical settings. It also takes a stand against pollution, building speculation and the destruction of coastal salt pans. As triumphs, it claims the setting up of Sicily's first nature reserve and protection of windmills, salt pans and marshes.

Trapani: Apparently Cronos, one of the Titans, castrated his father Uranus with a sickle and threw his genitals into the sea at Cape Drepanum. The result is modern-day Trapani. As a seafaring power, its history lies at the heart of the Mediterranean, trading with the Levant and Amalfi, Carthage and Venice. It remains an important port and an embarkation point for the Egadi Islands and the remote Moorish island of Pantelleria. Trapani's traditional industries of coral, tuna fishing and salt linger on. Salt, the symbol of perpetuity yet sterility, sums up the contradictions of a natural survivor, one that mislaid its spirit in the process. Trapani has an infamous reputation as a Mafia money-laundering centre, a rumour borne out by the city's countless private banks.

Visually, Trapani is appealing from a distance: a patchwork of shallow lagoons bounded by thin causeways; piles of salt roofed with red tiles. Close up, the spit of the old town has a superficial charm but even this is marred by the bland urban sprawl. The sights are not monumental: a graceful Gothic church; a fine arts and crafts collection; and a cluster of dilapidated baroque *palazzi*. The small Jewish quarter has a decayed charm epitomised by the **Giudecca** mansion, while the salty port offers *cuscusu* (fish soup) and lobster in boisterous fishermen's haunts.

About 3km (2 miles) north of the old town is **Santuario dell'Annunziata**, a Carmelite church in Chiaramonte-Gothic style. Its charms are a baroque belltower, a Gothic rose window and a doorway decorated in a zigzag pattern. Inside is a rococo nave and a cluster of exotic domed chapels. Dedicated to fishermen, the frescoed Cappella dei Pescatori rivals the sailors' Cappella dei Marinai. Within a Renaissance scheme, this chapel embraces Byzantine and Moorish elements, as well as a Spanish diamond-point design. Behind the high altar is a lavish chapel containing the **Madonna di Trapani**, a Gothic Pisan statue crowned in jewels. The venerated Madonna is credited with miraculous powers and, as the city symbol, is wor-

shipped by fishermen as well as the proverbial black-clad widows.

Museo Nazionale Pepoli, the city's eclectic museum, is housed in the adjoining former convent. Off the cloisters lie Gagini sculptures and sections devoted to the decorative arts. Exquisite craftsmanship is visible in the **coral** cribs and gilded figurines, the enamelled Moorish lamps, majolica tiles and vases. Gaudiest of all is a coral crucifix, with a salmon-coloured Christ against an ebony and mother-of-pearl cross.

The mystic mountain: Just north is a more enticing base than Trapani for exploring the African Coast. In spring, the winding road climbs past views of acacia, wild gladioli and waxy lemon blossom to the legendary **Mount Eryx**. Swathed in seasonal mists or in a carpet of flowers, **Erice** is an exquisite medieval town. The **Carthaginian walls** survive, rough-hewn slabs inscribed with Punic symbols. Nearby is the charming **Quartiere Spagnolo**, the 17th-century Spanish bastion.

This mystical city was founded by the Elymni (Elymians), mysterious settlers of Segesta who worshipped the Mediterranean fertility goddess. She was known as Astarte to the Elymni and the Phoenicians, Aphrodite to the Greeks, and Venus to the Romans. Each spring, the goddess flew off with an escort of doves to spend time at her shrine in Sicca Veneria, modern El Kef in Tunisia. Her return signalled the reawakening of nature in Sicily.

In Erice, the Romans followed earlier customs of worship, including the cult of sacred prostitution at the temple. According to the Sicilian historian Diodorus: "The Romans put aside the gravity of office and entered into play and intercourse with women amidst great gaiety." Despite countless invasions, Erice's sanctuary was inviolate.

Sights: Even without a goddess, the views from the **Balio gardens** justify a pilgrimage. Below stretch ragged turrets, wooded groves and vineyards; a tapestry of salt pans and sea slip all the way to the turtle-shaped Egadi Islands and to Cap Bon in Tunisia. As the blunt

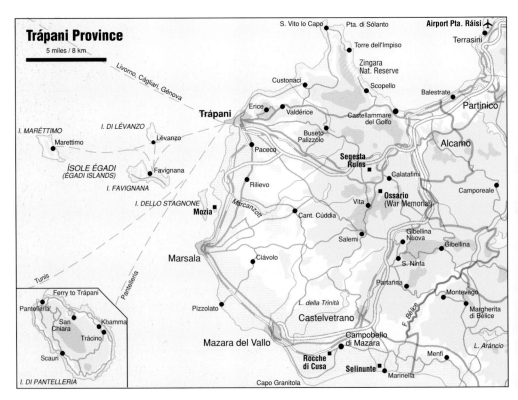

152

English poet Fiona Pitt-Kethley concludes: "If you want a good view, go up Eryx, not bloody Etna." Wintry weather is another story. Some older citizens wear a *burdigliuno*, a blue hooded cape worn as a wind shield or for soaking up the first spring rays.

On a rocky outcrop is the **Norman castle** overlooking **Torretta Pepoli**, a Gothic fantasy created by Count Pepoli. Inside the crenellated Norman castle is the **Tempio di Venere**, the battered marble remains of a sacred temple to Venus beside a well. After helping herself to a sliver of marble to bring luck in love, Fiona Pitt-Kethley said: "I expect centuries of lovers have done the same and that's why there's no temple left". Luckily, an enigmatic Greek alabaster bust of the goddess lies in the city museum. **Porta Trapani**, a medieval gate, leads to **Via Vittorio Emanuele**, a winding cobbled street lined with medieval *palazzi*. In Via Chiaramonte, just within the walls of this triangular town, is the severe Gothic **Duomo**. The crenellated facade is Aragonese and graced by a restored rose window. The blanched interior has fallen under the spell of Gothic Revivalism but is grandly convincing until one considers the waste of the original interior lurking under the trickery. At the end of the street is **Re Aceste**, a typical restaurant.

Virgil compared Erice to Mount Athos for its altitude and spiritual pre-eminence. Overlooking the green valley is the isolated white-domed **San Giovanni**, perched on a cliff. Most of the brownish stone churches are Gothic but suffer from baroque meddling. **San Pietro** has a sculpted doorway and fine medallions while **San Giuliano** is one of the most atmospheric spots, thanks to its mellow, caramel-coloured facade and elegant *campanile*. The weathered **Addolorata** retains its Gothic soul and stores the *Misteri*, the town's precious figures used in the Easter procession.

Not that Erice remains a sanctuary today. Orphanages and convents have become ceramic and carpet shops or night clubs and chic restaurants. Still, behind this public face lies a private

Below, Trapani harbour, with Erice in the background. Right, Castello di Venere at Erice.

Erice, one of wall-hugging alleys, grotesque baroque balconies, votive niches and secret courtyards. In keeping with Arab traditions, such courtyards were where women and children could sit in private, working or chatting by the well.

Erice is a paradox. In winter, it resembles a windy Umbrian hill town yet in summer bursts with bijou boutiques recalling the Côte d'Azur. The town is packed in season yet suffers from depopulation. This sleepy-looking citadel is home to the internationally-renowned **Centro Ettore Majorana**, a scientific and cultural institute set in a lovely old convent. Curiously, none of this affects the town's sense of harmony.

Erice has a tradition of *dolci ericini*, excessively sweet cakes. As elsewhere, these were originally made by novice nuns in a closed convent until the convent closed in 1975. Since then, locals lament that the sweets are not as "homemade" as before. Even so, Maria Grammatico vies for the title of best bakery in Sicily in her *pasticceria* in Via Vittorio Emanuele. She learnt the trade as a novice but fears that there is no one to follow her. Apart from *pasta reale* (marzipan), her sweets have such poetic names as *sospiri* (sighs) and *belli e brutti* (beauties and the beasts).

The former convent is in Via Guarnotti but sweet Sicilian memories spill over into the adjoining square of **San Domenico**. Near the baroque sculpted church is an equally baroque concoction of cakes in Pasticceria San Carlo. In La Pentollacia in Via Guarnotti, one can dine on *couscous* in a former monastery. This grey medieval town is a mistress of sensuality. Yet, as writer Carlo Levi realised, it is also "the Assisi of the south, full of churches, convents, silent streets and of the extraordinary accumulation of mythological memories".

Along the coast to Castellammare: This coast was once noted for its rich tuna-fishing grounds but most *tonnare* (tunneries) have fallen into ruin. However, the sea road passes the **Tonnara di Bonagie** on the way to Sicily's finest nature reserve. The **Riserva Naturale dello Zingaro** is set on a rocky head-

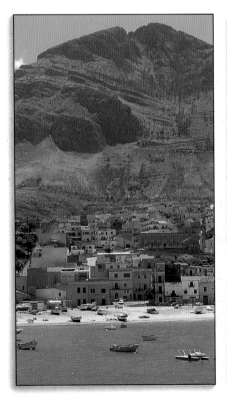

Left, Castel-lammare del Golfo. Below, Riserva Naturale dello Zingaro.

land pierced with coves and bays but containing no official roads. The reserve was created with the support of the council, citizens and ecologists but cynics say that it could not have been achieved without Mafia approval. Locals claim that these sheltered coves continue to be the destination for tiny fishing boats bringing ashore Turkish heroin. Whatever the truth of the matter, the reserve is a glorious home to buzzards and falcons as well as palms, carobs and euphorbia. Human vultures keep a low profile.

On the headland lies **San Vito lo Capo**, a burgeoning resort noted for its fine coast rather than its sophistication. The coastal road south skirts the reserve, passing primeval mountains, shepherds' bothies, abandoned tuna fisheries, ruined towers and ragged rock formations at sea. The ever-changing coastline continues to **Castellammare**, with the rugged journey made by boat, on horseback or on foot.

Scopello di Sopra marks the southern entrance to the reserve. This fishing village is based around a *baglio*, an imposing medieval farmstead. Apart from a rustic *trattoria* and a chance to buy farm-fresh cheese, the only site of note is the **Tonnara**, the finest tunnery in the bay below. The atmospheric complex contains a pink villa, chapel, storerooms and the barracks where the tuna crew stay in the fishing season. Above are a couple of rugged Saracen towers, designed to combat piratical invasions.

Castellammare del Golfo, an overgrown fishing village, enjoys panoramic views across the gulf. The sweet, pastel-coloured cottages, castle and idyllic harbour belie the town's bloody past as a Mafia haunt. In the 1950s, around 80 percent of the male population had been in jail and the internecine Mafia wars led the port to become the chief embarkation point to the United States. Today locals joke that so many of the old *mafiosi* were killed that only dumb innocents remain.

Gavin Maxwell lived among the tuna fishermen in the 1950s, recording their destitution and illiteracy in *Ten Pains of*

Approaching the island of Mozia.

Death. Yet, even then, there was a clash between old and new lifestyles: "From my eyrie in the castle I watched Castellammaresi women come down to the sea to bathe and swim fully dressed in their everyday clothes, and to meet, while so floundering, bronzed visiting nymphs in bikinis and snorkels."

In rolling countryside south of Castellammare lies **Segesta,** one of the most romantic Classical sites. Segesta was founded by the Elymni, a people whose language has yet to be transcribed. The settlers claimed to be refugees who escaped the Fall of Troy but some scholars believe them to be an iconoclastic tribe of Iberian-Ligurian descent. Yet the Trojan link would explain their hatred of the Greeks, an enmity which led to their role in the razing of Selinunte. Segesta itself was sacked by Siracusa in 307 BC.

The roofless Doric temple is unfinished, lacking a *cella* and fluting on the columns. It is no less lovely for that. The **Greek theatre** on the facing hill has an atmosphere of poetic desolation and stages Greek tragedies in the summer. But Goethe was irritated by Segesta: "The leeches, lizards and snails are no more beautiful in colour than ours; indeed all those I saw were grey."

The earthquake zone: In 1968 a major earthquake struck western Sicily, including Calatafimi, Salemi, Partanna and Gibellina. Over 50,000 people were left homeless and many are still in temporary accommodation. The reasons are unclear but involve bureaucratic inefficiency and the curious disappearance of funds earmarked for the project.

Salemi, a benighted hilltop town, is the most intriguing of the earthquake spots. Since the 13th-century castle has been ineffectually propped up, the main interest lies in the narrow, blackened medieval alleys and crumbling churches.

Ruderi di Gibellina, the rubble of a devastated city, has been left as it fell in 1968. A primitive stage has been erected on the ruins and is used for performances of "memorial" concerts and Greek tragedy. The citizens moved to **Gibellina Nuova**, a strangely ugly town domi-

Left, Salemi's castle is held together with metal bands. Below, Segesta's classical temple.

nated by futuristic architecture that bears little relation to Gibellina's history. Open-air exhibits such as a petal, plough and tomato overlook lifeless streets.

The African coast: South of Trapani is the so-called African coast, closer to Tunisia than to mainland Italy. It is known for its **salt pans**, a reminder of an industry that has flourished since Roman times thanks to ideal conditions: low rainfall, regular tides, and the absence of estuaries which would dilute the salinity. In **Nubia** is **Museo delle Saline**, a working museum rescued as a sea salt-extracting complex, with its scenic windmill and outbuildings. A stretch of salt pans and shallow lagoons embrace the marshy but fairly polluted **Isole dello Stagnone.**

A Phoenician causeway leads to **Mozia** but most visitors prefer the boat, even if accompanied by the boatman's randy dog. Poetic views across the shallow salt pans are intensified at sunset. Mozia, first known as Motya, is Sicily's chief Punic site, looming on the far side of the mosquito-infested **Stagnone lagoon**. The island was bought by the Marsala merchant, Joseph Whitaker, who made the excavations his life's work. Here, the Phoenicians established a trading centre based on glass, ceramics, ivory, ebony, textiles and metalwork. The colony minted coins depicting the Gorgon's head and worshipped Astarte and Baal, as well as sun and moon goddesses.

During Dionysius I's siege of Motya, a mole was constructed to move the siege engines close to the city walls. Perched on a spindly platform resembling a modern oil rig, his troops had to lean across a sheer drop to do battle with defenders on roof tops: it was a ring of aerial combat that saw citizens plunging to their deaths in the swampy lagoon. Those who survived the massacre or slavery founded a colony at Lilybaeum (Marsala). Since Mozia was never recolonised, Whitaker discovered a secret city more complete than Carthage.

Sights: The jetty leads to lush vegetation in an oddly subdued landscape. Plane trees, agaves, verbena and mari-

golds grow in the swampy soil and are interspersed with monolithic stone blocks. Nearby is the **Cappiddazzu** site, thought to have been a temple. A genteel **museum** of Whitaker's dusty collection conceals one treasure, the Greek statue of the *ephebe*, a sinuous youth in a tunic. The writer Dominique Fernandez waxes lyrical about "the liquid turbulence of the fabric, the firmness of his buttocks". Close to the museum are crude black and white pebble **mosaics** of a dragon, lion and bull. A path west leads to the **Cothon**, an artificial Punic dock with a paved canal running out to sea. It has been dredged after centuries of silt and misuse as a salt pan.

A trek north through vines, wild figs and almonds leads to a **necropolis** with stunted tombs and a sacrificial site. Known as the **Tophet**, this is where jars containing the remains of babies were found as well as charred offerings of kids, calves and cats. Sadly, the mosquitoes were not sacrificed and have survived longer than the Carthaginians.

Marsala occupies the next cape south, and takes its name from the Arabic Mars-al-Allah, harbour of God. The view of Capo Boeo was enjoyed by refugees from Mozia in 397 BC and became Carthaginian **Lilybaeum**. The site now houses the **Museo Nazionale Lilibeo**, with a reconstructed **Punic ship** that was sunk off the Egadi Islands during the First Punic War. It was manned by 68 oarsmen and boasts unrusty iron nails. In the adjoining archeological zone are **Roman mosaics** of a chained dog and a Medusa. Marsala was damaged in 1943 so historic sites are limited to the **Museo degli Arazzi**, a museum containing richly-coloured Flemish tapestries; and to the **cathedral**. It is dedicated to St Thomas of Canterbury and pillars destined for Canterbury Cathedral grace the nave.

The cape was also a view enjoyed by Garibaldi when his Red Shirts leapt ashore in 1860 and were astonished to find no resistance. Instead they visited the Marsala *cantine* and left their guns behind, where they remain to this day.

The **Stabilimento Florio** is one of the

Left, Mazaro del Vallo. Below, spreading the word in a square near the Duomo.

most typical of the Marsala distilleries, most of which are set in in *bagli*, traditional walled estates with elegant courtyards. The Florio founders are probably Sicily's greatest entrepreneurs but the amber-coloured dessert wine was pioneered by the British merchants, Ingham and Woodhouse. Woodhouse dealt in sherry and madeira but then discovered the potential of Marsala and established a trading post in the town.

Vergine, aged in oak barrels, is at least five years old and often drunk slightly chilled. It resembles a medium sherry but leaves an aftertaste of bitter almonds. *Superiore* is similar to sweet Tuscan *Vin Santo* and drunk as a dessert wine or an *aperitivo*. The Florio museum boasts a fine collection of vintages, including misleading bottles sent to the United States during Prohibition, Florio cunningly labelled the alcohol "seasoning" and "hospital tonic".

Near the seafront and ancient Lilybaeum is **San Giovanni**, an unprepossessing church built over a grotto to *Sibilla Sicula*, Apollo's prophetess. Her sanctuary was hewn into the rock and centred on a sacred spring. According to the cult of the sibyl, maidens drank her water and uttered incantations which the sibyl interpreted. This damp Delphic oracle still inspires devotion, from lovelorn girls to joyous citizens celebrating the *Ferragosto* festival.

Mazara del Vallo feels like a North African town and indeed flourished under Arab rule. A ragged **Norman castle** overlooks the seafront and palm-filled park. The **Norman cathedral** has been given a baroque veneer and contains two dramatic Roman sarcophagi. However, the best church is at **Porta Palermo**, in the heart of the fishing quarter. The crenellated Norman-Byzantine church of **San Nicolò Regale** overlooks the Tunisian port and contains abstract Roman mosaics.

The Mazaro river is packed with trawlers all the way to the fish market. **Via Pescatori** is full of Tunisian fishermen but the women are hidden away. Behind lies the **Casbah**, the Tunisian quarter, an intriguing den of arcaded, tapering

Selinunte in bloom: the area of Temples E, F and G.

alleys and backstreet charm. **Piazza Bagno** has a *hammam* with baths and massage. Nearby are a ritual butcher's and several Tunisian cafes with North Africans smoking hubble-bubbles. Locals may refuse to direct women to the Casbah but apart from the occasional drugged youth sitting in a doorway, it feels fairly safe.

As the most westerly Hellenic colony, **Selinunte** is a pocket of Greece in African Sicily. It was founded by colonists from Megara Hyblaea in 628 BC but, as Segesta's sworn enemy, became embroiled in clashes with the Carthaginians and Athenians. After being sacked by Carthage in 409 BC, the city never fully recovered and was destroyed in 250 BC. However, an aerial view of the collapsed columns reveals that they fell like dominoes, evidently the result of an earthquake.

Surprisingly for Sicily, the huge site is not overshadowed by building but is left in splendid isolation. The site is hemmed in by two rivers and **ports**, both of which are silted up. The main temples (E, F and G) are set on the **eastern hill** while temples A to D lie on the acropolis. Sited within a walled enclosure, the **acropolis** retains some of its original **fortifications**, communication trenches and gates. The site is poorly marked but not helped by the confusion of periods: in particular stone from Temple C and D was raided to build a 5th-century Byzantine village on the spot.

A startling new entrance directs visitors through tunnels in sandbanks to the reconstructed **Temple E**, possibly dedicated to Hera (Juno). Its lovely sculptures are in the Palermo museum, much to the chagrin of locals who would like the *metopes* and friezes to return, especially the statue of the *ephebe*, which was unearthed by a local farmer.

Temple F, constructed in Archaic style, is the most damaged of the trio, perhaps dedicated to Athena. **Temple G**, probably dedicated to Apollo, is now a vast heap of rubble with one restored raised column. Each column of this temple was built using stone drums weighing 100 tonnes and remained incomplete. Fragments of their painted stucco have been unearthed.

North of the acropolis is the ancient **Greek city** and, on either side of it, lie **necropoli**, quarters that have yet to be excavated. Selinunte is a tragic yet hauntingly lovely spot. The sight and sound of the waves merge with squabbling magpies and fast yellow-back lizards. In cracks of the ruins grow aromatic wild fennel, parsley, mandrake, acanthus and beds of yellow flowers. It is deeply therapeutic.

Just south of Campobello are the **Cave di Cusa**, the Classical quarries whose stone built Selinunte. Today, it is a rural site overrun with goats and wild flowers. Huge column drums have been chiselled, to be transported to Temple G at Selinunte, but have been abandoned. The fascination lies in the complex mechanics of construction. Old sketches show how half-carved capitals were levered and pillars were hauled to Selinunte in carts. The poignancy lies in the fact that all work stopped the moment Selinunte was destroyed. The vanquished city just disappeared under the sands.

Left, the massive slabs in the Cave di Cusa quarries. **Right**, sunset over salt pans on the Trapani coast.

THE EGADI ISLANDS

The Sicilian novelist Leonardo Sciascia once remarked upon how "most Sicilian towns make a show of turning their backs on the sea. For how could the islanders ever love a sea that does nothing but bear away emigrants and disembark invaders?" By this measure, the Egadi Islands are very unSicilian: this small archipelago lying off the western coast of Sicily is totally involved with the sea.

It is a particularly rich and beautiful sea that surrounds Lèvanzo, Favignana and Marèttimo. Its crystalline and multi-coloured waters, teeming with marine life, have provided the islanders with work and nourishment for thousands of years, isolating them in the bleak winter months and, in the calm of spring and summer, carrying off their produce as well as their offspring.

The sea is a paradise for sailors and scuba divers (and for those who prefer their fish served on a plate), but today discharges crowds of invaders, tourists who threaten to overwhelm the peaceful rhythm of island life. Fortunately, the summer weather lasts from mid-May to mid-October in the Egadi, and holidaymakers, mostly Sicilians, come in July and August.

In early and late summer tourism is minimal, and the three islands revert to their traditional patterns. June and September are the times to discover the subtle charms of each island, not to mention the renowned sunsets.

Ancient legacy: The Egadi have 15,000 years of history and boast the finest prehistoric cave drawings in Italy. As a Phoenician trading post, it finally lost out to Roman might in a battle that ended the Punic Wars. The Egadi were the springboard for the Arab conquest of Sicily. Under Norman and Aragonese rule, the Egadi were fortified. The Spanish contributed to the coral industry before selling the islands to the Pallavicini-Rusconi in 1637. These Genoese bankers were granted a barony with feudal fishing rights. The Egadi's lucrative links with Genoa and the Ligurian coast continued when the Florio family bought the islands in 1874.

The Egadi were once a land bridge linking Africa to mainland Italy. Such exotic race memories mean that Arab culture is pronounced, from the guttural local accent to the cube-shaped architecture. As for cuisine, a fishy *couscous* is as common as seafood pasta with tuna. On these parched islands, water is more precious than wine.

From the docks of Trapani, point of departure for the frequent ferries and hydrofoils, the islands resemble dark humps floating on a not too distant horizon. Close-up, however, contrasts emerge. Lèvanzo is rugged and friendly, Favignana the most developed and Marèttimo the loveliest.

Lèvanzo, the smallest island and the one closest to the mainland, bears witness to the islanders' bond with the sea. Much of the coast is still inaccessible, except by boat. The port of **Cala Dogana** consists of a handful of houses, a *pensione,* several cafés and *trattorie.* Its

Preceding pages: Favignana Port, the Egadi Islands. Left, hunting for tuna. Right, Favignana sculptor.

one tarred road turns into a dirt track as soon as it leaves town and winds along a gentle valley between the peaks of the Pizzo del Monaco and the Pizzo del Corvo.

The stony slopes are covered with *macchia mediterranea*, arid-looking grey-green scrub that turns lush with the winter rains and blooms in late spring. Equally lovely are the lavender, wild thyme and rosemary; the euphorbia and sea medick flowering in acid yellow; the bursts of white and purple on the caper plants; also the varied pinks of stonewort and Hottentot's Beard.

At the head of the valley the track forks: to the right are a few farmhouses and sheep-pens; to the left the path climbs and zigzags down the steep coast towards the sea, leading to the **Grotta del Genovese**. This deep cavern overhangs the rocky shoreline. If the sea is calm and the wind right, one can reach the grotto by boat, combining the carvings in the grotto with sailing and swimming from a craft hired at Cala Dogana.

The grotto walls hold Lèvanzo's great-est treasure: rock carvings dating from the Mesolithic period. Anthropomorphic dancers and wild animals, especially deer, are depicted in naturalistic poses. In addition, there is a series of rock paintings from the Neolithic period which are less fluid, despite dating from 5,000 years later. These are stylised figures of deities, people, animals and fish. A prominent image is the instantly recognisable tuna, still today the king of the Egadi waters.

Facing Lèvanzo is **Favignana**, the largest and most populous island. Seen from the air, it is shaped like a butterfly poised over the sea, its eastern wing a plain, criss-crossed with roads and pitted with abandoned tufa quarries, its western wing rising to the fortified peak of Monte S. Caterina. More prosaically, Favignana also presents itself as the land of tuna, tufa and tourism.

Farming has left less of an imprint on Favignana than tuna-fishing and tufa-quarrying. Ancient quarrying remodelled the landscape before it was brought to a standstill in the 1950s by the high **Scrubland on Lèvanzo.**

166

cost of extracting and transporting the porous limestone. The island is a homage to stone, its slopes dotted with tufa houses. Even cliffs and caves represent a pleasing spectrum of ochre, russet and cream-coloured rocks.

If cyclists peddling to one of the coves stop to peer over the roadside stone walls, they will discover an abundance of sunken gardens. Sheer stone walls, overgrown with wild thyme and capers, give shelter from the sweeping sea winds to the orange and lemon trees, as well as the figs and tomatoes planted on the floor of the abandoned quarries.

Other quarries were carved at the very edge of the sea so that the tufa could be loaded directly on to the boats transporting it to the mainland. Stone from the maze-like **Cala Rossa** built entire Moorish cities. The chiselled walls and eroded geometry of seaside quarries such as Cala Rossa and Cavallo make them popular picnic and swimming spots.

The *tonnara* (tuna fishery) of Favignana was once one of the most important in the Mediterranean, from feudal times until ownership by Ignazio Florio, the Palermitan entrepreneur. The tuna cannery closed recently, with the loss of 500 jobs, but processing is still carried out in Trapani. In Florio's time, a day's catch could be as high as 10,000 fish. Today, it has shrunk to under 2,000 a month because of over-fishing and deterrents such as pollution, noise and trawling. Even so, the tuna industry thrives, with traditional techniques allied to hi-tech sonar detection, used to spot the shoals.

On one side of the port, near where the ferry docks, stand beautiful vaulted warehouses in which the big black-bottomed boats, the long nets and the huge anchors of the *tonnara* are stored during the winter. **Villa Florio**, the eclectic summer residence of the Florio family, now serves as a gallery and cultural centre. The still waters of the harbour reflect the tiled roofs and stone smokestacks of the Stabilimento Florio, a cannery converted into a handsome monument to industrial archaeology.

The establishment has been bought

Where Ulysses landed, Favignana.

by the Sicilian government and is destined to become a marine museum and school for the fishing industry: a small sector may continue to produce canned tuna using the old procedures. There are also tentative plans to turn the archipelago into a marine reserve and to restrict future building on the islands.

However, Favignana does have a dark side. The Arab-Norman **Forte Santa Caterina** was a political prison in Bourbon times and is now a forbidden military zone. The Forte San Giacomo, formerly a Norman castle and Bourbon prison, performs a similar function today as a maximum-security prison for some of Sicily's *mafiosi*.

Marèttimo, the most mysterious, mountainous and greenest of the Egadi, lies to the west, separated from her sister islands by a stretch of sea rich in sunken archeological treasure. Here lie the remains of the Carthaginian fleet which was destroyed by the Romans in 241 BC. To Sicilian scholars, Marèttimo is a mythical island, nothing less than Odysseus' Ithaca.

The little port has no hotel but the fishermen of Marèttimo happily accept guests. Peace and natural beauty are what draw visitors here: scuba divers come to explore the 400 caves and grottoes scattered along the coast; plant-lovers can study the *macchia mediterranea* at its purest; the rest simply want swimming in aquamarine waters, boat trips to limestone caves, and walks in spectacular scenery.

Walks: Ambitious visitors will climb up to survey the island from Monte Falcone. An easier walk is an excursion to **Case Romane**, ruined Roman fortifications not far from the village. Beside the ruins is a crumbling Arab-Norman chapel, thought to have been built by Byzantine monks. An alternative hike leads north along the cliffs and cuts across an isthmus to Punta Troia, a rocky promontory dominated by a Saracen castle.

Originally a watchtower, the castle was enlarged by the Norman King Roger II, and converted into its present form five centuries later by the Spanish, who added an underground water cistern. When the castle was eventually turned into a prison by the Bourbons, the cistern became the most dreaded of gaol cells. Fortunately, such sombre thoughts quickly float away on this restful, thyme-scented island.

Even so, the islanders are torn between two schools of thought: the long-term but intangible benefits of cultural and environmental conservation, and the immediate financial rewards to be gained from tourism. In July and August, when the number of visitors peaks, tradition temporarily loses out. But luckily in the Egadi, summer outlasts the seasonal visitors.

However, if AGIP's oil exploration continues, the Egadi Islands may one day be rich but ruined. Even then, there will always be the *Fata Morgana* in Favignana. This hallucinatory mirage effect is often visible from Punta San Vituzzo. Islanders swear that it once saved Favignana from marauding Turks by conjuring up a vast fighting fleet. Would that modern invasions were so easily held at bay.

Sailing in the Med.

THE GREAT TUNA MASSACRE

Tuna fishing, along with swordfishing, is rooted in the Sicilian psyche. Nowhere is this more so than in Favignana, where it is considered the sea's ultimate challenge to man, as well as the island's traditional livelihood. The tuna's only predators are the killer whale, the Mako shark and man. But their ritual death is gruelling work. As the proverb says: "Tuna fishing shortens your arms and silences your tongue."

The fast-swimming tuna hunt off the coast of Norway but spawn in Sicily's warm spring waters. Here they are captured in a *tonnara*, a system of chambered nets introduced by the Arabs in the 9th century. The Arabs taught the islanders that tuna refuse to take bait before spawning, so harbour-wide nets were the logical death trap.

The season lasts from May to mid-June, with *la mattanza*, the ritual slaughter, the inexorable fate of a passing shoal. In the past, one day could determine the island's fortune for the rest of the year. Nowadays, this cruel ritual is both a gory tradition and a gruesome tourist spectacle.

Buoys mark out a 100-metre (330-feet) rectangle on the sea; up to 10 km (6 miles) of nets are suspended between the floats. Halfway along lie five ante-chambers. The innermost section is the *camera della morte*, a death chamber 17 fathoms (31 metres) deep.

At dawn, or when the winds are right, the black boats set off to check the nets. The helmsman leads the fleet in prayers, aided by an image of the Madonna. The 60-strong crew sings and chants the *cialoma* in guttural Arabic accents. Entreaties are uttered by the *rais*, a Moorish title given to the chief fisherman, who travels in a separate boat and constantly checks the entrance to the *camera della morte*.

The eight black boats encircle the nets. When the *rais* decides that the currents are right, the shoal is steered into the death chamber and the gate closed. As it fills with fish, the floating death trap sags, like a heavy sack. To the command of "*tira, tira!*" the net is pulled tight. The *rais* chants the fateful battle cry. Each verse of this bloodthirsty sea shanty has a chorus of "*aiamola, aiamola*", perhaps derived from *Allah! Che muoia!* (Allah, may it die!).

As the net is drawn in to the length of a football pitch, the fish circle frantically in the *sarabanda della morte*, the dance of death. The chanting stops and the slaughter begins. The frantic fish gasp and try to leap to freedom but their attempts are thwarted as they are stabbed and caught behind the gills with long pole gaff hooks.

Some of the tuna are man-sized and their razor-sharp tail fins can kill. As the silvery fish are pierced, the water is stained red. It takes a frenzied 15 minutes to slaughter about 200 tuna, although some die of heart attacks or over-oxygenation. With true Sicilian logic, the tuna's breeding grounds also become their tragic end.

Tuna processing can occupy the following three months. The biggest tuna need to be sawn up like tree trunks. *Bottarga* (tuna roe) is a delicacy, as are tuna steaks or *soppressata* (tuna salami). A variant is *tonno all'araba*, with peppers, capers and pistachio nuts.

The bulk of the harvest ends up in Japanese mouths. Yet some tuna reaches *El Pescador*, a restaurant run by Favignana fishermen. It's speciality is spaghetti with fresh tuna and capers, but few tourists have the stomach for it. ∎

Traditional tuna massacre (Mattanza).

VALLEY OF
THE TEMPLES

Siracusa may have been the most powerful city in Greek Sicily but **Agrigento** (Akragas) was the most luxurious. Pindar claimed that the people of Akragas "built for eternity but feasted as if there were no tomorrow". The city rivalled Athens in the splendour of its temples, but in its hedonistic lifestyle Akragas was the Los Angeles of the ancient world. Yet the modern approach could not be more disorientating, a sequence of motorway flyovers. At first, all Agrigento seems to share with Athens are nasty industrial outskirts, breeze-block monstrosities and smog.

Akragas was settled by colonists from Gela in 580 BC, attracted by the abundance of springs and a dreamy, well-fortified site. This most sybaritic of Sicilian cities was run by tyrants and sacked by the Carthaginians in 406 BC (*see page 32*). The city flourished again under the Romans and became the centre of the sulphur mining industry.

In AD 535 the Byzantines destroyed all the temples except one on the grounds that they were pagan. The medieval city abandoned Akragas and the Classical site was ignored until popularised by Goethe and the German Romantics. Winckelmann, father of modern archeology, wrote a celebrated book on the wonders of Agrigento which drew floods of artistic visitors. The wonder was that Winckelmann never set foot in Sicily.

The city abounds in Classical anecdote regarding its fabled wealth. The Tyrant of Akragas boasted reservoirs of wine hacked out of solid rock; each giant cellar contained 900 gallons (4,000 litres). Returning Olympic heroes were welcomed by cavalcades of chariots drawn by white horses, which were legendary in the Greek world. But the city's softness was equally notorious. The Gods provided peace and prosperity, but Agrigentine mortals failed when their non-intervention pact with Siracusa proved the downfall of Greek Sicily.

At the prospect of war with Carthage, soldiers on watch were under orders to make do with no more than two mattresses, two pillows and a blanket each. Gellias was a lavish city benefactor who accommodated a party of 500 riders who passed through town, giving them each a set of warm clothes. After Akragas fell to Carthage, the benefactor moved his precious possessions into a temple, set fire to it, and jumped in.

Valle dei Templi: Here, for a fleeting moment, the Classical world comes alive. The Valley of the Temples forms a natural amphitheatre, with a string of Doric temples straddling a ridge south of the city. This is still a valley of wild thyme, fennel, silvery olive groves and almond blossom. An ideal first glimpse of the temples is by night, during a drive along the Strada Panoramica and Via dei Templi. The temples glow in the black countryside, radiating a sense of cohesion, security and serenity.

An early start guarantees enough solitude to slip back into the Classical world. But unless planning to view the Temple of Concord from the elegant restaurant in Villa Athena, come armed with a

picnic. Otherwise, the on-site snack bar will bring one back to earth with a bump. From the valley, views of the modern town may offend purists. Yet while time cannot stand still, olive and almond groves mask the modernity.

Piazzale dei Templi, the entrance to the main temples, was once the *agora* and is alive to the ancient trading spirit. Bar staff double as guides while small boys demand money to protect tourists' cars from unknown dangers, a feature of Sicilian sites. This crest of temples was designed to be visible from the sea, both as a beacon for sailors and to show that the Gods guarded the sacred city from mortal danger.

Eastern zone: The first treasure visible is the **Temple of Hercules**. Built in 520 BC, this is the oldest temple, second in size to the Temple of Zeus and of roughly the same proportions as the Parthenon in Athens. Designed in Archaic Doric style, it once boasted a gorgeous entablature emblazoned with lions, leaves and palms but now presents an almost abstract puzzle. Although much is in

ruins, Alexander Hardcastle performed a Herculean task by re-erecting eight columns in 1924. The ruts of ancient cart tracks nearby are a reminder that Hercules himself would have recognised the stamina required to build such a temple

Villa Aurea, set in olive and almond groves beside the former Golden Gate, belonged to Hardcastle, the Englishman who devotedly excavated the site. The grounds are virtually riddled with catacombs and water cisterns which run under rocks and orchards the length of the Classical site.

A path on the left leads to the **catacombs**, which emerge in a necropolis on the far side of the villa. Now excavated and well-lit, the passages cut through the rock and reveal a cross-section of tombs and fossilised bones. Arches link circular rooms (*tholos*) containing circular honeycomb cells stacked high with shelf-tombs. The main passage is exposed to the air by means of a convex cistern resembling a well from above ground. While the oldest tombs

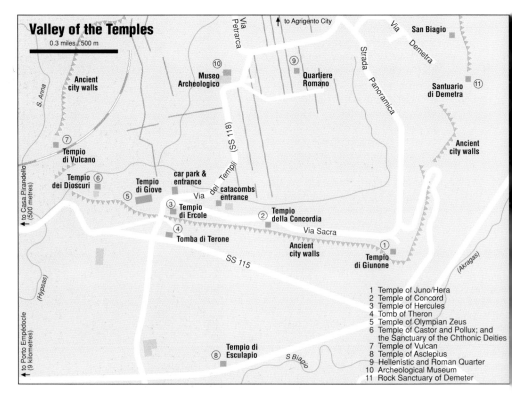

Valley of the Temples

0.3 miles / 500 m

to Agrigento City

Via Petrarca · Via San Biagio · Demetra · Strada Panoramica

⑩ Museo Archeologico

⑨ Quartiere Romano

Santuario di Demetra ⑪

Ancient city walls

S. Anna

SS 118

⑦ Tempio di Vulcano

Ancient city walls

Tempio dei Dioscuri ⑥ · car park & entrance · Via dei Templi · catacombs entrance

Tempio di Giove · ⑤

③ Tempio di Ercole

② Tempio della Concordia

Via Sacra

④ Tomba di Terone

Ancient city walls

① Tempio di Giunone

(Akragas)

SS 115

to Casa Pirandello (500 metres)

(Hypsas)

to Porto Empédocle (9 kilometres)

⑧ Tempio di Esculapio

S Biagio

1 Temple of Juno/Hera
2 Temple of Concord
3 Temple of Hercules
4 Tomb of Theron
5 Temple of Olympian Zeus
6 Temple of Castor and Pollux; and the Sanctuary of the Chthonic Deities
7 Temple of Vulcan
8 Temple of Asclepius
9 Hellenistic and Roman Quarter
10 Archeological Museum
11 Rock Sanctuary of Demeter

here date from 4 BC, the main Roman necropoli lie just to the south while Greek burial grounds are scattered around the city.

At the end of the Via Sacra lies the **Temple of Concord**, abutting ancient city walls. After the Theseion in Athens, it is considered to be the best preserved Greek temple in the world. Many Sicilian attributions are suspect and scholars argue that this temple was dedicated to Demeter, goddess of fertility and peace. The tawny temple slopes into the valley below, a pastoral scene at odds with its violent history: on this bulwark thousands were slain in the bloody battle against Carthage.

Dating from 430 BC, the temple was saved from ruin in the 6th century by being converted into a church. The peristyle was sealed by dry stone walls, and the *cella* opened to form twin naves. Sadly, the *metopes* and pediment were destroyed. Mass was celebrated here until 1788, the date when a local prince obtained permission to restore the building's Classical simplicity.

The tapering columns tilt inwards imperceptibly, creating an ethereal grace and airiness that belie the weighty entablature. A further refinement is that the fluted columns all have different spacing, narrowing towards the corners. They were originally coated with glazed marble dust to protect the flaky sandstone, then painted with vivid polychrome scenes, predominantly bright blue or blood-red. Now lichen-coated, the temple still represents sheer perfection in line.

The herb-scented air mingles with views of the sea and olive groves. The only jarring image is the distant cityscape and cemetery but, seen through a heat haze, even that shimmers obligingly. The temple is transformed by light: locals say that one has not lived until seeing Concord changing with the seasons, at dawn and sunset, dusk and moonlight.

The **Temple of Hera** surmounts a rocky ridge which formed the city ramparts. Known as Juno to the Romans, she was protectress of engaged and

The Temple of Concord.

married couples. Fittingly, Hera is held to be the most romantic of temples, set "high on the hill like an offering to the goddess". Yet Zeus's sister and wife was perceived as a bloodthirsty goddess, to be appeased by sacrifice at an altar beside the walls.

Part of the *cella* and 25 columns remain intact along with the drums of columns; the rest fell over the hill during a landslide. The stones bear reddish traces of fire damage where they were singed by flames. The valley views reflect Pindar's praise of Agrigento as "loveliest of mortal cities".

Western zone: After retracing one's steps to the entrance, cross the road to the **Temple of Olympian Zeus**. Even at the crest of its golden age, the temple was unfinished. As the largest Doric temple ever known, it was the size of a football pitch. The U-shaped grooves on the stone blocks represent primitive pulley marks formed during construction. Today's fallen masonry is a challenge to the imagination: its stone was plundered to build the port of Empedocle. A frieze on the east side depicted the battle between Zeus and the Giants, matched by the War of Troy on the western side.

Giants: The facade was supported by 38 *telamones* (giant figures) – a revolutionary concept for the time. In this way, the weight of the pediment was shared by the giants and by the columns of the peristyle. The *telamones* also had allegorical and aesthetic functions. They both broke up the uniformity of the peristyle and illustrated the war against Zeus; like Atlas, the defeated giants were compelled to carry the world on their shoulders.

A sandstone copy of a *telamone* lies on the ground, dreamily resting his head on his elbows. Four originals lie in the archeological museum. On the temple, these male *giganti* alternated with female caryatids and represented the three known racial types of the time: African, Asian and European.

West of the Temple of Zeus is the most confusing quarter, dotted with shrines dating from pre-Greek times.

Once this valley contained Sicily's most luxurious Greek city.

The sandy Via Sacra leads to the **Temple of Castor and Pollux** (or the Dioscuri), named after the twin sons of Zeus. Castor was mortal and Pollux immortal so they spent alternate days in Hades or on Mount Olympus. Although it has become the city symbol, the result is theatrical pastiche, erected in 1836 from several temples.

Even so, it is a graceful and evocative reconstruction. Locally, the temple is known as *tri culonni*, since only three of the four columns are visible from the city. Despite its name, the temple was first dedicated to Persephone and Demeter, Chthonic (Underworld) deities, along with Dionysus.

This theory is supported by the temples in the surrounding area. Known as the **Sanctuary of the Chthonic Divinities,** the quarter conceals sacrificial altars and ditches, a veritable shrine to fertility, immortality and eternal youth. Pale-coloured beasts were offered to the heavens but black animals were sacrificed to the gods of the Underworld. The altars took the form of flat, concentric circles or deep, well-shaped affairs. Now bounded by a gorge and an orange grove, this sanctuary of death was also the fount of life, with lush gardens and a lake full of exotic birds and fish.

Lesser-known temples: Close to Piazzale dei Templi lies **Theron's Tomb** (Tomba di Terone), a tribute to a benevolent Agrigentine tyrant. This truncated tower in Doric-Ionic style is essentially a Roman funerary pyramid, more a celebration of conquest than glory to a local hero.

Outside the ancient walls is the isolated **Temple of Asclepius**, half-hidden in an almond grove. Dedicated to the mysterious god of healing, it lies between the river Akragas and a sacred spring. It is of a curious design, with solid walls and no peristyle, possibly because the interior housed chambers for dream interpretations as well as wards for recuperation or for taking the waters. From here, the view embraces a phalanx of golden temples crowning the ridge.

From Piazzale dei Templi, a short

drive along Via dei Templi leads to Villa Athena restaurant, the archeological museum, the Hellenistic-Roman quarter and a clutch of pagan shrines. En route are fortifications, a reminder that Agrigento was once enclosed by walls, towers and massive gates, of which the perimeter and craggy foundations remain. The sandy landscape is dotted with olives and pines. Subsidence has created strange slopes and whirling patterns on the soil.

San Nicola is a Romanesque church whose severe but grand facade is reminiscent of monuments in ancient Rome. This is not so far-fetched given that the church is built from Greek stone raided from the ruins and also purports to be a Roman temple dedicated to the Sun god. The Cistercian church was altered by the Franciscans in the 15th century. A chapel contains the **Sarcophagus of Phaedra**, an exquisitely carved scene of Phaedra's grief at the loss of her lover and step-son Hippolytus.

Next-door is the **Archeological Museum**, incorporating a church, court-yard and temple foundations. The Graeco-Roman section is the centre-piece, along with a Bronze-Age urn from a Sican tomb and a three-legged *Trinacria*, the ancient symbol of Sicily. Exhibits include a wealth of painted Attic vases dating from 5th century BC, Greek lion's-head water spouts, an *ephebe* and a vibrant Roman mosaic of a gazelle. A poignant marble sarcophagus depicts the death of a child amidst weeping; a chariot spirits the child on to the afterlife. The highlight is a *telamone* in all its massive glory accompanied by other powerful giant heads. Elsewhere are votive offerings and statues associated with orgiastic rites: phallic donkeys compete with a libidinous pigmy and a hermaphrodite.

The Hellenistic-Roman Quarter lies opposite, an ancient commercial and residential area laid out on a grid system. The remains of aqueducts, terracotta and stone water channels are visible, as well as shops, taverns and patrician villas. The frescoed villas are paved with patterned mosaics and protected by glass enclosures.

Just east, on the far side of the Strada Panoramica is a stretch of Greek walls and **San Biagio**, a Norman church perched on a rocky platform. It is carved into an ancient Temple to Demeter and Persephone. Two circular altars lie between the church and another eerie tribute to the goddess of fertility. At the foot of the cliff is the **Rock Sanctuary of Demeter**, the oldest sanctuary in the valley, dating from 7 BC. A narrow rocky staircase leads down to a damp stone shrine carved into the hillside. A spring flowed into basins here and was used in a water cult. At sundown, the caves conjure up the Underworld only too readily.

Visiting Sicily in 1885, Guy de Maupassant was lucky enough to see the temples without tourists or modern desecration. The writer was struck by their air of "magnificent desolation; dead, arid and yellowing on all sides". Yet with falcons hovering above, lizards scurrying at one's feet, the air heavy with the scent of eucalyptus, today's landscape throbs with life.

Left, Classical necropoli. Right, the Golden Temple of Hera (Juno), Agrigento.

AGRIGENTO PROVINCE

People from Agrigento are a mysterious breed, often called *"né carne né pesce"*, neither fish nor fowl. Yet this elusive province has produced exceptional Sicilians: Empedocles, the pre-Socratic philosopher; Pirandello, the playwright; and Sciascia, the political novelist. All were gifted mavericks who shared a bitter-sweet relationship with their homeland. Empedocles committed suicide on Etna. Pirandello was the master of split personalities. Sciascia called his land a "wicked step-mother" yet rarely left, except to visit Paris.

Maverick province: In Agrigento's favour is the most complete set of temples outside Greece. Seen in spring, against a backdrop of almond blossom, the view is magical (*see the preceding chapter*). Outside the capital, the province is barely touched by tourism. There are also compelling links with the origins of Lampedusa's great novel, *The Leopard*. Agrigento's drawbacks are degradation and exceptional poverty, a cluster of Mafia strongholds, and a torpor conditioned by centuries of failure. This malaise is symbolised by a provincial tourist office that seems never to be open.

Modern Agrigento: It is ironic that a Classical city known for its luxurious lifestyle should have fallen so low. Not that the "modern" city is wholly poor or even modern. As always, Agrigento is a living contradiction. The town's medieval core is a maze of Moorish streets and substandard housing. However, this unaesthetic muddle conceals a fascinating urban mix. By contrast, the new quarter overlooking the temples is an attempt at bourgeois chic, which went horribly wrong when landslides aggravated by overcrowding and shoddy building killed many in 1966.

A scandal arose with the discovery that feckless Mafia surveyors had cut corners by not checking for subsidence and that contractors had used poor quality cement. Nowadays, charmless middle-class apartments gaze across at the temples. Sophistication is skin-deep: a handful of chic jewellers and restaurants resting on an economy beholden to the Mafia. The major Mafia round-up in 1992 was centred on Agrigento province. Operation Leopard netted 200 suspects in the southern hinterland.

City sights: Above Via Atenea is **Santo Spirito**, a fine Cistercian abbey founded in 1290. Often known as the **Badia Grande**, the complex of cloisters, chapter house and refectory is in Chiaramonte style. The church has a Gothic portal and rose window, plus a panelled ceiling and baroque stuccos attributed to Serpotta. The vaulted Gothic dormitory leads to a chapter house with mullioned windows and a bold portal, all with Arab-Norman geometrical motifs.

The abbey is currently undergoing restoration but the commercial spirit triumphs in Agrigento. The sacristan in the house opposite will gladly open the church for a tip while the Cistercian nuns sell sweet *cuscusu*, almond and pistachio pastries shaped like snakes, shells and flowers. Faced with such delights, the French writer Dominique

Preceding pages: the Moorish port of Sciacca. **Left**, mending the nets, Sciacca. **Right**, in the shadow of Santo Spirito, Agrigento city.

Fernandez was torn between the "baroque opulence" of the architecture and the "Arab unctuousness" of the cakes. The cakes won.

Cuisine: Apart from the sisters' sweetmeats, Agrigento offers a range of delicacies. Popular dishes are *coniglio in agrodolce* (sweet and sour rabbit), *salsiccia al finocchio* (pasta and fennel) or *involtini di spada* (stuffed swordfish) Combinations of shellfish, artichokes, pasta and pilchards are common. However, if pushed, Agrigentines plump for Arab staples such as *cassata* and *cannoli*.

Dominating **Piazza Purgatorio** is the church of the same name, a riot of baroque allegorical stucco-work by Serpotta. A lion guards an entrance to the ancient underground drinking water and drainage system. Linked to the hypogeum under San Nicola church, the system used conduits and cisterns to channel water to the city. There are plans to open the chambers to the public, including a Roman food store with a lava-stone grinding mill.

Further west is **Santa Maria dei Greci**, a Norman church set among Agrigento's Moorish alleyways. A Gothic portal leads to a Norman nave, a coffered ceiling and some Byzantine fragments. Below ground is the greatest surprise: the church is constructed around a Greek temple dedicated to Athena. A narrow gallery contains the bases of six fluted Doric columns, the remains of the temple peristyle and stereobate. The sanctuary spans Greek and Christian cults: tradition has it that St Paul preached here.

The **cathedral** surmounts a ridge in the west of the city. It is designed in eclectic style with Arab-Norman, Catalan-Gothic and baroque elements. The Norman-Gothic nave boasts an inlaid, coffered ceiling and a section frescoed to simulate a dome. Graceful baroque stucco-work in the choir contrasts with a severe Gothic chapel. Since this is Agrigento, the cathedral naturally occupies a prestigious Greek site: nothing less than the acropolis.

In summer, the Classical city comes alive with open-air performances of

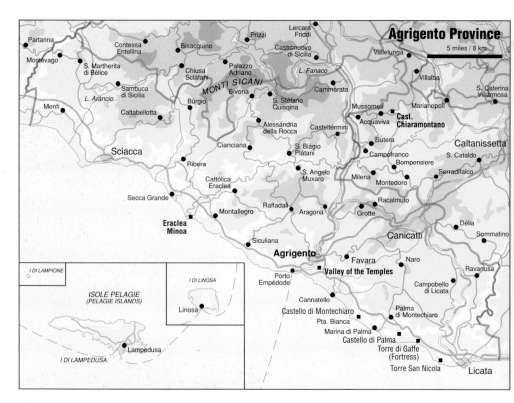

drama in tribute to Persephone. The modern city responds with *passeggiate* along tree-lined Viale Vittoria. However, like the Classical city, modern Agrigento is both sleek and scruffy. What could be more fitting for a city constructed by Carthaginian slaves yet inhabited by noble girls who built gold tombs for their song birds.

The interior: A rural drive north through the Platani valley leads to Bronze Age necropli near the village of **Sant'Angelo Muxaro**. This was the stronghold of the Sicani, the indigeous Sicilians who settled the west of the island. As a result, native Agrigentines stress Sicani roots, insisting that they are darker and swarthier than most Sicilians.

Pirandello in Caos: Just outside Agrigento is Pirandello's birthplace in the hamlet of Caos. The irony was not wasted on Pirandello, who called himself a "son of chaos". Now a museum, the house overlooks industrial sprawl. In accordance with the playwright's wishes, his ashes were buried under a pine tree on the edge of a cliff.

The East coast: Porto Empedocle, southeast of Agrigento, quarried the Classical site for stone to build its harbour walls. Perhaps in revenge, the temple gods cursed it with ugliness. The benighted city should be avoided unless a ferry trip to the remote Pelagie Islands makes a visit inevitable.

Southwest of Agrigento: Palma di Montechiaro strikes a romantic chord with readers of *The Leopard*. The novel's Donnafugata is based on a castle at Palma di Montechiaro founded in 1626 by Tomasi, Principe di Lampedusa. The Prince associated it with his idyllic childhood. Today, however, the town conjures up a catalogue of Sicilian ills: disturbing images of grinding poverty, emigration, unemployment, illiteracy, crime, child mortality, public indifference, despair and dogs. According to recent statistics, 30 percent of children are illiterate and 50 percent leave school at the age of seven.

Lampedusa's splendid *castello* is crumbling under the burden of serving as a trysting spot, prison and unofficial

Modern Agrigento, seen from the Valley of the Temples.

public lavatory. The town's only dusty glory is the **Chiesa Madre**, decaying under the weight of civic inertia. To qualify for funding, the church steps must be restored in the same stone as before. However, the original quarry is closed so Sicilian bureaucracy decrees that renovation is impossible.

Castles: Castello di Palma and **Torre di Gaffe** are striking castles, the remains of a string of fortifications along the coast. Downtrodden **Licata** also has a 16th-century *castello* and layers of *palazzi*. The neighbouring town of **Naro** encloses a Chiaramonte castle and baroque mansions within battlemented walls. From here, it is a short drive to Caltanissetta province.

The Southwest Coast: This is relatively unspoilt with patches of sheer loveliness. The coast borders a fertile valley and overlooks neat orange plantations and smoothly contoured fields. The Classical site of **Eraclea Minoa** squats on bleached soil and abuts olive-covered slopes. As one looks down from this idyllic spot beside the sea, there is a

view the white cliffs, golden sands and pine grove down below.

The Classical city was a satellite of Selinunte but suffered a grim fate at the hands of the Carthaginians, when it was depopulated and used as a no-man's-land in Greek and Punic territorial disputes. The name Minoa evokes the legend of King Minos of Crete who pursued Daedalus to Sicily, but the connection is tenuous. While the atmosphere is therapeutic, the excavations are not spectacular. So far, Eraclea has revealed city walls, a Hellenistic theatre, a necropolis, and ruined villas dating from Greek and Punic times.

Further along the coast is **Sciacca**, a working fishing port with a large Arab population. The name comes from the Latin and Arabic words for water (*aqua* and *xacca*), a reminder of Sciacca's origins as a Phoenician spa and Roman naval base. The town was evangelised by San Calogero and prospered in Arab times thanks to its location, midway between Mazara and Agrigento. In the 16th century, Sciacca was torn apart by two warring families, the Norman Perollo and the Catalan Luna. The town suffered a gradual decline until the revival of the port and thermal industry, aided by an injection of Mafia funds and close links with North Africa.

Sciacca lacks spectacular architecture but sea views and an ensemble of tawny, weather-beaten buildings justify a visit. It is a split-level town with the port overlooked by the natural balcony of the old town. A couple of tumbledown Norman castles, medieval gates and Aragonese walls provide an invitation to the eclectic array of architecture. The Moorish quarter is on the highest level, a raggedy mass of alleys, arches, courtyards and wary, illegal immigrants.

Sciacca's churches embrace all periods and styles. **San Calogero** and **San Domenico** are sober baroque works while the **Convento di San Francesco** combines clean lines with Moorish cloisters. **Chiesa del Carmine** is a Norman abbey with a Gothic rose window and a half-hearted baroque restoration. Facing it is a sculpted medieval gate and the Gothic portal of **Santa Margherita**. **Countryside near Cianciana.**

Further east, the ruined Romanesque **San Nicolò** contrasts with **Santa Maria della Giummare**, a Catalan-Gothic church with crenellated Norman towers and a baroque interior. Just within the Aragonese walls is **Badia Grande**, an impressive 14th-century abbey.

Corso Vittorio Emanuele has *palazzi* from all periods, including a Moorish mansion converted into a jeweller's. The loveliest civic building is the Renaissance **Palazzo Steripinto**, with a crenellated facade of diamond-shaped design, a style borrowed from Neapolitan architecture.

Piazza Scandaliato is the bustling centre, a scenic balcony for drinking in the views over an *aperitivo*. On summer evenings the square belongs to Tunisian hawkers flogging exotic clothes, leather goods or brightly painted Sciacca ceramics. Palazzo Comunale incorporates an Arab tower while, at the end of the piazza, the **Duomo** presents a confused image, with Arab-Norman apses buried in a baroque facade. Visitors tend to appreciate Sciacca for its sandy beaches and spa waters, or seafood and aubergine spaghetti at a rough portside bar.

Spa towns: Sciacca is one of the oldest spas in Italy, known since prehistoric times and praised by Pliny. Mud baths and volcanic vapours are available at the **Terme Selinuntine**, an aloof Art Nouveau establishment that attracts well-heeled Italians.

Just north, the **San Calogero** spa on Monte Kronio harnesses the powers of a "mini" volcano, bubbling hot springs and vapour-drenched grottoes used as saunas. The galleries, seats and water channels were hollowed out in ancient times by the Sicani or, according to the myth-makers, by Daedalus.

Castello Bentivegna, called the "enchanted castle", is a folly created by a peasant sculptor. Set among almond and olive groves just outside Sciacca, this forest of statues is the work of one man. In 1946, Filippo Bentivegna returned from the United States and bought a patch of land in his native town. Using the rocks at the foot of Monte Kronio as his material, he sculpted 3,000 primi-

Caltabellotta, clustered on a hill.

tive heads of devils, politicians and knights. Not content with his work above ground, the sculptor then set about carving heads from olive wood and creating frescoed caverns in the mountain.

The hinterland: Orchards, olive groves and chalky limestone peaks lead to the rural uplands. After glimpses of farmhouses and deep gorges, **Caltabellotta**, the loveliest village in Agrigento province, comes into view. It is spectacular whether seen through spring blossom or swathed in mist.

On the highest level, below the hulk of the ruined castle, is the Norman **Chiesa Madre** with its original portal and pointed arches. On the level underneath is the lopsided Piazza Umberto and handsome Chiesa del Carmine. Below stretch shadowy mountain views from the spacious Belvedere and the white **Chiesa San Agostino**. On the edge of the village lies San Pellegrino, a monastery with stupendous views of a mountainside studded with necropoli.

Thanks to *Agriturismo*, one can stay on local farms. The rural economy is

based on sheep and cattle breeding as well as olive pressing. The olive oil is famed for its herby fragrance and golden colour. The results can be tasted in *Trattoria La Ferla*. Local dishes include *fava* bean soup or pasta with ricotta and fennel.

West of Caltabellotta is **Sambuca di Sicilia** with its popular lake and facilities for watersports and barbeques. Amateur archaeologists are drawn to the neighbouring Iron Age village where huts and burial chambers have recently come to light.

Santa Margherita di Belice is Lampedusa country, bordering Palermo and Trapani provinces. However, in recent times it has become better known as the epicentre of the earthquake zone. Between Montechiaro and the coast lies Menfi, another earthquake-damaged town. Trapani province beckons to the West, with the Classical city of Selinunte still a fair match for Agrigento.

Pelagie Islands: This scorching archipelago of three islands lies amidst strong currents off the coast of Africa, closer to Tunisia than the Sicilian mainland. Although there are pockets of agriculture, the islands are unnaturally barren due to wanton deforestation. Fifty years ago, much of this lunar landscape was farmland bounded by dry stone walls.

Today, the local economy rests on fishing, from sponge fishing to canning. There are no outstanding sites but the waters are translucent, while the rugged native character and cuisine are distinctly Tunisian. Highlights include Moorish *dammusi* houses in local stone, excellent *couscous* and fish, quiet coastal walks and, except for August in Lampedusa, peace and quiet.

Linosa, the island closest to the shore, was created as a result of a marine eruption and forms a rocky turtle-shape indented by coves. In fact, Linosa represents the tip of a vast submerged volcano. The three visible cones may now be extinct but the beaches still coat the unwary in black dust. Since there is no escape from this windless, burnt island, it has periodically been used as a penal colony for *mafiosi*. Fertile soil produces prickly pears which are made into ani-

Sciacca's eclectic architecture.

mal fodder or fertiliser. There is little to do except rest, roast, swim, trek along dusty paths through vineyards or spot *dammusi*, pastel-coloured cubes with white window-frames.

Thanks to its location, **Lampedusa** is known as "a gift from Africa to Europe". The island was first settled by the Phoenicians and Greeks but was later owned by the Princes of Lampedusa. The family turned down a bid by Queen Victoria in favour of one by Ferdinand II of Bourbon in 1843. The Bourbons populated it with Sicilians but these have mostly been usurped by weather-beaten Tunisian fishermen.

Lampedusa port contains a rabbit warren of a casbah which reeks of spices, sardines, anchovies and goats. A bicycle trip across the flat, arid land reveals *dammusi* with hefty whitewashed walls, cupola-like domes and curtains for doors. In the centre of the island is **Santuario di Porto Salvo**, a church in a lush garden draped in bougainvillaea and surrounded by grottoes, once home to Saracen pirates. The sanctuary contains a venerated statue of the Madonna.

The wonderful marine life is similar to that off the North African coast. Parrot fish and seals abound in the limpid waters, while turtles lay their eggs on Isola dei Conigli, named after its huge rabbit colony. Cormorants and hawks wheel overhead; below is clay-coloured rock, dotted with cacti or prickly pears.

Its greatest claim to fame was as an American radar base for bombing Libya. In 1986 a Libyan launch fired rockets on the island in retaliation for the US bombing of Tripoli. When the islanders feared an imminent attack, some rushed to the airport, others to the port but the rest appealed to the town hall. In fact, Gaddafi's missiles landed harmlessly in the sea but the Italian government was concerned enough to close the US base.

Lampione, an uninhabited reef, is scorched dry thanks to man's negligence. Its drama lies underwater: the translucent sea is unpolluted and rich in marine life, from sponge beds to hungry sharks. Sicilian pleasures are notoriously double-edged.

Solitude at Eraclea Minoa.

CALTANISSETTA PROVINCE

"This is ancient Sicily, the land of *latifundia* (feudal estates), sulphur mines, hunger and insecurity." The French writer Dominique Fernandez is not alone in relishing the Wild West feel of Caltanissetta. Given the sparsely-populated nature of the province, the visitor will often be alone with this dramatic scenery. From the hill-top villages are spectacular views of mountain ridges and purple canyons, abandoned farms and ruined Norman castles.

Caltanissetta occupies a central position on a sulphur-bearing plain, its yellowish soil scarred with disused mines. Yet the province is far from uniform. There is a difference in character between the siege mentality of the bleak hill-top towns and the more accessible Greek flavour of Gela's coastal plains. This is a bitter province which feels betrayed by recent history: the sulphur mines brought hardship and a high mortality rate to the hinterland. Coastal industrialisation brought pollution but not prosperity. Although not the most poverty-stricken province, Caltanissetta is arguably the most aggrieved.

Caltanissetta, the provincial capital, is a harsh summation of the region's struggle for survival. Its name reflects its cosmopolitan past: Arab conquerors added the prefix of Kalat, Arabic for castle, to the Greek name of Nissa. As befits an ancient bastion, it is a closed city, its defences raised against outsiders. Modern war damage means that medieval monuments are restricted to the outskirts, along with the original Greek settlements. Architecturally, the city is mostly 19th-century, with only the occasional baroque monument to relieve the blandness.

Caltanissetta is no mere market town but the agricultural centre for the Sicilian interior, with grain and cotton long grown in the countryside. As the historic hub of the Sicilian mining industry, the city fell into decline in the 1960s with the collapse of the sulphur industry. Potassium and magnesium mining have now supplanted sulphur and the city has achieved modest wealth. Still, life here has always been tough, even by Sicilian standards, with sulphur miners treated like slaves.

Mafia lore: The Pope paid a pastoral visit in 1992, as part of his anti-Mafia mission to the island's crime-infested spots. Caltanissetta has Sicily's most understaffed and overworked magistrates' court. Cynics may say this is intentional, giving *mafiosi* suspects a head start. Despite public dismay, the town was entrusted with the investigation into the murder of Judge Falcone, his wife and bodyguards. Much to the astonishment of American FBI agents cooperating on the case, Caltanissetta magistrates hoped to compete with the Mafia without access to a computer.

City sights: Caltanissetta's heart, in so far as it has one, lies in Piazza Garibaldi. There, the baroque **Duomo**, flanked by belltowers, overlooks the ugly neo-Romanesque church of San Sebastiano, the baroque Town Hall and a rusty bronze statue of Neptune. The cathedral

Preceding pages: the breathtaking Castello Manfredinico at Mussomeli. **Left,** Umberto I gazes at Caltanissetta. **Right,** potter at work.

interior is an engaging explosion of kitsch. A frescoed ceiling by Borremans is complemented by baroque decor: pink pillars and dancing nymphs. In chapels to the right of the nave, saints in glittering glass cases compete for attention. A triumphal angel and cherubs adorn a gaudy glass and gold coffin, a Sicilian disguise for a rotting corpse.

Behind the Town Hall, Via Palazzo Paterno leads to the crumbling **Palazzo Moncada**. This was the home of the Moncada dynasty, the feudal rulers of the region from 1406 onwards.

The baroque mansion is emblazoned with snarling lions posing as gargoyles. Emblematic of Sicily, the building was never finished and its leisurely "restoration programme" implies that it never will be. The shabby **Museo Mineralogico** does not do justice to the importance of mining to the region.

Corso Umberto, the main street, is lined with dark, dilapidated buildings and scruffy bars. Oblivious to the rain, wizened men congregate outside to discuss politics or building permits. Inside,

dry-tasting pastries are washed down with Amaro, a reminder that Caltanissetta is the main producer of this famous *digestivo*. The unwelcoming atmosphere is pervasive. The Nisseni, the surly locals, are suspicious of outsiders.

The remaining sights are quickly dispensed with. The **Museo Civico** displays prehistoric and Greek remains from local settlements, including rock tombs. Finest are the Attic vases, painted urns, a terracotta model of a temple and the earliest Bronze Age figures found in Sicily. **Palazzo del Carmine**, a convent founded in 1371, is now the police headquarters. Nearby, the shabby **Villa Amedeo** gardens offer refreshing views over the rugged terrain.

Heavy baroque belltowers give the town a gloomy air. San Domenico is less impressive than **Chiesa Sant' Agata**, a severe baroque church with an exuberant interior. Although founded in 1300, it is largely a Jesuit's homage to St Ignatius. A marble inlaid altar piece vies with an allegorical depiction of the known world. Africa is represented by a

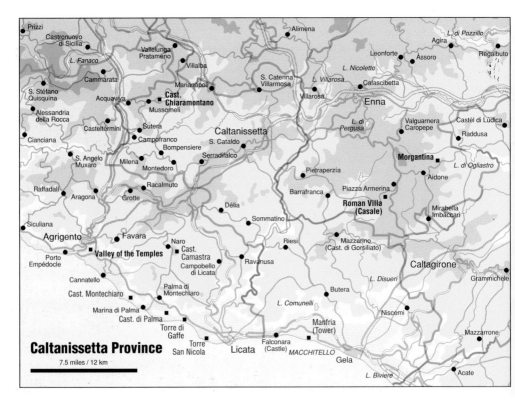

Caltanissetta Province

7.5 miles / 12 km

lion, Asia by a camel, America by a quiverful of arrows and Catholic Europe by the Papal crown. Beside the altar is a panel depicting St Michael driving a lance into a hydra.

Easter festivals: Here, as elsewhere in Sicily, Holy Week (*Settimana Santa*) with the Mysteries of the Passion, is the most important event on the Church calendar. Celebrations begin with mass on Palm Sunday and close with the veneration of the Black Christ on Good Friday. The highlight is the Maundy Thursday procession of the Mysteries of the Passion. Held since the 18th century, the *Misteri* is a melancholic parade of sculptures borne by the *maestranza* (guilds). Members of 15 local guilds, including bakers, marble-workers and miners, are joined by a cortège of wailing citizens. The mournful dirges are a throwback to Arab and Greek culture – a far cry from Italian mainland fun.

East of the town is **Santa Maria degli Angeli**, a ruined Norman church with a richly-carved Gothic porch. A little further on is the stump of **Pietrarossa Castle**, perched on a jagged spur. Frederick II sought refuge in this baronial fiefdom during his battle for supremacy with the Chiaramonte and Ventimiglia dynasties. However, the 1567 earthquake tossed the Norman-Arab castle into its present pitiful heap.

Environs: In the countryside just northeast of town lies the Romanesque abbey church of **Santo Spirito**. It was founded by Count Roger after the Norman victory over the Arabs and consecrated in 1153. The pink-tinged facade is topped by mini crenellations, relics of feudal fortifications. Such severity is softened by the delicacy of the treble apses. A key from the farmhouse next-door unlocks the basilica to reveal medieval frescoes of Christ in benediction and a Romanesque baptismal font.

Three miles (5 km) south lie the Arabic ruins of **Gebel Habib** on Monte Gibil Gabel, meaning Mountain of the Dead in Arabic. This prehistoric site was also home to a Hellenised settlement, the original site of Nissa. The city answered to the Greeks at Gela and

Caltanissetta fountains.

Agrigento but was abandoned at the end of 5 BC. Tumbledown fortifications remain, together with prehistoric and Greek tombs carved into the rock.

On the flanks of **Monte Sabucina** lies a more impressive prehistoric site. Take the old SS 122 road from Caltanissetta to Enna, leaving town through the barren Terra Pilata. The road crosses the Salso river at Ponte Capodarso, a delicate 16th-century Venetian bridge. Four miles (6 km) along the Enna road, a scenic route is marked to the archeological park of Sabucina.

This Bronze Age settlement was later occupied by Hellenised Siculi (Sicel) tribes. The community, influenced by Mycenaean culture, flourished from the 6th to 4th centuries BC. The Sicels lived within a square-towered fortress, parts of which survive. The remains include boundary walls, defensive towers, a sanctuary, two wells, the tracery of grid patterns and house foundations. The antiquarium contains finds from all the local necropoli but the best pieces are in Caltanissetta's **Museo Civico**.

Sabucina overlooks **Monte Capodarso**, a smaller Hellenistic (Sicani) settlement. The slopes are dotted with defensive walls and a necropolis. The exposed settlement was abandoned in 3rd century BC for the surrounding hills. From here, one can explore Caltanissetta's Wild West or the marginally tamer route south to the Gela plains.

The Wild West: Settlements are traditionally restricted to hill-tops, both for defensive purposes and as refuge from the malaria-infested plains. Feuding barons once inhabited these windswept castles. From such eyries stretch views of ravines and deserted plains, sulphurous hills and abandoned mines.

San Caterina Villarmosa's only claim to fame is its delicate embroidery and lace-making. **San Cataldo**, nestling in wooded hills, is noted for its crafts, especially terracotta pots and wrought ironwork. A ridge links it to **Serradifalco,** a dusty hilltop town. Once a ducal hunting estate, it is just one of the seemingly inaccessible settlements that characterise Caltanissetta. Acro-

The Castello Manfredonico at Mussomeli.

batic bends zigzag to **Bompensiere** and **Sutera**, ragged country towns set on rocky outcrops in old mining country.

Mussomeli, like many of the surrounding towns, has suffered from Mafia mythology and emigration. Still, Mussomeli's loss has been Watford's gain, at least as far as gardeners, carworkers and restaurateurs are concerned. As for the Mafia, New York received some of Mussomeli's finest in the 1960s.

Just east of town stands **Castello Manfredonico**, named after Manfredi Chiaramonte, Frederick II's son, killed defending his kingdom against Charles of Anjou. Set on an impregnable crag, the lopsided castle blends into the rock. From the fortress are vertiginous views over the desolate valley below.

Home to Uncle Joe: The town has always lived dangerously. Mussomeli was the hometown and political base of Don Genco Russo, the Mafia overlord from 1954 until the late 1960s. Mafia expert Clare Sterling describes him as a masterly political fixer despite being "a coarse, sly, half-illiterate ruffian loved

by none". Known as Zi Peppi Jencu (Uncle Joe the Little Bull), he helped organise the Sicilian takeover of the American heroin cartel. Only Lucky Luciano, the American Mafia boss, dared ridicule him as "not even a rooster, let alone a bull. He's just a big fat hen."

During his trial in the 1960s, the Don presented a petition with 7,000 signatures from Mussomeli alone. The petition claimed the Don had "dedicated his life to our welfare, setting an example in probity and rectitude." According to Sterling, the trial's turning point came with the threatened publication of telegrams from 37 Christian Democrat deputies, one a Cabinet Minister, thanking the Mafia's *capo di tutti capi* for helping them get elected. Don Genco Russo was acquitted and died a natural death in Mussomeli in 1976.

Villalba is another down-at-heel Mafia haunt, once held by Vizzini, Genco Russo's legendary predecessor. Don Calogero Vizzini was the main Mafia boss from 1942 until his death in 1954. As mayor, he ran this scruffy town like

a private fiefdom. His tombstone in Villalba cemetery laments the death of a gentleman and praises his Robin Hood status as a defender of the weak.

Luigi Barzini describes Don Calò as a prince holding court: "Villalba's piazza is a like stage, ready for *Cavalleria Rusticana* to begin, with the church on one side, *palazzi* and shabby houses all around." On to this set stepped Don Calò and was immediately petitioned by peasants, widows and young *mafiosi*. Open-air justice was dispensed, henchmen summoned, hands kissed and a humble petitioner withdrew satisfied.

Even before the rise of the Mafia, Villalba was doomed to be forever milked by absentee landlords. Along with other local Norman towns, it was a source of cheap labour for the feudal estate of Micciche. Now known as **Regaleali**, the famous estate has shrunk but remains a significant force in the community. **Vallelunga Pratameno**, a neighbouring town on the borders of Caltanissetta and Palermo provinces, is mercifully free of Mafia connotations but rich in wine. The surrounding vineyards belong to Regaleali, owned by Conte Tasca d'Almerita. This is a place to sample genuine Sicilian products, unlaced with dubious additives (*see Wine entry in Travel Tips section*).

South of Caltanissetta: Sinuous upland roads link the craggy countryside with the Gela plains to the south. The higher peaks abound in mountainous vegetation but the wooded slopes soon give way to olives and almonds. The journey south passes sleepy towns with populations reduced by emigration. They share a battered rural economy and dignified poverty. **Sommatino, Riesi** and **Niscemi** are typical of such spots, though **Delia**'s ruined castle helps distinguish it from its neighbours.

Mazzarino's modest reputation rests on Mafia lore and a ruined castle. Founded by the princes of Butera, the castle retains its original keep and some defensive walls. Ragged *palazzi* and a couple of undervalued churches add to the atmosphere of gentle nostalgia. Chiesa San Domenico contains a touch-

Contours of Caltanissetta in spring.

ing Madonna by Paladino. Chiesa dei Cappuccini houses an 18th-century marble tabernacle encrusted with ivory, ebony, coral and tortoise-shell.

In the 1960s this bedraggled country town hit the headlines as a Mafia stronghold run by a licentious abbot. Tales of the friars' orgiastic lifestyles were rife, gleefully embroidered by the press. Sensationalism aside, the good friars were far from blameless and admitted Mafia ties. The Mazzarino friars acted as messengers between the Mafia and their victims. At their trial in 1962, the friars were accused of extortion, intimidation and murder, as well as the creation and distribution of pornography. Under cross-examination, they admitted to writing some of the blackmail and ransom notes "but only because the *mafiosi* were illiterate and did not own a typewriter". Allegedly, verbal threats were delivered via the confessional.

Butera, a crumbling hill village perched on a chalky crest, is the most attractive in the province. The fief prospered under Spanish rule, held by the Branciforte family, the Princes of Butera. Although currently closed, the 11th-century castle is fairly well preserved, with a powerful keep and mullioned windows. The Chiesa Madre boasts a Paladino Madonna and a Renaissance tryptich. Nearby, the Palazzo Comunale (Town Hall) has an intricate 14th-century portal and panoramic views over the Gela plains.

Butera was a former Sicani colony, heavily marked by the Hellenistic influence at Gela. Sanctuaries, funerary rites and fortifications in the region owe much to Greek influence. North of town, step tombs dating from 8th century BC attest to this, their doors decorated with Greek spiral shapes. Just east of Butera is **Lago di Disueri**, a dam with a late Bronze Age necropolis on its rocky shores.

Southeast of Butera, on the N 117 bis, the curious mound of **Castelluccio** presents a dramatic break in the Gela plains. This tumbledown castle, jutting out of fields of artichokes, was built by the warlike Frederick II. Nearby is a modern **war memorial**, a reminder that these fields witnessed the Allied land-

ing in Sicily in 1943. Anglo-American forces fanned across the coastal plains, the Americans from Gela Bay and the British from the Pachino peninsula to the east.

Castelluccio overlooks the fertile **Gela plain**, rich in grain, wine and olives as well as artichokes and oranges, lemons and cotton. This land of plenty was once an open invitation to the Greeks, the first and most welcome wave of settlers. **Gela** is often called the only truly creative Greek colony. It was renowned for its entrepreneurial spirit, inspired military architecture and artistic excellence. It became a Doric colony in 688 BC, settled by Greeks from Rhodes and Crete. However, the indigenous Sicani tribe transmuted the superior Greek culture into a unique shape. Exquisite coins, terracotta figurines, sculpted walls, and flourishing agriculture remain a testament to these times.

From here, Hellenistic influence spread to the rest of Sicily. Yet Gela was sacked by the Carthaginians in 405 BC, a year after Agrigento's fall, and was

Mazzarino Duomo.

eventually razed by the Tyrant of Agrigento in 282 BC, who deported the entire population. The latest devastation was in 1943 when the Allies liberated Sicily and, in the process, bombed Gela to smithereens. Arguably, industrialisation has been the ultimate desecration, the Sicilian environment sacrificed to the northern Italian economy. The city is hideous and only those with a passion for Greek archaeology will brave the polluted outskirts.

Unlike the hill-towns of the interior, Gela has no tradition of aristocratic rule. As a result, it has no castles or noble *palazzi*, nothing linking its glorious Greek heritage with today's grim sprawl. Still, it is worth sifting through the industrial debris to reach the ancient city. Occupying the western slopes of Gela, the main archaeological site presents a strange slice of history. The walls built by Timoleon, the good Tyrant of Siracusa, are set amongst mimosa, eucalyptus and pines; just beyond the sand dunes are futuristic domes and glittering pipes.

The **Archaeological Museum** at the Corso Vittorio Emanuele is built over the ancient acropolis in the Molino a Vento quarter in the east of town. Recently excavated sections are open to inspection. The museum displays painted Attic vases, coins, Ionic capitals and terracotta sarcophagi. Gela terracotta was renowned throughout Magna Graecia, prized for its painted designs and the delicacy of the figurative work. The star piece is a noble terracotta horse's head from the 6th century BC, part of a temple pediment.

Parco della Rimembranza, close by, is a park with a single Doric column and the remains of a temple to Demeter (Athena). From here, there are views over the Gela plain, embracing the long horizon of the African sea, marred by the industrial mass on the beach below.

Capo Soprano fortifications, dating from the same period, are Gela's chief glory. Situated at the western end of town, these romantic walls were covered by sand dunes until 1948.

Running parallel with the sea, the battlemented ramparts were rebuilt by

The keep of Butera castle.

Timoleon after the Carthaginians razed the city. The thick walls are topped with angle towers and sentry posts, with the remains of barracks inside the northern sections. The lower walls are stone but, given the scarcity of stone, the upper sections were built with sun-baked bricks. The walls are unique, both in their state of preservation and in their severe yet stylish workmanship.

Also in the Capo Soprano quarter are **Greek baths**, the only ones to have survived in Sicily. Dating back to the 4th century BC, these are seated baths, one circular, the other horseshoe-shaped.

Fine feasts: Sicily's most depressing towns often have excellent cuisine. Gela, like Catania, proves the point. If marooned on the Gela riviera, at least sample macaroni with aubergines or *stigghuilata 'mpanata*, *focaccia*-style bread stuffed with vegetables, meat or fish.

Golfo di Gela: From here, one can visit the moonscape of the Gela coast, travelling northwest to Agrigento or east to Ragusa and Siracusa. West of Gela, the sandy shore is littered with pillboxes,

relics of Gela's most recent invasion. **Falconara**, to the west, is a small resort with two appealing beaches, Manfria and Roccazzelle. The stretches of golden sands beckon invitingly.

Castello Falconara, the local castle, is set in lush grounds overlooking the sea. Built in sandy-coloured stone, the feudal castle boasts crenellations and a 14th-century keep. This atmospheric spot is owned by Palermitan aristocrats and used as their summer residence.

If the oil-laden winds are blowing the wrong way, take the N 117 north across the plains, passing eucalyptus and cork plantations en route to Piazza Armerina and Roman Sicily. These are Virgil's celebrated **Campi Geloi**, the prairies in which the poet Aeschylus supposedly met his fate (*see page 30*). Archaeologists are still searching for the great tragedian's tomb. Quasimodo, the Sicilian poet, imagines Aeschylus still "measuring verses and inconsolable paces" on Gela's polluted shores. If so, Aeschylus's *Oresteia* should strike a chord with tragic industrial Gela.

Castello Falconara commands an unspoilt bay.

ENNA PROVINCE

To Ovid, Enna was "where Nature decks herself in all her varied hues, where the ground is beauteous, carpeted with flowers of many tints". Enna is still strewn with narcissi in spring but is otherwise a poetic, aloof province with its head in the clouds. In this mythological land, the cult of Demeter (Ceres) has lasted for over 2,000 years, offering a satisfying imaginative explanation for the changing seasons.

As the "navel of Sicily", Enna indulges in introspection. This desolate, sun-parched centre of Sicily is the only province with no outlet to the sea. Yet there is much to proclaim, from the Roman Villa at Piazza Armerina, one of the wonders of the ancient world, to a hinterland studded with hilltop towns and Norman castles.

Enna is considered a sacred city thanks to the cult of Demeter and the myth of Persephone. Apart from clashes with Siracusa, Enna was prosperous and relatively independent during Greek rule. Under the Romans, Enna merely worshipped the old fertility goddesses under the new names of Ceres and Proserpine. Enna became the anonymous breadbasket of Rome, despite several great slave revolts.

The Arabs also cultivated this region, planting a variety of crops including cotton, sugar cane and pistachio nuts as well as building solid fortifications. The city's formidable castle owes even more to Norman rule. Under the Bourbons, a cruel regime of "hangings and holidays" caused resentment and confirmed Enna's rebellious reputation.

Despite Persephone's gift of spring, Enna always feels cloaked in winter, shrouded in mist or blown by wintry gusts of wind. According to Vincent Cronin, Enna's citizens are as "remote, grey and ethereal as the city they inhabit". Yet, whatever the climate, the ancient cult of fertility cannot be crushed: Enna province remains agricultural, producing corn, olives, cheese, nuts and wine. The hill towns here are some of the

best places to sample *castrato*, charcoal-grilled castrated ram.

Sights: Enna's sights are fairly compact, but when the mist falls, expect to cling to the city walls between churches. Tradition has it that the **cathedral** was begun by Eleanor of Aragon but a fire in 1446 tragically swept away most of the treasures. The good news is that the coffered ceilings have been lovingly restored to their former glory and the chestnut panels gleam softly. However the bad news is that the charming belltower has been swaying dangerously for some time.

Nonetheless, the cathedral is a fascinating romp through Enna's mystical past. The elaborately carved white pulpit is encrusted with cherubs and rests on a Graeco-Roman base removed from a temple to Demeter, as does the marble stoup nearby. The quaint portico is matched by Gothic transepts and apses. The wrought-iron sacristy gate once graced a Moorish harem in the Castello di Lombardia.

The beloved statue of the **Black**

Madonna is stored within two sets of doors in a side chapel. On Good Friday, citizens sew ex-voto offerings on the Madonna's gold dress and parade her through the town. Enna's esoteric past makes it susceptible to pagan magic. The black basalt base of the capitals incorporate sculptures of Hades and demonic symbols in an attempt to crush evil forces by fair means or foul. A sacred 14th-century crucifix supposedly has supernatural powers, changing its expression in different angles and light.

Museo Alessi: The contents of this museum used to be crammed into a cupboard in the sacristy until common sense recently prevailed. As a result, the collection now has the care it deserves. In local eyes, icons, paintings, incense burners and candelabra are a poor second to the so-called Madonna's Crown, a sacred 17th-century diadem studded with diamonds.

Along **Via Roma** are a string of dignified mansions and churches, such as the Catalan-Gothic Palazzo Pollicarini and the baroque Chiesa San Benedetto.

At the bottom are sweeping views from the *belvedere* and **Torre di Federico II,** a tumbledown octagonal tower built by Frederick II. Secret passages link it to Castello di Lombardia at the top of the hill. Unfortunately, both the Torre di Federico II and the Castello di Lombardia are closed to the public while they undergo much needed restoration. Via Roma is pedestrianised for the evening *passeggiata* and contains a good *pasticceria* as well as cosy restaurants.

At the end of the bustling Via Roma is the **Castello di Lombardia**, one of the largest medieval castles in Sicily. This imposing fortress began as a draughty Byzantine castle but acquired towers with each wave of invaders, from the Normans to the Hohenstaufe Emperors. Six of its original 20 towers remain. A series of three courtyards leads to the majestic eyrie of **Torre Pisano**, and views over the whole of Sicily.

Rocca di Cerere, also known as the Temple of Demeter, is full of misleading promise. The reality is a sole rock and rural views but no sign of a temple.

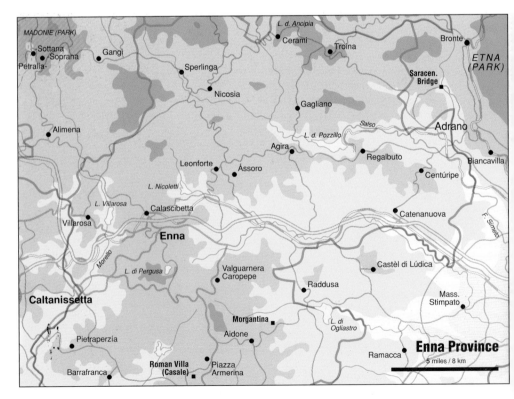

Legend has it that Demeter's daughter Persephone was abducted by Hades and swept off to the shores of **Lake Pergusa** and thence to the Underworld. Her mother's pleading won Persephone's freedom for part of the year, time to sow and spin the cycle of fertility. Hades' cavern is still on the south bank of the lake but his chariot and black horses are now Formula One. The lake is encircled by a racing track, a sacrilegious end to Persephone's memory and meadows of pure narcissi.

Facing Enna is **Calascibetta**, a decrepit hill village built by the Arabs while besieging Enna in 951. The Saracen stronghold was eventually taken by Count Roger but retains its intimate Moorish design. Rust-coloured buildings cling to the slopes and the Chiesa Madre is perched on top of a sheer cliff. In **Realmesi** necropoli nearby are curious oven tombs, hollowed out of the rock and dating from 9th century BC.

Northern hills: North of Enna is **Leonforte**, founded by the Branciforte in the 17th century. This erstwhile fief is best known for its colourful Good Friday procession and the **Granfonte**, a magnificent fountain. Set on the edge of town, the graceful arched fountain fills troughs from 24 spouts. As writer Paul Duncan says: "Its construction (in golden stone to match the surrounding cornfields) was an act of isolated benevolence at a time when feudal dependents were more likely to be given a kick in the teeth than fresh running water."

This testament to feudal largesse is watched over by the Branciforte. On the hill above, their tumbledown **family seat** and funerary chapel remain. The princely ghosts may still see their fountain appreciated by thirsty donkeys.

Sperlinga, north of Leonforte, may well be Sicily's most intriguing **castle**, with battlemented towers and bastions that reach to the bottom of the cliff. Above ground, the village is a string of modest cottages; below the castle, the rock is riddled with chambers, a secret underground city. Dating from 1082, the Norman castle passed from the Chiaramonte into the hands of the Natali,

Calascibetta seen from Enna.

Princes of Sperlinga in 1597. The citadel became a Bourbon prison and was donated to the town by Baron Nicosia, its feudal owner, in 1973. However, Sperlinga's heyday was Sicily's nadir.

After the bloody **Sicilian Vespers** in 1282, Sperlinga became the Angevins' last stand. The castle was besieged but the French forces within held out for over a year, aided by trap doors that deposited invaders in underground pits. The only access is still via a staircase hewn out of the rock.

Steep, switchback paths climb to the summit, festooned with warning notices. From the crenellations stretch sweeping views over oak woods, olive groves and pasture. (For the wary, Signore Modusa, a semi-official guide, is on hand for tours or found at Antico Mulino at the foot of the castle.)

The rocky slopes of the village are also pitted with caves, some of which have been inhabited since Sicani times. The cave dwellings were occupied by Sperlinga's poorest peasants and their livestock until the 1980s. Even today, many cottages open into chambers which function as store rooms or wine cellars.

Nicosia, southeast of Sperlinga, is set on four hills and ringed by rocky spurs. It has been a Greek city, Byzantine bishopric, Arab fort and Norman citadel. In the Middle Ages, it was riven by religious rivalry between Roman Catholic newcomers from the north and the indigenous population who, in Byzantine tradition, followed the Greek Orthodox rite. After pitched battles, the matter was settled in favour of the natives: San Nicolò triumphed as the city cathedral.

The town centre is dominated by **San Nicolò**, the 14th-century cathedral, with its lacey Catalan-Gothic *campanile* rooted in a gracious Moorish tower. Since the 1967 earthquake, the encircling Catalan porticos have overflowed with headless statues: Sicilian restoration at its slowest. After viewing a Gothic portal adorned with decapitated lions and cherubs, the baroque interior disappoints, despite its finely-worked choir stalls and Gagini statuary. But beyond

Granfonte, the imposing fountain, Leonforte.

the frescoed baroque ceiling lies the concealed 14th-century painted roof. The vivid panels feature phases of the moon, young noblemen, arabesques and floral motifs.

From the cathedral, Salita Salamone climbs to **San Salvatore**, a Romanesque church that would be at home in Burgundy. From the delicate portico is a view over the rooftops to Santa Maria Maggiore on the facing hill. Below are buildings made of yellow and grey local stone. On the next square down is **Palazzo Salamone**, the seat of Nicosia's most illustrious family, one that still exerts influence over city affairs.

Piazza Garibaldi is dotted with dingy bars and *circoli*, working men's clubs. Bandy-legged old men sit and chat in *gallo-italico*, a Lombard dialect stemming from northern settlers and shared with Aidone, Piazza Armerina and Sperlinga. Half the adult population emigrated between 1950 and 1970 and Nicosia has been further isolated by the route of the new motorway. A building boom has resulted in bland modern infill, fostered by Mafia interests.

Leading off Piazza Garibaldi, the main square, are myriad *vicoli*, crooked alleys climbing Nicosia's hills. From here, the steep **Via Salamone** winds above the cathedral, passing dilapidated *palazzi* and convents encrusted with garlands or gargoyles.

At the top is **Santa Maria Maggiore**, wedged between boulders. After an 18th-century earthquake, the Norman church was rebuilt in baroque style. This elegant shadow faces a montage of bells that fell down in the last earthquake. From the terrace, the tumbledown castle is visible, overgrown with cacti and thistles on a rocky spur. *Cardi* (fried thistles) are a rustic delicacy but the Trattoria La Pace in Via della Pace believes in heartier fare.

A meandering mountain road leads northeast to **Cerami**, a jagged village dominated by a ruined castle. The wooded countryside is interspersed with orchards and lolling cattle. Nearby is the scenic **Lago di Ancipa**, a lake set in a lush wilderness. East of Nicosia are windswept views across the bleak Nebrodi mountains. The wrinkled blue-brown slopes and undulating wheatfields shimmer in the heat.

Troina, the loftiest town in Sicily, occupies an Arab-Norman stronghold on a solitary ridge. This citadel has declined into an austere hill town with a nest of churches crammed into winding medieval alleys. Tall, draughty convents look out over scruffy terraces and the makeshift houses of returning emigrants.

The churches are suitably grand, as befits the first Norman diocese in Sicily. The Norman **Chiesa Matrice** has a fortified belltower, nave, crypt, tower and solid external walls. In this citadel Count Roger and wife were besieged by Saracens in 1064. The couple escaped by classic Norman cunning: while their enemies were lulled into a drunken stupor, the Normans scurried along secret vaulted passages that burrow deep under the ruined castle.

Inside, the fusty church has been revamped in baroque style, complete with flaking gold leaf and late Byzantine art. However, in the treasury Roger's ruby

ring remains as a memento. Outside, an arched walk slopes under the belltower and returns to the atmospheric Norman stronghold. The terraces are scarred with jagged bits of castle and chapel. On the belvedere, Troina's youth gather to enjoy rugged windswept views over the distant blue-grey hills.

Agira, south of Troina, is set on a hillside surmounted by a Saracen castle. The slopes once housed a Siculi settlement but are now given over to olives, grapes and almonds. These hills saw heavy fighting during the Sicilian campaign in 1943, hence the Canadian war cemetery on the town outskirts.

While not striking, the churches contain precious works of art. **Santa Maria Maggiore**, in the shadow of the castle, has a 15th-century triptych and sculpted Norman capitals while **Santa Maria di Gesù** contains a painted crucifix by Fra Umile da Petralia. Laden down by a 16th-century facade, the Gothic **San Salvatore** has a treasury containing a bejewelled medieval mitre.

Further east, past Lago di Pozzillo, an artificial lake, a minor road leads through orange and olive groves to **Centuripe**. The name supposedly comes from the Latin for steep slopes, justifying the town's tag as "balcony of Sicily" and its magnificent valley views to Catania and Etna. Like Agira, this strategic site witnessed the defeat of Goering's forces by an Irish brigade in 1943.

Cicero described this Hellenised Siculi settlement as the richest city in Sicily, thanks to its fertile soil, sulphur and salt mines. Classical statues, terracottas and vases are visible in the **municipal museum**. On the outskirts, further finds have been made at Castello di Corradino, the site of a clifftop Roman mausoleum. At the foot of Monte Calvario are the ruins of a Greek villa and, in the Bagni valley, the remains of Roman baths.

Southern hills: Southwest of Enna are a couple of isolated hill towns on the Caltanissetta border. **Pietraperzia**, stacked up on the slopes, lives off the land but once provided a living for the Barresi dynasty. As major landowners in Caltanissetta and Enna provinces, they placed a fortified **palazzo** at the heart of their battered fiefdom.

Barrafranca lies just south, set on a spur in the Erei mountains. This Roman outpost and Norman fief was swallowed up by the Branciforte feudal estates in 1530. The baroque **Chiesa Madre** has fine paintings while the hamlet of Bastia overlooks Byzantine ruins. Otherwise, pleasures lie in the sampling of local produce, including olives, almonds and grapes. The town is pitted with caves, used as wine cellars. This backwater bursts into life at Easter, with a colourful procession of giants and an exuberant Christian pantomime.

Further east is **Piazza Armerina** and the Roman Villa at Casale, Sicily's greatest wonder of the Roman world. As a town, Piazza Armerina is sorely neglected in favour of its Roman star. Yet while upstaged, Piazza Armerina is not overawed and has a faded elegance all of its own. Although the closure of the sulphur mines has cast a pall over the local economy, the town sees its salvation in tourism.

Church war memorial, Agira.

A series of flights of steps and alleys leads to the baroque **cathedral**, crowning the terraced hill. Theatrical staircases also accentuate the spacious belvedere and the Duomo's baroque facade. A Catalan-Gothic *campanile* with blind arcading remains from the original church and sets the tone for the lavish interior. Decorated like blue and white porcelain, the church boasts a Byzantine icon of a Madonna, a baroque tabernacle and a luminous *provençal* painted crucifix. Gilded organ cases, carved choir stalls and a sculpted arch complete this cluttered composition. Bordering the cathedral is **Palazzo Trigona**, a sober counterpoint to the baroque flights of fancy.

Old town: The hill-top quarter radiates from Piazza Duomo and Piazza Garibaldi. In keeping with 13th-century urban design, this is in fishbone formation, with tiny alleys fanning out delicately along the contours of the slopes. Beside Palazzo Trigona, Via Floresta leads to the picturesque Aragonese castle. Further south, the steep Via Castellina nudges the city walls and an old watchtower.

A stroll down the steep **Via Monte**, the medieval main street, reveals an evocative slice of history. This characteristic quarter passes *palazzi* dating from Norman and Aragonese times. Turnings right lead past turreted mansions to **San Martino**, a 15th-century church. A half-mile (1-km) stroll north from the compact hillside quarter reaches **Sant' Andrea**, an unadorned but delightful Norman priory with a frescoed interior designed in a Coptic cross plan.

A path signposted to **Villa Romana** cuts through the tumbledown side of town and hugs the foot of the hill into open country, with flashes of olives and forsythia. Nestling among oak and hazel woods at Casale, the Roman Villa lies on a Roman road. The excellent hunting in these forests was the bait that drew the villa's original owners.

Imperial glory: Whether hunting lodge or country mansion, the villa disappeared under a landslide for 700 years. The villa probably first belonged to

Taking a break, Nicosia.

Diocletian's co-Emperor Maximianus Heraclius (Maximinian) between 286 and 305, and then passed to later emperors. It was occupied throughout the Arab period but destroyed by the Norman King William in 1160. These fluid, impressionistic mosaics may have inspired the Normans in their designs for Palermo's Palazzo dei Normanni.

In splendour, the only rivals are Hadrian's Villa at Tivoli or Diocletian's palace at Split. But Sicily's mosaics better reflect the flux of Roman politics, with the emergence of separate Eastern and Western Empires. One theory is that after Diocletian realised that the Roman world was too vast to be ruled by one mind and retired to Split, so Maximianus withdrew to contemplation in Sicily.

After a hoard of treasure was found in 1950, the villa was seriously excavated. Much remains to be unearthed in the hazelnut orchards, from the slave quarters to the water system. Yet a Sicilian muddle caused excavations to be abandoned in 1985 and has delayed the restoration of mosaics that suffered flood damage in 1991. Many are discoloured, including those in the Great Hall.

If this were Venice, there would be a public outcry; since this is Sicily, manpower and funding focus on security, discouraging looters and fellow custodians from indulging in night raids. On top of everything, plastic roofing turns the site into a sauna in summer. Nonetheless, the mosaics triumph as "the last pagan achievement in Sicily executed under the old dispensation".

The villa: The vaulting is lost and the frescoes faded but the villa's magic lies in the 50 rooms covered in Roman-African mosaics. Their vitality, expressive power and free-ranging content set them apart from models in Tunisia or Antioch. The stylisation of these mosaics is undercut by humour, realism, sensuality and subtlety. Above all, the visual energy of the mosaics shines through.

A triumphal arch leads to an **atrium** surrounded by a portico and then crashes down to earth in the male **latrines**, in a composition of a Persian ass, ram and pouncing leopard. Despite the savagery

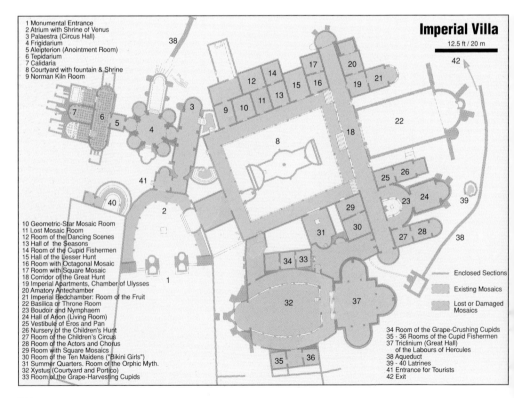

1 Monumental Entrance
2 Atrium with Shrine of Venus
3 Palaestra (Circus Hall)
4 Frigidarium
5 Aleipterion (Anointment Room)
6 Tepidarium
7 Calidaria
8 Courtyard with fountain & Shrine
9 Norman Kiln Room

Imperial Villa

12.5 ft / 20 m

10 Geometric-Star Mosaic Room
11 Lost Mosaic Room
12 Room of the Dancing Scenes
13 Hall of the Seasons
14 Room of the Cupid Fishermen
15 Hall of the Lesser Hunt
16 Room with Octagonal Mosaic
17 Room with Square Mosaic
18 Corridor of the Great Hunt
19 Imperial Apartments, Chamber of Ulysses
20 Amatory Antechamber
21 Imperial Bedchamber: Room of the Fruit
22 Basilica or Throne Room
23 Boudoir and Nymphaem
24 Hall of Arion (Living Room)
25 Vestibule of Eros and Pan
26 Nursery of the Children's Hunt
27 Room of the Children's Circus
28 Room of the Actors and Chorus
29 Room with Square Mosaics
30 Room of the Ten Maidens ("Bikini Girls")
31 Summer Quarters. Room of the Orphic Myth.
32 Xystus (Courtyard and Portico)
33 Room of the Grape-Harvesting Cupids

34 Room of the Grape-Crushing Cupids
35 - 36 Rooms of the Cupid Fishermen
37 Triclinium (Great Hall)
of the Labours of Hercules
38 Aqueduct
39 - 40 Latrines
41 Entrance for Tourists
42 Exit

— Enclosed Sections
Existing Mosaics
Lost or Damaged Mosaics

of the scene, the latrines look more civilised than most modern ones. The villa's centrepiece is the **courtyard**, with peristyle, pool and statue. The mosaics depict whimsical animals' heads, from a fierce bear and tiger to a horse with a stunted nose. The design has a symmetry, pairing domestic and wild or male and female animals; a butch ram thus sits beside a female deer.

The **Circus Hall** illustrates chaotic races at the Circus Maximus. Nearby is the **small latrine**, featuring bidets for women, and the complex of thermal baths. In the octagonal **frigidarium**, vestibules and plunge baths are adorned with tritons, centaurs and marine monsters. A fuzzy-haired maiden is shedding her robe while in the **anointment room** next-door, a man is massaged and perfumed by his naked servant.

The **Room of the Cupid Fishermen** depicts a naked mermaid clasping a dolphin in the presence of fishermen with bare buttocks or chests. Nearby is the **Hall of the Lesser Hunt**, with a frenetic deer hunt, the snaring of a wild boar, and a toast to a successful day's sport. To the Romans, hunting meant food, sport and sensuality, adventure and pleasure, preferably all at once.

Surrounding the main courtyard is the **Corridor of the Great Hunt**, a gloriously animated work meant to be appreciated while walking. In this swirling mass of movement, chariots, lions, cheetahs, rhinos and huge swans merge in lovely autumnal colours. A mosaic sea separates Africa and Europe, echoing the division of the Roman Empire. Africa is personified by a tiger, elephant and a phoenix fleeing a burning house. The exotic, bare-breasted Queen of Sheba is being ogled by a tiger as well as by heterosexual Romans.

Sport and erotica are often neatly entwined. The **amatory antechamber**, the Empress' suite, features Cupid fishermen netting a fine catch. The **Imperial bedchamber** is decorated with figs, grapes and pomegranites, snatching at Greek fertility symbols. The **Room of Ten Maidens** presents prancing girl gymnasts in costumes that prove con-

How little fashion changes: Villa Romana's "Bikini girls" in action.

clusively that the bikini was not invented by Coco Chanel in the 1950s.

The **Triclinium** (Great Hall) is the villa's masterpiece, a flowing mythological pageant based on the Labours of Hercules. It is a symphony of pathos and poetic vision worthy of Michelangelo: the gods are threatened by chaos and decay; tortured giants writhe in agony; and a mighty nude Hercules is glorified. Passion is present in Cerberus, the three-headed dog; and in the fierce Hydra which has a woman's face but snake-encrusted hair.

All the scenes normally excluded from Christian art lie here. The villa depicts a kaleidoscope of everyday life, highlighting intimate pleasures such as child's play and youthful dancing, massage and love-making. A timeless quality also infuses the mosaics' undisguised eroticism: the female nudes may have odd-shaped breasts but they dance in pagan abandon. The more accomplished male nudes are studies in virility, heightened by the use of *chiaroscuro* and three-dimensionality. Roman paganism worshipped heroism and masculine valour, a vitality crushed by cool Christian art.

Paganism: Amazons were admired rather than idealised. As the writer Vincent Cronin says of the "Bikini girls" mosaic: "Aphrodite is dead: the ideal goddess of beauty has been superseded by this plurality of particular girls, portrayed on a pavement where the feet of huntsmen can trample them."

Roman gods are only too mortal. For all their energy and realism, they have little inner life and lack the sacred dimension of Greek or Christian art. Emperor Constantine, the last Roman proprietor of the villa, only became a Christian on his death bed. This villa remains a temple of paganism.

If sated with Roman sights, consider picnicking in the pine and eucalyptus woods. Alternatively, **Aidone** represents a window on the Greek world. The town has a ruined castle and a clutch of austere churches enlivened by elaborate arches, warm brickwork and honey-coloured stone. **San Domenico** is noted for its diamond-point design on the facade.

Corridor of the Great Hunt: antelope on a leash.

The **Museo Archeologico**, set in a 17th-century monastery, is an introduction to the rural site of Morgantina, perhaps the most "legible" site in antiquity.

Morgantina occupies a rural paradise worthy of Persephone, its slopes covered in calendula, pines or olives and framed by grey-blue hills. This ancient Siculi settlement was Hellenised by a Chalcidian colony in 6 BC and survived for 500 years. After Morgantina fell to the Romans in 211 BC, the Greek population was sold into slavery and the farmlands given to Spanish mercenaries as a reward for subduing the city.

The remains are not aesthetically beautiful like Piazza Armerina but are supremely clear, an exposition of a Classical city in stone. The site reveals a civic and sacred centre bounded by a commercial district in the east and a residential quarter in the west. Cittadella, the hill site of the prehistoric city, is pitted with chamber tombs. Visible Hellenistic sections include: the *macellum* (covered market), designed alike a shopping mall; a schoolroom complete with benches; a gymnasium with an athletic track; the *bouleuterion* (town hall); as well as boutiques, a granary, and a theatre with good acoustics.

Several of the **noble villas** contain the earliest known mosaics in the Western Mediterranean, including a floor inscription saying welcome (*euexei*). Theatrical steps lead to the *agora*, complete with aqueducts and fountain. Nearby is a temple with a *bothros*, a round well-altar used as a sacrificial ditch. The presence of sanctuaries to the Chthonic gods shows that the city's focal point was a devotion to the cult of Demeter and Persephone.

This is a reminder that mystical Enna marked the crossroads of Trinacria, ancient Sicily's three provinces. According to one historian, Enna is the hub of a giant geomantic chart, lying on ley lines spanning the island. This network of sacred spots supposedly provides the key to the region's occult power. From here, return to earth in bustling Catania Province or remain in the clouds in lofty Caltanissetta Province.

The Queen of Sheba.

RAGUSA PROVINCE

Discreet well-being is the keynote to the region. Gesualdo Bufalino, regarded by many as Sicily's greatest living writer, describes his province proudly as "*un isola nell'isola*", an island within an island. It is perhaps not accidental that the province is a crime-free haven, surviving beyond the Mafia's reptilian gaze. Here the typical conditions for Sicilian crime are absent: a spirit of enterprise was established by Greek settlers; the feudal estates were administered better than most elsewhere and broken up earlier. Here the gap between rich and poor is smaller, thanks to favourable social conditions.

In the country, curiosity about new agricultural approaches has not destroyed rural traditions. Unlike much of Sicily, there is a civilised balance between ancient *cultura contadina* (peasant culture) and the creativity of the *borghesia*. As a result, the Ragusani are a hospitable people, more open than those in the mountainous interior.

As for scenery, Ragusa favours subtlety over drama: rolling countryside and sandy beaches border Classical sites and curious castles. Elegant towns seamlessly combine medieval and baroque styles. Yet, paradoxically, this is the finest corner of baroque splendour in Sicily: only Noto can rival the charms of Ragusa and Modica. However, tourism is so low-key that beds are scarce in the province (*see Travel Tips section*).

The provincial economy thrives on wine-growing and cattle-breeding as well as market gardening, especially hot-house flowers. But **Ragusa** has grown rich on asphalt and oil, the latter discovered in the 1960s. The mines, both underground and opencast, have produced asphalt that has paved the streets of London and Glasgow. During excavations, miners uncovered ancient quarries and Christian catacombs.

Ancient rivalry: Ragusa was a Norman stronghold which became a fief of the Cabrera dynasty. However, the 1693 earthquake devastated the province and reduced Ragusa to rubble. The merchant class responded by building Ragusa Alta, the new city on the hill. But the aristocracy refused to desert their charred homes so recreated Ragusa Bassa (Ibla) on the original valley site. The towns only merged in 1926 and the rivalry remains. Ibla remains an enchanting, timeless pocket of Sicily. By contrast, **Ragusa Alta** is a bland city, saved only by baroque mansions, churches and bustling restaurants. The urban design is a mess: baroque opulence interlaid with Fascistic monumentality and a modern sector riven by gorges.

San Giovanni, the theatrical baroque cathedral, has an ornate facade and soaring campanile. Its sense of sweeping movement is echoed by the bustle of the surrounding bars and veterans' clubs. Nearby, baroque mansions boast wrought-iron balconies with sculpted cornices. One such is **Palazzo Bertini** on Corso Italia. The sculpted masks represent "the three powers": a peasant, nobleman and merchant. On Corso Vittorio Veneto is the crumbling **Palazzo**

Preceding pages: view across the valley to Ragusa Ibla. **Left**, the town's medieval rooftops. **Right**, detail on Ragusa's Duomo.

Zacco. A gap-toothed monster sticks out his tongue, mocking the church of San Vito opposite.

The **Museo Archeologico**, oddly housed in the Mediterraneo hotel, is rich in finds from Camarina and Siculi necropoli. Exhibits include tombs, Greek vases, Byzantine mosaics and a reconstruction of a potter's workshop. The museum abuts a gorge criss-crossed by three bridges. One bridge was built by a friar who tired of the daily uphill slog to his parish. On the far side of the chasm is densely packed Ibla.

Ragusa Ibla: Ibla resembles a baroque city recreated on a medieval street plan. As such, old world intimacy prevails. Ibla is fawn-coloured stone mansions, filigree balconies hung with washing, oriel windows, dark courtyards popular with ambling dogs; secret arches, neglected shrines, baroque fountains and yellowing palm trees. The crumbling mansions would cost a fortune in Tuscany but cannot be sold in Sicily.

Santa Maria delle Scale, framed by parched hills, represents the gateway to Ibla. This Gothic church was remodelled after the 1693 earthquake. A medieval portal remains, as does the Catalan-Gothic nave, complete with Renaissance ornamentation and arches adorned with beasts and flowers. From this balcony over Old Ragusa, 250 steps zigzag down to Ibla. There is a commanding view over isolated farms and the blue-tinged cupola of the cathedral below.

Palazzo della Cancelleria, a baroque chancery, sits astride the winding staircase that links new and old Ragusa. The adjoining covered passageway, golden mansions and crumbling church make a quaint *chiaroscuro* introduction to Ibla. Next door, **Chiesa dell'Idria** is a chapel owned by the Cosentini, one of Ibla's leading families. Given the narrowness of the alleys, it takes time to gain a perspective of the robust belltower and majolica-encrusted dome.

Crushed between the church steps and Corso Mazzini is **Palazzo Cosentini**, an ancestral home adjoining the family chapel above. The sculpted balconies are a melange of bare-breasted

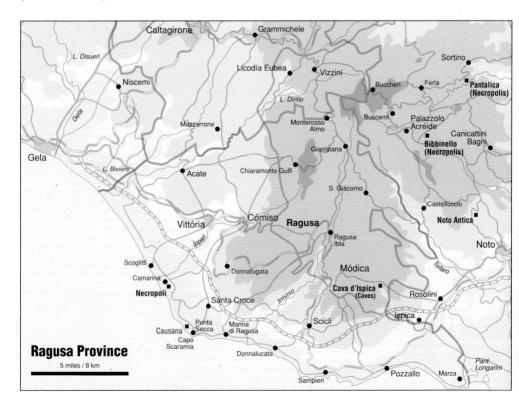

Ragusa Province

5 miles / 8 km

sirens and monsters with flaring nostrils. Leering faces proffer scorpions or serpents instead of tongues, a warning not to gossip.

On Piazza della Repubblica is **Chiesa del Purgatorio**, a dramatic baroque church surmounting an elegant staircase. The belltower is built on Byzantine city walls, visible from the steps of Salita dell'Orologio. A tortuous alley separates the church from **Palazzo Sortino-Trono**, an imposing baroque mansion with sculpted corbels.

After the cosy claustrophobia so far, the spacious **Piazza Duomo** comes as a shock. The square is lined with palm trees, baroque mansions and aristocratic clubs. The far end is dominated by Gagliardi's San Giorgio, a masterpieces of Sicilian baroque.

San Giorgio is the city centrepiece, a wedding cake of a cathedral. The sandstone church occupies a raised terrace and tricks one's eyes up from its convex centre, seemingly writhing with statues, to a crescendo of the campanile. The belltower is topped by a blue neoclassical dome that is a city landmark.

Its smaller imitator, also by Gagliardi, is **San Giuseppe**, which gains in subtlety what it lacks in theatricality. As Paul Duncan says of Gagliardi's work, the sweeping curves are always in the process of "moving into another plane".

Adjoining Piazza Duomo is the arched **Palazzo Arezzo** belonging to Baron Vincenzo Arezzo, whose family has had a stake in Ragusa for centuries. The facade is adorned with sculpted hedgehogs, the family crest. Their credo is one of enlightened paternalism. The Arezzo still own much of the province, from farmland to villas and a castle. In return, the family has endowed local hospitals, parks and churches. Ibla's nobles have always immortalised themselves in stone, linking grand baroque mansions to a graceful family chapel and even a chic gentlemen's club.

Nearby is the **Circolo di Conversazione**, a literary salon founded by local noblemen and the indefatigable Vincenzo Arezzo. The *Belle Epoque* interior boasts an allegorical *trompe l'oeil* ceiling but no conversation. Inspi-

rational busts of Michelangelo, Galileo, Dante and Bellini represent art, science, poetry and music. But the art of aristocratic conversation is dead in sleepy Ibla: taciturn old fogeys gaze on frescoed nymphs or ponder on cold coffee.

In the square, elderly *contadini* greet their masters with the honorific *baciolemani* ("I kiss your hands") and receive an imperceptible nod from the *signori* in response. Journalist Giuseppe Fava saw "the gentle melancholy of these last nobles" as proof of the city's petrification. "Nowhere in Italy has time stood still to the same degree as in Ibla."

The adjoining **Palazzo Donnafugata** was the nobles' private theatre, gallery and reading club until recently opened to a slightly wider membership. Still, the sculpted marble staircase, sumptuous salons and gallery adorned with old masters are not open to outsiders. Most symbolic is the heavily-shuttered loggia on the *piano nobile*, an example of a *gelosia*, a secret spot from which to view visitors.

Behind the cathedral is **Palazzo la**

Giardino Ibleo, the park of three churches.

Rocca, an austere baroque mansion transformed into the tourist office. The facade is enlivened by bizarre balconies, depicting 18th-century aristocratic entertainment. A lute player and cherub blowing a hunting horn vie with gawky, naked lovers clinging to each other in gauche poses.

The alleys in the shadow of the cathedral are what Italians readily term *suggestivo* (atmospheric). This is the heart of the ancient Jewish ghetto and artisan quarter. In Largo Camerina a cabinet-maker creates tables from olive, carob, cherry, cyprus and orange wood. Nearby, the majestic staircase of Palazzo di Quattro in Via Orfanotrofio shelters an antique shop. To discourage craftsmen from leaving, the covered market halls in **Via Mercato** are being restored. The last to flee will be Ibla's grandmothers, for whom lace-making remains an engrossing winter pastime.

Giardino Ibleo, an appealing park, is set on a spur. In spring, the statues, palm trees and pool are complemented by daffodils, broom and irises. Around the

grounds are three ruined churches, victims of the 1693 earthquake. The multi-coloured majolica dome of San Domenico overlooks San Giacomo, a Gothic church built on the site of a pagan temple. Next-door is Chiesa dei Cappuccini, a baroque church housing a monastic library, a collection of sacred art and a picture-restoring workshop.

On the far side of the gardens is the **Portale San Giorgio**, a Catalan-Gothic doorway depicting St George and the dragon. Carved in soft local stone, this is all that remains of the original church. From this quiet corner in Ibla, pensioners look out over terraces and dry stone walls to a valley embedded with ancient Siculi tombs.

Discesa Pescheria leads to **San Francesco**, a 16th-century church adorned with sculpted cherubs and housing the Arezzo mausoleum. All around are crumbling *palazzi* and views of orange trees. Opposite stands a collapsing Gothic doorway, now incorporated into an old people's home.

Snapshots of Ibla capture shrines, fountains and family crests. Shrines lurk in alleys, at crossroads, even on facades. They represent a need for reassurance as well as an expression of faith and a superstitious thanks for future miracles. Corso Mazzini contains a medieval *Flight into Egypt* as well as a shrine in memory of those who died of cholera. As for noble crests, the city is studded with symbolism, from the Arezzo hedgehogs to the Aragonese eagle.

Yet, despite its noble veneer, parts of Ibla are exceptionally poor. **The Pinnineddi quarter** is one of blind alleys, abandoned hovels and rock dwellings, side by side with remains of medieval, Byzantine and even pre-Christian Ragusa. The ancient Siculi tombs now tend to be used as storerooms, wine cellars or even garages.

Much livelier is the quarter of **San Paolo Gia Raffo**, set at the foot of an ancient quarry. Above is the jagged landscape of modern Ragusa. The valley floor is cut by a river that fed several mills until a decade ago. The scene is one of whitewashed cottages, steep steps, pots of geraniums, and peppers dried on

St George and the Dragon, Ibla.

walls Arab-style. The occasional impressive church, such as San Sebastiano, raises the tone of this ramshackle quarter. But more typical is the mill race, the air of lived-in scruffiness and the smell of woodsmoke.

Rustic cuisine: One of the old mills has been turned into the rustic Antica Macina restaurant. Elsewhere, Tunisian-run restaurants compete with local fare. Simple dishes include: *macco*, made with pasta and mashed fava beans; *scaccie*, pasta stuffed with broccoli or spinach; and *affocaparrini*, almond-encrusted sweets. This is *cucina contadina* (rustic cooking), following the seasons, from almond to olive harvests. Easter means *'mpanate* (lamb pies); pigs are slaughtered at Christmas so this is the time for pork *ravioli*.

From Ragusa the rural hinterland unfolds. On higher ground, olives, almonds and carobs abound but in well-irrigated areas greenhouse cultivation is gaining ground. Where there is enough water, on the coast or in river canyons, dwarf palms, holm oaks, plane trees, Aleppo pines and lentisks flourish. But on the plains, the view is of dust-coloured farmhouses, low dry-stone walls, endless fields, rugged limestone plains beaten to the colour of sandstone.

West of Ragusa: A dramatic descent from the Iblean hills leads across a vast plain to **Cómiso**, a muddled medieval and baroque town which had the misfortune to become a controversial NATO military base in the 1980s. Peace protests were the price residents paid for housing the last Cruise missiles located on European soil. As a bonus, 7,000 American soldiers subsidised the local economy until the final removal of the missiles in 1991. The troops' absence is felt in the bars, but essentially the town has reverted to its sleepy self with relief.

Ruled by the Aragonese Naselli dynasty from the 15th to the 18th centuries, Cómiso still boasts a feudal castle. The **Castello** retains its original Gothic portal and octagonal tower, converted from a Byzantine baptistry, but the rest was remodelled in the 16th century.

Although shattered by the 1693 earth-

Battered workshop in Ibla.

quake, fragments of Classical Cómiso survive. The Piazza di Municipio, for example, contains a **Fountain to Diana**, whose waters once gushed into the Roman baths. Legend has it that the city waters would not mix with wine when poured by unchaste hands.

Scruffy remains of the thermal baths lie behind the Municipio while a **Roman mosaic** of Neptune dancing with nymphs and dolphins can be seen in the municipal library.

The medieval town cowers under the baroque **Basilica dell' Annunziata** and Gagliardi's **Chiesa Matrice**, crowned by a similarly overblown dome. **Chiesa di San Francesco** dates from the 13th century and has an adjoining Renaissance funerary chapel for Count Naselli's tomb, a masterpiece sculpted by Gagini. The cupola of the curious chapel is joined to the square below in a nostalgic Arab-Norman pastiche. **Santa Maria delle Grazie**, the Capucin chapel, offers the town's most gruesome sight: mummified bodies of monks and benefactors stacked in horrific poses.

Vittoria, further west, is a wealthy, wine-producing centre on the slopes of the Iblean hills. The city was founded in 1607 by Vittoria Colonna, the daughter of a Spanish viceroy and wife of the Count of Modica. Since aristocratic power in parliament was closely linked to the size of the feudal estates, Vittoria tried to make the town as populous as possible. Today, this neat city remains wealthy rather than healthy: under the surface lurks a crime and drugs problem, proof of the Mafia's first toe-hold in the province.

Giuseppe Fava dismissed Vittoria as "a city built by those without the time, money, imagination or background to make anywhere better." Even so, the elegant **Piazza del Popolo** boasts the baroque church of Madonna delle Grazie. Amidst the bland modernity are bourgeois mansions with grand courtyards. The finest are the Renaissance Palazzo Pavia in Via Palestro, the Venetian-Gothic Palazzo Traina in Via Cancellieri and the Art Nouveau Palazzo Piazzese in Via Matteotti.

Mobile market, Cómiso.

From the city gardens are views across the fertile valley to the sea. Deforestation has made way for market gardening, with flowers and peaches added to the traditional crops of olive oil and wine. From here, it is a reasonable coastal drive northwest to Agrigento. The sand dunes seem to fly by more quickly after a glass of Cerasuolo di Vittoria wine.

South of Ragusa: An intriguing drive leads to a magical fake castle and, on the coast, beyond greenhouses of ripening tomatoes, ends beside two genuine archeological sites.

Castello di Donnafugata lies 20km (12 miles) southeast of the city. Despite its evocative name, the castle owes nothing to *The Leopard*, Lampedusa's novel, except a taste for excess shared by the Sicilian nobility since time immemorial. Set in a carob and palm plantation, this modern Moorish pastiche feels authentically Sicilian.

The castle dates from 1648 but was redesigned as a full-blown *Ottocento* fantasy by Corrado Arezzo, Baron of Donnafugata, in the 19th century. The

baron, a prominent politician and campaigner for Sicilian independence, was famed for his satires against the Bourbons. Donnafugata was his whimsical refuge from revolutionary politics.

The exterior is a Venetian palace transplanted by magic carpet to *One Thousand and One Arabian Nights.* The crenellated facade, inspired by an austere Arab desert fort, is softened by an arcaded Moorish balcony. Below the arched windows opens an amazing loggia in Venetian-Gothic style.

The Arab inspiration is not wholly fake: in the 10th century an Arab village named Ayn as Jayat (Fountain of Health) occupied the site. Saracen ceramics still turn up locally. Yet if the exterior echoes La Ziza in Palermo, the interior is a tribute to *fin-de-siècle* decadence.

This 120-room palace was lived in by descendants of the Arezzo family until the 1970s; their family emblem, the hedgehog, still covers the walls of the *salone degli stemmi* (the crested room). The finest rooms are naturally on the *piano nobiliare* and include a smoking

Fountain to Diana, sited over a Roman spring.

room, picture gallery, billiards room, winter garden and a salon for conversation. The frescoed music room illustrates the noble pastimes of painting, *bel canto* and piano recitals as well as tombola and chess. The bishop's chambers, set aside for Baron Arezzo's dearest friend, contain a painted woman on the ceiling to inspire heavenly dreams.

Although sumptuous, the palace is coated in charming Sicilian neglect. The barrel-vaulted chapel, suffused with light, makes a mystical spot. Still more atmospheric is the *salone degli specchi* (room of mirrors). The floating drapes, faded gilt, inlaid tables and dusty chandeliers conspire to create an atmosphere straight out of *The Leopard*.

In the grounds is the so-called coffee-house, a pavilion the baron favoured for morning refreshments. During World War II, the Luftwaffe commandeered the pavilion, along with the rest of the castle. However, the troops respected Donnafugata so all the baron's quirky touches remain, from the cute well and the children's maze to the artificial grotto and the silly seat which squirts out water. The only damage done was to "the friar's joke", a game in which an unsuspecting visitor is embraced by a mechanical friar as he enters the house. Not unsurprisingly, a Nazi officer disliked the joke and shot the friar to smithereens.

Before leaving the castle, glance at the warehouses, stables and servants' quarters. It is easy to believe that in its heyday the estate supported 1,000 labourers. Nowadays, Donnafugata provides for little more than the rustic Tre Fontane restaurant.

The Classical site of **Camarina** lies on the coast just 7 miles (12 km) east of Donnafugata. Founded in 598 BC, two centuries after Siracusa (the ferocity of the native Siculi tribes was a deterrent to earlier settlement), this sophisticated piece of urban planning covered three hills at the mouth of the Ippari river. The city of perfect parallel lines was destroyed by the Romans in AD 258.

The **Antiquarium** marks the centre of the site, an array of dispersed city walls, a tower, tombstones and sar-

Left, Piazza del Popolo, Vittoria. **Below**, the town's Teatro Communale.

cophagi. The foundations of a **Temple to Athena** lie beside the museum. Nearby, the **House of the Altar** has rooms radiating from a central courtyard. In the centre is an altar with a Doric frieze surrounded by a battered mosaic floor and once frescoed walls. Other Hellenistic dwellings include a merchant's house, confirmed by the presence of scales and measuring devices. At the foot of the cliffs is the chic Kamerina Club Med, providing a reminder that French hedonism is only a stone's throw away.

Between here and **Santa Croce Camarina**, the landscape is dotted with early necropoli and settlements. In Mezzagnone district just outside the village is an early Byzantine necropolis with weird honeycomb-shaped tombs. In the neighbouring Mirio district is an early Christian cemetery carved into the chalk and a Byzantine rock church. Necropoli along the coast have thrown up statues and simple earthenware, most of which are in Ragusa's museum.

At Punta Secca, the headland just south of Camarina, the Roman port of **Kaukana** is still being excavated. The port was partly preserved by sand, as at Gela northwest, further down the coast. The lush site is lovely but inscrutable, a puzzle compounded by the discovery of Hellenistic amphora, Roman coins and Jewish candelabra. Amidst the rubble, the clearest find is a Byzantine church with a colourful mosaic of a goat.

Leave the shady umbrella pines for a picnic on the sandy beaches below or consider a fish lunch at the modern resort of **Marina di Ragusa**, just east of Kaukana. In summer, this winter ghost town turns into a bustling resort, with 10,000 villas let to outsiders.

Southeast of Ragusa: Beyond farmsteads and stone walls are two high road bridges and a sudden glimpse of a grey-brown town buried in a deep valley. **Mòdica**, the former county capital, has an illustrious history as the most powerful fiefdom in Sicily. The prosperous Arab citadel of Mudiqah became a fief of the Chiaramonte family in 1296 and merged into the county of Mòdica. After

What's left of the Roman port, below the Camarina Archaeology Museum.

succumbing to Spanish influence, it passed from the Caprera viceroys to the Henriquez, Spanish absentee landlords. Around town are the family crests of the three dynasties: respectively, mountains, a goat and two castles.

Although once known as "the Venice of the South", Mòdica suffered a disastrous flood in 1902 and as a result, all its rivers were diverted and canals covered over. Since watery perspectives are no longer a feature, today's charm lies in the contrast between the sumptuous churches and sombre houses.

Perched precariously on a slope, **San Giorgio** makes a bold entrance against a backdrop of rocky terraces. The church surmounts a flight of 250 steps. The writer Vincent Cronin said: "After such a meandering introduction, which arouses our hopes to the highest pitch, all but the greatest building would appear to fail." But Gagliardi's masterpiece does not disappoint: its imagination, movement and magic encapsulate Sicilian baroque. This frothy concoction of flowing lines and curvy ornament seems barely rooted to the spot. The vision is one of rococo splendour, shadowy recesses and a soaring belfry silhouetted against the sky.

After such spectacle, other churches play walk-on parts. San Giorgio's only rival is the opulent **Duomo di San Pietro**. It is reached by a theatrical staircase along which tiers of apostles welcome visitors much like latter-day party greeters. Nearby, in Via Grimaldi, is the frescoed Byzantine chapel of San Nicolò Inferiore, under the baroque church of the same name.

Several Gothic churches survived the earthquake. **Chiesa del Carmine** retains a graceful Norman rose window while **Santa Maria di Betlemme** still has a sculpted Gothic-Chiaramonte chapel with the familiar decorative portal.

Museo Ibleo is a museum dedicated to rural culture and crafts. Workshops present the skills of the stonemason, saddler, cabinet-maker, carter, cobbler and pastry-cook.

Cakes are a local art, especially chocolate pastries and *cubbaita*, an Arab sweet

Chromatic shades of Mòdica.

made from almonds, honey and sesame seeds. Mòdicana steak, aubergines and sausages with fennel are also specialities. If driving to the coast at **Marina di Mòdica**, consider a meal en route at the 18th-century Villa Serrauccelli, a rustic restaurant.

From Mòdica, it is a short drive south to baroque Scicli and the coast or southeast to the Ispica canyon and Siracusa province. **Cava d'Ispica** is a 7-mile (11-km) limestone gorge whose ghostly galleries and caves have been inhabited almost continuously since prehistoric times. The southern end of the narrow valley is overlooked by the **Castello**, a rock shaped like a castle. Below is a lush valley floor overgrown with oleanders, prickly pear and carobs. The better tombs lie in the northern end of the gorge. The honeycomb of galleries conceal native Siculi "oven" tombs, Greek necropoli and early Christian tombs.

La Grotta della Signora is a Byzantine sanctuary a stone's throw from Baratavilla, Bronze Age grottoes. **San Nicola** and **Santa Maria** caves contain faded Byzantine frescoes of a Madonna and saints as well as a shrine. Nearby are 5th-century Christian catacombs known as **La Larderia**. The multi-tiered **Il Convento** may represent the early Christian concept of an office block.

Southwest of the canyons is **Scicli** and the coast. Scicli is a neglected baroque gem in mothballs. Anthony Blunt went into raptures over Scicli. The fusty city churches and fantastic baroque mansions feel out of place in this sleepy market town. To Sicilians it is less celebrated for its stylish churches than for citrus fruits, carobs, wine and flowers.

Piazza Italia opens with **Chiesa San Ignazio**. Its gilded interior holds a Neapolitan nativity scene and a painting of an historic battle between the Turks and Christians in 1091. **San Giovanni**'s restored concave-convex facade is matched by an exuberantly stuccoed interior. **Santa Maria della Croce** contains a 16th-century fresco accompanied by script in Sicilian dialect. At the foot of the rock are the majestic cupola and domed apses of **Santa Maria la Nova**, the heart of Scicli's best pre-

served quarter. Modest houses, alleys and steps overflow with vases of flowers and pot plants.

Palazzo Beneventano has beautiful balconies. Fantastic corbels represent mythical beasts, Moors and ghoulish human masks. **Palazzo Fava** is a riot of galloping griffons and horses ridden by cherubs. For more baroque balconies, scan Via Mormino Penna.

Overlooking the town is a ruined castle and **Chiesa San Matteo**, set on the site of the original Siculi settlement. From here, secret passageways, dating from Saracen sieges, are said to lead out of town. The hill is pitted with caves which were inhabited until the 1980s. They still serve a purpose as wine cellars, garages and store rooms.

The coast is less than 6 miles (10 km) away, with sandy beaches at Donnalucata rapidly being swamped by greenhouses. Further east, at the port of **Pozzallo**, the beach and industrial complex are too close for comfort. From here, escape to the baroque masterpiece of Noto (*see pages 244–47*).

Gawping cherubs on Palazzo Beneventano, Scili.

SIRACUSA PROVINCE

Cicero called it the loveliest city in the world: the island of Ortygia, separated from the mainland by a narrow channel. Its name resounds as Syracuse in academic circles abroad. It prides itself on discerning tourism, as sophisticated as the city itself. Subtracting the Arab link, Siracusa is the summation of Sicilian splendour, with an emphasis on Greek heritage. The un-Arab approach is often cited to explain the city's lack of Mafia ties. It is oddly fitting that Siracusa should hold the International Institute of Criminal Science.

The cultivated city supposedly witnessed the birth of comedy in its Greek theatre. Today Siracusa boasts the only school of Classical drama outside Athens. Apart from tales of Artemis and Apollo, Siracusa gave the world architectural beauty with a baroque heart. Ortygia's facades are framed by wrought-iron balconies as free as billowing sails. As Sicily's greatest seafaring power, Siracusa indulges an affinity with the sea that pervades city myths and art. Siracusa's sensual sculpture of Venus emerging from the breeze-swept sea embodies this cult of water.

Classical glory: The city was founded in 733 BC, a year after Naxos, by Corinthian settlers who maintained links with Sparta. Although it was ruled by a succession of cruel but occasionally benevolent Tyrants, Siracusa rose to become the supreme Mediterranean power of its age under Dionysius the Elder. The decisive battle was Siracusa's defeat of Athens at sea in 415 BC.

During a despotic 38-year rule, Dionysius personified Sicilian tyranny. He was a demagogue, a megalomaniac, a military strategist, an inspired engineer and an execrable tragedian. He was the most powerful figure of his era. He was also a monumental builder who presided over Siracusa's golden age, with the grandest public works in the Western world, surpassing Athens in power and prestige.

As an empire builder, he ruled wherever his writ ran. He secured eastern Sicily, southern Italy, Elba, Corsica, and challenged the supremacy of Carthage. He differed from other Tyrants in his vision of a homogeneous Sicily which entailed destroying the Phoenician and Siculi cities and extending Sicilian influence to the Italian mainland. He was also an early convert to "ethnic cleansing", uprooting populations at whim to create a favourable constituency elsewhere.

After the sun set on ancient Greece, Siracusa became a Roman province and was supposedly evangelised by St Peter and St Paul on their way to Rome. Certainly, the city catacombs are the finest outside Rome. Siracusa became the capital of Byzantium, albeit briefly, in the 7th century and produced several Popes and patriarchs of Constantinople. After being sacked by the Arabs in 878 and the Normans in 1085, the city sunk into oblivion but quietly prospered under Spanish rule.

Sights: Siracusa is a diffuse, segmented city whose ancient Greek divisions are

Preceding pages: sailing through papyrus on the River Ciane. Left, statuary surrounding the Fonte Aretusa, Ortygia. Right, Ear of Dionysius, Neapolis.

still valid. **Ortygia**, the cultural heart of the Greek city, is still beating. This welcoming quarter is built on a human scale even if it looks primarily Catalan and baroque. On the mainland lay **Tyche**, the northern quarter studded with catacombs; **Achradina**, the commercial quarter, bordered Ortygia; west of Achradina lay the public arena of **Neapolis**; further north-west was **Epipolae**, the military zone centred on Castello Eurialo. While Tyche and Achradina suffered bomb damage in 1943, much of Siracusa is unscathed.

After an earthquake in 1991, sections are currently cordoned off "*per restauro*", including most catacombs and parts of Neapolis. However, encouraged by a dynamic tourist board and civic good will, hopes for a rapid restoration are high. The ugly modern church of **Madonna delle Lacrime** is a useful landmark, visible from most of the city. In 1953 a statue of Mary reputedly cried and the spot became a shrine in the shape of a giant teardrop, now a popular pilgrimage centre.

Neapolis, the archaeological park, is set among shady fir trees and olive groves but the Classical sites are still sweltering in summer. After running the gauntlet of boisterous coach parties and stalls selling papyrus pictures, independent travellers can quickly melt into the spacious Greek ruins. The following route through Neapolis may change as new sections are re-opened.

A stroll to the Greek theatre passes the rubble of **Hieron II's Altar** (Ara di Ierone), a sacrificial altar once decorated by imposing *telamone* (giants). Surrounded by trees, the vast **Teatro Greco** seats 15,000 and is often called the masterpiece of ancient Greece. This astonishing accomplishment dates from 474 BC although much was altered in the 3rd century BC. The *cavea* is divided into two by a *diazoma*, and vertically cut into nine tribunes. These seating blocks contain inscriptions to deities and dignitaries.

A satisfying climb to the top provides striking views over modern Siracusa and the sea. On the terrace is a *nymph-*

Pitcher from Fusco necropolis (in Museo Archeologico).

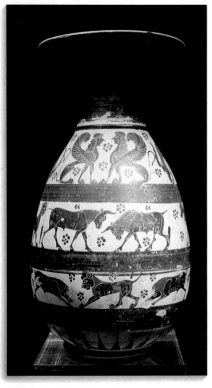

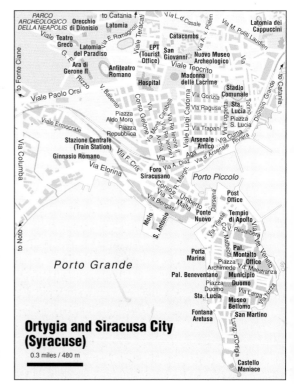

Ortygia and Siracusa City (Syracuse)

0.3 miles / 480 m

aeum, a complex of waterfall, springs and grotto that once contained statues and niches for votive offerings. In the Roman era, the theatre was used as an amphitheatre. Water was dammed and diverted to flood the orchestra for mock naval battles or gladiatorial combat.

In Hellenistic times it was a theatrical rather than sacred forum, witnessing the staging of Aeschylus's *Prometheus Bound*. Aeschylus's tragedies were first performed here and the theatrical tradition is maintained today. In summer the dramas of Sophocles and Euripides are played on a stage once viewed by spectators as illustrious as Plato and Archimedes.

Via dei Sepolcri, the path of tombs, is partially open: the higher level reveals cave tombs and carved niches. The lower level leads down to the *latomie*, giant quarries used as prisons in Classical times. A wooded path slopes behind the back of the Greek theatre to a secret rocky arch and the lush **Latomia del Paradiso**. These Classical quarries were once vaulted but are now open to the sun, bursting with olives and citrus groves or overgrown with cacti and ferns.

The **Ear of Dionysius**, shaped like an upside-down ear lobe, was named by the poetic painter Caravaggio. He fancied that this echoing, dank weirdly-shaped cave was used by Dionysius to eavesdrop on his prisoners. More mundanely, the adjoining **Cordari Cave** was used by rope-cutters to stretch out their ropes. Currently sealed, the grotto's multicoloured rock is scored with chisel marks.

These days a tunnel links Latomia del Paradiso with **Latomia Intagliatella** and a rocky arch leads on to **Latomia di Santa Venere**, lemon-scented quarries pitted with votive niches. It is hard to imagine today that these lush gardens were once torture chambers. After Siracusa's decisive victory over Athens, the captives were flung into these pits. There was no need to mount guard: keeping prisoners alive involved no more than lowering a slave's half-rations and a drop of water.

Plutarch records that "ten weeks long

The glorious Greek theatre, Neapolis.

ARCHIMEDES

The idea of Archimedes deep in thought in his bath and jumping up with a cry of "Eureka!" is, alas, untrue. While testing a gold cup suspected of being a mere alloy, Archimedes realised that the water displaced by an object was equal to the object's weight, not its volume. The object either floats or sinks so *Eureka*: Archimedes had the principle of specific gravity and the basis of hydrostatics.

Archimedes, born in 287 BC, worked for Hieron, the Tyrant of Siracusa. While watching the Tyrant's builders and marine engineers at work, he devised theories worth a "Eureka!" each. His greatest work was the formulae for the areas and volumes of spheres, cylinders and other shapes which anticipated the theories of integration by 1,800 years.

Archimedes was not a mere theoretician. He was intensely practical in an age when Siracusa was the most inventive place on earth. Dionysius's think-tank devised the long-range catapult which saved Siracusa from the Carthaginian fleet.

Archimedes built on this tradition with the Archimedean screw, still used for raising water, and with siege engines which did sterling service against the Romans. Polybins says the Romans "failed to reckon with the ability of Archimedes, nor did they foresee that, in some cases, the genius of one man is more effective than any number of hands."

Like many inventors, Archimedes could be carried away. "Eureka" apart, he is often quoted as saying "Give me a place to stand and I will move the world", implying that he understood the principles of leverage. It is unlikely that he anticipated the laser beam by arranging magnifying glasses to set fire to the Roman fleet at long range. But he did produce a hydraulic serpent contraption which enabled one man to operate a ship's pumps.

Archimedes played a part in the construction of Hieron's amazing 4,000-ton ship. Enough timber to build 60 conventional ships was brought from Mount Etna for the hull, which was then covered with sheet lead. Naval historians still marvel over this, since the secret of synchronising three banks of oars was rediscovered only in the 1980s.

The ship had three decks, one of which had a mosaic floor depicting *The Illiad*. The upper deck boasted a gymnasium, a lush garden with shady walks and a temple to Venus paved with Sicilian agate. The state cabin had a timepiece, a marble bath, and 10 horses in stalls on either side. Yet this was no pleasure craft. It mounted a long-range catapult, a device fitted to the masts which swung out over an attacking vessel and disgorged a huge rock, and also had a "cannon" which fired 18-ft (5.5-metre) arrows. Archimedes designed a system of screws which was made for launching a vessel. It was then loaded with corn, 10,000 jars of Sicilian salt fish and 500 tonnes of wool and despatched to Ptolemy in Egypt as a gift.

Keen to exploit Archimedes' genius, the Roman commander Marcellus wanted him taken alive when the Romans occupied Siracusa. However, a Roman soldier came across a codger apparently doodling in sand. Archimedes was dabbling in his latest brainwave and protested sharply when the soldier unknowingly stepped on his drawing. The soldier drew his sword and, with a foolish laugh, killed one of the greatest men in the world. ■

Statue of Archimedes, Porta Liceo.

they died, and yet they were not all dead; and when the sun was declining, and the people of Siracusa went out to taste the sea breeze, many came and stood at the edge of the quarry, on the windward side, lest their nostrils should be offended, and looked down at men who were rotting alive. The fine ladies of Siracusa held little vials of scent to their noses and leaned upon their slaves' arms, and looked down curiously; for the Athenians had been handsome men."

At last, the non-Athenians were hauled out and sold as slaves. The Athenians were left to suffer before being branded with the mark of the Siracusan horse and sold as slaves. Allegedly, some of the Athenians astonished their captors by being able to recite passages from the works of Euripides, a favourite in Siracusa. They were released because the Siracusani "had a passion for his poetry greater than that of any other Hellenes outside Greece".

A separate entrance leads to the **Roman Amphitheatre**, ringed by trees but drowned by traffic noise. While this tumbledown affair is not comparable with the amphitheatre at Nîmes, the site has charm. A path of stone sacophagi leads to the theatre, complete with rectangular animal pits and the base of an Augustan arch. Between the Greek theatre and Roman amphitheatre is **San Nicolò**, a Romanesque church concealing a Roman cistern. A circuit along **Viale de Rizzo** reveals a cross-section of the Classical city, including an aqueduct, the tomb-laden Via dei Sepolcri and rear views of Neapolis.

Further uphill lie the **Grotticelli Necropolis,** a collection of Hellenistic and Byzantine tombs, including the supposed **Tomb of Archimedes**, framed by a dignified Roman portico. The Romans insisted that Archimedes' death was accidental, despite his creation of diabolical death traps used against them during the city siege. This quarter is ancient Tyche.

Nearby are the **San Giovanni Catacombs** and the entry to the persecuted world of the early Christians. Escorted by a reluctant friar, visitors view early

Mending nets in the Porto Piccolo.

Christian sarcophagi, a 4th-century drawing of St Peter and a mosaic depicting Original Sin. The ceiling, punctuated by light-giving *tholos,* opens into space-creating rotondas. On the walls are primitive frescoes and arcane symbolism, with a mysterious fish-headed boat or dead dove bound by an *alpha* and *omega*. Does it represent a secret Christian code or a pagan transmigration of souls? Academics disagree.

In the wild garden outside is the shell of **San Giovanni Evangelista**, with its rose window and sculpted door often masked by monastic underwear drying in the sun. This modest church was Siracusa's first cathedral and is dedicated to the earliest bishop. Crooked steps lead down to **Cripta di San Marziano**, linked to the catacombs. Light filters in on faded frescoes of Santa Lucia, sculpted cornices and an altar supposedly used by St Paul. Amidst Greek lettering and crosses are primitive depictions of a phoenix and a bull.

Probably the finest archeological collection in Sicily lies in the **Museo Archeologico**, fittingly built over a quarry and pagan necropolis. In succession, the well-organised museum reveals the prehistoric, Classical and regional sections from Siracusa and its colonies, ending with finds at Gela and Agrigento. In the prehistory section, the stars are reconstructed necropoli, earthenware pots from Pantalica, and depictions of Cyclops and dwarf elephants.

In the Classical sections, the tone is set by two strikingly different works: the "immodest modesty" of the headless Venus Landolina and an Archaic sculpture of a seated fertility goddess suckling her twins, found in Megara Hyblaea. Elsewhere, the collection bursts with beauty and horror: lion's head gargoyles, Aztec-like masks, a Winged Victory, a terracotta frieze of grinning gorgons; a Medusa with her tongue lolling out. Away from the horrors, smoothly virile marble torsos of *kouroi* await. Beauty, both pure and sensual, lingers in the Roman sarcophagus of a couple called Valerius and Adelphia or in fragments of friezes from Selinunte and Siracusa.

Painting on papyrus, Siracusa.

Around the corner, **Istituto Siracusano del Papiro** displays collections of papyrus and presents Egyptian paper-making techniques. Studios throughout the city offer to reproduce anything in papyrus, from old masters to holiday snapshots.

Off the adjoining Via Von Platen are the **Vigna Cassia Catacombs**, galleries of burial chambers and frescoed chambers. The catacombs lead to **Latomia dei Cappuccini**, the most picturesque quarries. Set on the coast, these huge honeycombed quarries are matched by sculptural vegetation and are used for private parties during the summer season. From the adjoining Piazza Cappuccini are wild views of the rocky shore.

Further south are a series of catacombs surrounding **Santa Lucia al Sepolcro**, a Byzantine church founded by San Zosimo, the first Greek Bishop of Siracusa. The treasury of Siracusa Cathedral houses a glorious Antonello da Messina painting of the saintly bishop. Yet the Byzantine church essentially belongs to Santa Lucia (St Lucy), the city's patron saint.

On the **Porto Piccolo** are the scanty remains of the city's ancient **arsenal** and rough-hewn boat houses. Nearby are a **Byzantine bath house.** Here legend has it that Emperor Constans II was assassinated with a soap dish. On Piazzale del Foro Siracusa, just behind the port, is the so-called **Forum,** actually the *agora* of Achradina. This was the commercial centre of the Greek city but sadly suffered bombing by both the Allies and the Luftwaffe in 1943.

Further west lies the **Roman Gymnasium**, sited on a picturesquely flooded spot. Its origins are obscure, but it was conceivably dedicated to Oriental deities. The raised portico is well-preserved and shimmers obligingly. Nearby, the **Porto Grande**, where Dionysius defeated the Athenian navy in 415 BC, is now an industrial and mercantile port.

Ortygia: The island was dedicated to the huntress Artemis, with the chief temple known as "the couch of Artemis". In Christian times, she fused with Santa Lucia, and her cult is still celebrated in city festivals. On this romantic stage

set, Theocrites wrote his erotic verse. The Greek poet's *Idylls* recount such tales as "the kissing contest" in which a every young male queued up to kiss the lips of a young Adonis who, after amorous exhaustion, designated the winner.

A stroll across **Ponte Nuovo** leads past prettily moored boats and pastel-coloured Venetian *palazzi* to the **Darsena**, the inner docks. On the far side is Ortygia, with views of a tumbledown bridge and grand *palazzi* lining Riva Garibaldi.

Heralding the entrance to Ortygia lurks the **Temple of Apollo** in the middle of an unprepossessing square. Now sunken and dishevelled, it is the oldest city temple, built in 565 BC and discovered by chance in 1862. This Archaic-Doric temple was dedicated to Artemis (Diana) as well as her brother, Apollo whose name is legible on the steps of the *stereobate*. The squat temple has accrued Byzantine and Norman remains.

San Pietro, just east, was supposedly founded by St Peter before being converted into a Byzantine basilica. The

San Giovanni Evangelista, the city's first cathedral.

8th-century apses and blind arcading are incorporated into a 15th-century shell. Just west, Via XX Settembre contains tracts of **Greek walls**. Dionysius was an indefatigable builder, and this immense wall, 3 miles (5 km) in length and built in 20 days by 60,000 men on double overtime, is still visible in other parts of the city.

From here, it is a short stroll to **Piazza Archimede**, the grandiose centre of Ortygia. This baroque stage set, planted with a newly-restored fountain, is framed by dignified mansions. The atmosphere is sustained by the mysterious **Via Maestranza**, the heart of the old guilds quarter. Amidst the sombre courtyards and swirling sculpture, local *pasticcerie* literally represent the icing on the cake.

A return to the sea at **Porta Marina** presents the heart of the Catalan-Gothic quarter, centred on **Santa Maria dei Miracoli**, a finely-sculpted 15th-century church. Just beyond is a graceful Catalan-Gothic archway and the remains of the city's medieval walls. Via Gemmellaro, one of the Moorish alleys off the piazza, hides some of Ortygia's best restaurants.

Following the shore leads to **Fonte Aretusa**, a freshwater spring that is the symbol of Siracusa. Legend has it that the nymph Arethusa was pursued by Alpheus, a river god. As she reached the sea, Artemis kindly transformed her into a fountain and she reached Ortygia safely. There Alpheus pulled her under the waves and "mingled his waters with hers". Whether this was rape or the reuniting of lovers, Siracusani disagree.

After a 17th-century earthquake, the spring is supposed to be mingled with sea water. In any case, upside-down ducks and clumps of reedy papyrus plants make a romantic love nest. At night, the fountain sees a parade of Siracusa's youth, accompanied by flirtation, exposed thighs and the revving of ice-cream splattered motorbikes. The nymphs still seem to have a ball on harbour-side terraced cafés.

Just inland is **Santa Lucia alla Badia**, a baroque church, under restoration. Even so, graceful wrought-iron balus-

Fruit market, Siracusa.

trades and barley stick columns are visible. The neighbouring Via Cappodieci is home to **Palazzo Bellomo**, the loveliest Catalan-Gothic mansion in Ortygia. Its cool courtyard leads to the newly-restored **Galleria Regionale,** housing Caravaggio's masterpiece, the *Burial of St Lucy* and Antonello da Messina's *Annunciation.* Other highlights include 14th- to 18th-century works, from Byzantine icons to Catalan and Spanish paintings and Sicilian jewellery.

From here, a flight of steps leads to the **cathedral**, a Temple to Athena masquerading as a Christian church. Classical columns bulge through the external walls in Via Minerva, a sign that the temple has only been encased in a church since the 7th century. Before then, the temple was a beacon to sailors, with ivory doors and a gold facade surmounted by the goddess Athena bearing a glinting bronze shield. It is humbling to think that Dionysius himself worshipped at this temple.

Yet the exterior conjures up a Spanish spell: a baroque facade with dramatic *chiaroscuro* effects, including an inside porch boasting twisted barley stick columns. Yet the cool, striking interior betrays its Greek origins. The worn but lovely fluted Doric columns belong to the Temple to Athena (Minerva). Notwithstanding a Greek soul, the temple also glories later conquerors. A Norman baptismal font rests on bronze lions; above is a medieval wood-panelled ceiling; a baroque choir and Byzantine apses strike new notes; only the Arab presence is missing. The apses were slightly damaged in the 1991 earthquake but the Greek sandstone fluted columns survived, as they are fated to do.

Outside, the **Piazza del Duomo** is a baroque jewel of sculpted facades, gracious courtyards and overblown balconies. Palazzo Beneventano is a mass of elegant pillars and foliage motifs. No night stroll could have a more romantic ending.

Porto Piccolo: At night or siesta time, this atmospheric port is quiet except for the crashing of waves. Locals warn lone travellers against exploring the port at

night yet with care it is worth risking the occasional *scippatore* (bag-snatcher) for the rough and ready restaurants, crumbling *palazzi* and sea views. Even so the former Jewish ghetto, the dark alleys behind Via Nizza, are slightly ominous. By contrast, the strip between Porta Marina and Fontana Aretusa is a summer fashion parade.

Sea strolls: The Fonte Aretusa marks the central section of gentle *passeggiate* or bracing sea walks along the east of Ortygia. The island's dilapidated western shore is no less interesting but is best explored by day. **Lungomare di Levante**, in particular, offers a facade of battered *palazzi* and warehouses, some of which have been undergoing much-needed restoration.

The fortified hulk of **Castello Maniace** divides the two shores and dominates the point but this Staufer fortress retains its military purpose. Visitors who peer too long at the delicate Gothic doorway are discouraged by nonchalant soldiers waving bazookas. Beyond, **Lungomare d'Ortygia** offers somewhat safer, windswept views over the rocky shore.

Cuisine: After a surfeit of temples and baroque curlicues, browse among the chic boutiques and bars along Via Matteotti. While the more clinical international restaurants are centred on the modern hotels in the east of town, the atmospheric restaurants are in the back streets of Ortygia. Specialities include seafood, particularly swordfish and shrimps; roast peppers; stuffed artichokes and *stimpirata di coniglio*, a rabbit and vegetable flan.

Outskirts: Close to the city are sandy beaches and two unique spots, a Greek castle and a dreamy riverside pocket of papyrus. Just south of Siracusa lie **beaches** at Arinella and Fontane Bianche. In the height of summer the beaches are full of golden bodies rather than golden sands. However, Lido Sayonara, a spot overlooking sculpted rocks, is less crowded. However, a more atmospheric swimming spot is 12 miles (20 km) from Siracusa: Brucoli, a rocky beach set around a Spanish castle, enjoys

The storm-lashed bastions on Ortygia.

wonderful views of Etna on clear days.

North-east of Siracusa is **Castello Eurialo**, the fifth component of the Greek pentapolis and the most magnificent of all Greek military sites. Designed by Dionysius, the castle protected Siracusa's most exposed flank, the meeting place of the northern and southern city walls. Apart from amazingly solid walls and moats hewn out of the rock, the castle had a keep surrounded by five towers. Labyrinthine tunnels let soldiers move about easily.

As a final security measure, the only entrance was concealed by a patchwork of walls. When Dionysius was in residence, he would not allow his wives into his bed without first being searched. According to legend, his bed was surrounded by a moat, and his wives reached it across a little wooden drawbridge, which he then drew up.

Just south of the city is **Fonte Ciane**, a picturesque spot close to the ruined Temple of Olympian Zeus. Ciane is a mythical river dedicated to a nymph who was transformed into a spring after trying to thwart the rape of Persephone by Hades. A boat trip leads through groves of papyrus with tendrils as delicate as cobwebs. The origins of papyrus are obscure: this wild plant was either imported from Egypt or native to Siracusa. Either way, its habitat is endangered but survives in this idyllic backwater, named after the Greek word for blue.

After the collapse of the Greek city, little matters in this backwater. As Vincent Cronin says, the spirit of "Archimedes, Gelon and Dionysius are more real to the people of Siracusa than of any citizens since the Greek period". Since then, the greatest city of the Classical age has slumbered.

However, despite a lingering nostalgia, Siracusani are aware that they can live off their past while creating a forward-looking commercial city. This fusion is personified by actress Grazia Visconti who loves acting tragedy in "her" Greek theatre: "the sacredness of the site fills the actors with a sense of grandeur and destiny". She even

nte Aretusa,
e papyrus-
led spring,
tygia.

practises singing in the vaulted chamber known as Dionysius's Ear.

SIRACUSA PROVINCE: Siracusa is a supremely cultured province, with an ancient *savoir-faire* that Mafia money cannot mimic or buy. This south-eastern corner of Sicily also has an elegance, grace and honesty unmatched by other provinces. It is reputedly a crime-free haven of hospitality, although in recent years the Mafia's tentacles have stretched into the industrial heartland around Augusta. Even so, it feels light years away from the brooding intensity of Palermo.

The Greeks colonised the province two centuries after settling the rest of eastern Sicily. Since then, Siracusa believes it has led from the front, parading its Greek heart and Levantine soul. Culturally, the province enjoys the effortless superiority of natural aristocrats. Economically, a perceived enterprising "Greek" outlook to business contrasts with the lethargic "Arab" approach. A thriving economy helps foster a sense of *discreto benessere*, discreet well-being. However, Siracusani are still regarded as *baba* (naive), devoid of cunning, compared with the sharp operators of Catania and Palermo.

Outside Siracusa city, the province offers a cross-section of Sicily: a blend of baroque, Classical and prehistoric sites. **Noto** is the finest baroque town in Sicily, both blatantly theatrical and deeply rational. Visitors praise its grace, proportion, symmetry, spaciousness and innate sense of spectacle. Sicilians call it simply "a garden of stone". Yet much is crumbling in the garden and many museums and interiors are closed for eternal restoration. Luckily, on this open-air stage, Noto's chief pleasures are on permanent display.

After Noto Antica was destroyed in the 1693 earthquake, Prince Landolina instigated its rebuilding, planting the new Noto on the flanks of a distant hill. Giuseppe Lanza, a Sicilian-Spanish architect, was entrusted with the urban design. Noto was composed around three parallel axes running horizontally across the hillside. To create interest, he conceived of three squares, each enlivened by a scenic church as a backdrop. He clothed his design in warm, golden limestone and used monumental flights of steps to enchant with tricks of perspective. The realisation of this ambitious plan was the work of Gagliardi and Sinatra, gifted local architects who also worked in Ragusa province.

Under Spanish rule, Noto was an aristocratic, conservative and royalist city which supported right-wing religious factions and the retention of feudal privileges. Its loyalty to the Bourbons was rewarded by its promotion to provincial capital, thus deposing Classical Siracusa. After the 1848 revolution, the city paid dearly for its Bourbon allegiance and was deposed by Siracusa.

Since the 1986 earthquake, much has been under restoration, aided by UNESCO and European Community funds. Sadly, the glowing limestone is fragile and susceptible to erosion and pollution. However, Noto council's idea of restoration is to convert the finer mansions, such as Palazzo Trigona, into congress centres. More imaginatively, the vast

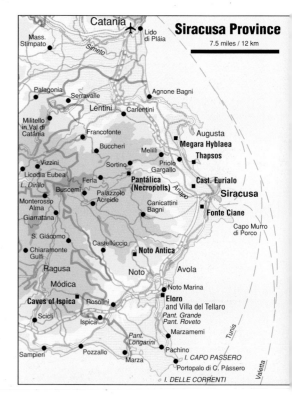

244

monastery of San Tommaso has been transformed into a sinister prison.

Urban theatre: On the lower slopes, three scenic squares unfold in a succession of theatrical perspectives sculpted in burnished stone. Yet in this hierarchical city, even the streets knew their place. The main thoroughfare was called a *corso* and dedicated to the King while the second street was a *via* named after the chief minister. The lower part of town was designed as the civic and religious centre whereas the upper town was laid out as a cramped *quartiere popolare*. Even so, the two-tiered city looks entirely homogeneous.

Piazza XVI Maggio is graced by gardens of palms, monkey puzzle trees and a fountain of Hercules taken from Noto Antica: water gushes through a dolphin's nose while cherubs frolic below. Behind these shady gardens lies **San Domenico**, a curvilinear Gagliardi church influenced by Roman and Spanish baroque. Facing it is the ornate Teatro Emanuele, with its gilded interior under restoration. Also lining the spacious

square is **Collegio dei Gesuiti**, another tragic casualty of neglect and earthquake damage. Now propped up by scaffolding, this fragile wreck was a *conservatoire* until the rumblings of the 1989 earthquake drowned the baroque music within.

Stately Via Vittorio Emanuele leads to **Piazza Municipio**, Noto's stage set. The golden grace of the buildings matches the majestic proportions of the design; the set is framed by amber hills, a natural note intruding on man-made scenery. The lavish baroque facade of Palazzo Landolina heralds the triumphant progress to Piazza Municipio.

Palazzo Ducezio, the elegant town hall, borrows from French architecture with more than a nod at Versailles. Opposite is San Nicolò, a splendid cathedral surveyed from a theatrical staircase and curiously framed by two belltowers. In one sense, the city of Noto is a facade for disappointing interiors. Baroque splendour is bathed in a golden light that erases the complexity of a *chiaroscuro* canvas. Still, the town

Castello Eurialo, Siracusa.

hall atrium, with its lavish marble floors, shimmers softly, while the cathedral interior is a cool pastel composition. The adjoining **Palazzo Vescovile** makes a mundane showing, an episcopal palace resembling functional stables.

Palazzo Villadorata, in Via Nicolaci, is Noto's pride and joy. Don Nicolaci, a patron of the arts, donated a wing of the palace to the city library. Also known as Palazzo Nicolaci after its noble owners, this baroque jewel has recently been restored to its former glory.

Around the windows are friezes of mythical monsters, a snarling parade of griffons, sphynxes, sirens, centaurs and cherubs. Arabesques climb the walls, clashing with crested cornices and billowing wrought-iron balconies. The sloped courtyard was designed for carriages and includes an access ramp so that the prince could ride directly into the *piano nobile*.

Palazzo Villadorata plays a starring role in the city drama but secondary characters should not be overlooked, especially the convents and churches.

Even the walk-on parts are worthy of attention: Via Giovanni XXIII runs behind the cathedral and reveals such subtle details as niches for statues, sculpted cornices and bulging "goose-breast" balconies.

Two Gagliardi churches deserve mention: **Santa Chiara**, with an oval-shaped interior; and **San Carlo**, with a colonnaded concave facade. Gagliardi's **Santa Maria dell'Arco** demonstrates his versatility, with three strikingly different portals. But his assistant, Vincenzo Sinatra, created the **Carmine**, from its concave facade to a doorway guarded by two *putti*, the symbol of the Carmelite order. The elaborate white interior, studded with stucco work, is at odds with Noto's emphasis on minimalist baroque interiors.

The spacious lower town was only for the clergy and the aristocracy. Above the grandiose public face of Noto rises the *popolare* district, based around the hill site of Piazza Mazzini. Hierarchy aside, the style of this working-class quarter suggests that Bourbon feudal

246

lords were no less unenlightened than 20th-century Sicilian town planners. The **Crocifisso**, a domed Gagliardi church that dominates Piazza Mazzini, has a portal flanked by Romanesque lions rescued from Noto Antica. Inside is a Francesco Laurana Madonna, an incongruously serene sculpture amidst the frenzy of baroque.

The **Giardino Pubblico** is a peaceful end to any visit. The ancient weeping fig trees form a verdant roof over the park. Nearby is an open-air *gelateria*, a popular hot spot for Noto's bored youth, tactfully placed outside the city walls. Alternatively, the chic Mandelfiore *pasticceria* and *gelateria* beckons invitingly from Piazza del Carmine. Noto may look good enough to eat but restaurants and bars are scarce in this baroque stage set.

Noto Antica nestles in the foothills of the Iblei mountains, a memory of the phoenix that never rose from the ashes. It was a complex city full of Classical, Romanesque and baroque churches, convents and mansions. All this was submerged under rubble in the 1693 earthquake. An eyewitness recorded the earthquake as "so horrible that the soil undulated like the waves of a stormy sea, and the mountains danced as if drunk, and the city collapsed in one terrible moment killing more than a thousand people." The fallen masonry represents one of Sicily's three capitals in Arab times; each controlled a third of the island. Today, a ruined castle, bastions, tombs and crumbling mansions are all that remain.

The southern coast: East of Noto lies **Eloro**, a Classical site on the unpolluted coastline that stretches to Capo Passero. This is the site of Elorus, a city founded by Siracusa at the end of the 8th century BC. Well-preserved turreted walls survive, as do porticoes, a pair of gateways, the *agora* and a Sanctuary of Demeter.

Just outside the site stands the **Colonna della Pizzuta**, a curious Hellenistic funeral column which looks like a tower or chimney stack. In the neighbouring hamlet of **Caddeddi**, a villa from the same period has been unearthed,

A Gagliardi facade overlooks the Giardino Pubblico.

along with interesting mosaics depicting hunting scenes.

Beside this wild site are rocky and sandy **beaches** which tend to be deserted. The journey south to the deserted **Vendicari wetlands** passes citrus and almond groves. As a nature reserve, the Vendicari salt pans are popular with nesting and migrating birds but most Siracusani flock south to **Pachino** and the sandy beaches on the Capo Passero.

In July 1943 the Allied invasion of Sicily took place on these shores. While General Patton and the American forces landed near Gela, General Montgomery and the British 8th Army landed between Pachino and Pozzallo. Nowadays, Pachino is a quiet wine-producing centre with a faded baroque heart. The hinterland is devoted to market gardening but the coast is rapidly becoming the acceptable face of Siracusa's resorts.

Beyond is **Capo Passero**, the southern-most tip of the province, and home to several low-key seaside resorts. Until recently, these were villages dependent on tuna fishing and processing. However, only one tuna fishery remains, run by Don Bruno di Belmonte. The baron blames the collapse of the tuna trade on Japanese over-fishing and the vagaries of the tuna migrations but pollution is certainly also a factor. Nearby, Scandinavian visitors collapse on beaches after a surfeit of full-bodied red Pachino wine. The more energetic can row to the islet off Portopalo, a spot with nothing but sea between an isolated Sicilian beach and Africa.

The eastern coast: Swimming is not advisable north of Siracusa. As the coastline with the highest concentration of chemical effluents in Europe, this area is an ecological disaster. Petro-chemical plants based around Augusta have destroyed 30 miles (48 km) of beach.

Yet there is some hope on the polluted horizon: Mare Nostrum, the ecological group, together with local factory workers, have begun clean-up operations in earnest. Factory worker Emanuele Salerno laments the fact that his father might be the last fisherman in these waters because of pollution caused by

The prehistoric Necropoli di Pantalica.

his son's factory. "We who are responsible for damaging the coast should save it," he says with an unSicilian public-spiritedness.

But for the moment, the Greek tragedy has placed **Thapsos** out of bounds. The Classical site on Peninsola Magnisi is too close to the belching fumes to be acceptable. Acrid fumes also threaten to engulf the important site of **Megara Hyblaea**, one of the earliest Greek cities in Sicily. Cypresses shield it in poetic desolation but industrial blight is tangible. A wall and a group of sarcophagi front the ramparts of a Hellenistic fortress. Beyond are the foundations of an Archaic city, as yet unexplored.

As a smaller mirror image of Siracusa, **Augusta** once had charm. However, while its islet setting, double harbour and faded baroque centre remain, so does rampant industrialisation. Cement works and petro-chemical plants blight views of the park, **Castello** and quaint causeway. Augusta's good restaurants provide little compensation.

Inland from Siracusa: The rocky, wild, sparsely-populated hinterland is one of Siracusa's charms. The parched slopes and odd mounds conceal several significant Classical sites. The desolate countryside has an austere appeal matched by the dusty baroque country towns along the route. This is Sicily with its roots laid bare, a prehistoric and Siculi land that predates Siracusa city by centuries.

Despite their importance, the **Necropoli di Pantalica**, are off the tourist trail, at least to most foreign visitors. Siracusani have long been drawn to the lush gorges, a verdant paradise remote from the barren landscape above. Apart from the loveliness of the site, Pantalica offers a slice of Sicily's earliest history: this Siculi necropolis contains rock tombs dating from 13th to 18th century BC. It is the largest cemetery in Sicily, with over 5,000 tombs carved into the sheer cliffs of a limestone plateau.

The tombs lie at the end of a gorge studded with citrus trees and wild flowers. The Anapo river has carved a path through the cliffs and is invitingly cool

Making tracks on Capo Passero.

for swimmers. In this secret garden lie tiered **rows of tombs**, a honeycomb-pitted surface of jagged rectangular openings cut into the pale rock. Pantalica's history is shrouded in mystery but tradition claims it as Hybla, the capital of the Siculi king who allowed Greek colonists to occupy Megara Hyblaea. Certainly, some of these gaping holes are 3,000 years old.

Pantalica was deserted in 733 BC but inhabited again in Byzantine times and used as a safe haven during later invasions. Apart from the tombs, a Byzantine rock chapel remains, as do early Christian frescoes. It is hard to return to the windswept plateau, leaving behind this sacred chasm bursting with snapdragons, asphodel and daisies.

A country drive leads to **Palazzolo Acreide**, a sleepy town with an air of surprise that outsiders should stray so far. The baroque centre displays several theatrical set-pieces, whose charms are only diminished by the air of abandon. Scruffy bars confirm the impression given by tumbledown *palazzi* and half-

hearted restoration. Piazza Michele was not alone in being damaged by an earthquake in December 1991.

The town's rough-hewn charms are apparent in **Palazzo Zocco** on Via Umberto, with its chaotic baroque ornamentation. **Chiesa Annunziata**, an early baroque church, boasts a portal guarded by Spanish barley-shape columns. However, many of the town's rewards are low-key: the occasional gargoyle, carved door post or billowing balcony. A road signposted to Teatro Greco leads to the Classical city of Akrai.

Akrai is another sentinel of the past, a Greek site set on high windy moorland. The attractive walled park encloses a Greek theatre, quarries and temples founded in 7th century BC by Siracusa. In Byzantine times, the site was used as a place of worship and altars and basins were installed at the bottom of the quarry. The site contains stone carvings, votive niches, commemorative plaques, a necropolis, catacombs and the scant remains of a Temple to Aphrodite. The most impressive views are of the deep quarries framed by dry stone walls, firs, bay trees and wild olives.

The lovely site suffers from poor management, with temples and sculptures often arbitrarily locked. The **Santoni** (Holy Ones) is a series of 12 crudely-carved sculptures. They were made in honour of the goddess Cybele, the Magna Mater whose esoteric cult originated in Asia. These precious finds lie a few fields away but require a custodian's presence. Sadly, the *Beni Culturali*, the bureaucratic watchdogs of artistic Sicily, do a nice line in padlocked green metal gates.

Leading out of town, the so-called **Strada Panoramica** lives up to its name, offering views across the Greek settlements towards Ragusa province. After falling under the spell of Pantalica's primeval atmosphere, Vincent Cronin was moved to remark: "Here is Sicily of the Stone Age, intent on nothing higher than the taking of food and the burial of the dead." Artistic Siracusa City certainly had higher concerns, but the hinterland is closer to the heartbeat of primitive Sicily.

Left, Chiaramonte Gulfi. Right, decorative doorway of San Sebastiano, Ferla.

CATANIA PROVINCE

Catania province hugs the Ionian Coast to Taormina and is bounded by the fertile but dull Piana di Catania to the south. In a sense, this is Catania province without its soul since the fascinating routes around Etna are explored on pages 267–277. However, exceptions must be made for Acireale, Caltagirone and Catania City itself.

Coastal Catania turns away from the volcanic hinterland and a peasant culture. This is commercial Sicily, profiting from its entrepreneurial roots as a Greek trading colony. Catania boasts budding resorts and significant commercial centres. Yet it is a mass of contradictions: forward-looking but wary; clean-thinking yet corrupt; the province looks quite prosperous but the capital is poor and politically divided.

Catania has a different heritage from the west of the island and an equally long tradition of distaste for Palermo. Since the decline of Messina, Catania is the only modern rival to Palermo. As Mary Simeti says of the Catanesi: "They feel Greek as opposed to Arab, commercially enterprising as opposed to parasitic, honest as opposed to *mafioso*".

This East versus West dispute has a yin and yang feel. As the writer Mary Simeti admits, Catania is just two and a half hours away by motorway from her home in Palermo, yet it feels as foreign as it once did, with "ill-kempt roads gutted with potholes".

Catania embodies the best and worst of this odd province. As the writer Ian Thomson says: "Catania has the feel of a real city, quite without the gracious suavities of Siracusa." This is double-edged: Catania has culture but little charm; it has bold yet neglected baroque architecture. Catania is also in the clutches of the Mafia and holds the highest crime rate on the island.

Giuseppe Fava, the investigative journalist murdered by the Mafia, made impassioned pleas for Catania, his adoptive homeland. His refrain was to compare it to the proverbial tart with the heart of gold: "It is a vulgar, dirty, duplicitous whore." Yet he loved "her spirited vices and subtle tricks of the trade." In 1984 he was murdered by a spirited but treacherous Catanese.

Catania is a city of contradictions: brash, belligerent and beleagured yet also vibrant, cultured and resilient. It is a commercial success, boasts a dynamic arts scene and is a showcase of Sicilian baroque. Catania should be comfortable but is deeply uneasy, understandable for a city living in Etna's shadow. The edgy tone is captured by Etna, glittering red on a menacing Catanese night.

Under the volcano: The approach to Catania along the *circonvallazione* (ring road) reveals the extent of nature's wrath. Recent volcano flows are visible between the grim tenements or piled like slag heaps by the roadside. The pot-holed welcome to Catania reveals the citizens to be Sicily's most reckless drivers, especially if they espy a Palermo number plate or a law-abiding tourist.

This ancient Siculi settlement was colonised by settlers from Naxos in 729

BC. As an ally of Athens, Catania incurred the wrath of Siracusa and citizens were sold into slavery in 403 BC. By contrast, the Roman conquest spelt prosperity, particularly under Augustan rule. But in AD 253 St Agata, the city's beloved patron saint, suffered martyrdom by being rolled in hot coals and having her breasts cut off. A February festival records her horrendous life and she is tastelessly commemorated by breast-shaped jellies and cakes.

St Agata's statue is still used to ward off impending lava flows, with mixed success. The 1669 eruption struck the city centre while 12,000 people were attending Mass and the 1693 earthquake killed two-thirds of the population. The 1983 eruption caused panic. The city's fears of becoming a latter-day Pompeii are based on hard facts.

Under Spanish rule Catania was "a city of gentlemen, merchants and masons", dominated by landowners like Prince Biscari. By the 1960s, Catania won plaudits as "the Milan of the South" but chaotic city politics and corruption in both cities now give the slogan a hollow echo. Catania's crime rate has earned it the label of "little Chicago". As Sicily's commercial soul, Catania has recently sold out to property speculation, leading to the neglect of the baroque centre. According to reports from *pentiti* (Mafia turncoats), *Cosa Nostra* has also switched key operations from Palermo to Catania. Still, the city is in the throes of shaking off a lethargic city administration so change is in the air.

Baroque: After the earthquake, a handful of nobles were allowed to rebuild their *palazzi* on the city walls. As a result, the baroque mansions near Porta Uzeda hug the Spanish bastions, with religious buildings sited in the east. While the architecture is less ebullient than in Noto or Siracusa, this is still trail-blazing baroque, with spacious streets and sinuous churches. In addition, it has what writer Dominique Fernandez calls "a secret opulence". An aerial view reveals vast square mansions with concealed courtyards often bursting with statuary or banana trees.

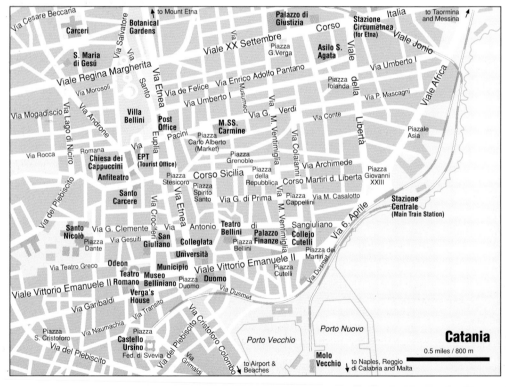

Sights: Catania seems the most homogeneous Sicilian city. From 1730 it was stamped with the vision of one man, Vaccarini, an architect influenced by grand Roman baroque. His work has a sculptural quality allied to a native vigour. Billowing balconies, sweeping S-curves and a taste for *chiaroscuro* are intermixed. Until one's eyes adjust, the colour of the volcanic stone seems depressing but the clever chromatic effects are a tribute to Vaccarini's skill.

Piazza del Duomo is the baroque centrepiece, a dignified composition on a grand scale. The buildings in the square make use of flat facades, restrained decoration, elegant windows and huge pilasters. The ensemble seems homogeneous, despite being designed by several architects. In the centre is the city symbol, **Fontane dell'Elefante**, Vaccarini's fountain: an antique black volcanic elephant is surmounted by an Egyptian obelisk taken from the Roman circus.

The **cathedral** was begun by Count Roger in 1092 and rebuilt by Vaccarini after the earthquake. It is a confused summation of Catanese history: Roman theatres were raided to adorn the lugubrious baroque facade with granite columns. Norman apses are still visible from number 159 Via Vittorio Emanuele. The interior conceals vaulted subterranean Roman baths; a Romanesque basilica lies under the nave; while Roman and Byzantine and Roman columns line the transepts. A Roman sarcophagus contains the ashes of the Kings of Aragon. Opposite is Queen Constance of Aragon's graceful tomb. St Agata's chapel is a gaudy shrine of multicoloured marble. If you miss the ridiculous opening times, bribe the sacristan.

Just east is **Palazzo Biscari**, in Via Museo Biscari, the most accomplished baroque mansion in Catania. It is still owned by the Biscari but the public can attend concerts in the *salone della musica*. This suite represents a rococo wonder, with a grand staircase, minstrel's gallery and allegorical ceiling. Via Dusmet offers the best view of the facade, with its frolicking cherubs, caryatids and grinning monsters.

Via Crociferi, created on top of a lava flow in the 17th century, is the most charming street, a succession of baroque churches and noble *palazzi*. **Chiesa San Giuliano**, designed by Vaccarini, delights in a graceful loggia.

The baroque facade of **Casa di Bellini** conceals a charming museum of musical memorabilia and the original scores of the composer's work. The father of *bel canto* is also commemorated in the newly-restored Teatro Bellini, which opened in 1890 with his opera, *Norma*. Nearby, in Via Sant'Anna, is the birthplace of another celebrated Catanese. Verga's house is an endearing museum stuffed full with the writer's original furnishings.

Further along Via Crociferi lies **San Benedetto**, a mammoth, unfinished monastery. Brydone, an 18th-century visitor, was awed by "a facade almost equal to that of Versailles". The austere interior contains a zodiac sundial, 17th-century choir stalls and a rococo sacristy. Brydone was later informed that the San Benedetto was "a convent of fat Benedictine monks who were deter-

Mosaic pavement in the courtyard of Catania University.

mined to make sure of a paradise at least in this world, if not in the other".

Opposite is **Chiesa San Nicolò d'Arena**, resembling a grim religious factory rather than a church. As the largest church in Sicily, this desolate 16th-century work was conceived on a vast scale. It has an eerie, amputated look, with truncated stumps of columns framing the door like rotten teeth. Inside is a Hollywood-esque folly, Sicily's first classical staircase. Anthony Blunt, an expert on baroque, bluntly dismissed it as "a monstrosity".

This neglected baroque square leads north to **Chiesa di Santo Carcere**. Its charm lies in the Romanesque portal moved from the cathedral after the 1693 earthquake. Sculpted with griffons and glowering beasts, the door conjures up suitable horrors for a Roman prison, the church's original function. According to legend and graffiti on these Roman walls, it was here that St Agata was reputedly held captive.

Via Etnea, the main city thoroughfare, runs parallel to Via Crociferi and

climaxes in a stunning view of Mount Etna. The street passes the university, baroque churches and a Roman amphitheatre. However, the Catanesi prefer the evening *passeggiata*, a parade past chic shops selling jewellery, shoes, fruit sorbets and nougat ice cream.

Directly south is **Castello Ursino**, a Staufer castle built on a steep bastion. It commands a view of what was once the harbour: the moat was filled in by the lava flow of 1669, which also left the castle marooned inland. Now the city museum, it was the Aragonese seat of government in the 13th century and became a palace under the Spanish viceroys. The eclectic collection delighted Goethe but has rarely been open since. Newly-restored, the Museo Civico represents a cavalcade of Sicilian history, with fine Hellenistic and Roman sculpture, including an Eros riding a dolphin.

Classical Catania: The considerable remains clash with one's expectations of gleaming marble theatres or golden sandstone temples. Instead of the lofty, spacious theatre in Taormina, Catania offers cramped, low-lying monuments in sombre black lava stone. Yet for visitors prepared to traipse down unpromising alleys, the rewards are worthwhile. While most Classical remains enjoy splendid isolation, Catania's are fully integrated in the urban tissue. The main Graeco-Roman theatres are in the dilapidated city centre and every second turning reveals the odd Roman column, tomb or hypocaust.

Teatro Romano (off 266 Via Vittorio Emanuele) retains its underground passages and *cavea* as well as some of the *scena* and orchestra. Originally coated in marble, the site was plundered by the Normans to embellish the cathedral. Next door is the semi-circular **Odeon**, used for oratory and rehearsals. The building materials were chosen for their contrasts: volcanic stone, red brickwork and marble facing. It was first excavated in the 18th century when demolition of encroaching buildings began. However, the intimate site is still hemmed in by a medieval and baroque quarter.

For further Roman ruins, walk along

Aci Castello, with its castle built onto basalt rock.

Via Rotonda to the Graeco-Roman **baths** and the simple domed church of Santa Maria della Rotonda, remodelled in Byzantine times. In the Cortile San Pantaleone are the remains of the **forum**, built over the ancient *agora*. Many Roman porticos and columns were removed to construct the arcades in **Piazza Mazzini**.

In Piazza Stesicoro lies the **Anfiteatro Romano**, the battered remains of the largest amphitheatre in Sicily. This was where St Agata supposedly met her doom and where earthquake ruins were dumped in 1693. Ancient **necropoli** stretch north and east of this site and are visible in many spots, including below the Rinascente store in Via Etnea.

Hidden dangers: The colourful portside area is given over to fishing and crafts. **La Pescheria**, the popular fish market, encircles Via Dusmet, a haunt of *scippi* (bag-snatchers). The ill-lit castle quarter and the impoverished San Cristoforo to the west are dangerous at night, as are suburban ghettos and the rough port. Ominously, Via Ursino, the road lead-ing back from the castle to the centre, specialises in coffins.

A recent film about Catania's Malaspina juvenile prison made it famous as a finishing school for criminals. The city has the worst juvenile crime rate in Europe: one in three teenagers is unemployed while one in five plays truant. According to social workers, Catania's youth want *"soldi senza faticare"*, money for nothing. A customised Vespa is every teenager's dream, budding criminals included.

To dispel any sense of menace or simply to escape Catania's constant bustle, retreat to the delightful **Giardino Bellini** in the north of the city. One section is named *labirinto* after the maze of paths, all leading to aviaries and an Oriental bandstand. Between the *ficus*, palms and playing children are snow-capped or smouldering views of Etna.

Cuisine: A visit to **Fera o Luni** market on Piazza Carlo Alberto creates an appetite for Catania's varied cuisine. Made with basil, aubergine and ricotta, *pasta alla norma* is named after Bellini's op-

Swimming off the Isole Ciclopi, Cyclops' haunt.

era. Grilled seafood or swordfish steaks (*pesce spada alla griglia*) are good in many places but especially in the chic Il Timeo Ristorante.

Culturally, this is an energetic university city with an active arts scene, including good drama, classical music and a spring jazz festival. But to end a stay in traditional style, consider a boisterous puppet show. Catania's last remaining puppet shows are staged in Pino Correnti's restaurant at number 61 Via D'Amico. This simulated violence is Catanese exuberance at its safest.

The coast: Heading north from Catania is a welcome release: sea breezes sweep away images of Catania's dirty tenements. Since an offshore eruption in 693 BC, the coastline has receded or advanced in response to Etna's serious lava flows. The last time was in 1978–79 when the lava reached the chapel doors at Fornazzo, a village near Giarre. Yet another miraculous intervention is claimed after the molten lava was threatened by a statue of the Madonna.

Etna's wrath: Like Californians living on the San Andreas Fault, Sicilians are waiting for "the big one", the earthquake or eruption that will reverberate down the centuries. Until then, however, they are happy living the good life, picking nature's riches from the trees. Over 20 per cent of Sicilians live on the flanks of the volcano. Farmers are drawn by the fertile soil while wealthy city residents construct villas for the views, cool summer climate, and for winter skiing on the slopes.

But Etna calls in her dues. Vulcanologist Franco Barberi calls it, "a beautiful battle, where the lava has the brute strength and we have the intelligence". An eruption is as long as a piece of string: it can last 15 minutes or 10 years, like the 1614 eruption. As Giovanni Giuffrida says: "Lava is like a mole, it takes cover, burrows and reappears where you are not ready to catch it."

Within 20 years volcanic ash is ideal for producing sun-drenched fruit, wine and aubergines. Unlike Sicilian earthquakes, Etna's eruptions destroy property but are rarely life-threatening. Even so, tourist offices play down the amount of damage caused by volcanoes and earthquakes. There is always an acknowledgenment of Etna's prior claim. "Etna has taken back my orchard," cried a farmer in 1992, as the river of lava swept past his fruit trees.

This is sometimes known as the "Coast of Cyclops" after Homeric myth. The **Isole Ciclopi** are jagged lumps jutting out of the sea just off the coast of Aci Trezza. Legend has it that these rocks were flung at the fleeing Odyseus by an enraged, blinded Cyclops. The rocks are now used as a marine physics station by Catania University.

Aci Castello, near Catania, is memorable for its dramatic castle perched on a rocky crag overlooking the sea. The crenellated Norman fortress is well-preserved despite frequent eruptions and a fierce attack by the Aragonese. From here, locals potter on the rocks or wander down to one of several fish restaurants along this gnarled coast.

Aci Trezza, a fishing village hoping to become a resort, is celebrated for its connection with Verga and his novel on

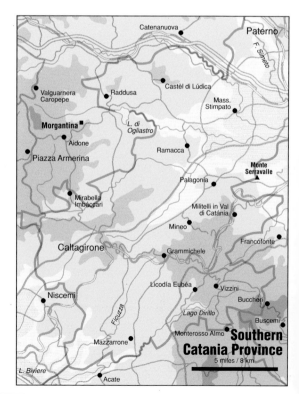

a fishing community here. *I Malavoglia (Under the Medlar Tree)* depicts the benighted lives of a fishing family with humour, perception and an intuitive sympathy. Visconti also filmed *La Terra Trema* on the same spot. Verga was a master of such lines as: "Unfortunately the boy was conscientiously built, as they still make them at Aci Trezza." More tellingly, he feared the sea: "Property at sea is writ on water."

Acireale is proud of its royal appellation and stands aloof, both from the over-commercialised resorts and the rural hinterland. The city is admired for its sense of balance and quality of life, which could make it too popular in future. As Akis, the Greek settlement fared badly in the face of eruptions and earthquakes. Thanks to the ravages of Etna and the talent of local craftsmen, it is predominantly baroque.

The **Duomo** occupies centre stage, its 17th-century grandeur tampered with this century. However, the peeling interior is original enough, with *trompe l'oeil* decoration and stucco in musty browns and yellows. In the gloom, it is just possible to make out a gilded chapel and frescoed ceiling. The inlaid marble floor contains an appealing 1848 Meridian Line.

The Palazzo Comunale represents the first flowering of Catanese baroque. It has an elegant, graceful facade and delicate wrought-iron balconies. French writer Dominique Fernandez considers this town hall a masterpiece, "full of imagination and rustic ingenuity". During carnival, the square becomes a lively outdoor theatre or concert hall.

San Pietro e Paolo is a white baroque church which has been restored. It is possible to glance inside and take a look around before returning to the lemon-scented courtyard. **San Sebastiano**, in Piazza Leonardo Vico, is such an exuberant baroque church that the riot of cherubs and fancy carving on the facade threatens to spill into opera.

Carnival: Acireale advertises itself as having *il più bello carnevale della Sicilia*, the best carnival in Sicily. This is borne out by the illuminations, the

Aci Trezza, the fishing village immortalised by Verga in *I Malavoglia*.

inventiveness of the floats and the enthusiasm of the crowds. Stalls sell masks, shoddy toys, feathered costumes, nougat, nuts and mushroom pastries.

In the compact historic centre, the grandiose baroque buildings are gathered around Piazza Duomo. There is a curious contrast between the spacious public squares and the small-scale design of the town beyond the grand *piazze*.

Yet the tiny, dark alleys yield rewards in the form of pastry shops or the **Teatro dei Pupi** (Via Alessi), one of the last traditional puppet shows. The plays are performed in dialect, but there's enough action and audience participation to help you follow these chivalric tales.

Cuisine: Acireale is credited with inventing sorbets, aided by a profitable monopoly on snow held by the local archbishop until modern times. Nino Castorino, in Corso Savia, is famed for his ice cream, pastries and *pasta reale*, decorated marzipan concoctions.

Unlike neighbouring Giarre or Giardini-Naxos, Acireale is a proper living town rather than a satellite or ugly resort. Compared with the other coastal towns, even Acireale's modern blocks of flats are respectable and unshoddy. From the Giardino Pubblico a pleasant sea walk leads from the park to **Santa Maria la Scala**, a quaint fishing village.

Santa Venera, a spa to the south of town, exploits the healing properties of Etna's radioactive waters. Sulphurous lava mud baths have supposedly been beneficial for rheumatism and skin conditions since Roman times.

Fiumefreddo di Sicilia, further north, is named after a cooling river which flows through thick clumps of papyrus. This feudal town has a tumbledown Phoenician tower and two castellated mansions. The **Castello dello Schiavi**, the stranger of the two villas, has sculpted stone slaves leaning over an 18th-century parapet.

But the chief attractions are clear: coastal views and clean beaches. Fiumefreddo is a calming interlude before the volcanic hinterland. Alternatively, the town is a springboard to chic Taormina.

The southwest is occupied by **Piana di Catania**, a dullish plain which is a poor second to Etna's attractions. The plain was reputedly the abode of the mythological cannibal Laestrygones. Until the 19th century it was better known as a malaria bed and, as a result, there are few farmhouses. Still, the orchards, citrus groves and pasture now make the plain a touch more cheerful.

Militello in Val di Catania is the only significant centre. It has a medieval quarter and a ruined castle as well as several baroque churches. Even so, it is a place best visited by accident not design. By contrast, a couple of towns in the hilly southern interior have considerable charm, especially Caltagirone.

Grammichele is a bizarre baroque town, a champion of bold town planning after the 1693 earthquake. Within a hexagonal design, roads radiate from the **central square**, like spokes of a wheel. The Chiesa Madre and town hall personify the city's cool baroque image and clean geometric design. However, the clinical effect is mocked by the shabby, down-at-heel population.

Caltagirone is a charming city cov-

Caltagirone's stairs are covered with candles during the July festival.

ering three hills. The name derives from the Arabic words for castle and cave but its history is more ancient. It was settled by the Greeks but the mood is dramatic baroque. Like Acireale and Noto, Caltagirone feels like a grand theatre, with spacious squares and majestic mansions. Most churches seem truly monumental and contain grand works of art. Yet Caltagirone is best known as the capital of Sicilian ceramics.

The upper town is surprisingly grand for this part of Sicily. The finest and most imposing public buildings are clustered around the **Piazza Municipio**. The **Corte Capitaniale** is a dignified mansion decorated by school of Gagini sculptures. The remodelled **Norman cathedral** is essentially true baroque. **Museo Civico**, below Piazza Umberto, was once a fearsome Bourbon prison. The barbaric, spike-studded metal doors remain but inside is a museum with archaeological finds and ceramics.

Ceramics: Caltagirone is renowned for its decorative majolica. Signs of the industry are everywhere: ceramic designs occupy tiles, niches, ledges, and even parapets. Ceramic flowers even grace a bridge, **Ponte San Francesco**. The lovely formal gardens are home to the **Ceramics Museum**, a collection of Sicilian pottery from prehistoric times to the present. Also in the gardens is the **Teatrino**, a majolica-decorated folly with ballustraded terraces.

The star is the **Scalazza**, a staircase linking the old and new sections of the city. Each step is decorated in vivid ceramics depicting mythological scenes. In July, a colourful festival, "the tapestry of fire", takes place on the steps. Every year, this ingenious carpet of light is reinvented in different designs. The carpet consists of 5,000 tiny oil lamps on the steps; these are covered by delicate paper cylinders called *coppi*.

From here, one can explore Enna, Ragusa or Siracusa. Alternatively, visit Catania's fascinating volcanic landscape *(see next chapter)*. This smouldering or snow-capped cone will already be a familiar, perversely comforting presence in Catania province.

Life on the farm.

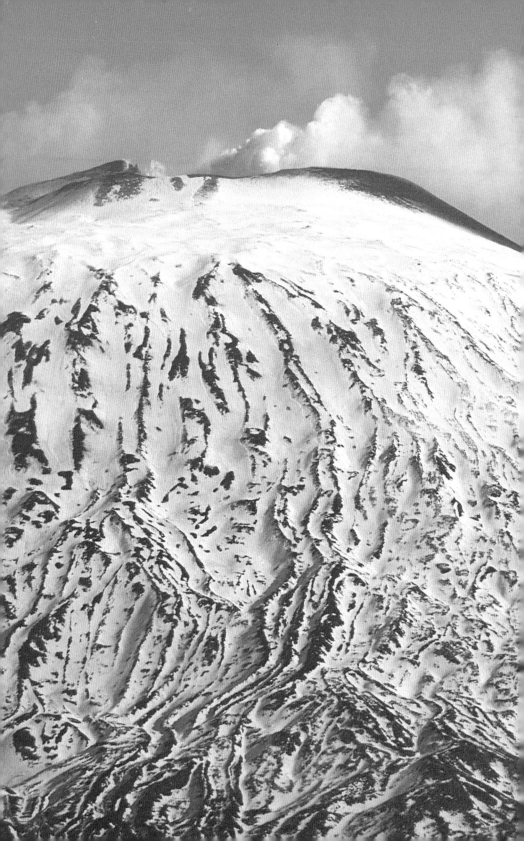

ETNA ENVIRONS

Etna is the gaping chasm where the heart of Catania province should be. The volcano munches Messina too, with new lava mouths opening all the time. Locals joke that not even the Mafia can close Etna's myriad mouths.

Mongibello, the Sicilian name for Etna, comes from the Arabic for mountain. Locally, Etna is known as *"a muntagna"* (the mountain). The volcano is addressed as "she", even though the word is masculine. Place names are symbolic: Linguaglossa is a corruption of *lingua grossa*, referring to a fat tongue of lava that engulfed the village.

The native Siculi worshipped Etna long before the arrival of the Greeks. Adranus, their God of Fire, inhabited the turbulent depths of the volcano. To the Greeks, Etna was Hephaistos' forge, moulding black magic from incandescent lava. To present-day Sicilians, Etna is still an atavistic god. As Pino Torrisi, a carpenter, says: "You must never speak badly of Etna. She was here 200 million years ago, and we are guests on her slopes; we are nothing against her will."

The sense of appeasing the mountain gods still survives in Zafferana Etnea, a village in the path of the 1992 eruption. Before abandoning his farmhouse to the volcano, Giuseppe Fichera left bread, cheese and wine to satisfy "the tired and hungry mountain". Even gods of destruction need food and rest.

Routes to Etna: The circular journey to Etna is a game of light and shade. From the Ionian coast to the fertile Etna foothills is a feast of glistening citrus and olive groves, orchards and nut plantations. But clinging to Etna's flanks are dark volcanic villages and ruined Norman castles. It is a strange trail from green slopes to the moonscape above.

From Taormina, a scenic railway runs to Randazzo, travelling along the valley floor, crossing a bridge made of lava blocks and even disappearing inside a lava cutting. But to appreciate Etna's grandeur, drive around the base or follow a similar route on the Circumetnea single-gauge railway from Catania or Giarre. (If planning an ascent of Etna, consult the *Travel Tips* section for advice before setting out.)

Dramatic canyon: Leave the coast near Taormina for a foray into the Alcàntara Valley, starting with **Gole dell' Alcàntara**, a delightful gorge discovered in the 1950s when a Taormina film director was so enchanted with the prospect of a secret gorge that he had a tortuous path built down to the river. He was the first of many to capture Alcàntara on film.

Seen from above, the view is of wooded crags descending to a weirdly pitted river canyon. The bed is rocky, the remains of a prehistoric lava flow that created the peninsula of Capo Schisò. The canyon was created not by erosion but by the splintering collision of volcanic magma and cooling water. The impact threw up lavic prisms in monstrous shapes. These warped boulders resemble a cross-section of a fossil.

A lift leads down to the grey-green river. In summer, low water levels make

Preceding pages: Mount Etna's snowy slopes. <u>Left</u>, ski resorts are growing in popularity. <u>Right</u>, the bizarre gorge of Gole dell' Alcàntara.

the initial section accessible to visitors in waders or swim suits. The athletic can clamber to caves but a waterfall with a sheer drop is a barrier to further exploration of the gorge. Beyond are dangerous whirlpools and fast-flowing currents in ever-narrowing tracts.

Linguaglossa, set on Etna's northern flanks, is a ski resort and logging centre. The **Chiesa Madre** pays tribute to the forests, with 18th-century choir stalls and wood panels. Treks lead through pine forests to **Grotta del Gelo**, a lava stone cave with weird light effects.

Castiglione di Sicilia beckons, an ancient jumble perched on a crag. Although Greek ramparts remain, this bastion is better known as a Norman fiefdom. Narrow alleys wind to the crumbling lava stone church of San Pietro and the grander Maria della Catena. The **Norman castle** dominates the valley, with its jagged lookout tower, walls and roofs. This rocky citadel compels respect, as do the ominous views of rubble trailing from Etna's summit.

Francavilla di Sicilia, just north, is set in a fertile valley of citrus plantations and prickly pears. Like Castiglione, it is also on the Circumetnea rail route. Founded by King Roger, Francavilla prospered under Spanish rule. Roger's **ruined castle** occupies a lone mound in the valley and once guarded the route to Randazzo. The other Norman relic is the hermitage of **La Badiazza**, perched atop a rocky platform and victim of the 1693 earthquake.

The **Chiesa Madre** has a Gagini Madonna, matched by the sculpted Gagini fountain in Piazza San Paolo. The **Matrice Vecchia** boasts a Renaissance door with a vine-leaf motif. The finest sight is the **Convento Dei Cappuccini**, a 16th-century monastery on a lovely hillock, protected by Spanish sentry boxes and marble parapets. Inside is a profusion of *intarsia* work and carving, the handiwork of 17th-century monks.

Between Francavilla and Randazzo, the **Alcàntara valley** offers a slice of rural architecture, from dry-stone shacks to gracious villas, all in grey-mauve lava stone. Most curious are the Sicilian

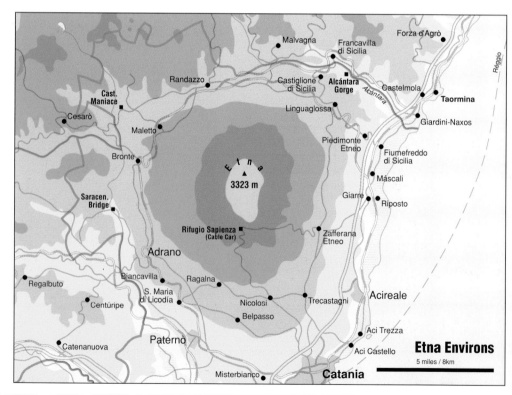

Etna Environs

5 miles / 8km

shepherd bothies, dry-stone refuges built in beehive style.

Overlooking the hamlet of **Mojo Alcàntara** is the eccentric extinct volcano that in prehistoric times vomited lava to the coast and created Capo Schisò. In open country below the truncated cone is **La Cuba**, a ruined honeycomb church, a rare relic of the mighty Byzantine empire in eastern Sicily.

An old bridge leads to **Randazzo**, the most atmospheric medieval town on the northern slopes of Etna. Originally settled by Greeks fleeing from Naxos, it reached its apogee under the Normans. During the Hohenstaufen dynasty, Randazzo was a summer court and retreat from the heat of Messina. It remains a market town, with crenellated churches and sturdy 14th-century walls.

For a town in the jaws of Etna, Randazzo has survived magnificently. The 1981 eruption threatened to engulf the walls and blocked surrounding roads and railway lines. But human beings are to blame for any damage to the medieval core. Allied bombing in 1943 destroyed much of the Nazis' last stronghold in Sicily, including the fortress and finest *palazzi*.

Until the 16th century, a competition for supremacy fuelled the three rival communities. Each parish church took its turn as cathedral for a three-year term: the Latins were centred on the church of Santa Maria, the Greeks had San Nicolò and the Lombards San Martino. The churches were fiercely battlemented and ostentatious. Ultimately, the Catholics triumphed and Santa Maria is now the cathedral.

Randazzo's sights: Porta San Martino, one of two surviving city gates, marks the entrance to the walled medieval town. The elegant Piazza San Martino is the heart of the shell-damaged Lombard quarter, set against the city walls. Appropriately, **Chiesa San Martino** boast a 13th-century Lombard *campanile*. This banded lava and limestone belltower is matched by an early baroque facade in grey and white stone. The interior holds a Renaissance marble font and tabernacle as well as a cool Gagini *Virgin of*

Randazzo, a lava-built town of great antiquity.

Mercy. Most significant is the so-called *Crucifix of the Rain,* named after its miraculous powers of producing rain in times of drought.

Virtually next-door is the **Castello-carcere**, a medieval castle transformed into a Bourbon prison. Beside the lava stone windows is an inscription to Philip II and bullet holes which attest to the Nazi defeat in August 1943.

Via Umberto contains symbols of Randazzo's past role as a royal city, including the **Palazzo Reale**, the severe Hohenstaufen summer palace now demoted to a mini-market. Yet surprising signs of wealth remain in the chic jewellery shops, occasionally daubed with anti-Mafia slogans.

Via Umberto ends in the spacious **Piazza Municipio**, the bustling heart of Randazzo. Competing offices of the political parties remain a legacy of ancient rivalries. A giant outdoor chessboard is a chance to settle old scores. The square is dominated by the **Palazzo Comunale**, the well-restored town hall. Leave the crowds by turning down **Via degli Archi**, a quaint arcaded alley, to Piazza San Nicolò and the Greek quarter. In one corner is Santa Maria della Volta, a 14th-century shell of a bombed church. In the centre of the square is the impressive Greek **Chiesa di San Nicolò**, with its original 14th-century apses and huge early baroque facade and tapering campanile. Inside the church are several Gagini sculptures – including, appropriately, a St Nicholas.

Nearby, in Via Duca degli Abruzzi, is **Palazzo Finocchiaro**, a Renaissance mansion with mullioned windows. The road continues to Porta Aragonese, the city walls and market.

At the end of Corso Umberto is **Chiesa Santa Maria**, the Latin church, well-sited opposite the smartest bar in town. It is an elegant grey lava stone church in Norman-Swabian design, with Norman apses and walls and side portals in Catalan-Gothic style. The facade was clumsily remodelled in the 19th century, as were the *campanile* and spire. The odd interior contrasts Satanic-looking black columns and altar with a pure

Randazzo, long in Etna's shadow.

270

Gagini font and a 15th-century view of the town.

Between Randazzo and Bronte extends a wooded, volcanic landscape to **Maletto**, noted for its wine and strawberries. Maletto marks the highest point on the Circumetnea line and offers views of recent lava flows. From Maletto, take a right fork to Admiral Nelson's abbey at Maniace or continue south to Bronte.

Nelson's fiefdom: Following signs to the Castello di Nelson leads to **Abbazia di Maniace**, one and the same. Set in a wooded hollow, the abbey was founded by Count Roger. The chapel commemorates a Saracen defeat on the site in 1040. With Norman help, the Byzantine commander, Maniakes, routed the Arabs and regained Sicily for Constantinople. But the estate is better known as the fiefdom of Nelson, Duke of Bronte.

The title and estates were presented to Nelson by Ferdinand IV in gratitude for the Admiral's part in crushing the 1799 rebellion in Naples. As Duke of Bronte, Nelson never visited his vast Sicilian domains, despite wistful dreams of retirement here with Emma Hamilton. The closest he got was in Emma's affectionate nickname for him, "My Lord Thunder", a reference to Bronte, the mythical giant who forged thunderbolts for Jupiter.

Nelson's descendant, Viscount Bridport, only relinquished his Sicilian seat in 1981, when the 30,000-acre (12,500-hectare) estate was broken up and the orchards, nut plantations and dairy farms sold. Nevertheless, Nelson memorabilia remains, including paintings of sea battles and the Admiral's port decanter.

Inside the castle compound, the best part of the Benedictine abbey owes nothing to Nelson. The late Norman **chapel** boasts an original wooden ceiling, doorway and statuary. Treasures include a Byzantine table, a medieval winged altarpiece and an ancient icon presented to the abbey by Maniakes.

The original castle is unrecognisable, thanks to the 1693 earthquake and heavy anglicisation. It resembles a gracious Wiltshire manor from outside, an image confirmed by the English cemetery.

Almond trees on Etna's fertile slopes.

Even the gardens are home to neat hedges as well as cypresses and palms. As for the interior, it is genteel English.

Between Maletto and Bronte are subtle shifts in scenery. Walnut and chestnut groves on the higher hills are dotted with jagged volcanic clumps, including the lava flow of 1823. Around Bronte, the slopes are covered with small nut trees, a reminder that 80 per cent of Italy's pistachio crop comes from these well-tended terraces.

Bronte, founded in 1520 by Charles V, is an ill-planned town sandwiched between two lava flows. As the administrative centre for the 24 hamlets of the Dukedom of Bronte, the town flourished but its present status is one of mere market. It is resolutely shabby, its dingy charm residing in the neglected late Renaissance churches with crenellated towers. It is indeed a pious town: even ragamuffins cross themselves when passing a church.

In Piazza Pio IX the **Chiesa Madre** has a fine mosaic ceiling. **Chiesa San Sebastiano** opposite has faded frescoes

and Greek-style columns. Other late Renaissance churches include **della Trinità**, with Romanesque remains, and **dell' Annunciata** with a sandstone portal and Gagini sculpture. The rococo **Chiesa del Sacro Cuore** adjoins **Collegio Capizzi**, the college that educated the ruling class in the 18th century.

Chiesa San Giovanni boasts a baroque belltower and fountain in the adjoining square while the Renaissance **Chiesa del Rosario** has also been given a gilded white baroque facelift. This strange church displays stars and masonic symbols.

About 3 miles (5 km) away is the **Masseria Lombardo**, a Sicilian farm converted into a museum of rural culture. (Follow signs for *museo dell'antica civiltà locale*.) Constructed around an Arab-Norman monastery, this odd artisan centre displays the bygone monastic crafts of paper-making and hide-curing.

South of Bronte, the prosperous air of solid chalets on the alpine plains gives way to ramshackle dwellings and rough scrubland. The pistachio plantations cede to scruffy, cacti-strewn slopes, with lumps of lava interspersed with white lava-coated trees. The makeshift mood reflects a region devastated by the 1985 eruption: everything has been built in haste but, given Etna's whims, there will be no time to repent at leisure.

Adrano, set on Etna's south-west slopes, is a shabby market town with mythical roots. On the outskirts are the remains of a grander past: the Greek city of Adranon was founded by Dionysius I in 4th century BC. In antiquity, the city was celebrated for its sanctuary to Adranus, the Siculi god of fire.

Its battered charm lies in the busy **Piazza Umberto**. Like Randazzo, political associations and social welfare clubs are clustered around the main square. Here, too, is the austere **Norman castle**, sitting on its squat Saracen base. This powerful bastion was rebuilt by Roger I in the 11th century and remodelled by the Aragonese. The interior, once a Bourbon prison, houses a museum with minor Greek sculptures and Siculi ceramics. On the floor above is Queen Adelaide's chapel, a mysteri-

Adranus, the god of fire, erupts again on Etna's north-east crater.

ous room decorated with purplish lava stone capitals by Roger's third wife.

Beside the castle, the **Chiesa Madre** is a Norman church disfigured by clumsy restoration. The dilapidated interior displays a luridly coloured polyptich and dusty missals. The heavy basalt columns conceivably came from the Greek Temple to Adranon that once occupied the site. Plutarch records a dramatic eve of battle appeal to the gods: in response, a bronze statue of Adranus suddenly quivered into life. A final twinge of nostalgia for ancient Adranon is evoked by the **Greek city walls**, lying at the end of Via Buglio.

In Via Roma, adjoining Piazza Umberto, is **Santa Lucia**, a symbol of Norman times. The sprawling convent was founded by Count Roger's niece but transformed beyond recognition in the 17th century. Now a school, its rococo chapel is more reminiscent of a ballroom than a convent, with its swirls of silk brocade and blue and gold stucco.

Equally bizarre is the August festival. A child dressed as an angel "flies" along a cord linking the old city powers: the castle, town hall and a statue of the god of fire himself. So far, Adranus has kept his city safe from fiery Etna.

Five miles (8 km) west, in open country near Carcaci, is the **Ponte Saraceno**, a sinuous hump-back Saracen bridge over the Simeto river.

Biancavilla, built on a basalt escarpment, was founded by Albanian refugees in 1480. Some of the 1991 influx of latter-day Albanians were resettled here but transferred to Palermo province. The sole Albanian link now is the Madonna of the Alms, an icon brought over by the first refugees. It is visible in the comically grandiose **Chiesa Madre**.

If Biancavilla is today best known for its prickly pears, **Paternò** is famous for its oranges, the juiciest in Sicily. The town is of baroque inspiration but the **Norman castle** on a hilly volcanic site is more striking. The severity of the 14th-century lava stone keep is echoed by the Great Hall and frescoed chapel. Frederick II died here while journeying to his favourite fortress of Enna.

Etna's unique vegetation: the lava-rich hills of Linguaglossa.

Nearby is the **Chiesa Madre**, a Norman church with a Gothic facelift and the ruined Gothic **San Francesco**. More recently, the Nazis used this hill as an observation post and drew heavy Allied fire, leading to the death of 4,000 people. Known as the **Rocca Normanna**, the castle quarter now enjoys happier associations. In summer, visitors can attend concerts, sample the local stuffed aubergines, or simply drool over terraces glistening with orange groves.

From Paternò it is a short drive back to the coast via **Misterbianco**, Catania's Mafia-infested satellite town. Infinitely more pleasant is a trip through the fertile southeastern foothills, or, time and weather conditions permitting, an ascent of Etna.

Nicolosi, east of Paternò, is both a charmless ski resort and the gateway to Etna's wine and walking country. Lying east of the wooded Monti Rossi twin craters, the town was wiped out by the 1669 eruption. Today it marks the start of short but bracing treks to spent cones and the interior of prehistoric craters.

(The offices of Etna National Park, based in Nicolosi, can advise on routes.) Along the road to Trecastagni, the lava beds of 1886 and 1910 are visible. Once a medieval fiefdom, **Trecastagni** is noted for the **Chiesa Madre**, a Renaissance church probably designed by Antonello Gagini, as good an architect as he was a sculptor. The interior is somewhat marred by a garish Florentine chapel. Nearby, the 15th-century Chiesa del Bianco has a quaint, low belltower while the Lombard-Romanesque Sant' Antonio di Padova boasts 17th-century lava stone cloisters.

Traditional crafts: Sicilian carts are still made in these lava stone streets. Etna's craftwork embraces wrought iron, basket-weaving, painted ceramics and, best of all, carving in lava stone or gnarled olive wood. Nor are Trecastagni's almond biscuits, sorbets and red wines to be sneezed at.

ASCENDING ETNA: Etna is not to everyone's taste. Circling the volcano is intriguing and safe but an ascent requires caution. When it works, it is wonderful.

Adrano's Convent church of Santa Lucia (left) and its imposing Norman castle (below).

But if conditions are misty, you might as well be in your hotel room breakfasting on bad eggs or rotting cabbage.

Zafferana Etnea lives dangerously. This unprepossessing mountain resort hit the national headlines for a month in 1992 when Etna threatened to engulf the village. The resort had barely recovered from the 1984 earthquake and a minor eruption in 1986. The baroque **Chiesa Madre** was the focus of fervent prayers, as vineyards and citrus groves all around were swallowed up. It is only 500 metres from the crater on Monte Serra Calvarina and landslides are still common.

During the 1992 eruption, the Americans were called in to save Zafferana. A Navy and Marine task force, accompanied by the world's largest helicopters, set up base in Sapienza. The force made forays to the mouth of the crater, depositing blocks of concrete in the seething river of lava. They whiled away the time between missions by painting erupting volcanoes on their helmets.

Route to the top: From here, a road leads to Sapienza and an ascent of Etna. Given the regularity of volcanic activity, access roads may be barred or blocked. The cautious are better-off going on an organised trip, where the costs are known and risks restricted. Local firms can even offer a night excursion ending at dawn. Always check current options before setting out (*see Travel Tips*). For sheer adventure, a private alpine guide is recommended.

As one climbs the scenic **Casa Cantoniera** road, wooded slopes give way to a wasteland of lava flows, bare slabs of brown rubble half-covered by snow. Even in deepest winter, snow is unevenly distributed, thanks to the heat generated by the volcano. Recent volcanic debris lies in folds, a desert of bluish clinker. Occasionally, Etna violets and broom struggle for survival.

Rifugio Sapienza is a refuge and hostel run by the Italian Alpine Club. It has recently been rebuilt after an eruption, depicted in lurid Technicolor inside. For starters, glance at the spent cone just in front of the refuge, one of

The scorched Silveri crater, Mount Etna.

many extinct cones nearby. Take the cable car to the top, leaving behind the tacky bars and shops selling lava stone ashtrays.

Qualified guides are available for hire but discuss what there is to see. Depending on the season and Etna's mood, the menu may include a mere mass of clinker, a spent cone, a smoking cone, or even a seething lava front (*fronte lavica*).

The **cable car** trip may be made in the company of skiers comparing eye-witness accounts of Etna's latest devastation. En route are grim views of a burnt-out cable car destroyed in the 1983 eruption, along with ruined access roads, the wreckage of a ski lift and the original mountain centre.

At the summit, feebler visitors can simply admire the snow-capped views, usually best in the morning, before sloping off to the mountain bar and videos of the volcano in action. Without a guide, suitably-clad explorers can clamber about at their own risk. Even so, it is essential to get advice on routes and weather conditions from the refuge personnel. Torre **del Filosofo**, Empedocles' observation post, wrecked in a recent eruption, currently marks the highest point one can go unaccompanied. Daring skiers peer into an active cone at their own risk.

Empedocles did not live to tell the tale. The Greek philosopher allegedly leapt into the main crater in 433 BC in a vain attempt to prove that the gases would support his body weight. The charitable interpretation is that it was also a quest for divine consciousness in death. But, as his sandal was found on the edge, perhaps he merely slipped.

Views from the top: The sights will depend on volcanic activity and weather conditions, particularly the prevailing winds: it is vital to avoid the gases emitted from active craters. At most, you may see an active crater belching out sulphurous vapours or exploding *bombe*, molten "bombs". The bottom of the misty cone bubbles with incandescent lava. In periods of intense seismic activity, the volcano spits out molten rock or fireballs, a dramatic sight at night. A lava front some distance away from the volcano is bathed in mist and a stench of sulphur. It sounds like the clinking of china cups or the hissing of some chained animal.

Sunset on Etna can be glorious or tedious, as Evelyn Waugh found when confronted with Etna "glowing on the top and then repeating its shape, as though reflected, in a wisp of grey smoke, with the whole horizon behind radiant with pink light, fading gently into a grey pastel sky. Nothing I have ever seen in Art or Nature was quite so revolting."

Going down: The descent of Etna may not be an anti-climax, if you can visit a lava front. (Without a guide or local help, it is impossible to find one: visitors are discouraged.) The main 1992 lava front spread from a secondary crater to the Valle del Bove, filling the valley before lurching to Zafferana. Sand gushed up to 2,000 ft (600 metres) in the air and fell like rain, crushing roads and houses in the volcano's path.

Valle del Bove, best seen from Milo, is a former gaping chasm that acted as a natural reservoir for lava in recent eruptions, thus sparing the valley towns. However, it was partly filled by lava in 1986 and again in 1992. Today the volcanic dykes are barely visible under new lava. During the 1992 eruption, forest rangers rescued two French tourists who thought they could safely walk over molten lava: a fall in Valle del Bove proved their folly.

Etna's riches: sample the mountain cuisine before returning stiff-limbed to Catania or the coast. Roast lamb or sausages seasoned with fennel are good but the fruit, honey and wine are best. Try luscious prickly pears, chestnut or citrus blossom honey, conserved peaches and fresh grapes. Fruit finds its way into crunchy nougat and delicious sorbets. Avoid Fuoco di Etna, an explosive but evil-tasting liqueur.

In response to the often posed question of why people choose to live by an active volcano, a Catanese vulcanologist, Romolo Romano, muses: "It's the same reason people live in places like the San Andreas Fault: they are beautiful spots, so beautiful that you sometimes forget how dangerous they are."

Right, mysterious Etna.

TAORMINA

Taormina is Sicily's most dramatic resort, a stirring place celebrated by poets from Classical times onwards. Goethe waxed lyrical about the majestic setting: "Straight ahead one sees the long ridge of Etna, to the left the coastline as far as Catania or even Siracusa, and the whole panorama is capped by the huge, fuming, fiery mountain, the look of which, tempered by distance and atmosphere, is, however, more friendly than forbidding." D. H. Lawrence was equally enamoured of the Hellenistic city, calling it "the dawn-coast of Europe".

Yet this elemental site has been domesticated into a safe, sophisticated, unSicilian pocket. A century of tourism has toned down the subversive Sicilian spirit, effaced poverty and displaced undesirables. French visitors liken Taormina to a Sicilian St Tropez, stylish but unreal. In fact, it is more like an old Soviet-style hard currency shop, its luxury goods beyond the reach of most locals. Still, after Catania's street crime, or the wariness of mountain villages, who wants reality?

The terraced town was once a wintering place for frustrated northerners and gay exiles. Today, this safe haven appeals to romantic couples of both sexes, sedate shoppers and the cultured middle classes. Local gossip has it that the town is uncontaminated by corruption because even the Mafia likes a crime-free holiday haunt. Yet despite blasé langour and designer glamour, the site's majesty is not manufactured. Nor is the heady decadence.

A long history: Taormina started as a Siculi settlement at the foot of Monte Tauro. It was an outpost of Naxos until the Greeks fled the first colony for Taoromenion in 403 BC. Under the Romans, the city acquired a garrison and the new name of Tauromenium. The town prospered in medieval times

Preceding pages: Taormina's Teatro Greco.
Left, Corso Umberto, out of season.

and became the capital of Byzantine Sicily in the 9th century. Aristocratic leanings drew Taormina into the Aragonese camp and support for the Spanish. The town's richly decorated *palazzi* reflect the Catalan legacy.

Taormina's *raison d'être* is the **Teatro Greco**, a setting that is pure drama, with the *cavea* hewn out of the hillside. In Greek theatres, sea and sky were the natural backdrop; the Romans preferred proscenium arches. Where the Greeks worshipped nature, the Romans tried to improve on it. The Hellenistic theatre was built under Hieron in 3 BC and enlarged by the Romans in AD 2. Like Tindari's Greek theatre Taormina's was turned into an arena for gladiatorial combat. Roman theatrical conventions caused the view to be obscured by arches. By adding a double portico and colonnades behind the stage, they showed insensitivity to the natural setting.

Romantics side with the Olympian gods in seeing Roman grandiosity unequal to the timeless character of Greek art. However, Roman erudition is evidenced in the well-preserved *scena*. But in the 19th century, the granite columns and Corinthian capitals were wrongly repositioned on the site. Still, Greek purists are delighted to see the Roman *scena* crumble, the better to appreciate the Greek atmosphere.

Not that cats sunning themselves on the ruins distinguish between Greek marble and pinkish Roman brickwork. Views from the terraces above the *cavea* and *parascenia* (wings) reveal a perfect fusion of the elements. Writer Vincent Cronin likened the theatre to a seagull suspended between sky and sea. The scene is shrouded in mystery by a smouldering volcano or snow-capped peak. Citrus groves carpet the slopes while the cliff face is a tangle of cacti and orchids. Below stretches a craggy coastline and the romantic islet of Isola Bella.

Piazza Emanuele lies beyond, a noisy market square built over the Roman forum. Bordering the piazza is **Palazzo Corvaja**, an historic mansion where the Sicilian Parliament met in 1411. Now a tourist office and exhibition centre, this

People-watching on Via Teatro Greco.

eclectic building incorporates a crenellated Saracenic tower, a secluded courtyard, sculpted parapet, and Catalan-Gothic decorative details around the doorway and windows.

On the far side of the square stands the medieval gate of **Porta Messina** and, through the arch, the tiny church of **San Pancrazio**, built over a Temple to Isis. Nearby is the **Odeon**, or Teatrino Romano, a Roman concert auditorium partly hidden by the church of Santa Caterina.

Corso Umberto, the main street, is a feast for shopaholics. The 15th-century *palazzi* are converted into craft shops, boutiques and bars. Luxury food emporia display bottled peppers, candied fruit, marzipan animals and fresh kumquats. Majolica tiles, leather goods and traditional puppets vie with chandeliers and reproductions of Classical statuary.

Just off the Corso lies the **Naumachia,** a hybrid construction second only to the Greek theatre in importance. Originally a vaulted cistern connected to the city baths, it evolved into a Hellenic nymphaeum and Roman gymnasium. The an-

cient arched buttress walls remain, propping up the Corso.

Halfway down the Corso, **Piazza Aprile** offers glittering views of Etna and close-ups of preening poseurs at chic cafés. **Sant'Agostino**, the forbidding 15th-century church on the square, has been converted into a cosy library. The city churches feel more like social than spiritual centres. **San Giuseppe**'s rococo interior overflows after a Sunday service. After much hand-shaking, the congregation spills into the cafés, disdaining the odd blind beggar outside.

The Corso continues beyond the Porta di Mezzo, a clocktower marking the city's medieval quarter. Steps lead to the Catalan-Gothic **Palazzo Ciampoli**, now the Hotel Palazzo Vecchio. After admiring its Aragonese battlemented facade and mullioned windows, climb to Via Venezia, a charming alley by the Corso, or walk down to the Duomo.

Piazza del Duomo is a central meeting place. At the first sign of spring sun, kids start roller-skating and the *jeunesse dorée* pose. Matrons still swan around

An operatic evening in the Teatro Greco.

in weighty furs: in Taormina, the fur coat parade lasts until May. The **cathedral** itself has a crenellated stone facade, a severity that survived Renaissance remodelling. Outside is a baroque fountain sporting sea horses, cherubs and a podgy female centaur. This weird mythological creature is the city symbol – confirmed by a stone centaur unearthed on the Greek site.

Opposite the fountain, steps lead to Piazza del Carmine and the **Badia Vecchia**, a battlemented Norman abbey. Although over-restored, the abbey boasts Trecento flourishes, arched windows, fretwork and friezes. Set on a lower level, **Palazzo di Santo Stefano** is a gracious ducal palace and Taormina's loveliest medieval building. Highlights are the Norman-Gothic windows, delicate lava stone cornices, and the lacey frieze of *intarsia* work, a Saracenic legacy.

From here, Via del Ghetto winds down to **San Domenico**, a 15th-century monastery converted into a *de luxe* hotel. During the war, it was Marshal Kessel-

ring's headquarters and suffered bomb damage, although the cells and cloisters were spared. The cells are now distinctly unspartan bedrooms. It is a short stroll to the **Giardino Pubblico**, a lush park bequeathed to the town by an eccentric Englishwoman in the 1920s. Florence Trevelyan adorned her hanging gardens with pagoda-style follies and observation towers for bird-spotting. The tiered gardens are linked by mosaic paths and wind past caged peacocks and tropical plants, from spiky cacti and lilies to dull English hedges.

English connection: St George's Anglican Church also dates from Trevelyan's time. Her contemporary, D. H. Lawrence, lived for a few years in a villa in Via Fontana Vecchia. When King George V visited, Lawrence was the only British resident to ignore him. Undeterred, the King called on the writer and helped water his garden. In Taormina, the sickly Lawrence chose to live a solitary life, writing of sensuality.

As the first international Sicilian resort, Taormina had a sizeable pre-war

The resort's churches are a reminder of a less sybaritic age.

foreign community and was known as a "fashionable loafing place". Although anti-Mafia raids closed down many nightclubs in 1992, the town remains Sicily's most sophisticated resort. Taormina is fun, from the summer cultural season to the Sunday posers. The chic crowd wears Valentino ties and Armani suits; even dogs are clad in little coats. The backdrop is equally vivid: balconies hung with geraniums and bougainvillaea; inner courtyards resplendent with sculpted cornices, grape-carved motifs, and miniature lemon trees.

Taormina by night is a fitting farewell. The Catalan-Gothic facades are illuminated and the squares tinged pink in the moonlight. From the belvedere, Etna's fiery cone glitters before dissolving into the sea, stars and smoky peaks. Strollers slip into a fashionable restaurant in the aptly-named Vicolo Stretto (narrow alley). Solitary walkers climb Salita Ibrahim to the Carmine, a tranquil monastic spot with a tower and wild garden behind. Dreamers take Via Caruso to the Badia Vecchia and bay views,

a reminder that Taormina, like Vancouver, is a setting in search of a city.

Below Taormina, sheer cliffs drop to the tempting islet of **Isola Bella.** A cable car links the city to the pebbled beach at **Mazzarò**. Nearby are entrances to underwater caves, where scuba divers spot shrimps, red starfish, perch, scorpion fish and sea urchins. If you prefer your fish on a plate, leave the sea for the grey and pink cliffs above Taormina.

From Taormina, a winding road climbs to **Castelmola**, a hamlet perched on a limestone peak. From this natural balcony over the sea, there is a sense of what Taormina used to be. Out of season it is home to old craftsmen and part-time potters. But in summer, it resembles a tourist trap: visitors are too tired by the climb to do anything but collapse into trinket shops and bars. Caffè San Giorgio is the place for celebrity autographs, a reminder of (separate) visits by Churchill and Kesselring. Once Churchill's local, it is now devoted to hearty German drinkers downing beer or local almond wine.

Taormina and Castelmola.

MESSINA PROVINCE

"*Monte e Mare*" is Messina's official slogan, a promise of sea and mountains through the "gateway to Sicily". Messina delivers rugged ranges and contrasting coastlines. The Tyrrhenian coast is one of rocky inlets, saltwater lakes, sand dunes and dry gravel-beds; citrus groves are fringed by myrtle, broom and prickly pear. The Ionian is a gentler but equally exotic coastline with sandy shores and similarly bland resorts. Both coasts boast Classical sites, stumpy castles, seafood dishes and an enticing hinterland.

Coastal refinement is set against a backdrop of ancient mountain culture, with lifestyles aeons apart. The raggedy hinterland is the place for Moorish churches and for those on the trail of Madonnas by Antonello Gagini, Sicily's greatest sculptor. The wooded hillsides abound in bizarre festivals and peasants on mules. After this, Taormina comes as a shock, an international oasis. But the coastal glitz of Taormina is grafted on to self-contained rural Sicily.

This stretch of coast is awash with myths. Greek sailors north of Messina were wary of the twin demons of Charybdis, the whirlpool, and Scylla, the six-headed sea monster. It took an 18th-century scientist to demystify the whirlpools as the meeting of clashing currents. Although diverted after the 1908 earthquake, strange counterflows still exist, colourfully known as *bastardi*. Messina was a Phoenician-Punic colony eventually settled by the Greeks in 730 BC. Its apogee was as a Norman stronghold and Crusader port but the city thrived for centuries as a seafaring power. Decline set in with the outbreak of plague in 1743, followed by earthquakes and, in the 1800s, by a naval bombardment and cholera epidemic.

But the greatest calamity was the 1908 earthquake which killed 84,000 people in 30 seconds. The shore sank by half a metre and the reverberations were felt in Malta a day later. In 1943, Messina represented the Nazis' last stand: the city was devastated and 5,000 people died during Allied bombing. Such disasters have engendered a salvage mentality: every recoverable stone has been reused or recreated.

The ensuing fresh start favoured economic enterprise. Today, the province has pockets of industry at Messina and Milazzo, with oil, tyres, terracotta and cement replacing the dependence on fruit production. Tourism is important and hotels abound, ironically thanks to the well-organised Mafia infrastructure. However, the province's long-term prosperity depends on better communications and the building of a suspension bridge over the Straits. As yet, the benighted bridge is only a gleam in the regional government's eye.

Messina city: The wide boulevards, grid system, imposing public buildings and matter-of-factness make **Messina** the most American-looking Sicilian city. While not instantly appealing, Messina's apparent blandness conceals a handful of sunken treasures. As a touring base, however, Taormina or a Tyrrhenean coastal resort are preferable.

The port: In Classical times, the sickle-shaped harbour earned the city the name of Zankle, also reputedly referring to the sickle with which Zeus castrated his father. The port's protectress is the Madonnina, the tall statue built on ancient harbour walls. Curved around the sickle is the cittadella, the remains of the 16th-century Spanish bastion.

At the Maritime Station, trains are dismantled, devoured by the cavernous ferry and shipped over the Straits. The harbour welcomes grey NATO warships docked in deep water and long-prowed feluccas in pursuit of swordfish. Ever-present are the boats of the Guardia di Finanza, the efficient fraud squad on the trail of drug-smugglers. Despite the bustle, the overwhelming feeling is one of space and sweeping views; the townward side of the harbour has no walls. Unlike Palermo, Messina does not turn its back on the sea.

The **Duomo** symbolises the stubbornness of the natives: this Norman cathedral has survived medieval fires, earthquakes and wartime American fire-bombing. It is set on a lower level than the surrounding streets that were redeveloped after the earthquake. The sculpted main portal and much of the Gothic facade are original, including the vivid farming scenes.

The designer pink and grey interior impresses with its pleasing proportions. Restored treasures include a painted wooden ceiling, 14th-century mosaics in the semi-circular apses, glittering Renaissance altars and a Gagini statue of St John. The high altar boasts an extravagant Madonna, a vision of Sicilian literalism adorned with a silver crown and Byzantine gold background.

The Orion fountain, outside the cathedral, is a masterpiece by Giovanni Montorsoli, a pupil of Michelangelo. The restored Renaissance fountain is a tribute to Orion, a mythical city founder. It is also a celebration of water, from the Tiber to the Nile. This riot of cherubs and watery figures is overshadowed by a free-standing Flemish belfry. The old campanile contains an astronomical clock from Alsace. Its most spectacular

Clocking in at the Duomo's campanile.

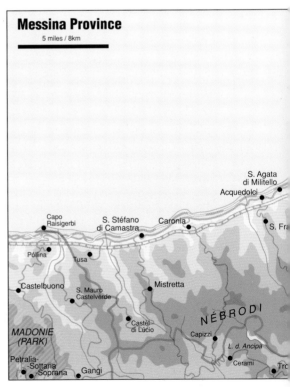

Messina Province

5 miles / 8km

S. Agata
di Militello
Acquedolci

Capo
Raisigerbi
S. Stéfano
di Camastra
Caronia
S. Fra

Pόllina
Tusa

Castelbuono
S. Mauro
Castelverde
Mistretta

NÉBRODI

MADONIE
(PARK)
Castel
di Lúcio
Capizzi
L. d. Ancipa

Petralia-
Sottana
Soprana
Gangi
Cerami
Tro

performance is at midday: to the accompaniment of a cock crowing and a lion roaring, religious and mythological scenes are played out.

Piazza Antonello, the next square north, houses a cluster of Art Nouveau public buildings leading to the vaulted Vittorio Emanuele gallery, an elegant Art Nouveau concoction.

In a neighbouring square is **Chiesa dei Catalani**, a sunken Arab-Norman church with Byzantine echoes. Built on the site of a Temple to Neptune, this eclectic church has Norman arches, blind arcading, 13th-century portals and honeycomb apses. The facade features a star-shaped abstract design on the domes. Inside, the three naves boast barrel and cross-vaulting, spindly capitals and a cupola resting on Byzantine plumes. The mellow stonework is often festooned with flowers: as Messina University chapel, it is much in demand for academic weddings.

The city churches are a wayward mixture of restoration and invention. However, Chiesa di Santa Maria degli Alemanni is an authentic roofless Gothic ruin, founded by the Order of Teutonic Knights. Behind it is the severe 17th-century Sant'Elia church, named after a patron saint who failed to save the city from the 1743 plague. Less subdued churches are San Giovanni di Malta, a hymn to Sicilian baroque; and San Tommaso, a fusion of Byzantine and Arab-Norman designs.

Messina's disastrous recent fortune gives it the right to raid its illustrious past. This magpie approach to architecture is illustrated by the neoclassical Town Hall, mock-Renaissance Chamber of Commerce, Fascistic Tribunal and Art Deco Prefecture. Contemporary churches can be Rhenish, Bavarian, Spanish or, like San Giuliano, a Byzantine pastiche. Even genuine relics are given a contemporary twist by an incongruous setting. Chiesa di San Francesco, a Gothic fortress of a church, overlooks a frothy ice cream parlour.

In Piazza Unità is Montorsoli's Fountain of Neptune; the original Renaissance sculpture lies in the **Museo**

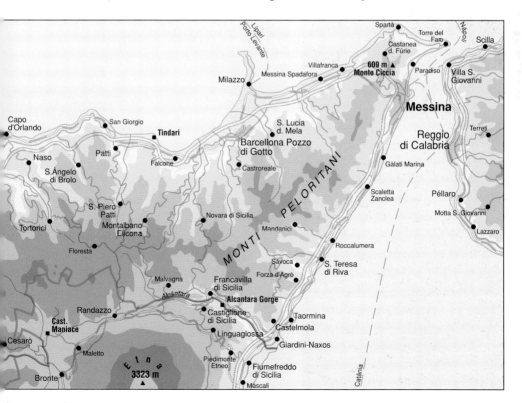

Regionale. This museum is noted for its works by two honorary citizens. Antonello da Messina is Sicily's master painter and southern Italy's greatest Renaissance artist. His moving St Gregory Polyptich blends Flemish technique with Italian delicacy and a Sicilian sense of light. The best-preserved panel is the *Virgin and Child*. Caravaggio, an equally influential figure, worked in Messina and his theatricality imbues Sicilian art. His familiar dramatic poses and doomy shadows are present in *The Adoration of the Shepherds* and *The Raising of Lazarus*.

Messina by night: Writer Rodolfo de Mattei likens the city to "a sailing ship, low in the water, ready for a night cruise". Mercantile Messina only looks romantic at night, its lights glittering along the harbour front. Summer strollers take a *passeggiata* from the seafront to the lively cafés on Piazza Cairoli. Seafood pasta is eaten in such restaurants as Alberto, whose chef was a favourite of Ernest Hemingway. After dinner, under-age lovers enjoy the scenic, wind-ing drive up Viale Umberto to the botanical gardens.

In summer, city life shifts to Mortelle, a small resort 6 miles (10 km) north of Messina. En route, the coastal road passes the Ganzirri lake, once famed for its mussel beds, and Torre del Faro, the tip of the toe of Italy. This peninsula was once graced by a Temple of Neptune whose columns ended up in Messina Cathedral. Today's view is of gigantic pylons and power cables that supply Sicily with electricity. Mortelle, just around the cape, offers sandy beaches, open-air films and pop concerts. However, for sophisticated international night-life, the Messinesi prefer Taormina. This stretch of coast is devoted to popular summer tourism and swordfishing. As a result, the air is heavy with a peculiar combination of petrol fumes and grilled fish.

Death of a swordfish: Weighing up to 660 lbs (300 kg), this huge fish is the local delicacy par excellence. Swordfish are traditionally pursued in tiny, black, fish-shaped boats with a har-

Left, tossing back a *spremuta* (fresh fruit juice). **Below,** *Annunciation* by Antonello da Messina, famous for his luminous Renaissance style.

poonist perched on the end. But given the profitability of swordfishing, fast fleets of feluccas are gaining ground. These 30-ton monsters are equipped with a look-out post and a platform on the prow for the harpoonist.

Once the prey is sighted, a blessing is shouted to St Mark ("*Viva San Marcu biniditu*") and the harpoon gun fired. If the victim is female, the grief-stricken male often thrashes around in sympathy and charges the boat. This final gesture of love leads to the capture of the male in what Sicilians see as "a sublime and mysterious synthesis of love and death". Fatalism, if not forgotten, is double-edged: it is the swordfish's fate to end up as juicy *spada alla messinese*.

The Tyrrhenian Coast: From Messina to Milazzo and the coast, follow the SS 113, the old Roman road, for the best scenery. The first stretch climbs the Monti Peloritani, winding past pine groves, broom, oleanders and geraniums. But even from the motorway are dazzling glimpses of azure inlets through the pines. On the way out of town are views of three ruined forts and apricot-coloured churches in the hills.

Just before the SS 113 passes under the motorway, take the rough road on the right to the Badiazza. This fortified Benedictine convent is set in an overgrown gully. Local lore has it that these 12th-century ruins were converted from a Byzantine granary. What is not in dispute is that the abbey was the meeting place of Eleanor of Anjou and her future husband, Frederick of Aragon.

The SS 113 allows panoramic views of pine forests and the Straits, particularly from Portella San Rizzo, the road leading along the crest of the Peloritani range to Monte Antennamare. The coastline from Messina to Palermo has been heavily fortified since Aragonese times. The headlands are still dotted with defensive towers built by the Spanish and exploited by the French. The Napoleonic forces boasted of being able to transmit a message to Naples in under two hours by lighting a string of fires in the coastal towers.

In the hinterland, halfway between

The ferries disgorge train carriages as well as passengers.

Villafranca and Milazzo, is **Roccavaldina**, a medieval hill village with an imposing baronial hall. A period pharmacy-cum-herbalist's shop is adorned with a collection of Renaissance majolica from Urbino. Amidst the gleaming woodwork lie painted pestles and mortars beside jugs decorated with cherubs and mermaids. Medicinal potions were stored in these exotic pots, bottles and jars until the 19th century.

From Messina, tunnels thread through pine and olive groves to **Milazzo**. The vision of this verdant peninsula is slightly marred by the presence of an oil refinery. Compensations lie in the welcoming breezes and dramatic castle, with views of the jagged green spit stretching towards the Aeolian Islands (Isole Eolie). This is the place to while away the time waiting for a ferry by sampling swordfish or bottarga (mullet roe).

Known as Mylae in Classical times, Milazzo is the legendary site of Ulysses' shipwreck. Traces of ancient civilisations include a Bronze Age settlement north of the castle and a Greek necropolis in Piazza Roma. From the Norman era onwards the citadel of Milazzo was regularly besieged; the victors could hold sway over the Tyrrhenean Sea.

The unprepossessing commercial centre lies at the foot of the castle, clustered around the isthmus, but the historic nucleus is the walled city. **Palazzi** with baroque balconies and elegant stonework embellish the lower town, particularly Via Umberto I. Here too, Duomo Nuovo, the new cathedral, is memorable for its Renaissance paintings in the apse. But the most satisfying churches are the 15th-century San Giacomo and Chiesa del Carmine, a 16th-century Carmelite convent.

Salita San Francesco, a steep stairway, climbs through the Spanish quarter to the medieval castle, its flanks encrusted with churches. The 17th-century San Salvatore belonged to a Benedictine abbey whereas San Rocco represents an older, fortified church. San Francesco di Paola is a frescoed 15th-century shell with a baroque facelift. The cluttered interior contains a Ma-

Torre del Faro, the tip of Messina province.

donna and Child by Gagini. Facing the castle is the Chiesa del Rosario, once a seat of the Spanish Inquisition. This Dominican church is studded with stucco, an oddly fluffy vision for the rigorous interrogators.

The **Castello**, perched beside a rocky precipice, occupies the site of the Greek acropolis. Originally Arab-Norman, the citadel later fell into Hohenstaufen, Aragonese and Spanish hands. The castle was even a British base during the Napoleonic Wars. But its finest hour was in July 1860 when its seizure by Garibaldi's forces spelt the rout of the Royalists and the Republican conquest of Sicily. Garibaldi himself led the hand-to-hand combat against the Bourbons.

The surviving fortress is of 13th-century Hohenstaufen dynatic design with Aragonese walls. A Gothic gateway leads to the keep and parliamentary Great Hall, a museum. Also within the castle walls, the Mannerist Duomo Vecchio, the ruined former cathedral, overlooks an open-air theatre. Despite atmospheric views of watchtowers and walls, the citadel's size and symmetry are best appreciated from the sea.

Boat trips to the **Baia del Tono** visit reefs, coves and grottoes, including favoured swimming spots such as the Baia San Antonio or Baia la Renella. Near the Baia del Tono is **Grotta di Polifemo**, Polyphemus' cave, where Ulysses blinded the Cyclops. The 4-mile (7-km) boat trip around the peninsula from Al Faro (the lighthouse) to Baia del Tono affords views of Sicily's two active volcanoes, Etna and Stromboli.

A stroll along the Al Faro promontory from the lighthouse to **Capo Milazzo** leads through lush vegetation to the cape. Just around the headland is San Antonio da Padova, a hermitage hewn out of the rock and inhabited by the saint in 1220. For the energetic, a climb to the heights of Monte Trinità is a chance for a lingering look over to the Aeolian Islands.

Santa Lucia del Mela, just inland from Milazzo, is a Saracen village with a Norman castle. It rose to prosperity in the 16th century as a trading post on the

Below, the bastion of Milazzo. Right, Santa Maria di Pollina.

Lombard silk route. The churches are well-endowed with works of art, thanks to the wealth generated by the local silver mine.

The **Norman cathedral**, revamped in 1607, contains a Gothic portal and 16th-century treasures including an Antonello Gagini statuette of St Lucy. The church attached to the castle seminary boasts a Gagini Madonna while the library has a collection of illuminated manuscripts. Garibaldi stayed in the monastery of San Francesco, and viewed the Milazzo plain where he fought his decisive battle against the Bourbons the following day, 20 July 1860.

The fertile coastal plain is rich in vineyards, olive plantations and orange groves, not to mention money-making spas. **Castroreale Terme**, facing the Aeolian archipelago, is a noted thermal resort. It claims cures for liver congestion, gastritis, constipation and genital diseases. Dubious treatments include "mud baths, hot-humid inhalations and tympanic insuflations", in conjunction with the drinking of sulphurous waters.

Inland-bound: After bland Castoreale Terme, the hinterland beckons. **San Biagio** has a Roman villa built in the first century. The baths feature a black and white mosaic depicting fishermen and dancing dolphins. Rough roads lead to a cluster of inland villages. **Longane**, near Rodi, on the edge of the Peloritani mountains, is a megalithic and Sikel settlement razed by Messina in 5th century BC. The remains of a turreted fort are visible and Bronze Age cavity tombs are found in the nearby necropolis.

Just east is **Castroreale**, a shabby upland village dominating the Micazzo valley. Founded by the Siculi in 8th century BC, the settlement flourished as a medieval barony but a ruined tower is all that remains of Frederick II's summer home. If trapped overnight in this medieval time-warp, male visitors may consider staying or dining with the lonely abbot at the crumbling Collegio dei Redentori, a depopulated monastery.

Many churches were damaged by the 1978 earthquake but retain their original treasures. Santa Maria degli Angeli contains a fine Nativity and Renaissance Madonna while Sant'Agata has a Gagini Annunciation. But the sculptor's masterpiece is the statue of St Catherine in Chiesa Matrice, a restored Renaissance church overlaid with a baroque veneer.

A return to the coast at **Oliveri** is a chance to exchange churches for seafood and excellent beaches. Between here and Cefalù is arguably the cleanest stretch of coastline on the island. Oliveri itself is a standard Sicilian resort with a Norman-Arab feudal castle and sandy beaches. On the seafront is a converted *tonnara*, the traditional tuna-processing plant, a reminder of life before tourism. Yet the tuna, aubergine and pasta dishes show that life post-tourism retains something of its original flavour.

Oliveri is on the **Golfo di Patti**, a wilder spot than the Gulf of Milazzo, stretching west to the rocky ridges of Capo Calavà. Its bays are framed by the moody Nebrodi mountains.

The coastal road crosses *fiumare*, wide, dry torrent-beds, and overlooks World War II pill-box defences.

Castoreale, Frederick II's summer retreat.

Tindari, christened Tyndaris, was one of the last Greek colonies established in Sicily. Set on a bold headland, the city was founded by Dionysius in 396 BC as an outpost against the Carthaginians. Tyndaris was peopled with Greeks fleeing from the Peloponnesian War and named after the colonists' native battle gods, the brothers of Helen of Troy. Pliny records that in 70 AD much of the city slipped into the sea. Despite subsidence and earthquake, the Greco-Roman city prospered until razed by the Arabs in 836 AD.

The **archaeological park**, overrun by goats, is pleasingly wild. Italian visitors are more impressed by the sacred Black Madonna housed in the church bordering the park. The Greek city covers a Bronze Age site and has left its mark in impressive boundary walls and assorted public buildings. The Greco-Roman theatre cannot compare with Taormina's but enjoys a superb natural setting overhanging the bay. The *decamanus* links the theatre to the vaulted basilica. This Augustan basilica was once a grand entrance to the *agora*, a ceremonial space for meetings and festivals. Nearby are the remains of Roman baths, villas, workshops and taverns. One villa is adorned with geometrical mosaics while the thermal baths enclose mosaics of dolphins, bulls, warriors and the *Trinacria*, the symbol of Sicily. The antiquarium displays sculptures, ceramics, a tragic mask and a bust of Augustus.

Santuario della Madonna Nera, built onto an old chapel, stands on the site of the acropolis. This glittering church is a contemporary effusion of kitsch beloved by Sicilians. It is revered all over Southern Italy as a shrine built to a black-faced Byzantine icon with miraculous powers. The **Madonna Nera** boasts a "black but beautiful" motto: *Nigra sum, sed hermosa*. Amongst other miracles, she is credited with providing a magic mattress to cushion a child's fall over the cliff. It is a mecca for wailing pilgrims, particularly on the Madonna's 8 September feast day.

Below Cape Tindari is the **Oliveri**

Chewing the cud near Mazzarò.

lagoon, one of Sicily's loveliest natural havens. A walk along the beach reveals lagoons swarming with fish and birdlife. Migratory birds, including grebes, coots and egrets, are drawn to the pale green saltwater pools and wide beaches of translucent grey pebbles. The lagoon's capricious sands are a sublime spot, yet also the place for a picnic of fresh bread and local *caciocavallo* cheese.

Patti is set on a low hill overlooking a cultivated plain. The **medieval quarter**, linking Via Ceraolo and the cathedral, has a quiet charm and several art-filled churches. San Nicolò and San Michele boasts works by Gagini while the 15th-century Sant' Antonio Abate contains Corinthian capitals supporting delicately rounded arches. The remodelled **Cattedrale di San Bartolomeo** is home to remarkable treasures: a subtle Madonna by Antonello da Saliba and the Renaissance sarcophagus of Queen Adelasia, the wife of Roger I, complete with the original Norman effigy. Traces of Norman rule also lie in the ruined tower, gateway and stretch of city walls.

Sadly, this historic hilltown is ringed by a jagged necklace of new development. Even so, Patti has recently unearthed its greatest attraction, a **Roman villa** at Marina di Patti.

Its fate is indeed curious. This sumptuous late-Imperial villa was destroyed by an earthquake in 4 AD but restored and then occupied until Byzantine times. After centuries of oblivion, it was rediscovered during the construction of the motorway in 1973.

The gracious rooms lead off a porticoed peristyle, looking incongruous beside the motorway flyover. The mosaics display geometric, animal, figurative and floral motifs, often of African inspiration. The stylised compositions and subtle chromatic range make for a satisfying whole. But like the finer villa in Piazza Armerina, Patti suffers from periodic waterlogging and wilful neglect. After a surfeit of art and architecture, picnic amongst the poppies, as did the Roman aristocracy, or retreat to the beaches of **Marina di Patti**.

From Patti to Capo d'Orlando are a

The sinuous Oliveri lagoon, seen from Tindari.

cluster of bland resorts fighting a battle against coastal ribbon development and the Mafia. From the sandy resort of **Gioiosa Marea**, one can walk up to the ghost town of Gioiosa Guardia, abandoned after an 18th-century landslide. **Brolo** has a crenellated Saracen tower, crumbling city walls and several grand palazzi. But food is the real incentive: fish soups and squid dishes, as well as strong-tasting salami from the hills behind Brolo.

From Brolo, a rural inland foray visits Raccuja, Tortorici and Castell'Umberto. Citrus groves give way to pine forests. This is the **Madonie** mountain range, parched in summer and dotted with ski resorts in winter. The hilltop villages enjoy views over to the Aeolian islands. **Tortorici**, best known for its Mafia activities, has several fine churches with school of Gagini sculptures.

In winter, one can continue south to the ski resort of **Floresta**. Galati Mamertino, a medieval village west of Tortorici, is a noted halt on the Gagini trail. Just north is **Castell'Umberto**, a former feudal domain with a long Dominican tradition. Constant landslides persuaded the citizens to abandon the historic centre for a new home. Nonetheless, the *centro storico* still has a whimsical, rustic charm, with its ruined castle and vine-hung churches.

Capo d'Orlando is a windswept headland subject to sudden storms. Set on the edge of a fertile plain, the town is geared to tourism and citrus farming. There is little of interest in this sprawling resort save a sandy beach strewn with whale-shaped boulders or a climb to the ruined medieval castle and church perched on the cape.

From here, an inland road leads to **San Marco d'Alunzio**, famed for its Temple of Hercules converted into a Christian church.

Mafia strongholds: Capo d'Orlando, Tortorici, Sant'Agata, Fratello: Messina's towns are a recitation of Mafia strongholds. Yet in 1992 the Mafia's stranglehold over this coast was seriously challenged. For the first time, local businesses resisted the clan's

Nature reserve in the Madonie.

extortion demands. Shopkeepers formed an anti-racket association to combat payment of the *pizzo* (protection money). Interior Minister Nicola Mancino used the occasion of the 1992 Ferragosto festival to visit Capo d'Orlando. As well as offering moral support, his visit was symbolic, a way of showing that the state exists in Sicily.

Sant' Agata di Militello, the next resort, boasts the Castle of Princes di Lanza di Scalea e Trabia and a folklore museum in Palazzo Gentile. Before travelling inland, try the *granite* (sorbets).

A drive to **San Fratello** and **Cesarò** is a chance to appreciate the rugged hinterland of the Nebrodi and Madonie ranges. San Fratello is one of the most characteristic villages, particularly colourful during its famous demonic festival, the Easter Feast of the Jews, a shrieking costumed chase through the village. It is not so much anti-semitic as Sicilian, hence a sacrifice of subtlety to spectacle. Founded by Roger I, this Lombard colony retains its distinctive Gallic dialect dating back to Norman

times. This scenic mountain village boasts a Norman church and a 15th-century Franciscan monastery.

The road continues through beech plantations to **Lago Biviere di Cesarò**, a swampy lake popular with wild fowl. The rounded silhouettes of the Nebrodi are all around. Also known as the Caronie mountains, this is remote, rugged hill-walking country.

A return to the coast at **Santo Stefano di Camastra** is an excuse to visit one of Sicily's best centres of pottery production. The rows of vivid street-side wares make purchase a mere formality. Just west of Santo Stefano is **Halaesa**, a Siculi settlement that flourished under the Greeks. Excavations are in progress Sicilian-style, bribery and political clout permitting. From Halaesa, leave Magna-Graecia for Mafia country or Messina's lush Ionian coast.

The enchanting N 117 road leads across the Nebrodi range to **Mistretta**, a rust-coloured town commanding a ridge. The stone town is noted for power rather than piety, despite its 22 churches. The Mistretta Mafia clan, led by Giovanni Tamburello, is adept at extortion. However, the jury at the 1992 trial failed to convict Tamburello, despite damning evidence by supergrass Antonino Calderone. With its ruined feudal castle, sculpted Chiesa Madre, red-tiled houses and cobbled streets, the town has a faded charm. Since it is not visibly wealthy, Mafia money must be stashed away elsewhere.

The Ionian Coast: From Messina, the motorway hugs the shore to Taormina. The exotic coastal vegetation, ravaged by rampant development, is wilder further south. On leaving Messina, consider visiting the neoclassical city cemetery on Via Catania. Set among luxuriant gardens, the Cimitero Monumentale is one of the grandest in Sicily. From the old coastal road south, tempting tracks explore the hinterland.

South of Messina is **Mili San Pietro**, a neglected hamlet with a derelict Byzantine monastery. Equally remote is **Itala**, boasting the multi-coloured Arab-Norman church of **San Pietro e Paolo**. Just south, hairpin bends lead to **Alì**, a

The rural pace of Tusa.

hamlet with an imposing Chiesa Madre overlooking wooded slopes.

Monti Peloritani: If travelling on the motorway, at **Santa Teresa di Riva** leave the coastal crowds for mountain air and curious hamlets. Despite the proximity of Taormina, this is timeless Sicily, as remote as anywhere on the island. The scenery is stark: skeletal peaks and brooding ravines; mountains gouged by winter torrents and scorched brown in summer. Such fierceness is softened by sweet-scented scrub and the curves of Moorish monasteries.

The battered mountain village of **Sávoca** is best-known for its macabre mummies, embalmed in a crypt by local monks. The monastery was in use until 1970 and awaits restoration by a Catholic mission. The catacombs of the **Convento Dei Cappuccini** contain 32 ghoulish mummified corpses dating from the 17th century. At a time when corpses were thrown into the communal ditch, genteel mummification was a tradition among noble families. The bodies were drained, sprinkled with salt and left to dry for a year before being washed in vinegar, aired and then dressed in their original clothes.

These gruesome, wizened faces and shrunken puppet-like forms are mummified abbots, lawyers, noblemen and priests. Others lie naked in caskets or as skulls crushed into high niches.

After this macabre scene, leave the monastery for the evocative medieval village. Sàvoca's name derives from *sambuca*, the elder trees that still perfume the hills. A paved path climbs cacti-dotted terraces and olive groves to the heart of the village. The roads were repaved with the proceeds of *The Godfather*, filmed on location here. Coppola found his perfect setting in the dusty piazza, the windswept church, shots of Etna smouldering in the distance, and the shimmer of the Ionian Sea below.

Equally atmospheric are the churches overgrown with prickly pear, the tumbledown dovecote, abandoned houses and the terraces slipping into the sea. The church of San Nicolò lost its choir in a landslide but kept its dignity. None-

Have book, will travel.

theless, this once prosperous Saracen stronghold has slid into decline.

Gothic **San Michele** has been clumsily restored but the **Chiesa Madre** retains all the charm that caught Coppola's eye. This solitary church, on a narrow ridge overlooking the sea, was renovated with film money. The Moorish portal, Aragonese doorway and capitals are delightful. All the eclectic churches contain panel paintings, flaking frescoes and gilded statues. (Collect keys to the churches at Casa del Parocco, the priest's house in Via San Rocco.)

The quarter beyond the medieval city gate seems abandoned. On the highest point is a *calvario*, a stumpy castle and the Archbishop of Messina's ruined summer palace. Sàvoca is still a cool summer retreat away from the city heat. The scruffy **Bar Vitelli**, immortalised in Michael Corleone's wedding banquet, comfortably hosts peasants and *borghesi*, united in their thirst for a cool *granita di limone* (lemon sorbet).

Casalvecchio Siculo, set above Sávoca, is a livelier but less complex village. The **Chiesa Madre** boasts a gilded interior full of chanting crones. Nearby are windswept views over terraces. Outside the village, take the first turning left, a steep road sign-posted to **SS Pietro e Paolo**, a monastic church down in the Val d'Agro.

SS Pietro e Paolo is the most significant Norman church in Eastern Sicily, despite its desolate location on the bank of the dry Agro river. The twin-domed exterior is reminiscent of a Turkish mosque. A banded facade combines red brick, black lava, cool limestone and grey granite. Blind arcading and mosque-like decor complete the picture.

A knock at the adjoining farmhouse rouses the farmer's wife to a tour, including memories of her wedding here.

A Greek inscription over the west portal names Gerard the Frank as the master builder, an imported craftsman who oversaw talented artisans. Restored in 1171, the church is a synthesis of Byzantine and Norman styles. Moorish roundness and decorative flourishes compete with Norman verticality and

Messing about in boats on the Ionian Coast.

austerity. Yet the interior is a happy marriage between stylish Arab stalactites and solid Norman squinches. It is, as the locals say, "a pure bastard" hence uniquely Sicilian.

For rugged scenery but few sites, drive back to the coast via Limina and Melia. Well-tended terraces are interspersed with ravines and paltry streams. Alternatively, break this journey to Taormina with an inland trip to **Forza d'Agro** and views of orange, lemon and olive groves.

A twisting road climbs to Forza d'Agro, with its cramped stone cottages and brooding Norman castle. In 1117 Count Roger presented the village to Basilian monks, an Orthodox order which still survives. Despite school of da Messina paintings in the churches, the scenery hogs the limelight: visions of Calabria and the Straits unfold. From here, rejoin the road to Taormina and 20th-century sophistication.

Before ascending to Taormina, consider visiting neighbouring **Naxos**, the first Greek colony in Sicily. It was founded on an ancient lava flow by Euboans in 735 BC and became a springboard for colonisation of Catania and the east coast. But after supporting Athens against Siracusa, the colony was destroyed by Dionysius in 403 BC. The archaeological site occupies the top of **Capo Schisò**. A stretch of Greek city walls remains but the elusive Temple of Aphrodite is still being excavated. The museum houses Greek, Roman and Byzantine exhibits, including the head of Silenus, god of fertility and wine.

The Greeks would bewail the great colony's degeneration into a down-market resort. Lemon groves are giving way to ribbon development, Naxos' fate as Sicily's fastest-growing resort. Still, for the young crowd there are compensations: wide beaches fringed by volcanic rocks and a riotous, brash nightlife Silenus might have sympathised with.

Legendary Taormina lies just above Giardini-Naxos. But if Messina province palls, see the Alcántara Gorge in Catania province or the dramatic Etna lava fields. Messina is indeed the "Gateway to Sicily".

Capo Sant' Alessio, close to Taormina.

AEOLIAN ISLANDS

Like Sicily's earliest history, that of its Aeolian islands is shrouded in mystery. Were they accidentally formed by the fire god when he angrily threw away bits of rock, or did the devil create these places of wind and fire as a punishment site for miscreants?

Homer, in his *Odyssey*, says the winds were created when Odysseus opened a parting gift from Aeolus, King of the Islands, too soon. The king, wishing to make his guest's journey to Ithaca a smooth one, graciously gave him a bag of wind, which was to remain sealed until the ships were well at sea. But the curious sailors opened it in sight of land, the winds escaped and immediately blew the boat back into the harbour. The furious king vowed that his winds would never again leave the islands.

Located off the north coast of Sicily, in the Tyrrhenian Sea, the Aeolian archipelago consists of seven inhabited islands: Lipari, Vulcano, Salina, Stromboli, Panarea, Filicudi and Alicudi, the result of volcanic activity millions of years ago. The surrounding waters are some of the cleanest and clearest in the Mediterranean and the weirdly-shaped underwater lava formations attract a rich variety of marine life.

The first recorded inhabitants arrived in the 4th century BC; they were probably traders from Asia Minor. It was the subsequent discovery of obsidian, a hard volcanic glass used as a cutting tool, that enabled Lipari's residents to prosper. With the advent of the metal ages, obsidian became obsolete, making a stop on Lipari no longer compulsory. Tourism is replacing pumice quarrying, agriculture (olives, grapes and capers), and fishing as the primary source of income.

Although the islands share a common volcanic heritage, each has its own distinct character and charm. Few sights can rival the vision of Stromboli or Alicudi rising from the morning mists, or the sensual feel of strolling along the oleander-bedecked paths of Panarea. Hermits can find solace in deserted countryside and, for the adventurous, there is at least one volcano on each island.

LIPARI: Two hours by ferry from Milazzo, the archipelago's main island hoves into view. Lipari is all hills and winding roads, craggy shorelines with a few black, sandy beaches. The four volcanic peaks spewed their last lava in 18 BC; but it was **Monte Pilato's** eruptions which gave the island its first economic base: the lava hardened into pumice and obsidian.

Dominating Lipari city is the **citadel**. Via Garibaldi, the town's shopping street, hugs its base and Via del Concordato leads upwards from it. The Spanish walls enclose the castle, cathedral and a superb archaeological museum.

The **archaeological park** contains the remains of Greek and Roman villas and offers a superb view of rugged hills and the sea beyond. The **Site of Diana**, containing the remains of Greek towers and fortifications, is in the lower town.

The fishing village of **Canneto** enjoys black, sandy beaches and views of craggy, emerald hills. For a closer look

at the obsidian fields, take the road signed **Forgia Vecchia** and **Pierra**.

Quattropani is an upland town; yellow broom and purple thistle line the road. **Pianoconte** has the largest vineyards on Lipari, but are not as extensive as those on Salina. From here, a gravel road leads down to **Terme di San Calogero,** the island's only thermal baths. Legend has it that the curative baths were discovered by San Cataldo, a follower of St Paul. At **Quattrocchi**, the **belvedere** is a place to rest and view Vulcano across the narrow channel.

VULCANO: Approaching the belching volcano which dominates the island brings to mind Hephestos, the god of fire and blacksmiths, and the myth that the volcano was his workshop.

The first sensation after landing is a sulphurous smell from **Acqua del Bagno** and **Acqua Bollente**. These are shallow pools of mud, and rubbing the greyish liquid over oneself or sitting submerged in the glob is considered beneficial.

On the northern end of the island is **Vulcanello,** the youngest of Vulcano's three volcanoes. Lava formed a bridge to Vulcano, creating the isthmus and the two ports. The climb to the top is easy, and inside the crater is a small cave where alum was once mined.

It is, however, the 952-ft (293-metre) high **Fossa di Vulcano** which demands attention. The volcano last erupted in 1890, but there is still volcanic activity in the form of greenish-yellow sulphuric gases rising from the crater. For the reasonably fit, climbing La Fossa should take less than two hours. Walking around the rim of the crater and peering into its eerie depth is infinitely exciting.

An excellent road connects the ports with inland towns and **Gelso,** located on the extreme southern tip. As the road climbs the side of a massif, La Fossa looms on the left, sitting in its own treeless bowl. There are few trees on the island, yet even in high summer broom covers the hillsides, creating bright patches among the brown rocks.

SALINA: It is the two volcanic peaks which gave the island its original name: *Didyme* (twin). Both cones are covered

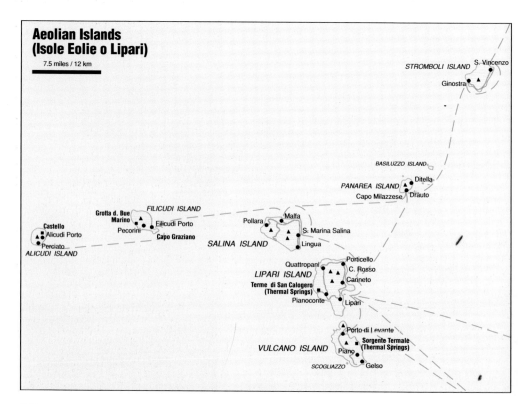

**Aeolian Islands
(Isole Eolie o Lipari)**

7.5 miles / 12 km

with verdant foliage, a result of the island's natural springs. Salina takes its modern name from the former salt pans near Lingua. Tourism is undeveloped and Salina gives the impression of being a working, rather than playing, island.

As one heads north from Santa Marina, the lighthouse at **Capo Faro** is the first landmark. This is a wealthy area which produces *malvasia* wine.

Malfa's **old port** is more interesting than the modern town – except as a place to buy *malvasia*; follow signs to *porto vecchio*. There is no concession to gentrification; the weather-beaten buildings and boat sheds remain a delight.

Pollara, situated at the extreme western end of the island, has a beach of black lava sand. **Rinella**, a seaport on the rugged southern coast, is reached via the **Valdichesa**, a rich valley of small farms and neat homes running between the two volcanoes. The 16th-century **Madonna del Terzito Convent** is also here; on 14 August, tourists can join the throng of pilgrims celebrating the Assumption.

STROMBOLI: "Stromboli is ever at work, and for ages past has been looked upon as the great lighthouse of the seas." Patrick Brydone's comments in his 1773 book, *A Tour Through Malta and Sicily*, are true today. The sight of crimson smoke and belching fire is stirring. It's easy to see how the island received its original name: *Strongyle* (spinning top). Residents are not bothered about being devoured by lava: it flows down a well-trodden path, the **Sciara del Fuoco** (fiery trail), to fall harmlessly into the sea.

The climb to the top of **Serra Vancura** (3,003 ft/924 metres) which overlooks the **crater** can end in disappointment for those expecting great showers of smoke and fire. Although the volcano erupts with regularity, all are not equal, and days of gentle belching and slight dribbling can be common. Participants sit at the crater's rim for an hour then bolt down the mountain in total darkness and a whirl of lava dust. Careful preparations for the trip are advisable.

An alternative might be to watch from the sea; boats anchor off the **Sciara**, and

Volcanic Stromboli.

the shower of sparks, no matter how small, still excites. If cruising past the Sciara during the day, notice the disparity between the delicate green of the island and the black scar created by centuries of molten lava.

PANAREA: The centre of its own miniature archipelago, ancient *Euonymos* (of good omen) is the smallest of the seven major islands. It is also the most fashionable: in summer, sleek yachts descend on the harbour. The boutiques stock designer fashions; restaurant *habitués* exude a "watch me" attitude.

As Panarea becomes the latest holiday magnet, a controversy rages. One faction would create a Mykonos double in white and turquoise; another favours pink buildings with white trim in order to complement the rampant oleander; the rest wish to leave things as they are. Whatever the result, Panarea will hopefully remain delightful and decadent.

The **prehistoric village** of Punta Milazzese is a collection of beehive huts located at Panarea's southern end. Beyond Ditella is **Calcara**, noted for its

fumaroles. In ancient times, they were thought to house evil spirits; Neolithic people, in order to appease them, dug great holes around the *fumaroles* then filled the pits with offerings. Today, the richly coloured stones, steam rising from them, give only visual delight.

Panarea is surrounded by uninhabited volcanic islets. **Basiluzzo** is the largest, a mass of stratified lava formed into weirdly shaped columns. At its landing stage, the remains of an old Roman dock lie just under the water.

FILICUDI: Shaped like a blowfish, the island is named after the ferns which once blanketed it. The "body" of the fish is topped by the high **Fosse delle Felci Vulcano,** while the "tail", connected to the larger part by a narrow strip of land, is topped by **Capo Graziano**. This is the oldest inhabited part of Filicudi, with ruins of a **Bronze Age village**.

Tourists usually come to enjoy the excellent snorkelling in the azure waters. There are several rocky beaches, the largest located between Porto and the Capo. Climbing enthusiasts have three peaks to conquer.

The best way to see the island is by boat. To the west is a collection of *faraglioni* (pillars formed by lava rock). Just beyond Peccorini, an archway marks the entrance to the **Grotta del Bue Marino**, named after Mediterranean monk seals; you can swim in the amazingly clear waters which change colours as the sun crosses the sky.

ALICUDI: Originally called *Ericusa* after its heather, this near-perfect circle is the western-most Aeolian. The island owes its shape to an extinct volcano, the **Filo dell'Arpa**. Prehistoric lava-stone tombs lie on Piano del Fucile, prompting speculation that Alicudi was used solely as a necropolis.

Sightseeing is limited; most visitors come looking for a peaceful and simple vacation. Energetic souls may want to climb the volcano, pausing in their ascent at the **Timpone delle Femmine**, a place where the island women sought sanctuary during pirate invasions. Easier diversions include the boat trip around the island, admiring the variety of lava pillars which thrust up from the sea bed.

Left, sampling a sulphur bath on Vulcano. Right, leaving luxurious Panarea. Overpage, Sicilian sunset.

INSIGHT GUIDES
Travel Tips

Insight Guides portray destinations in depth, providing the complete picture and the top photography

Insight Pocket Guides focus on the best choices for places to see and things to do and include large fold-out maps

Insight Compact Guides' portability makes them the perfect books to carry with you for on-the-spot reference

Three types of guide for all types of travel

INSIGHT GUIDES Different people need different kinds of information. Some want *background information* to help them prepare for the trip. Others seek *personal recommendations* from someone who knows the destination well. And others look for *compactly presented data* for on-the-spot reference. With three carefully designed series, Insight Guides offer readers the perfect choice. Insight Guides will turn your visit into an experience.

The world's largest collection of visual travel guides

CONTENTS

Getting Acquainted

Area: 25,700 sq. km (9,920 sq. miles).
Capital: Palermo
Highest point: Mount Etna (3,323 metres/10,906 ft)
Population: 4,990,000
Language: Italian
Religion: Catholic
Time zone: Central European Time (GMT plus one hour)
Currency: lira
Weights & measures: Metric
Electricity: 220 volts AC (50 cycles), two- or three-pin plugs
International dialling code: 39

Government

Sicily is an "autonomous region", Italy's first and still the one with the greatest degree of independence from central government. As such, it has its own parliament and many of its other institutions are separately organised.

The nine Sicilian *provincie* have considerable independence, electing their own councils, as do the *comuni*, the towns and villages. Town councils are regularly dissolved on the grounds of corruption. During the 1993 political purges, over 20 percent of local administrators were investigated for possible Mafia links.

Deputati (Deputies or Parliamentarians) in the Sicilian Regional Assembly are highly paid, and their large monthly salaries excludes a massive sum for support staff and travel expenses.

The politicians ensure political support by dubious means. In their wake come a legion of unnecessary postal workers, false invalids and incredibly young pensioners.

The influence of *clientelismo*, the granting of favours in return for support, is still common. A local politician can and does expect practical support from those he has helped, and such support readily becomes a pre-condition for help. The practice of *tangenti*, kickbacks for contracts, although not unique to Sicily, is widespread.

The Economy

Sicily suffers from its distance from the main European markets. The difficulty of communications is compounded by poor rail and postal services. On paper, Sicily falls well below EU averages for income and productivity, and is more dependent on its traditional agricultural skills than the rest of Italy. But its poverty should not be exaggerated. The black economy ensures that cities such as Catania and Palermo come near the bottom in national league tables of productivity but score highly on consumer spending.

In the main inland areas of the *latifundia* durum wheat (used for pasta) is the main crop. In the more fertile and lower lying areas, such as the Conca d'Oro, the slopes of Etna, around Catania, and in the low-lying western part of Trapani province, intensive farming produces fruit, olives and wine. On the coast south of Ragusa around Comiso vast greenhouses stretch for miles.

Italy's largest fishing fleet sails out of Mazara del Vallo, heading for international waters. Inshore fishing has declined in importance, although it still provides fresh fish to restaurants. Tuna (*tonno*) are still fished in the traditional manner in Trapani province, as are swordfish (*pesce spada*) off Messina. Processing and packaging of agricultural produce is Sicily's healthiest, if small scale, industry.

Some areas (Augusta, Gela, Termini Imerese and much of Catania) have large industrial complexes which provide work and inject cash into local economies. They have also injected pollution into the nearby coastal waters, and sometimes into the drinking water.

Climate

Sicily is deservedly renowned for its sunshine. The hottest months are July and August, when high temperatures are intensified by lack of rain and the cities empty as people head for the beaches.

Along the coasts winters are short and generally mild. The Etna ski resorts are usually open December to March. From February onwards the coastal areas bloom with spring flowers, the almond blossom is out, and Sicily defies its parched image by turning spectacularly green. Temperatures remain comfortable into May or June, but the landscape begins to turn browner as the winter rains lessen.

Average Temperatures

	Dec–March	April	May	June
°C	12–15	18	21	24
°F	50–58	64	70	76

	July	Aug	Sept	Oct	Nov
°C	28	28	24	22	18
°F	85	85	76	72	64

Much of this industry is dependent on government subsidies and, far from the main markets in the north, this is unlikely to change.

Tourism has become essential to the island's economy, fuelling much of the construction and service sectors and bringing with it a typical pattern of seasonal work.

Unemployment, under-employment, and continuing emigration are significant. Emigration from the country to the cities continues, fuelling Palermo's and Catania's population growth, building boom and social problems.

Difficult to measure, but undoubtedly important, is the black economy: not only the drug trade with its associated money laundering, but submerged money-generating activity in apparently legitimate businesses.

The island suffers from the entrenched privileges of the political system, and the criminal under-ground that supports and is supported by it.

Planning the Trip

What to Bring

Sicilian summers (May to October) are hot and you will need light clothing. Remember, however, that many churches and cathedrals will not allow bare legs (i.e. no short skirts or shorts) or bare shoulders. In spring (April to May) and autumn (October to November) come armed with light clothes, including a summer jacket or sweater for the evenings. Between December and March, it is advisable to bring some warmer clothes since the winters, particularly in the mountainous central areas of Sicily can be very cold. Hotels and houses tend to be less well heated than is usual in northern climates: indoors is sometimes chillier than out! Mount Etna is often (spectacularly) snow-covered in winter, and its lava-based rock requires strong footwear at any time of year. (*See Mount Etna* in *Excursions, page 358*).

Casual wear is accepted in all but the grandest hotels and restaurants, but most Sicilians will dress smartly when dining out. Visitors will feel more comfortable (and may be treated better) if dressed elegantly for chic clubs, hotels and city *ristoranti*.

Photography

Sicilian summer light is extremely bright. You will need to allow for this, both in choosing film and in setting the camera. Film and most photographic equipment is expensive in Italy. Buy film before you travel.

For reasons of safety, do not leave cameras or photographic equipment visible in a car.

Flash and camera stands are generally not allowed in museums. In churches, exercise discretion about photography, in particular about using flash.

Entry Regulations

Visas & Passports

For visits up to three months, no visas are required by visitors from EU countries, the US, Canada, Australia or New Zealand. A valid passport (or in the case of those from EU member countries, a valid identification card) is sufficient. Nationals of most other countries require a visa. This must be obtained in advance from an Italian Embassy or Consulate. For a list of Consulates in Sicily and Embassies in Rome, *see Practical Tips, page 321*.

Customs

Used personal effects may be imported and exported without formality.

The import of narcotics, weapons and pirated materials is forbidden (except to members of Cosa Nostra, of course!). Certain items (e.g. alcoholic drinks, tobacco, perfume) are limited as to the amount one may take in or out, and these amounts vary for those coming from the EU, other European countries or outside Europe. This can seem confusing, particularly since the amounts also vary depending on whether the goods were bought duty paid (i.e. in Italy) or duty-free (i.e. at the airport or on a plane or boat).

For EU citizens: Provided goods obtained in the EU are for your personal use there is no further tax to be paid. EU law sets out recommended guide levels and if you bring in more than these amounts you must be able to show that the goods are for your personal use. The guide levels are: Cigarettes – 800, cigarillos – 400, cigars – 200, smoking tobacco – 1kg, spirits – 10 litres, intermediate products (such as port and sherry) – 20 litres, wine – 90 litres (of which not more than 60 litres sparkling), beer – 110 litres.

For US citizens: The duty-free allowances remain: 200 cigarettes, 50 cigars, or 3 lbs of tobacco; 1 US quart of alcoholic beverages and duty-free gifts worth up to $100.

If planning to import or export large quantities of goods, or goods of exceptionally high value, contact the Italian Consulate and your own customs authorities beforehand to check on any special regulations which may apply.

The customs authorities are quite active in Sicily, partly to combat smuggling from North Africa, and partly because of the level of Mafia activity and the associated movements of goods and money. This is, however, very unlikely to affect the ordinary tourist.

For more information on UK import regulations, contact HM Customs and Excise, tel: 0171-202 4227, or your local Customs and Excise office.

Note that different regulations apply to all types of commercial import and export. For further information, contact the Italian Consulate in your own country or your own customs authorities.

Animal Quarantine

It is not advisable to take animals to Italy from the UK because of the six months quarantine required by the British authorities on your return. However, if you do decide to take a pet you need to have a vaccination certificate for rabies and an officially stamped document stating that the pet is healthy. This must be obtained no more than one month before you travel. For further information, contact the Italian Consulate in your country.

Health

EU residents are entitled to the same medical treatment as Italians. Visitors will need a form E111 before they go. This covers medical treatment and medicines, although you will have to pay a prescription charge and a percentage of the costs for medicines. Note that the E111 does not give any cover for trip cancellations, nor does it provide for repatriation in case of illness. If you wish to provide for this, you will need to buy private insurance.

If you are not covered by a reciprocal scheme, you should ensure that you have adequate private health cover for your trip.

The **International Association for Medical Assistance to Travellers** (IAMAT) publishes for its members a directory of English-speaking doctors abroad. IAMAT offices: **Canada**: 1267 St Claire Ave, W. Toronto, M6E 1B8. **New Zealand**: PO Box 5049, Christchurch 5. **US**: 417 Center Street, Lewiston, NY 14092.

If you are taking medicines on prescription, ensure that you have adequate supplies to cover the period of your trip. You should also take details of the prescription in case the medicines are lost.

If you need medical treatment whilst in Sicily, take form E111 to the **Unità Sanitaria Locale** (local health office), who will direct you to a doctor covered by the state system and supply you with the necessary paperwork.

In an emergency, you can go direct to a hospital or doctor, but you may have to pay for treatment. If so, ensure that you have receipts: you can claim reimbursement in the UK. The same applies if you have private insurance. In many areas in summer, there is a **Guardia Medica Turistica** (tourist emergency medical service) which functions 24 hours a day. Telephone numbers are available from hotels, chemists, tourist offices and local papers. The Guardia Medica or **Pronto Soccorso** (first aid) for the area are able to help in an emergency.

Lists of duty pharmacists are published in the daily papers (*Giornale di Sicilia* for Palermo and the west or *La Sicilia* for Catania and the east).

The general emergency phone number is **113**.

Water Supply

Tap water is safe to drink in most places. Italians generally prefer to drink mineral water, however, and this will usually be offered in restaurants. In some places the water supply becomes erratic or "part-time" in summer. In a few places, particularly in the south of the island, the ground water has become polluted by industrial effluents, and the water from village pumps may not be good to drink. If in doubt, ask the locals. Water supplies marked *Non potabile* should not be used for drinking or cooking.

Mosquitoes

There are a lot of mosquitoes in Sicily, as you will quickly discover if you leave your light on and the window open for any length of time. Green, slow-burning mosquito repellent rings can be bought cheaply and are effective, as are the small electrical devices which plug into a standard socket. Take and use mosquito repellent.

Public Holidays

Banks and most shops are closed on the following public holidays:
New Year's Day (Capodanno)
1 January
Epiphany (*Befana*)
6 January
Easter Monday (*Lunedí di Pasqua*)
Variable
Liberation Day
25 April
May Day (*Festa del Lavoro*)
1 May
August holiday (*Ferragosto*)
15 August
All Saints (*Ognissanti*)
1 November
Immaculate Conception
8 December
Christmas Day (*Natale*)
25 December
Boxing Day (*Santo Stefano*)
26 December

Banks may close early the day before a public holiday. If a holiday falls on a Tuesday or a Thursday,

many offices may also close on the preceding Monday or the following Friday. This is known as a *ponte*, bridging the gap.

In addition, most towns and villages have at least one holiday of their own (*feste del Santo Patrono*) during the year.

Getting There

By Air

Sicily has two main airports, at Palermo (Punta Raisi) and Catania (Fontanarossa). There is also a small airport at Trapani. Messina uses the Reggio di Calabria airport on the mainland across the Straits. Lampedusa and Pantelleria, two of the smaller islands, may also be reached by air from Palermo or Trapani.

Alitalia (*see Practical Tips, page 320*) is the main agent for flights to Sicily. The journey by scheduled flight from Heathrow, Ireland or Canada is usually via Milan, Rome or Naples. There are no direct flights from the Republic of Ireland to Sicily. There are direct flights to Palermo from New York. For more information contact: Alitalia, the national airlines or travel agencies.

There are direct charter flights from several UK airports (Gatwick–Catania, Luton–Palermo) to Sicily. Information may be obtained from the **Magic of Italy**, 227 Shepherds Bush Road, London W6 7AS, tel: 0181-748 7575, or any travel agency.

For information on buses from Palermo and Catania airports to the city, *see Getting Around, page 323*. For Sicily airport and other airline information, *see Practical Tips, page 320*.

By Car

Travelling to Sicily by car from the UK or Ireland is not cheap. Costs include petrol, motorway tolls, hotels en route and the ferry crossing to the island. If you wish to have the use of a car in Sicily, consider Fly-Drive options (flying and hiring a car). *See Getting Around, page 326* for information on car hire and driving in Sicily.

If you do decide to travel by car, you will require a current driving licence (with an Italian translation unless it is the standard EU licence) and valid insurance (green card). Additional insurance cover, which can include a get-you-home service, is offered by a number of organisations including the British and American Automobile Associations.

Insurance in the UK: Europ-Assistance, Sussex House, Perrymount Road, Haywards Heath, West Sussex RH16 1DN, tel: 01444 442442.

Insurance in the US: Europ-Assistance Worldwide Services Inc., 1133 15th Street, Suite 400, Washington DC 20005, tel: 202-331 1609. You must carry your driving licence, car registration and insurance documents with you.

The total journey from London to Palermo is around 2,650 km (1,660 miles). London to Milan is around 1,150 km (720 miles). From Milan to Villa San Giovanni is 1,300 km (810 miles) and Messina to Palermo is 200 km (130 miles). It is advisable to take several days for the journey. This allows you to visit places en route as well as making the entire trip more pleasant.

The usual route through France is via the Mont Blanc tunnel.

From the north of Italy, take the Autostrada del Sole (A1), a motorway which starts in Milan, down to Villa San Giovanni. From there, ferries run approximately every 20 minutes across the Straits of Messina. The crossing takes about 30 minutes, but in the high season there may be long queues. It is not possible to book. There are also ferries from Reggio di Calabria to Messina, but these are much less frequent.

Fuel is expensive in Italy, so it's advisable to fill up in France. The A1 is a toll motorway from Milan to Salerno (south of Naples). Pay either cash or with magnetic cards (Viacard) bought from ACI offices at the border or at motorway services. Large cars, campers, caravans and boats cost extra. The last stretch from Salerno is free.

In the past, the Italian government provided tourists with special coupons allowing reductions on both petrol and motorway tolls. These have now been discontinued.

By Rail

The train journey from London takes approximately 42 hours, changing at either Milan, Turin or Rome. There is no direct service to Sicily but there is normally one direct service from Calais to Milan and Rome a day, or you may travel via Paris, from where there are frequent services. The cost is about the same as flying.

Train timetables change twice a year, so for up-to-date information, contact Rail Europe at Victoria Station, London SW1, tel: 0990-848848, or the Italian tourist offices. In Italy, stations and travel agents have details of train times and can make reservations. There are also detailed timetables published commercially and available for a small fee, from newsstands.

For those under 26, youth rail cards (Interail and Eurail) give use of the European rail system for a month, and may work out cheaper than the standard tickets. In Italy, there are also a number of special deals available: the *chilometrico*, which allows one or more persons to travel 3,000 kilometres (1,864 miles). Enquire at stations or travel agents for details of current offers.

The advantages of travelling by train are the chance to see some of Europe's most beautiful landscapes and to make stops along the way. It is also a very sociable way to travel.

There is a daily *rapido* service between Rome and Palermo, Catania and Siracusa.

The crossing from Villa San Giovanni to Messina is an experience in itself: the train carriages are literally (and time-consumingly) shunted into the ferry, and then shunted off again at Messina. If arriving on overnight trains, your first view of Sicily from the ship's deck may be of early morning sunlight on the sea and the mountains.

By Sea

If you wish to avoid the long drive or train ride through Italy, you may take advantage of the following ferries:

Genoa–Palermo: Grandi Traghetti (20 hours)
Genoa–Palermo: Tirrenia (20 hours)
Livorno–Palermo: Grandi Traghetti (19 hours)
Naples–Palermo: Tirrenia (11 hours)

There is also a ferry run by Siremar from Naples via the Aeolian islands to Milazzo. This is a good route for anyone arriving by train and heading for the Aeolian islands themselves.

Ferries may most easily be booked through your local travel agent but booking is also possible direct through the Italian offices. For addresses in Sicily, *see Getting Around, page 324*. The following are the addresses in mainland Italy.

In Genoa:
Grandi Traghetti, Via Fieschi 17, tel: 010-589331.
Grandi Navi Veloci, tel: 010-589331.

In Naples:
Tirrenia Staz. Marittima, Molo Angionio, tel: 081-720 1111.
Linee Lauro, tel: 081-551 3352/091-611 1616.

Cabins are available on all of the services, but in the high season they must be booked early.

Travelling this way can work out to be expensive but there is a considerable saving on petrol, motorway tolls and an overnight stop. Grandi Traghetti is privately owned, and tends to raise its prices in the high season. Tirrenia gets booked up early.

Arriving by boat in Palermo is certainly more relaxing than the trip down the length of Italy's boot. You also have the satisfaction of following in the footsteps of travellers in previous centuries. Arriving by boat from Naples on 2 April 1787, Goethe memorably described his first views from the deck of the ship: the city backlit, Monte Pellegrino rising above it and the Conca d'Oro, green with spring in the afternoon sun.

By Coach

This is not an easy way to reach Sicily from Northern Europe as there are no direct coach services. If you are already in Italy however, there are express coach services from Rome to Messina, Catania and Siracusa, with connections from Catania to Palermo. For information, enquire at travel agents in Italy.

Useful Addresses

Tourist Information Abroad
Canada: Office National Italien de Tourisme, 1 Place Ville Marie – Suite 1914, Montreal, Quebec. H3B 2C3, tel: 514-866 7667/8.
UK: Italian State Tourist Board, 1 Princes Street, London W1R 8AY, tel: 0171-408 1254.
Also helpful: The Italian Institute, 39 Belgrave Square, London SW1 8NX, tel: 0171-235 1461.
US: Italian Government Tourist Office, 630 5th Avenue – Suite 1565, New York, NY 10111, tel: 212-245 4822/3/4.

Package Holidays

From the UK, Ireland or the USA, a package holiday is usually the easiest and most economical way to visit Sicily. It can be an advantage to travel with a company that has good local representation on the island. Most package holidays visit Taormina or Cefalù, the chicest resorts, but some travel companies are more adventurous and cast their net further afield. Current brochures should be available from your travel agent.

Travel Agencies

The following are among several UK companies which specialise in travel to Sicily.

The **Magic of Italy** at 227 Shepherd's Bush Road, London W6 7AS, tel: 0181-748 7575 can arrange Fly-Drive and individual tailored holidays in addition to their standard packages, which offer a good choice of accommodation and resort and the presence of an English-speaking courier or tour representative.

Many of the large British package holiday companies (CIT, Thomsons, Cadogan, Rambler's Holidays, Saga) run holidays to Sicily. Two-centre holidays are increasingly popular, with a chance to stay in a major city, followed by a week at a coastal resort.

Italian Expressions, 104 Belsize Lane, London NW3 5BB, tel: 0171-435 2525, offers various packages including multi-centre and fly-drive holidays, to Sicily alone, or in combination with destinations in mainland Italy and France.

Page & Moy, 136–140 London Road, Leicester LE2 1EN, tel: 0116-250 7000, arranges package tours in spring and autumn, and also two-centre holidays in Taormina and Cefalù, and tours of the island.

Practical Tips

Business Hours

Shops are generally open 9am–1pm and 4–7.30pm. Except in tourist resorts, shops are closed on Sundays. Food shops and petrol stations are also closed on Wednesday afternoons. In cities other shops are closed on Monday mornings.

Bars and restaurants are legally obliged to close one day a week: a notice indicates which day.

Office hours are normally 7.30am–12.30pm and 3.30–6.30pm. Public offices are frequently open to the public only in the mornings.

Banks

Banks are open Monday–Friday 8.30am–1.30pm. Some are also open in the afternoon 2.30–4pm or 3–4.30pm. You will need to have your passport or identification card with you when changing money. Remember that this can be a slow operation. Allow plenty of time and ideally visit in the morning.

You may sometimes be asked to leave handbags, cameras and metal objects such as keys in a secure locker at the entrance. This is intended to prevent robberies: for a tourist laden with luggage it can be inconvenient since the lockers are usually small. Not all banks will provide cash against a credit card, and a few of the smaller local banks may refuse to cash traveller's cheques in certain currencies. Generally speaking, the larger banks (those with a national or international network) will best handle tourist transactions.

Media

British and other American and Northern European papers can be found in cities and in tourist resorts, generally one day after publication. The *International Herald Tribune* is also quite widely available. In less-touristy areas, you may have difficulty finding non-Italian papers.

The main Italian papers (*Corriere della Sera, La Repubblica*) publish southern editions, but the local dailies have a higher circulation in Sicily. They carry far more local information; particularly useful for the visitor are the sections covering current boat, train, air and bus timetables, together with daily information on duty chemists, petrol stations etc. This is presented in a clear fashion so visitors with a smattering of Italian should understand it.

All the Sicilian papers provide details of musical and theatrical events.

Newspapers

Il Giornale di Sicilia, Palermo's morning paper, covers the western part of the island and provides a supplement for each of the western provinces. It offers the most complete practical listings (timetables, etc.).

La Sicilia, Catania's main paper, also has provincial supplements for Siracusa, Ragusa and Enna. Identified with right-of-centre politics, *La Sicilia* occasionally contains some interesting reporting, but is as unlikely to rock boats as *Il Giornale*.

La Gazzetta del Sud is not strictly a Sicilian paper: it is based in Messina and Reggio di Calabria. It is the highest circulation daily in Messina province and is somewhat less parochial than the purely island papers.

Magazines

The following are Sicilian publications that may be of interest to visitors.

Sicilia Magazine – a glossy, highly illustrated magazine written in Italian and English. It includes articles on art, culture and personalities. It is published in Catania four times a year.

Sicilia Illustrata – this glossy monthly covers Sicilian current affairs, politics and culture.

Kalos – this is a highly illustrated bi-monthly on art and history.

Sikelia – this is an academically-orientated journal on Sicilian art, history and culture. It appears in black and white, and is published bi-monthly.

Sicilia Tempo – an economic and political monthly.

Radio & Television

There are dozens of private stations, most of them awful. The commercial radio stations provide a mix of pop and phone-ins. The national radio stations (RAI) include news, current affairs and documentary-type programmes, and also, particularly on RAI 3, some classical music.

Reception of the BBC World Service is only possible in the short wave band and not usually good in Southern Italy.

There are some local news programmes on the national television channels. Occasionally a local travelogue or documentary makes it onto the local television stations. On the whole, however, the local television ranges from bad to appalling.

If you have children, be aware that Italian private television sometimes shows pornographic films of a type that would be encoded or banned elsewhere.

Postal Services

Post Offices are generally open Monday–Friday 8.30am–1.30pm. In Palermo, the main post office in Via Roma (near Piazza Domenico) is open 24 hours (full service from 8am–8pm).

Stamps (*francobolli*) are available from *tabacchi* (tobacconists).

The postal service is not renowned for its speed. If you need to send an urgent letter, send it *espresso* (express). In a real emergency, send a telegram. This may be done from a post office, telecom office, or by dialling 186 from a private phone. It is possible to have mail sent *poste restante* to main post offices. Letters should be marked *fermo posta*.

Tipping

It is the norm to tip various people for their services. The following are general guidelines. In hotels, provided good service has been given, leave about 10,000 lire a week in your room for the maids, and give about the same to the head waiter for the dining room staff. These tips are usually divided among the staff concerned. In restaurants, service is included unless the menu indicates otherwise.

Taxi drivers will expect around 10 percent of the fare, although 5 percent is acceptable on very short trips. Tips to local guides depend on their ability and the length of the trip: between 2,000 and 5,000 lire per person is normal. The driver will expect a similar tip. In many small towns and villages, churches and other monuments may appear to be permanently closed for lunch: there is usually a custodian (or elderly "helper") somewhere nearby who will be pleased to open the door. A tip of around 2,000 lire per person and many *grazie* are then appropriate.

Telephones

Public telephone boxes take 100, 200 and 500 lire coins. There are also card phones. Cards may be bought at bars, newspaper kiosks and post offices. It is not uncommon to find telephone boxes out of order, particularly in the large cities. More reliable are the public telephones available in many bars and some other commercial premises.

Telephone directories are available at main offices of Telecom in cities and at Palermo and

Catania airports. You can also make phone calls here. The call is metered and you pay when you have completed the call.

If making phone calls from a hotel, you will usually pay an additional charge which can be high. Cheaper rates apply to calls made between 6.30pm and 8am on weekdays, on Saturday after 1pm and all day Sunday.

Call **12** for directory assistance for all of Italy (L1000).

To make international calls, dial 00, then the appropriate country code (*see below*) followed by the number (omitting any initial 0).

International dialling codes:

Australia: 61
Canada and US: 1
Ireland: 353
UK: 44

Telephone offices in Palermo and Catania:

In Palermo:
Piazza Giulio Cesare: 24 hours.
Piazzale Ungheria 22:
8am–9.30pm.
Via P. Belmonte 92: 8am–8pm.
At the port: 8am–8pm.
At the airport: 8am–10pm.
In Catania:
Via A. Longo: 24 hours.
Piazza Giovanni XXIII: 8am–8pm.
At the airport: 8am–8pm.

Airlines

Palermo

Alitalia. To buy tickets, use a travel agency. For information on national and international flights, tel: 1478-65643 toll-free, or from a portable telephone, tel: 06-65643.
KLM, Via Amm. Gravina, 80, tel: 091-331207.

Catania

To buy tickets or for information on **Air France**, go to Corso Martiri della Libertà 184–186, tel: 095-532210. Open: Monday to Friday 9am–12.30pm and 4–8pm, Saturday 9am–12.30pm. Also at Fontanarossa airport, tel: 095-345921.

For tickets and information on **British Airways, Lufthansa, Air Malta, Meridiana, Alitalia,**

Swissair, KLM, Air France and **A. Eagles** try a travel agency or go to Catania airport *Biglietteria*, tel: 095-345367. Open: 24 hours.
Qantas/TWA, Corso Martiri della Libertà, 38, tel: 095-535054/534961. This is a private tour operator. Open: Monday to Friday 8.30am–1pm and 3.30–7pm, Saturday 8.30am–noon.

Airports

Punta Raisi, Palermo Airport, tel: 091-591698. This is the Tourist Information office. Open: Daily 8am–midnight.
Flight information: internal flights, 091-6019111; international flights, 091-591275-95
Fontanarossa, Catania Airport, tel: 095-311711.
Messina (Reggio di Calabria airport on the mainland: connection via hydrofoil from Messina), tel: 0965-320287.

Tourist Information

Most Sicilian tourist offices have some staff who speak English, French or German. Availability of these staff varies however, as does their ability.

Many have a wealth of information on their province, including detailed brochures, maps and books. Again, however, there is considerable variation in their enthusiasm for sharing this. The best are excellent; the worst appear to see their function as preventing disturbances to the daily newspaper reading and coffee drinking.

If writing for information, be prepared for a long wait: the postal service is not speedy.

The provincial tourist offices are theoretically now all called AAPITs (*Azienda Autonoma Provinciale per l'Incremento Turistico*), but they still occasionally hide under their old title of EPT or are abbreviated to APT. The local offices are usually called *Azienda Autonoma per il Turismo*. In small places they are sometimes called Pro Loco, and may have rather restricted opening hours.

AGRIGENTO PROVINCE

Agrigento

Azienda Autonoma per il Turismo, Via Empedocle, 73, tel: 0922-20391. Open: Monday to Saturday 8am–2pm.
AAPIT, Viale della Vittoria 255, tel: 0922-4013524. Open: Monday, Wednesday, Thursday and Saturday 8am–2pm; Tuesday and Friday 8am–2pm and 3.30–7.30pm.

Sciacca

Corso V. Emanuele, 84, tel: 0925-21182. Open: Monday to Saturday 8am–2pm and 4–6pm.

Caltanissetta

AAPIT, Corso Vittorio Emanuele 109, tel: 0934-530411. Open: Monday, Wednesday, Friday and Saturday 8am–2pm and 4–7pm; Tuesday and Thursday 8am–2pm.
Information office, Viale Conte Testasecca, tel: 0934-21089. Open: Monday to Saturday 8am–noon.

CATANIA PROVINCE

AAPIT, Via Cimarosa 10, tel: 095-7306211.
There are also information offices located at the airport and in the railway station.

ENNA PROVINCE

Enna

Azienda Autonoma per il Turismo, Piazza N. Colaianni, 6, tel: 0935-500875. Open: Monday to Saturday 8am–2pm.
AAST, Via Roma 411, tel: 0935-528288. Open: Monday, Tuesday, Thursday and Saturday 9am–1pm and 4–7pm; Wednesday and Friday 9am–1pm and 3.30–6.30pm.

Piazza Armerina

AAST, Via Cavour, 15, tel: 0935-680201. Open: Monday to Saturday 8am–2pm.

MESSINA PROVINCE

Messina

AAPIT, Via Calabria 301, tel: 090-640221. Open: Monday to Saturday 9am–noon.

Taormina
Palazzo Corvaja, Piazza S. Caterina, tel: 0942-23243. Open: Monday to Saturday 8am–2pm and 4–7pm; Sunday 9am–1pm.

Giardini Naxos
Via Tysandros 54, tel: 0942-51010. Open: Monday to Saturday 8am–2pm and 4–7pm.

AEOLIAN ISLANDS
Lipari
Azienda Autonoma di Turismo, Corso Vittorio Emanuele, 202, tel: 090-988 0095. Open: Monday to Friday 8am–2pm and 4.30–7.30pm; Saturday 8am–2pm. July and August: Monday to Saturday 8am–2pm and 4–10.30pm.

Vulcano
Porto di Ponente. Summer only, tel: 090-9852028. Open only June to October.

PALERMO PROVINCE
Palermo
The regional tourist office covers the whole of Sicily although it is not open to the general public. The address is Via Emanuele Notarbartolo 9/b, tel: 091-696 8201.

Palermo Province and city are covered by the **AAPIT**, Piazza Castelnuovo 34, tel: 091-583847. Open: Monday to Friday 8am–8pm; Saturday 8am–2pm. There are also information offices at the airport (tel: 091-616 591698) and the station (tel: 091-616 5914).

The local tourist office for Palermo itself is illogically situated a 40 minute walk outside the city centre:
Azienda Autonoma di Turismo, Palermo e Monreale, Villa Igiea, Salita Belmonte 43, tel: 091-540122. Open: Monday, Tuesday, Wednesday and Friday 8am–2pm; Thursday 8am–2pm and 3–6.30pm.

Cefalù
Azienda Autonoma di Turismo, Corso Ruggero 77, tel: 0921-421050. Well-informed, plenty of documentation, helpful. Staff speak either English or French. Open:

Monday to Friday 8am–2pm and 4–7pm; Saturday 8am–2pm.

Ustica
c/o Ass. Turistica Pro Loco, Piazza V. Longo, tel: 091-844 9190.

RAGUSA PROVINCE
AAPIT, Via Capitano Bocchieri 33, Ragusa, tel: 0932-621421 (near the archaeological museum). Well-informed and helpful staff, most leaflets available only in Italian. Open: Monday to Saturday 8am–2pm.

SIRACUSA PROVINCE
AAPIT, Via San Sebastiano 43, Siracusa, tel: 0931-481232. Open: Monday to Saturday 8am–2pm.
Azienda Autonoma per il Turismo, Via Maestranza 33, Siracusa, tel: 0931-65201. Helpful and friendly staff and a wealth of information available. The town office is in Ortygia, and the provincial one is near the archaeological museum. Not all staff speak English. Open: Monday, Wednesday, Thursday and Saturday 8.30am–2pm; Tuesday and Friday 8.30am–2pm and 4–7pm.

TRAPANI PROVINCE
Trapani
AAPIT, Via San Francesco D'Assisi 25, tel: 0923-548817. An active well-informed office, with plenty of documentation available and enthusiastic and helpful staff. Open: Monday and Wednesday 8am–2pm and 3–6pm; Tuesday, Thursday, Friday and Saturday 8am–2pm.
Information office EPT, Piazzetta Saturno, tel: 0923-29000. Extremely helpful and well organised office. Open: Monday to Saturday 8am–8pm; Sunday 8am–noon.

Erice
AAPIT, Via C. A. Pepoli 11, tel: 0923-869388. Open: Monday to Saturday 8am–2pm in summer.

Embassies & Consulates
In Naples
US Consulate: Piazza della Repubblica, tel: 081-533 8111. Open: Monday to Friday 8am–noon, 8–10am (for visas).
UK Consulate: Via Crispi 122, Naples, tel: 081-663511. Open: Monday to Friday 9am–12.30pm and 2–4.30pm.

In Rome
Australian Embassy: Corso Trieste 25/c, tel: 06-852721. Open: Monday to Thursday 9am–noon and 1.30–5pm, Friday 9am–noon.
Canadian Embassy: Via Zara 30, tel: 06-445981. Open: Monday to Friday 8.30am–12.30pm and 1.30–4pm.
Irish Embassy: Piazza Campitelli 3, tel: 06-697 9121. Open: Monday to Friday 10am–12.30pm and 3–4.30pm.
New Zealand Embassy: Via Zara 28, tel: 06-440 2928. Open: Monday to Friday 8.30am–12.45pm and 1.45–5pm.
South African Embassy: Via Tanaro, 14–16, tel: 06-841 9794. Open: Monday to Friday 8.30am–noon.
UK Embassy: Via XX Settembre 80/a, tel: 06-482 5441/487 3324. Open: Monday to Friday 9.30am–1.30pm.
US Embassy: Via Veneto 121, tel: 06-46741, 487 0235. Open: Monday to Friday 8.30am–noon.

Emergencies
Security & Crime
The vast majority of tourists have pleasant, trouble-free holidays in Sicily. Although the Mafia have a strong hold on the island, it is highly unlikely that the average tourist will knowingly come into contact with them. The following information will help in all unfortunate eventualities.

The main problems for tourists is petty crime: pick-pocketing and bag-snatching (by young criminals known as *scippatori* or *scippi*) together with theft from cars. Theft of all sorts is more likely in

Palermo, Catania and the historic centre of Siracusa. Most tourist resorts require caution however, but Taormina and Cefalù are normally extremely safe. You can greatly reduce the possibility of theft by taking some elementary precautions. Remember too, that very little violent theft occurs: the chances of being mugged are very much higher in London or New York.

Expect the police to have a casual attitude to petty crime and a slightly suspect attitude to a woman on her own. Expect, also, to have to prove who you are and where you are staying before even beginning to embark on your tale of woe. A serious criminal investigation can be held up while the innocent party tries to explain that a passport stating "England" or "United Kingdom" represents the same part of the world as "Great Britain".

In the event of a serious crime, contact your country's consulate or embassy as well as the Carabinieri (a national police force which is technically part of the army). Following that, try the Sicilian approach: summon the most influential Sicilian you know on the island and request advice. Having friends in the right places helps.

Emergency Services

Police/Carabinieri: 113/112
Vigili del Fuoco: 115 (Fire brigade and ambulance service.)
ACI: 116 (The Italian automobile club: assistance in case of breakdown).

Anti-theft Precautions

Avoid looking like a tourist and do not wear your wealth ostentatiously: carry your camera out of sight, and do not wave money or wallets. Avoid wearing jewellery, or at least ensure that it is not visible. If carrying a handbag, keep it on the side away from the road (one speciality is the motorbike snatch and drive). It is best to leave money and valuables in the hotel safe. It hardly needs saying that a wallet poking out of a back pocket is an easy target, nor

that you should keep a separate record of credit card and cheque numbers, just in case.

Cars: never leave luggage or valuables visible in a car; in fact, if possible leave nothing visible in a car. Cars are best parked off the street (e.g. in a hotel car park, of which there are sadly very few). You must have all the car documents with you when driving, but take them with you when you park: if you should be unlucky enough to have the car stolen, they will help you record the theft.

Particularly in Catania and Palermo, some *scippatori* specialise in what could be called mobile crime: stealing from "moving" cars. It works something like this. You are crawling in a traffic jam. Suddenly a motorbike swerves in front of you. You brake. A youth approaches the car, pulls open the door, grabs whatever is reachable, leaps on the back of the motorbike and is gone. For the thief, the pickings are good: typically cameras or handbags placed beneath the driver's legs or seat. The moral: lock the car doors when driving. Particularly if the windows are open, which they will be if it is hot, put valuables in the boot, rather than in the car.

If you are robbed: Report it as soon as possible to the local police. You will need a copy of the declaration in order to claim on your insurance. Even more importantly, it is highly likely that part of your property will be returned, often very rapidly. There is apparently an unspoken agreement between police and thieves: provided documents and credit cards are returned and that no violence is used, the police apply minimum effort to arresting those responsible. So although your camera, blank film, cash and traveller's cheques have gone for good, the thieves may helpfully call the police to report the whereabouts of your passport, credit cards, exposed film and possibly even your empty wallet within hours.

The feeling of the thieves and of

some police is that the tourists are, by their standards, rich and should be insured, especially if foolish enough to be driving around with foreign number plates.

Thieves are usually in their mid-teens or early twenties. The unemployment rate for this group is over 33 percent. Many regard stealing from tourists as playing Robin Hood. The damage that they do to Sicily's image does not concern them.

Tips for Female Travellers

If blonde, expect attention: you will certainly get it. Sexist though it may be, you will probably enjoy Sicily better if you think hard about your dress and behaviour, particularly if travelling alone, and most particularly outside the known tourist resorts.

Either dress down or very formally (as Italians do). Wear a wedding ring and refer to your husband as if he is travelling with you, but is at a conference at that precise moment. (The wedding ring alone may be viewed as a challenge!)

Reject offers of lifts or guides, and try to avoid sitting alone in parks or on beaches. This last may be impossible: be prepared to ward off the over-friendly. Sometimes an alliance with a convenient family party may help. Avoid city centres alone at night, especially side streets. Ask the hotel's advice on the safety of the particular area. If you are going out in the evening, consider taking a taxi to your destination.

You are unlikely to be in any danger, but the Sicilians' determined pursuit may begin to feel like a hunt with you as the quarry. If you do feel in real danger, appeal to other women, particularly those accompanied by men: if you successfully claim a man's protection, you will probably put yourself off-limits to both him and others.

Possible Danger Zones

Palermo, Catania and Ortygia in Siracusa are the most likely places for *scippi*. Avoid the station areas of Palermo and Catania, and also the myriad unlit back streets of Palermo's historic centre after dark. La Kalsa in Palermo is fairly safe during the day, provided you take the anti-theft precautions mentioned, but should be avoided by night. Also avoid the San Cristoforo area of Catania (behind the castle) at all times and be wary in the portside fish markets. In Siracusa, by all means visit the characteristic restaurants, but steer clear of the Via Nizza port area late at night unless there are plenty of people about. In Mazzara del Vallo, explore the Moorish Casbah but ideally in company.

Drugs

As you would expect from the world's Mafia headquarters, drugs are in plentiful supply on the streets. This is true even in small towns and villages. It is widely assumed that raw heroin is brought in along Sicily's coasts, processed and shipped out again to markets across the world. Some part of this production finds its way into the local marketplace. Cocaine also seems to be in good supply. Do not, however, be tempted to buy. Apart from the possible legal penalties (jail, fines, expulsion), you are touching the edge of a truly criminal world. You would probably prefer to have no deeper contact with it.

Getting Around

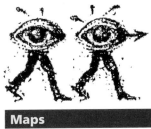

Maps

The Sicilian tourist offices can supply maps which may be adequate if you are staying in one place. If touring, you will certainly need a good map. The best Italian maps are those produced by the Touring Club Italia (TCI). Their map covers the whole of Sicily together with the islands. The scale is 1:200,000, 1 cm to 2 km.

In the UK, the TCI maps can be bought from Stanfords Map Shop, 12 Long Acre, Covent Garden, London WC2E 9LP (tel: 0171-836 1321). In Sicily, maps should be available from bookshops, and some garages.

Travel within Sicily

Hiring a car will certainly make travelling around easier. However, public transport is a reasonable alternative, particularly if time is short. By combining bus and train, you can reach most parts of Sicily quite easily, although you may occasionally find yourself waiting for some hours for a connection. If you are going to any of the smaller islands, a car may be a liability rather than an asset: the smallest islands have no roads to speak of. A car is better left behind, which means paying for a garage.

Bicycles are only selectively useful, unless you are a professional cyclist or a masochist. Much of Sicily is simply too mountainous and too hot to be comfortably visited by bike. Bikes can be hired in the places where the terrain suits them, such as the smaller islands and the flat parts of Trapani Province.

Hitchhiking tends to be slow. The risk of getting stranded in the middle of nowhere is high. Women are strongly advised to think six times before trying it, and then take the train.

The main Sicilian newspapers carry details about local flights, boats, train and bus schedules. This is by far the best way to get up-to-date and accurate details on all of these. For information on Sicilian newspapers, see *Media, page 319*.

BY AIR

From **Palermo Airport** (Punta Raisi) regular buses run to and from Palermo's main station, stopping at Piazza Ruggero Settimo in front of the Teatro Politeama. The buses are run by Ditta Prestia & Commandè, tel: 091-580457.

Timetables vary according to the season and are displayed at both the airport and the station. The first journey to the airport is at 5.45am, and the last one is around 10pm. From the airport, the first journey is at 9am, and the last is around midnight. The journey takes about an hour. The last bus usually waits for the final flight of the day.

Getting out of Palermo airport by car: If you are not going into Palermo, then avoid it. It is not the easiest first experience of Sicilian driving. If you are going west simply take the A29 direction Trapani. If you are going towards Cefalù or Catania, then take the A29 towards Palermo, but follow signs for the A19 and A20 for Catania, Enna, Messina. This will keep you on the ring road around Palermo (Viale della Regione Siciliana). It is wide, usually full of traffic and slightly chaotic, but much easier than the centre of Palermo.

Catania Airport: *Alibus* runs from 5am–midnight to the train station (every 20 minutes). Tickets can be purchased from tobacconists.

Getting out of Catania airport by car: If you are heading for Siracusa, then follow the Siracusa signs to turn south as you leave the airport. If you are going towards Palermo, then follow signs for the A19. The motorway starts a few kilometres from the airport. If you are heading north towards the A18 for Taormina and Messina, you have to cross Catania first. Follow the signs for Catania Centro and Catania Porto. These will take you along the seafront into Catania. Then follow the signs for the A18. If going to Giardini Naxos, leave the motorway at Taormina Sud. Remember that you will need Italian currency to pay the toll. For Taormina itself, leave the motorway at the second Taormina junction, Taormina Nord. From here the road winds steeply up into the town.

Other airports: In addition to Palermo and Catania, Trapani, Lampedusa and Pantelleria have commercial airports. Most of the traffic from these three is domestic.

Trapani Birgi, tel: 0923-841130 for information. Flights from and to Palermo and Pantelleria. Open: daily from dawn to dusk.

Lampedusa, tel: 0922-970299. Flights from and to Palermo, Milan and Rome. Open: daily 8am–4pm.

Pantelleria, tel: 0923-911398. Flights from and to Palermo. Direct flights from and to Rome and Milan in the summer. Open: daily 8am–4pm.

For telephone numbers for Airlines and for the airports at Palermo (Punta Raisi), Catania (Fontanarossa) and Messina (Reggio di Calabria), *see Practical Tips, page 320.*

BY BOAT

Ferries *(traghetti)* and hydrofoils *(aliscafi)* are the main transport to Sicily's smaller islands. The frequency of service varies according to the season. In summer, boats and hydrofoils leave for the main destinations several times a day, but in winter some of the smaller islands are only visited once a week. If the weather is stormy, which it often is, islands may be cut off for days at a time.

Ferry prices tend to be low. Where more than one company runs ferries or hydrofoils on a particular route, they normally work in competition, not collaboration, i.e. your ticket will only be valid on

the ships of the carrier from whom you bought it. This sometimes makes single tickets a better bet than return ones.

For the Aeolian Islands: Ferries and hydrofoils run frequently from Milazzo (Messina Province). Milazzo can be reached by train from Messina and Palermo, by bus from Messina and from Catania airport.

In the summer, there are up to 11 hydrofoils a day to Lipari and Vulcano, and six a day to Salina. There are ferries direct to the other islands several times a week, but all of the islands can best be reached from Lipari. The ferry takes about 2 hours to Lipari and the hydrofoil about 30 minutes. Lipari or Vulcano make a good base from which to explore all of the islands.

There are also boats to the Aeolian Islands from Cefalù, Messina, Palermo and Naples.

For the Egadi Islands and Pantelleria: From Trapani, ferries and hydrofoils run several times a day – even in the low season – to Favignana, Lévanzo and Maréttimo (the Egadi Islands). The crossing to Favignana by ferry takes 45 minutes. To Pantelleria (daily in the summer, Monday to Saturday in the winter), the ferry takes about 5 hours. (Trapani can be reached by train or by bus from Palermo.) Bikes are usually available for hire on Favignana. The island is relatively flat and a bike is a good way to get about.

For the Pelagie Islands (Linosa and Lampedusa): Ferries run once a day (in fact overnight) in summer from Porto Empedocle (Agrigento Province) to Lampedusa stopping at Linosa on the way. In winter, there are ferries six times a week. It is worth taking a cabin if one is available. The ferry carries cars, but in summer it can be booked up. In summer there is also a hydrofoil service between the two islands. Agrigento can be reached by train or by bus. A town bus runs about every 30 minutes from Agrigento to Porto Empedocle.

For Ustica: In summer, ferries and hydrofoils operate daily services between Palermo and

Ustica. In the low season, there are ferries only.

Boat Companies

Note that in some cases, these are agencies, rather than the boat companies themselves.

Milazzo

Siremar, Via dei Mille, tel: 090-928 3242. (Ferries and hydrofoils). **NGI**, Via dei Mille, tel: 090- 928 4091. (Ferries).

Messina

SNAV, tel: 090-362114.

Trapani

Siremar, tel: 0923-27780. (Hydrofoils to the Egadi Islands). **Siremar**, Via Amm. Staiti, tel: 0923-540515. (Ferries to the Egadi Islands). **Traghetti delle Isole**, tel: 0923-22467.

Tickets at **Egatour Viaggi**, Via Amm. Stoiti 23, tel: 0923-21754. (Ferries to the Egadi Islands and Pantelleria). **Alivit Due**, tel: 0923-24073. (Hydrofoils to the Egadi Islands). **Aliscafi SNAV**, tel: 0923-27101. (Hydrofoils to Pantelleria).

Favignana

Siremar, tel: 0923-921368. (Hydrofoils and ferries).

Levanzo

Siremar, tel: 0923-924003. (Ferries & hydrofoils).

Marettimo

Siremar, tel: 0923-923144. (Ferries & hydrofoils).

Porto Empedocle

Siremar, tel: 0922-636640.

Lampedusa

Siremar, tel: 0922-970003. (Ferries).

Linosa

Siremar, tel: 0922-972062. (Ferries).

Palermo

Grandi Traghetti, Via M. Stabile 179, tel: 091-587404.

Siremar, Via F. Crispi 120, tel: 091-582403. (Ferries and hydrofoils).
SNAV (agency), Via P. Belmonte 51, tel: 091-586533. (Hydrofoils).
Tirrenia, Palazzina Stella Maris, Via F. Crispi, tel: 091-333300.

Ustica

Siremar, Piazza Vito Longo, tel: 091-8449002. (Ferries and hydrofoils.)
SNAV, Via S. Bartolomeo, tel: 091-8449077. (Hydrofoils)

For more information about companies operating services from Genoa, Livorno and Naples *see Getting There, page 317*.

BY TRAIN

The train service is adequate provided you want to go where it does: primarily along the coast from Palermo to Messina, on to Catania and Siracusa. These two lines also offer wonderful scenery. Try to sit on the sea side of the carriage. Agrigento, Siracusa, Trapani and Enna can all be reached by train, but it takes patience and time. If you want to explore the interior of the island, the south or west coasts, or to hop between smaller destinations you may have to wait several hours for a connection, even if your train does arrive on time, and there are many places the train simply does not go near.

Italian railways have several types of train:

rapido: fast, often on time; a supplement is usually payable and you may have to book a seat in advance. Some *rapidi* have first-class accommodation only.

espresso: a main line long-distance train that does not stop at every small station.

diretto: a main line long-distance train which stops at some smaller stations. Timetabled to run more slowly than an *espresso* (although not necessarily much more so).

locale: a local train, not long-distance. It tends to be slow and stops everywhere.

Train Information and tickets can be obtained at stations or in most travel agents. Particularly if you wish to reserve seats, couchettes or sleepers, this is often quicker and more efficient than going to the station (where there are often long queues). Call 147-888088 toll-free.

BY BUS

Fast buses link Sicily's main towns and are a good way of getting around the island, particularly the interior and the south. Buses are usually more reliable and quicker than trains but cost more. The main exception where the train is generally better is the Palermo–Messina route. Following is a list of the most important and popular routes and the bus companies which operate them.

From Palermo

SAIS, Via Balsamo, 16, tel: 091-616 6028): Buses go to Caltanissetta, Catania, Enna, Piazza Armerina, Gela, Messina, Siracusa, Noto, Cefalù, Gangi, Petralia, and Termini Imerese.
Cuffaro, Via Lincoln, tel: 091-616 1560. Buses go to Agrigento.
Autoservizi Salemi, Piazza Marina. Buses go to Castelvetrano (near Selinunte), Marsala, Mazara del Vallo, and Salemi.
AST, tel: 091-617 5411/616 7102.

From Agrigento

City buses leave from outside the station in Piazza Marconi. The main bus station for the rest of Sicily is in Piazza Roselli, near the Post Office. Main bus companies:
SAIS, Via Ragazzi del 199, 12, tel: 0922-595260.
S. Lumia, Via F. Crispi 87, tel: 0922-20414.

From Catania

The bus terminal is in front of the central station.
AST, Piazza Giovanni XXIII, tel: 095-347330). Buses connect with Acireale, Etna Rifugio Sapienza, and Caltagirone.
SAIS, Via d'Amico, 18, tel: 095-536168. Buses go to Messina, Taormina, Enna, Agrigento, Caltanissetta, Palermo, Nicosia, Siracusa, Noto, Pachino.

From Caltanissetta

Buses leave from Via Catania.
SAIS, Via Calabria, tel: 0934-592597. Buses go to Palermo, Catania, Agrigento, Enna.

From Enna

SAIS, Viale Diaz, tel: (0935) 500902. Buses leave from Piazza Scelfo in the lower town and connect with Piazza Armerina, Catania, Palermo, Caltagirone.

City Buses

In Palermo, Catania and Messina, the city buses are frequent and are the easiest way to get around. Tickets must be bought before boarding the bus, either from a bus company office or from tobacco shops (*tabacchi*). Tickets are then 'cancelled' on entering the bus.

From Messina

Giuntabus, Via Terranova 8, Milazzo, tel: 090-673782.
SAIS, Piazza della Repubblica 6, tel: 090-771914. Buses connect with Taormina, Catania, and Palermo.

From Ragusa

All buses stop outside the railway station. Destinations include Catania, Messina, Siracusa, Caltagirone, Piazza Armerina, Rome.

From Siracusa

AST, Piazza delle Poste, tel: 0931-462711. Buses go to Lentini, Catania, Comiso, Ispica, Mòdica, Noto, Pachino, and Ragusa.
SAIS, Via Trieste 28, tel: 0931-66710. Destinations include Catania, Noto, Pachino, Palermo and Taormina.

From Trapani

City buses and those for the rest of Trapani province leave from Piazza Umberto.
AST, Piazza Montalto, tel: 0923-21021.

For Palermo and Agrigento, buses start from Piazza Garibaldi.

Taxis

Taxis may be hailed, found at taxi ranks or telephoned. There are additional charges for luggage, on Sunday and holidays, and a special supplement to or from the airport.
In Palermo, **Autoradio taxi**: tel: 513311/513198.
In Catania, **Radio Taxi**: tel: 333216/330966.

Driving

Motorways: There are toll motorways between Messina and Catania and on the northern coast from Messina to Capo d'Orlando (with the rest due to have been built years ago). The quickest route from Messina to Palermo is to take the motorway to Catania, although it is not the shortest route on paper. The northern coastal road, whilst offering some beautiful scenery, has a slow, twisting, lorry-infested stretch between Sant' Agata di Militello and Cefalù.

Non-toll: The motorway from Catania to Palermo is toll-free, as are those from Palermo to Trapani and towards Mazara del Vallo in the west of the island. The motorways are well-surfaced and fast. They are rarely blocked with traffic. Several of them curve spectacularly high above the valleys on stilts. The curves are sometimes necessary to avoid marshy ground, but were sometimes a means to extract additional finance from government contracts. Many of the dead of Sicily's Mafia wars are assumed to be buried in the concrete of the stilts: these are victims of *lupara bianca* ("white deaths"), deaths where bodies were never discovered.

Other roads: *Strada Statale* are the main non-motorway roads. They are numbered and appear on maps and in addresses as SS 115 etc. SS roads are usually well signposted and surfaced.

The surfacing of other Sicilian roads varies from excellent to appalling, sometimes within a few hundred metres. Road works sometimes cause entire sections of road to become impassable. There are several notorious roads which have been closed for over 10 years (notably one near Montelepre). Roads in the interior tend to suffer from flooding in the winter. Main roads and junctions are usually well-signposted, but in the countryside signs are sometimes missing or misleading. A good map is useful.

See Language, page 368 for some common road signs.

Speed limits are as follows: 50 kph (31 mph) in towns; 90 kph (56 mph) on ordinary roads outside towns; 110 kph (68 mph) for small cars (up to 1100 cc) on motorways; 120 kph (74 mph) for all other traffic on motorways.

Seat belts are compulsory, but few Sicilians wear them. The cars with local number plates and belted passengers are usually rented. Motorcycle helmets are compulsory. Fines are high for those the police choose to catch without.

Infants up to 9 months must occupy a baby seat. Children between 9 months and 4 years must be seated on the back passenger seat.

Driving in the cities: Nervous drivers are advised not to make the Palermo or Catania rush hours their first experience of driving in Sicily. Parking in both cities is hard to find.

Palermo is best negotiated by reference to a number of main roads such as Via Roma, and Via Maqueda which are bisected by Corso Vittorio Emanuele. *Quattro Canti* is a clear central point as is the *Teatro Politeama*. The *Politeama, Palazzo Reale* (or *dei Normanni*) and the station are signposted on main roads into the city, albeit slightly erratically. You may find it easiest to head for one of these initially. Many of the small streets in the centre, although heavily used by traffic, are unsuitable for use by nervous drivers. Apart from the risk of getting lost, visitors find the narrowness of the streets and the disregard of one-way signs

alarming, not to mention the sight of underage drivers.

Both main cities have ring roads, which are frequently packed with traffic, but much easier to negotiate than the cities themselves. If crossing the area, or travelling from Palermo airport to Cefalù, the ring road is the best route.

The driver and the pedestrian: Sicilian pedestrians believe they own the roads. Sicilian drivers allow them to continue in their belief. You need to become quickly acclimatised to chaotic street sense: pedestrians will walk out in front of you, or stand in the street and hold conversations. As a driver, you are expected to expect this.

Petrol stations are few and far between on the many small roads in the interior. Fill up in the towns whenever possible. Petrol stations often close for lunch 1–5pm. On Sunday, a single petrol station in each area will be open: local newspapers list these. Around Palermo and Catania there are self-service petrol stations which can be used 24 hours a day. Lists appear in the local papers.

Parking in the larger towns and cities is difficult. *Rimozione forzata* means that cars will be towed away. Do not leave anything visible in the

Car Rental

Car hire is readily available all over the island. International car hire companies are all represented, and have agents in most resorts. Cheaper rates may be on offer from some of the local companies, particularly in the low and off-peak season. Check exactly what is included in the hire agreement. It is often better value to arrange and pay for car hire through a travel agent in your home country before you travel.

Here are toll-free numbers for the major companies:
Eurodollar, tel: 167-018668.
Hertz, tel: 167-234679.
Avis, tel: 167-863063.
Budget/Maggiore, tel: 1478-67067.

car. Even apparently uninteresting items (plastic bags, newspapers) may suggest to a thief that you have perhaps left something more interesting under the seat. Leaving camera equipment or valuables in a parked car is highly risky. Radios are also at risk. Italians carry their car radios with them. Consider doing the same. Car theft is less likely, but the car should be left in a guarded car park if possible.

In Palermo: There are car parks run by ACI (the Italian motoring organisation) at the following locations:

Piazza Castelnuovo, Piazza Verdi, Piazza Marina, Piazzale Ungheria. In the city centre car parks (such as the Teatro Politeama), it is not uncommon to leave the car keys with the official in charge, who will then move the car around in the course of the day. Use your judgment as to whether this is safe.

At archaeological sites: At most of the key archeological sights (such as the Roman Villa at Piazza Armerina and the Greek temples at Selinunte), there are semi-official car parks where a fee is payable to the watchful attendant. Elsewhere, at other sites, ragamuffins may offer to 'keep an eye on' your car. It is wise to accept and pay a small fee in the reasonable assurance that the vehicle will still be there, undamaged, on your return.

Organised Tours

One way to get to know more about the area you are staying is to take one of the organised tours. Virtually every travel agency in the main tourist resorts organises tours with English, French, German or Scandinavian-speaking guides. These can be good value for money. In the high season, tours from Taormina usually include: Vulcano, Lipari, Siracusa, Agrigento, Palermo, Gole dell' Alcántara, Piazza Armerina, Enna, Etna and an Etna sunset. From Cefalù, tours include Palermo, Agrigento, Piazza Armerina, Gangi, Petralia Sottana, and other destinations west of Sicily. See *Tourist Information, page 320.*

Where to Stay

Hotel Accommodation

Sicily has over 500 hotels of various grades.

Outside the main resorts, hotel standards are generally not as high as in northern or central Italy. For reasons of comfort, quality and security, consider staying in accommodation a grade above the one you would normally choose.

Hotel categories: Hotels are classified according to a star rating system: five-star, of which there are only three on the island, are de luxe. four-star are first class and exceptionally comfortable. Three-star are comfortable and economical. Two-star are hotels with fairly basic accommodation. One-star hotels are simple to frugal.

There are considerable differences in price and quality depending on the market, i.e. availability and demand in a particular region. In Ragusa, for example, where there is a shortage of hotel accommodation, prices are much higher than in Palermo. Also expect to find a huge difference in quality between hotels of the same grade in "tourist" and "non-tourist" towns. Off the beaten track, hotels will be very basic but conceivably cost the same as in better resorts.

Unless otherwise stated, hotels accept all major credit cards. Prices may vary considerably between cities and small towns.

The provincial and local tourist boards issue up-to-date lists of hotels which include prices. Hotels are not allowed to charge more than the price written on the rate card – usually located on the inside of the door – for each room.

Note that some hotels are open only in high season (approximately May to October). When busy, hotels may insist on guests taking either half or full board (i.e. evening meal, lunch). This policy is a feature of many Sicilian resorts. Conversely, in the low season, it is worth asking prospective hotels if they are able to offer reduced rates. Outside certain cities and resorts, most will, certainly if you look or sound doubtful about staying. Request a *sconto* (discount) because it is *bassa stagione* (low season).

Payment: Most hotels listed in the three-, four- and five-star categories will accept the usual credit cards, and will also take payment by Eurocheque. Traveller's cheques are less common. It is advisable, however, to check when booking. Sicilian society generally looks upon cash payment with particular favour.

Jolly Hotels is a hotel group operating in Sicily which is represented in the UK; tel: 0800-7310470 for reservations.

Price Categories

$$$$: L200,000–L400,000;
$$$: L140,000–L200,000;
$$: L100,000–L135,000;
$: L55,000–L95,000.
Price categories are based on the cost of a room including breakfast

TIPS FOR TOURING VISITORS

Sicily does not always have accommodation in the most obvious or appealing places. Where it does, the hotels tend to be quickly booked, so reserve well in advance in season. In the case of Cefalù, Ragusa and Taormina, accommodation should always be booked well in advance. Even if touring out of season, it is worth calling a day ahead to reserve rooms.

Since distances in Sicily are so great, it is possible for touring travellers to find themselves stranded with nowhere to stay. The following list of accommodation also suggests contingency hotels. (The comments below make it clear which resorts are positively recommended and which are merely there for contingency purposes).

A note of caution: Remember that there is a gulf between urban and rural Sicily. In the mountainous hinterland, particularly in lower grade hotels, advise the hotel if you expect to check in late at night. If you are female (even several women together) and travelling alone off the beaten track, expect to be interrogated on the absence of a male companion by a mistrustful hotel-keeper. However, once you are accepted as "respectable", the atmosphere changes to friendly acceptance.

Hotel safety: In general, the higher grade hotels are in safer and more salubrious areas. However, particular care should be taken in choosing hotels in the old quarters of Catania and Palermo. Families or women travelling alone are strongly advised to choose a hotel on a main street or in a modern quarter. In general, parts of historic Palermo and Catania can be deserted or slightly intimidating at night, with a greater prevalence of *scippatori* (street thieves).

Hotel reference: For easy reference between *Travel Tips* and the *Places* section of the book, accommodation has been listed under provinces, in the order they appear under Places. The provincial capital is covered first, followed by towns/resorts in alphabetical order. The hotel listing below contains a flavour of each city/resort to help you select the ones most suitable to your needs.

Villas: Villas are a popular alternative to hotels in Cefalù, Taormina, Mondello, Castellammare del Golfo and the more salubrious coastal and mountain resorts. As an independent traveller, it is difficult to book villas on the spot since most are booked well in advance or have tie-ins with foreign agents. As a result, villa holidays tend to be booked as part of packages through travel agencies and holiday companies in your country of origin.

PALERMO CITY

Visitors need to choose between staying in the bustling centre of Palermo (ideal for seeing the historic sites) or in the select resort of Mondello, just outside town.

In Palermo city, accommodation is reasonably-priced and easier to find than in most parts of the island. It is, however, advisable to choose a higher grade hotel in Palermo than you might elsewhere. For safety's sake, choose a hotel on a main street (*see Hotel Safety*).

There is a large concentration of hotels at the southern ends of Via Roma and Via Maqueda, between the station and Corso Vittorio Emanuele. Further along the Corso, the hotels are more expensive. The modern Viale della Libertà quarter, within walking distance of the historic centre, is a good choice from many points of view, offering safety, convenience and fashionable neighbourhood bars. There are a few very inexpensive places around La Kalsa, but this area is best avoided.

Centrale, Corso Vittorio Emanuele 327, cap 90134, tel: 091-336666; fax: 091-334881. A 2-star hotel with dilapidated 30s charm near Quattro Canti old quarter. **$$$$**

Excelsior Palace, Via Marchese Ugo 3, tel: 091-625 6176; fax: 091-342139. 4-star. Extremely comfortable. Refurbished but in the original 19th-century style. Rooms vary considerably so you may wish to see the room before booking. A good location opposite a park in the chic part of Palermo. Friendly staff. Excellent restaurants. **$$$$**

Grande Albergo delle Palme (Hotel des Palmes), Via Roma 398, tel: 091-583933; fax: 091-331545. 4-star. One of the oldest hotels in the city centre. Wagner completed Parsifal here in 1882. Slightly shabby grand Victorian style. The Art Nouveau lobby is much grander than the modern bedrooms. Even if not staying, at least come here for a preprandial cocktail. **$$$$**

Jolly Hotel, Foro Italico 22, tel: 091-616 5090; fax: 091-616 1441. A large, modern hotel with a garden

and pool, it borders the seafront and the ramshackle Kalsa quarter. Walking around the area at night is not advised. A shuttle takes guests into the modern centre at Teatro Politeama. **$$$$**

Villa Igiea Grand Hotel, Salita Belmonte 43, tel: 091-543744; fax: 091-547654. 5-star. Originally a villa built by the Florio family (one of the great entrepreneurial and political families of the 19th century), the hotel has been carefully restored to its turn of the century glory. From its position in Acquasanta on a cliff above the city and the bay, the view stretches across to the Conca d'Oro. Facilities include a piano bar and restaurants. Expect to pay for the privilege. **$$$$**

Cristal Palace Hotel, Via Roma 477/D, cap 90139, tel: 091-6112580; fax: 091-612589. 3-star modern hotel across the street from the Grande Albergo delle Palme. Centrally-located for the historic quarter. Comfortable. **$$$**

Ponte, Via F. Crispi 99, cap 90139, tel: 091-583744; fax: 091-581845. 3-star. **$$$**

Moderno, Via Roma 276, cap 90133, tel: 091-588683; fax: 091-588683. 2-star. Centrally located, clean and good value. **$$**

Albergo Orientale, Via Maqueda 26, cap 90134, tel: 091-616 5727; fax: 091-616 5180. 1-star, so basic. Half of the rooms are en-suite. Former palazzo with marble courtyard and plenty of atmosphere. Not far from the railway station. **$**

Alessandra, Via Divisi 99, cap 90100, tel: 091-616 7009; fax: 091-616 5180. 1-star. Fairly basic but clean modern hotel with large rooms. Near the station. Good for independent travellers. **$**

PALERMO MONDELLO LIDO

For families with young children or those seeking hectic nightlife, Mondello makes a better summer base than Palermo city. It also offers a greater level of safety than the city centre. During the season, much of fashionable Palermo moves to the resort. Mondello's hotels are then popular so early reservation is advisable. The best hotels tend to have private beaches. Elsewhere, most beaches tend to charge a fee.

Mondello Palace, Viale Principe di Scalea, cap 90151, tel: 091-450001; fax: 091-450657. 4-star modern, luxury hotel on the seafront. Private beach, pool, restaurant and bar. **$$$$**

Conchiglia d'Oro, Viale Cloe 9, cap 90149, tel: 091-450359; fax: 091-450032. 3-star. **$$$**

Splendid Hotel la Torre, Piano Gallo 11, cap 90151, tel: 091-450222; fax: 091-450033. 3-star concrete block, but built on the rocky point of the bay, at the far end of Mondello Lido. It is on the beach with a pool and tennis courts. Many rooms overlook the sea or garden. **$$$**

Price Categories

$$$$: L200,000–L400,000;
$$$: L140,000–L200,000;
$$: L100,000–L135,000;
$: L55,000–L95,000.
Price categories are based on the cost of a room including breakfast

PALERMO PROVINCE
Bagheria

As the first of Palermo's garden suburbs, Bagheria is bursting with dilapidated 18th-century villas, none of which has yet been turned into villa-hotels.

Zabara Park Hotel, on the SS 113 road, cap 90011, tel: 091-907111; fax: 091-903104. Out of town 3-star motel with swimming pool and tennis courts. **$$$**

Cefalù

Along with Taormina, Cefalù is Sicily's most appealing resort. Convenience, good infrastructure and safety make it an ideal choice for families or elderly people. The beaches are closer and far better than at Taormina. Like Taormina, the resort feels perfectly safe and free from petty crime. There is a wide range of accommodation to suit all pockets. Visitors out of

season would do well to avoid hotels located on the beach since the beaches tend not to be very clean in the low season.

Baia del Capitano, Località Mazzaforno, cap 90015, tel: 0921-420005; fax: 0921-420163. 3-star. A pleasant hotel about 5 km (3 miles) west of Cefalù. Modern, but well-built and set in an olive grove. Swimming pool, tennis courts and nearby beach. **$$$$**

Carlton Riviera, Località Capo Plaia, cap 90015, tel: 0921-420304; fax: 0921-420264. 3-star. About 5 km (3 miles) west of Cefalù, a large modern hotel right on the cliffs. Tennis courts, swimming pool. **$$$$**

Riva del Sole, Via Lungomare 25, cap 90015, tel: 0921-421230; fax: 0921-421984. In the town, but on the seafront. Large rooms, some with a view of the sea or the old town. A good restaurant. **$$$$**

Kalura, Località Caldura, cap 90015, tel: 0921-422501; fax: 0921-423122. 3-star. About 3 km (2 miles) east of Cefalù. Slightly shabby, but most rooms have a sea view; pleasant terrace. Reasonable value. **$$$**

Le Sabbie d'Oro, Località S. Lucia, cap 90015, tel: 0921-421565; fax: 0921-422213. 3-star. About 2 km (1½ miles) from Cefalù. Modern, not far from a sandy beach. **$$$**

Tourist, Via Lungomare, cap 90015, tel: 0921-421750; fax: 0921-421750. A friendly 3-star hotel with a reasonable restaurant. "Packaged" breakfasts. **$$$**

Isola Delle Femmine

Creeping pollution makes this an undesirable location, but its lingering popularity with visitors remains.

Saracen Club, Via dei Saraceni 1, cap 90040, tel: 091-867 1423; fax: 091-867 1371. 3-star. **$$$$**

Hotel Eufemia, Via Nazionale 28, cap 90040, tel: 091-867 7800; fax: 091-867 8002. 3-star comfort. **$$$**

Monreale

This pleasant cathedral town makes a low-key alternative to accommodation in Palermo City.

Carrubella Park Hotel, Via Umberto 1st floor, 233, cap 90046, tel: 091-640 2187; fax: 091-640 2189. 3-star. About 1 km (half a mile) from Monreale, with wonderful views across the Conca d'Oro. **$$**

Il Ragno, Via Provinciale 85 (Località Giacalone), cap 90040, tel: 091-419256. In the countryside about 10 km (6½ miles) from Monreale in the direction of S. Giuseppe Jato. A good option for those travelling by car, who wish to stay outside the Palermo conurbation. **$**

Montelepre

Once the haunt of the Bandit Giuliano, this mountain village makes an unusual base within easy reach of Palermo. (A car is essential, however.)

Rose Garden, Via Circonvallazione 120, cap 90040, tel: 091-878 4360; fax: 091-878 4192. 2-star. **$**

Isola Di Ustica

This lovely island off Palermo is extremely popular with swimmers and nature-lovers. It attracts a large number of German, Scandinavian and Sicilian visitors. Hotels tend to fill up very fast but there are many opportunities to rent rooms: call in at the Pro Loco tourist office (*Vito Longo*) if the fishermen at the port haven't already made you an offer. Alternatively, book a room through a lettings agency:

Agenzia Osteodes Travel Agency, Via Magazzino 5, cap 90010, tel: 091-844 9210; fax: 091-844 9210.

Diana, Contrada San Paolo, cap 90010, tel/fax: 091-844 9109. 2-star. **$$$**

Grotta Azzurra, Loc. San Ferlicchio, tel: 091-844 9048. 3-star. **$$$**

Punta Spalmatore, Loc. Spalmatore, tel: 091-844 9388. 3-star. A village with bungalows and rooms for rent. Open June to September with prices varying depending on the season. For reservations and/or information throughout the year, call **Orizzonti Gestioni**, tel: 02-583 96325; fax: 02-583 96430. Minimum one week rent. **$$-$$$**

Stella Marina, Via C. Colombo, 33, cap 90010, tel: 091-844 9014; fax: 091-844 9325. 2-star. **$$$**
Ariston, Via della Vittoria 5–7, cap 90010, tel: 091-844 9042; fax: 091-844 9335. 2-star. **$$**
Clelia, Via Magazzino 7, cap 90010, tel: 091-844 9039. Located on the main square, Clelia is the oldest *pensione* in town. Wonderful fish restaurant. **$**
Locanda Castelli, Via S. Francesco 16, tel: 091-844 9007. 1-star. Three apartments for two people. Minimum one week rent. **$**

TRAPANI PROVINCE
Trapani City
Astoria Park, Lungomare D. Alighieri, San Cusumano, cap 91016, tel: 0923-562400; fax: 0923-567422. (Set 3 km/2 miles along the seafront towards Erice.) Comfortable 3-star hotel with restaurant, bar, tennis courts, pool, private beach. **$$$**
Vittoria, Via Crispi 246, cap 91100, tel: 0923-873044; fax: 0923-29870. Central city location with some sea views from this 3-star hotel. **$$$**
Cavallino Bianco, Lungomare Dante Alighieri 5, cap 91100, tel: 0923-21549/23902; fax: 0923-873002. 3-star hotel by the sea, half the rooms with views. **$$**

Castellammare del Golfo
This charming fishing port and small resort is an ideal base for families or for independent travellers wishing to be close to Palermo yet in a quieter, more manageable location. It also appeals to those wishing to swim in clean waters near the nature reserve of Lo Zingaro. Consider renting a villa in Castellammare.
Al Madarig, 7 Largo Petroio, cap 91014, tel: 0924-33533; fax: 0924-33790. Modern 3-star hotel overlooking the port. **$$$**

Castelvetrano
Castelvetrano is not an especially interesting town but its hotels are mostly on the beach and are handy for the Greek ruins of Selinunte. (*See Selinunte* for hotels too.)

Lido Azzurro, Via Marco Polo 98, tel/fax: 0924-46256. 1-star. **$**
Zeus, Via Veneto 6, tel/fax: 0924-905566. 2-star comfort. No credit cards. **$**

Erice
Erice is a perfect base and an extremely attractive village. In summer, its hilltop site makes it far more comfortable than Trapani itself. However, in season accommodation is in great demand so early booking is recommended.

Price Categories
$$$$: L200,000–L400,000;
$$$: L140,000–L200,000;
$$:L100,000–L135,000;
$: L55,000–L95,000.
Price categories are based on the cost of a room including breakfast

Elimo, Via Vittorio Emanuele 73, tel: 0923-869377; fax: 0923-869252. A small 3-star hotel in the old town with a pleasant restaurant, bar and roof terrace. **$$$$**
Ermione, Via Pineta Comunale 43, tel: 0923-869138; fax: 0923-869587. Set in a pine grove just outside the walls of medieval Erice, this unattractive-looking 2-star hotel has large rooms, great views, a pool and an average restaurant. **$$$**
Moderno, Via Vittorio Emanuele 63, cap 91016, tel: 0923-869300; fax: 0923-869139. A 3-star hotel in the old town. Fairly intimate with a terrace and a good restaurant. **$$$**
Edelweiss, Cortile Padre Vincenzo, tel: 0923-869158. This basic but quiet *pensione* has a distinctly alpine feel. **$$**

Marsala
Hotel Cap 3000, Via Trapani 161, tel: 0923-989055; fax: 0923-989634. Comfortable 3-star hotel with an uncovered pool. **$$**
Acos Hotel, Via Mazara 14 (on the SS. 115 road), tel: 0923-999166; fax: 0923-999132. A rather bland 3-star motel. **$$**
Albergo Garden, Via Gambini 36, tel: 0923-982320; fax: 0923-

982320. 2-star comfort. Credit cards are not accepted. **$**

Mazara del Vallo
Hopps Hotel, Via G. Hopps 29, tel: 0923-946133; fax: 0923-946075. 3-star. Relatively expensive, but traditional service; recommended for its hospitality and good cuisine; pool and garden. **$$$**
Kristal, Via Valeria 36, tel/fax: 0923-932688. 3-star; comfortable; shuttle service to the beach. **$$$**

San Vito Lo Capo
This is an up and coming resort near Castellammare with a wild west feel about it. But it is pleasant and safe, a good choice for families or those on a limited budget. The most popular hotels are around Via Savoia and Via Mulino.
Vecchio Mulino, Via Mulino 49, tel: 0923-972518. A 2-star hotel with panoramic terrace views and a good restaurant. **$$$$**
Hotel Capo San Vito, Via San Vito 3, tel: 0923-972284; fax: 0923-972559. This large 3-star hotel is 6 miles (10 km) south of Capo San Vito and situated on the beach. There is a private beach for guests, gardens and tennis courts. **$$$**

Selinunte
Selinunte has a number of standard beach hotels.
Paradise Beach, Contrada Belice di Mare, tel: 0924-46333; fax: 0924-46477. Set beside the sea 6 km (4 miles) from Marinella. An impressive hotel-club with sports facilities, a pool and tennis courts. Closed November to February. **$$$$**
Alceste, Via Alceste 23, Marinella, tel: 0924-46184; fax: 0924-46143. A terrace, garden and solarium. **$$**

EGADI ISLANDS
In July and August accommodation can be very difficult to find: book well in advance for this period. However, the ferries tend to be met by local people offering rooms to rent.
Egadi, Via C. Colombo 17, Favignana, tel/fax: 0923-921232. 2-star. Closed October to April. **$$$**

Albergo Bouganville, Via Cimabue 10, Favignana, tel: 0923-922033. Quiet rooms. **$$**

Paradiso, Via Lungom Mare 8, Levanzo, tel: 0923-924080. 1-star. **$**

PANTELLERIA

This volcanic, mountainous island is not part of the Egadi archipelago. It is nearer Tunisia than Sicily. (There is a daily hydrofoil from Trapani in summer.) Giorgio Armani and other famous names have villas on this intriguing island. Holiday accommodation is limited, but there are villa rental possibilities.

Agadir, Via Catania, tel: 0923-911100. 2-star. **$$**

Cossyra, Loc. Cuddie Rosse-Mursia, Mursia, tel: 0923-911154; fax: 0923-911026. (2 miles/3 km from Pantelleria port.) This 3-star hotel has pleasant grounds, a pool, tennis courts and a private beach. **$$**

Miryam, Corso Umberto 1, tel: 0923-911374; fax: 0923-911777. 2-star. No credit cards. **$$**

AGRIGENTO PROVINCE

Agrigento City

While Agrigento city is well provided with good quality hotels, this is not true of the rest of the province. This section covers Valley of the Temples.

Albergo della Valle, Via Ugo la Malfa 3, cap 92100, tel: 0922-26966; fax: 0922-26412. 4-star comfort. **$$$$**

Villa Athena, Via Passeggiate Archeologiche 33, cap 92100, tel: 0922-596288; fax: 0922-402180. This serene 4-star hotel overlooks the Temple of Concord offering lovely views of the temples. The hotel is set in charming gardens and there is a pool available. It is the only hotel within the Valley of the Temples so it is certainly worth making the most of the spot for lunch or dinner graced by serene views. Patchy service. **$$$$**

Jolly Dei Templi, Parco Angeli, Villagio Mosé, (on the SS 115, 3 km/2 miles east of the ruins), cap 90100, tel: 0922-606144; fax: 0922-606685. This crisp 4-star

hotel is a typical conference centre. Swimming pool; good restaurant. **$$$**

Colleverde, Strada Panoramica, cap 92100, tel: 0922-29555; fax: 0922 29012. This 3-star hotel is set further up the slope from Villa Athena, at the start of Strada Panoramico. Lovely views of the temples. Reasonable restaurant. **$$$**

Tre Torri, Contrada Fegotto, Villaggio Mosé, cap 92100, tel: 0922-606733; fax: 0922-607839. This large 3-star hotel lies just east of the temples. Restaurant; bar; pool. **$$$**

San Leone (Coast)

Pirandello Mare, Via G. de Chirico 17, cap 92100, tel: 0922-412333; fax: 0922-413693. Unattractive but very comfortable 3-star hotel; restaurant and bar. **$$$**

Akragas, Via Emporium 16, (located at the edge of the Valle dei Templi, between the sea and the town), cap 92100, tel: 0922-414082; fax: 0922-414262. 2-star coastal hotel with restaurant and bar. Ideal location for families. **$**

Cammarata

Rio Platani, Scalo Cammarata, Str. Agrigento–Palermo, cap 92022, tel: 0922-909051. 2-star. **$**

Canicatti

Italians use Canicatti as a synonym for Timbuktu – an emergency stop only.

Belvedere, Via Resistenza, 22, cap 92024, tel: 0922-851860; fax: 0922-851860. 2-star. **$**

Licata

This historic but down-at-heel town is a possible overnight stop should Agrigento hotels be full.

Piccadilly, Via Panoramica, cap 92027, tel: 0922-893626; fax: 0922-893626. 3-star. **$$**

Al Faro, Via Dogana 6, cap 92027, tel: 0922-773846; fax: 0922-773087. 3-star. **$**

Porto Empedocle

Porto Empedocle is not recommended as a base but makes

a sensible overnight stop for those catching a ferry to the Pelagie Islands.

Dei Pini, (SS 115. Loc. Vincenzella), cap 92015, tel: 0922-634844; fax: 0922-632895. 4-star. **$$$**

Sciacca

Sciacca is a possible base in Agrigento province. While the town is rather scruffy, it is popular with Italians and Germans undergoing thermal cures in this spa town.

Grande Hotel delle Terme, Viale delle Terme 1, cap 92019, tel: 0925-21838; fax: 0925-21746. This 3-star hotel has a thermal treatment centre. **$$$**

Garden, Via Valverde 2, cap 92019, tel: 0925-26299; fax: 0925-26299. 3-star accommodation. **$**

La Paloma Bianca, Via Figuli 5, cap 92019, tel: 0925-25130 or 25667; fax: 0925-25667. 2-star hotel. **$**

PELAGIE ISLANDS (ISOLE PELAGIE)

Lampedusa

Gattopardo, Contrada Cala Creta. Reservations/information, tel: 011-812 4089; fax: 011-817 8387. High season, tel: 0922-970051. All inclusive (daily boat trips and full board, free cars as the place has no access to the sea). Open June to October. Minimum one week stay. **$$$$**

Alba d'Amore, Via Favorolo 33, cap 92010, tel: 0922-970272; fax: 0922-970786. 3-star. **$$$**

Baia Turchese, Contrada Guitgia, cap 92010, tel: 0922-970455; fax: 0922-970098. 3-star. Open summer only. **$$$**

Martello, Piazza Medusa 1, cap 92010, tel: 0922-970025; fax: 0922-971696. 2-star. **$$$**

Lido Azzurro, Contrada Guitgia, Lampedusa, cap 92010, tel/fax: 0922-970225. 2-star. **$$**

CALTANISSETTA PROVINCE

The province has limited accommodation and, while the hinterland is lovely, Caltanissetta city itself is dull and is not a good base. For those who wish to stay in the mountains, go instead to Enna.

Caltanissetta
San Michele, Via Fasci Siciliani, tel: 0934-553750; fax: 0934-598791. 4-star hotel with restaurant. $$$

Butera
Lido degli Angeli, Contrada Falconara, tel: 0934-349133. Hotel-restaurant located on the coast, close to Falconara Castle. $

Gela
Gela is only a sensible stopping place if you have to do business there: it has a large oil refinery and a high rate of petty crime.
Motel Agip, Loc. Giardinelli SS. 117/1, Via Venezia, tel: 0933-911144; fax: 0933-907236. $$$
Delle Mimose, Viale Indipendenza 11, cap 93012, tel: 0933-935217; fax: 0933-822703. 3-star. $

Mazzarino
Hotel Alessi, Via Caltanissetta 20, tel: 0934-381549; fax: 0934-381549. A basic 2-star hotel. $

ENNA PROVINCE

Enna
Enna itself has very few hotels so reservations are advisable. Because of Enna's altitude, take warmer clothes and expect to find views from your hotel window swathed in mist.
Grande Albergo Sicilia, Piazza Colajanni 7, cap 94100, tel: 0935-500850; fax: 0935-500488. 3-star. Comfortable and reasonably efficient. Central. Some rooms have fine views. Daily car parking fee is quite high. $$$
Plaza, Via Gaetani 5, tel/fax: 0934-583877. $$$

Enna Pergusa
Lakeside resort good facilities, set around Lago di Pergusa, about 5 km (3 miles) from Enna.
Park Hotel La Giara, Via Nazionale 125, Villaggio Pergusa, cap 94100, tel: 0935-541687; fax: 0935-541521. 3-star. $$$
Riviera, Villaggio Pergusa 21, cap 94100, tel: 0935-541267; fax: 0935-541260. 3-star. Can be noisy at weekends and on festival days, as it's inside the autodromo. $$$

Garden, Villaggio Pergusa, Via Nazionale, cap 94100, tel: 0935-541694; fax: 0935-541690. 3-star. $$

Nicosia
This untouristy inland town is a refreshing base for exploring Enna's hilly interior.
Pineta, Loc. San Paolo 35/A, cap 94014, tel: 0935-647002; fax: 0935-646927. 3-star hotel. $$
Vigneta, Contrada San Basilio, Vigneta, tel: 0935-638940. 3-star. $

Piazza Armerina
This appealing town makes an excellent overnight stop for visitors wishing to see the Roman Villa, one of Sicily's great attractions.
Park Hotel Paradiso, Contrada Ramaldo, cap 94015, tel: 0935-680841; fax: 0935-684908. 3-star comfort. $$$
Selene, Via Gen. Gaeta 30, tel: 0935-682254. 3-star comfort. $$$
Hotel Mosaici, Contrada Paratore, tel/fax: 0935-685453. Close to the Villa Romana. $$

Troina
This quiet town makes a good alternative to Nicosia.
La Cittadella dell'Oasis, Loc. S. Michele, cap 94018, tel: 0935-653966; fax: 0935-653660. Unpretentious 3-star comfort. $$

RAGUSA PROVINCE
The province is easily accessible on day trips from Ragusa. However, the sudden economic boom of modern Ragusa means that city accommodation is scarce. Tourism is so low-key that unless visitors are lucky enough to find a bed in Ragusa or the resort of Marina di Ragusa, they may need to be based in Siracusa. However, on the plus side, part of the province's charm lies in its lack of tacky tourism and in its warmth towards foreign visitors.

Ragusa
Sadly, there are no hotels in Ragusa Ibla (the medieval 'lower' town). The only hotels are in Ragusa Alta (the baroque and modern 'high' town). Parking can be

tricky and the town's sign-posting and one-way system is confusing. Existing hotels are fairly similar: standard, mid-range, patronised by the business community. Higher quality hotels are currently under construction so enquire at the tourist office prior to booking.
Mediterraneo, Via Roma 189, cap 97100, tel: 0932-621944; fax: 0932-623799. 4-star. This central hotel is a convenient second choice to the Montreal. $$$$
Montreal, Via San Giuseppe 8, cap 97100, tel/fax: 0932-621133. This 3-star hotel is arguably the most pleasant but is not outstanding. It is centrally located in Ragusa Alta, the 'high' town. $$
San Giovanni, Via Traspontino 3, cap 97100, tel: 0932-621013; fax: 0932-621294. Near the railway station. $

Modica
Modica is an appealing provincial town and makes an acceptable, if less convenient, alternative to Ragusa.
Motel di Modica, Corso Umberto, tel: 0932 91022; fax: 0932-941077. 3-star hotel. $

SIRACUSA PROVINCE
Siracusa
A booming economy means that Siracusa is currently building hotels. The majority of existing hotels are sited in safe modern quarters. Compared with much of Sicily, the hotels are more 'international' and efficient, if occasionally a little characterless. Bear in mind that most hotels tend to be some distance from the archaeological sites and the island of Ortygia. This means that public transport or a car will be required, and the same may be true if you are planning to eat out in one of Siracusa's many excellent restaurants.
Jolly Hotel, Corso Gelone 45, cap 96100, tel: 0931-461111 or 64350; fax: 0931-461126. This 4-star hotel is in the bland shopping district but as a mid-town base is most convenient for the sights. $$$$

Motel Agip, Viale Teracati 30, cap 96100, tel: 0931-463232; fax: 0931-67115. 4-star business hotel. Despite rising out of a petrol station, it is the most convenient hotel, close to the archaeological park. **$$$$**

Park Hotel, Via Filisto 80, Siracusa, cap 96100, tel: 0931-412233 or 32758; fax: 0931-38096 . Elegant 3-star hotel with fairly expensive restaurant and pool. Set in the modern quarter to the east of the town; in a quiet residential area. Ample parking. **$$$**

Albergo Bella Vista, Via Diodoro Siculo 4, cap 96100, tel: 0931-411437; fax: 0931-37927. 3-star comfort. **$$$**

Como, Piazza Stazione 11, tel: 0931-464055; fax: 0931-464056. 3-star. Convenient location midway between the Archaeological Park and Ortygia. **$$**

Gran Bretagna, Via Savoia 21, cap 96100, tel: 0931-68765. As the only cheap *pensione* on Ortygia, it is often full. No credit cards. **$$**

Augusta

This is an emergency overnight stop for those catching an early ferry the next day.

Noto

Club Eloro, Contrada Pizzuta, Noto Marina, cap 96017, tel: 0931-812244; fax: 0931-812200. 3-star hotel on the Noto coast. **$$$$**

Stella, Via Francesco Maiore 44, cap 96017, tel: 0931-835695. This *pensione* is Noto's only hotel in the baroque town, so book ahead. **$**

Portopalo di Capo Passero

Jonic, Via Vittorio Emanuele 19, cap 96010, tel: 0931-842723; fax: 0931-842615. An inexpensive hotel in the southern-most resort. **$$$**

El Condor, Via Vittorio Emanuele 38, tel: 0931-842016. 1-star hotel. Open mid-June to September. **$$**

CATANIA PROVINCE

Catania

It is advisable to choose accommodation in the smaller town outside Catania, but if you are intending to stay in the city, take a

superior hotel in the centre.

Excelsior, Piazza G. Verga 39, cap 95129, tel: 095-537071; fax: 095-537015. This comfortable 4-star hotel and restaurant is open all year round. **$$$$**

Central Palace, Via Etnea 218, cap 95131, tel: 095-325344; fax: 095-715 8939. This convenient if old-fashioned 4-star hotel is situated on the main shopping street. **$$$$**

Jolly Trinacria, Piazza Trento 13, cap 95129, tel: 095-316933; fax: 095-316832. Business-like 4-star hotel in the city centre; no parking. **$$$$**

Nettuno, Viale di Lauria 121, cap 95127, tel: 095-712 5252; fax: 095-498066. 3-star comfort; pool and restaurant. **$$$$**

San Domenico, Via Cifali 76/B, cap 95123, tel: 095-438480. A well-situated but modest 2-star hotel. **$**

Price Categories

$$$$: L200,000–L400,000;
$$$: L140,000–L200,000;
$$: L100,000–L135,000;
$: L55,000–L95,000.
Price categories are based on the cost of a room including breakfast

Aci Castello & Aci Trezza

This stretch of coast north of Catania makes a good base. The good quality hotels tend to have sea views of rocky bays and good restaurants. Taormina and Catania are close by.

Catania Sheraton, Via A da Messina 45, Cannizzaro, cap 95020, tel: 095-271557; fax: 095-271380. Luxurious 4-star hotel with pool and a renowned restaurant – *Il Timo*. **$$$$**

Aloha Dioro, Via A. De Gasperi 10 (Strada Panoramica), Aci Castello, cap 95024, tel: 095-604344; fax: 095-606984. 4-star hotel beside the sea with 2 pools (one with jacuzzi) and one of the area's best restaurants. Highly recommended. Thirty minute drive from Catania on the road to Messina. **$$$$**

I Faraglioni, Lungomare dei Ciclopi 115, Aci Trezza, cap 95026, tel: 095-276744; fax: 095-276609. Set

in a fishing village, this 3-star hotel has its own private platform and a good regional restaurant. **$$$**

I Malavoglia, Via Provinciale 3, Aci Trezza, cap 95026, tel: 095-276711; fax: 095-276873. 3-star comfort. **$$$**

Eden Riviera, Via Litteri 57, Aci Trezza, cap 95026, tel: 095-277760; fax: 095-277761. 3-star comfort. **$$**

Acireale

Orizzonte Acireale, Via C. Colombo, tel: 095-886006; fax: 095-765 1607. 3-star comfort. **$$$$**

Santa Tecla, Loc. Santa Tecla, Via Balestrate 100, tel: 095-763 4015; fax: 095-607705. 3-star. Great view of the sea; no restaurant. Closed from November to mid-March. **$$$$**

Caltagirone

Grand Hotel Villa San Mauro, Via Porto Salvo 10, tel: 0933-26500; fax: 0933-313661. This 3-star hotel is the best, with a pool, a couple of unexceptional restaurants and high prices. **$$$**

ETNA ENVIRONS

Alcantara

Il Vulcanetto, Via Vittorio Veneto, 34. Mojo Alcantara, tel: 0942-963042; fax: 0942-963042. 2-star hotel, not far from the weird Alcantara gorge. **$**

Linguaglossa

On the northern slopes of Etna, along with Nicolosi, accommodation tends to be fully booked during the skiing season.

Happy Days, Via Mareneve 3, tel: 095-643484. Small, 2-star, basic hotel. Open in wintertime only. **$$**

Nicolosi

If planning to stay for winter sports, book early. There are mountain walks from Nicolosi, planned through the local tourist office, all year round.

Biancaneve, Via Etnea 163, tel: 095-911176; fax: 095-911194. 3-star. pool and tennis courts. **$$**

Gemellaro, Via Etnea 160, tel: 095-911060; fax: 095-911071. 3-star. **$$**

Belvedere, Via Etnea 110, tel: 095-911406. 1-star. Open wintertime only. **$$**

Paternò
Sicilia, Via Vittorio Emanuele 391, tel: 095-853604; fax: 095-854742. 2-star and often full; surly management but the only hotel. **$**

Zafferana Etnea
On the southern slopes of Etna. A very good base for skiing.
Airone, Strada Mareneve Sud. Via Cassone 67, tel: 095-708 1987; fax: 095-708 2142. 3-star. **$$**
Del Bosco, Via Cassone 75, tel: 095-7081888; fax: 095-7082438. 2-star. No credit cards. **$$**
Primavera dell'Etna, Via Cassone 86, tel: 095-708 2348; fax: 095-708 1695. 3-star. **$**

TAORMINA

During the Taormina peak season (April to May and July to September) many hotels insist upon a half-board arrangement.
Bristol Park, Via Bagnoli Croce 92, tel: 0942-23006; fax: 0942-24519. 4-star. Dramatic location; pool; private beach; restaurant of some standing; covered parking. Pleasant atmosphere. **$$$$**
Excelsior, Via Toselli 8, tel: 0942-23975; fax: 0942-23978. This 4-star hotel commands a promontory and enjoys lovely grounds and a spectacularly sited pool. The facade is Neo-Gothic and the interior is modern. Good restaurants. Parking. Off-season reductions. **$$$$**
Grande Albergo Monte Tauro, Via Madonna delle Grazie 3, tel: 0942-24402; fax: 0942-24403. An ugly exterior conceals a good value 4-star hotel. **$$$$**
San Domenico Palace, Piazza San Domenico 5, tel: 0942-23701; fax: 0942-625506. 5-star. This beautiful former monastery is now a luxury hotel. There are magnificent views from many rooms and from the terrace towards Etna and the sea. The monks no doubt paid less for the privilege, but they had no swimming pool and presumably the cells were less comfortable. Along with Palermo's Villa Igiea, it is the

finest hotel in Sicily. Excellent restaurant. **$$$$**
Villa Paradiso, Via Roma 2, tel: 0942-23922; fax: 0942-625800. 4-star. Fine views and private beach. **$$$$**
Villa Belvedere, Via Croce Bagnoli 9, tel: 0942-23791; fax: 0942-625830, e-mail: hotbelve@cjs.it. 3-star. **$$$$**
Villa San Michele, Via Damiano Rossi 11, tel: 0942-24327; fax: 0942-24328. 3-star. Bed and breakfast only. **$$$**

Price Categories

$$$$: L200,000–L400,000;
$$$: L140,000–L200,000;
$$: L100,000–L135,000;
$: L55,000–L95,000.
Price categories are based on the cost of a room including breakfast

Palazzo Vecchio, Salita Ciampoli 9, tel: 0942-23033; fax: 0942-625104. Charming if quaint medieval mansion in the town centre. Sea views. 2-star. Visa accepted only. Closed November to 21 December and 10 January to February. **$$$**
Villa Kristina, Via Leonardo da Vinci 23, tel: 0942-28366; fax: 0942-28371. 3-star. Can be rather noisy in the height of the season, but is good value for money. Closed December to February. **$$$**
Ariston, Via Bagnoli Croce 168, tel: 0942-23838; fax: 0942-21137. 3-star. American Express not accepted. **$$**
La Campanella, Via Circonvallazione 3, tel: 0942-23381; fax: 0942-625248. 2-star. Pleasant but not suitable for invalids. No credit cards. **$$**
Corona, Via Roma 7, tel: 0942-23022; fax: 0942-23022. 2-star. Bed and breakfast only. No credit cards. **$$**
Svizzera, Via Pirandello 26, tel: 0942-23790; fax: 0942-625906. 1-star. Clean and well run. No credit cards in low season. **$$**
Villa Greta, Via Leonardo da Vinci 46, tel: 0942-28286; fax: 0942-24360. 2-star. **$$**

Villa Schuler, Piazzetta Bastione 16, tel: 0942-23481; fax: 0942-23522. An individual 2-star hotel with lots of charm. Closed December to February. **$$**
Terra Rossa Apartments, Via Bongiovanni 12, tel: 0942-24536; fax: 0942-23188. Situated between Taormina and the beach. Fairly basic flats. Better to have a car. Not suitable for older people or invalids. Substantial discounts for one week's rent. No credit cards. **$**

Taormina Mazzarò
This is the beach level area of Taormina, below the old town. A cable car connects the resort to the hill-town of Taormina. Its popularity is confirmed by a variety of lively restaurants and clubs which tend to be less expensive than those in Taormina. Nightlife is more frenetic.
Grande Albergo Capo Taormina, Via Nazionale 147, tel: 0942-24000; fax: 0942-625467. This sleek 5-star hotel is perched above the beautiful bay of Mazzarò. Salt-water pool built into the cliff. All rooms have private terraces. Private beach. **$$$$**
Villa Sant'Andrea, Via Nazionale 137, tel: 0942-23125; fax: 0942-23838. 4-star comfort near the sea. **$$$$**
Ranieri Principe, Via Nazionale 228, tel: 0942-23962; fax: 0942-24716. 3-star accommodation. **$$$**
Baia Azzurra, Via Nazionale 240, tel: 0942-23249; fax: 0942-625499. 3-star comfort. **$$**
Villa Esperia, Via Nazionale 244, tel: 0942-23377; fax: 0942-21105. 3-star. Bed and breakfast only. Closed October and November. **$$**
Villa Moschella, Via Nazionale 240, tel: 0942-23328; fax: 0942-23328. 1-star. Large garden; all rooms with sea views. No half board (breakfast only). Closed November to Easter. Visa only. **$$**

Castelmola
Villa Sonia, Via Porta Mola 9, tel: 0942-28082; fax: 0942-626047. 2-star. **$$**
Panorama di Sicilia, Via A. De Gasperi 44, tel/fax: 0942-28027. 2-star. **$**

MESSINA PROVINCE
Messina
Jolly Hotel dello Stretto, Via Garibaldi 126, tel: 090-363860; fax: 090-5902526. Well-organised 4-star. **$$$$**
Royal Palace Hotel, Via Tommaso Cannizzaro 224, tel: 090-6503; fax: 090-292 1075. A comfortable but unremarkable 4-star hotel. **$$$$**
Paradis, Via Consolare Pompea 441, tel: 090-310682; fax: 090-312043. Modern hotel overlooking the strait. **$$$**
Excelsior, Via Maddalena 32, tel: 090-293 8721; fax: 090-293 8721. 3-star. **$$**

Messina Lido Mortelle
Giardino delle Palme, Road SS. 113, tel: 090-321017; fax: 090-321666. Modern 3-star hotel near the beach. Half a mile from the lake. **$$$**
Faro, Via Circuito 45, tel: 090-321762; fax: 090-326670. Simple 2-star. **$**

Capo D'Orlando
La Tartaruga, Via Consolare Antica 70, tel: 0941-955012; fax: 0941-955056. 3-star. **$$$**
Il Mulino, Lungomare Andrea Doria 46, tel: 0941-902431; fax: 0941-911614. 3-star. **$$$**
Amato, Via Consolare Antica 150, tel: 0941-911476; fax: 0941-912734. 3-star. **$$**

Giardini-Naxos
This lively but downmarket resort is popular with families and young holidaymakers.
Arathena Rocks, Via Calcide Eubea 55, tel: 0942-51348; fax: 0942-51690. 3-star. Recommended but a little off the beaten track. Closed from November to Easter. **$$$$**
Hellenia Yachting, Via Jannuzzo 41, tel: 0942-51737; fax: 0942-54310. Fine but unexceptional. **$$$$**
La Sirenetta, Via Naxos 177, tel: 0942-53637; fax: 0942-53637. **$$$**

Gioiosa Marea
Capo Skino Park, Contrada Capo Skino, tel: 0941-301167; fax:

0941-301340. 3-star. July and August minimum rent one week full board. Closed November. **$$$**

Letojanni
Antares, Loc. Poggio Mastropietro, tel: 0942-36477; fax: 0942-36095. 3-star. Great views. Not suitable for disabled or older clients due to its position, although a lift is installed. **$$$$**
San Pietro, Via L. Rizzo, tel: 0942-36081; fax: 0942-37012. 3-star comfort; private beach. Closed November to Easter. **$$$$**
Da Peppe, Via L. Rizzo 346, tel: 0942-36159; fax: 0942-36843. 2-star. **$**

Milazzo
This is the port for the Aeolian Islands: it is not a particularly panoramic or interesting town, but convenient for an overnight stop if you intend to cross to the islands.
Silvanetta, Via Acquaviole 1, tel: 090-928 1633; fax: 090-922 2787. 3-star comfort. **$$$**
Riviera Lido, C. da Corrie, Via Panoramica, tel: 090-928 3456; fax: 090-928 7834. Ask for a room with a sea view. **$$$**

AEOLIAN ISLANDS
The islands have a number of *pensioni/locande* but you should expect to have full board – the custom on the Aeolian. Islanders keen to let rooms to tourists will greet each ferry, however.

Alicudi
Ericusa, Via Perciato, tel: 090-988 9902; fax: 090-988 9671. Basic but fine accommodation. A restaurant is attached and half-board arrangement is usually possible. No credit cards. Closed October to May. **$$$$**

Filicudi
Hotel Club Phenicusa, Via Porto, tel: 090-9889946; fax: 090-9889955. For reservations/information, tel: 0941-302501; fax: 0941-301188 all year round. 3-star comfort. Open January to 1 October. **$$$$**

Lipari
Carasco, Porto delle Genti, tel: 090-981 1605; fax: 090-981 1828. As the best on the island, this 3-star hotel enjoys its own private rocky beach and has exquisite views. Good buffet lunches at low prices. Closed 15 October to Easter. **$$$$**
Augustus, Via Ausonia 16, tel: 090-981 1232; fax: 090-981 2233. 2-star. **$$$$**
La Filadelfia, Via F. Mancuso 2, tel: 090-981 2485; fax: 090-981 2486. 2-star. **$$$**
Poseidon, Via Ausonia 7, tel: 090-981 2876; fax: 090-988 0252. 2-star. Closed 15 November to early March. **$$$**
Albergo Casa Vittorio, Vico Sparviero 15, tel: 090-981 1523. This basic hotel is set among 18th-century palazzi in a secluded part of the island. Rooms or apartments are available. No credit cards. **$**

Panarea
Cincotta, Via San Pietro, tel: 090-983001; fax: 090-983211. 3-star. Closed October to mid-April. **$$$$**
Lisca Bianca, Via Lani 1, tel: 090-983004; fax: 090-983291. 3-star. Large garden and balconies in each room. **$$$$**

Stromboli
La Sciara Residence, Via Soldato Cincotta, tel: 090-986004; fax: 090-986284. A comfortable 3-star hotel, one of Stromboli's best, as reflected in the price. Closed 20 October to mid-April. **$$$$**
La Sirenetta, Via Marina 33, tel: 090-986025; fax: 090-986124. 3-star. Closed November to Easter. **$$$$**
Miramare, Via Nunziante 3, tel: 090-986047; fax: 090-986318. Very basic. Closed 7 October to mid-April. **$$**
Pensione La Nassa, Via Fabio Filzi, tel: 090-986033. Terraced double rooms. **$$**

Price Categories

$$$$: L200,000–L400,000;
$$$: L140,000–L200,000;
$$: L100,000–L135,000;
$: L55,000–L95,000.
Price categories are based on the cost of a room including breakfast

Vulcano

Arcipelago, Loc. Vulcanello, tel: 090-985 2002; fax: 090-985 2154. 3-star. Seawater pool. Minimum rent 3 days. Closed November to Easter. **$$$$**
Garden Vulcano, Loc. Porto Ponente, tel: 090-985 2338. This is an old-fashioned 3-star hotel lying in exotic gardens and is owned by a retired sea-captain who has decorated the rooms with his 'treasures'. **$$$$**
Orsa Maggiore, Loc. Porto Ponente, tel: 090-985 2018; fax: 090-985 2415. 2-star. Closed 20 October to 20 April. **$$$$**

Youth Hostels

There are only three youth hostels on Sicily. They have a tendency to be closed when you want them. The private hostel in Siracusa is the most reliable and generally the most pleasant.
Aeolian Islands: Via Castello 17, Lipari Island, tel: 090-981 1540; fax: 090-981 1715. Hostel card required. No reservations in August. Lock out 9.30am–1pm and 3–6.30pm, curfew midnight–1am. 25 beds.
Enna: Via Nazionale, Lago di Pergusa, just outside Enna. No telephone. Unless you like Grand Prix, check that no race is scheduled during your stay. The race-track runs around the lake, close to the youth hostel.
Siracusa: Albergo per la Gioventù, Viale Epipoli 45, Siracusa, tel: 093-711 118; fax: 093-377922. Azienda rents out private apartments close to the beach for a minimum of four days, from June to September. Equipped kitchen and sheets are provided. Good location in the country, 23 km (14 miles)

from Catania, 40 km (25 miles) from Siracusa. The apartments are inside old farmhouses.

Rural Holidays

Agriturismo describes a holiday stay in the country, often on a working farm. *Agriturismo* is officially illegal in Sicily since the appropriate legislation has yet to be passed. In practice, it is accepted but is not as developed in Sicily as in other parts of Italy. It can offer an interesting alternative to a hotel-based holiday. At its best, it provides a real opportunity for contact with Sicilians and a traditional way of life. At its worst, it is occasionally an exploitative business venture. Most *agriturismo* locations are, naturally enough, in small villages or in the country. Book in advance.

AGRIGENTO PROVINCE
Contrada Capello, 6 km (4 miles) from Sciacca. Minimum one week rent. No heating or sheets, equipped kitchen, cheap. Green surroundings.

SIRACUSA PROVINCE
Noto, Azienda Agricola Roveto. For information: Sig. Giuseppe Loreto, Via Adige 3, Siracusa, tel: 0931-66024; fax: 0931-36946. Although this has no *Agriturismo* there are flats to rent – at a minimum of 3 days for two people – inside a nature reserve.
Siracusa, SS. 115. 3–5 km (2–3 miles) south of Siracusa, Azienda Agricola Rinaura, tel: 0931-721224. No *agriturismo*. One room flats in farmhouse. Open all year.
Villaggio le Grotte, Viale Lidi, Fontane Bianche, tel: 0931-790625. Bungalows. Open July and August.

CATANIA PROVINCE
Azienda Agrituristica Fondo 23, Via San Giuseppe La Rena Fondo 23, tel: 095-592521. No *agriturismo*. Flats inside a 14th century farmhouse. Open all year.
Giarre, Azienda Agricola Russo Tocca, Loc. Mascari, tel: 095-931229; fax: 095-779 4765. No *agriturismo*. Flats near the sea. Open all year.

MESSINA PROVINCE
Capo d'Orlando, Azienda Agricola F.P. Milio, Loc. S. Gregorio, tel: 0941-955008/0336-924666; fax: 0941-955281. English spoken.

PORTOPALO DI CAPO PASSERO
Villaggio Turistico Capo Passero, Via Tagliamenti 22–26, tel: 0931-842030. Two room apartments available all year. Without kitchen. Full *pensione* available.

Camping

There are over 80 official camp sites on Sicily, mainly on the coast. The sites are ranked from 1- to 4-star according to their facilities. 1-star sites are basic, 4-star luxurious. Hot water may not always be available. Some sites cram in large numbers in high season. Many sites will provide sleeping bag space for those without tents. Prices are generally reasonable, but vary greatly between provinces. Always phone ahead: sites may be full – or closed if trade is slack.

Camping rough is frowned upon, and is illegal in the national parks. In summer, beware of starting fires which can be dangerous and destructive.

The following is a small selection of camp sites.

PALERMO PROVINCE
Palermo
Eolie Yachting Spa, Via Principe di Belmonte, tel: 091-321419.

Cefalù
Costa Ponente, Loc. Ogliastrello, tel: 0921-420085. Open 1 April to 31 October.
San Filippo, Loc. Ogliastrello, tel: 0921-420184. Open April to October.

Sferracavallo
Trinacria, Via Barcarello 26, tel: 091-530590. Open all year.

Termini Imeresi
Himera, Stazione di Buonfornello, tel: 091-8140240. Open all year.

TRAPANI PROVINCE

Castellammare del Golfo
Ciauli, Contrada Ciauli, tel: 0924-39042. Open July and August only.
Lu Baruni, Scopello, tel: 0924-39133. Open all year.
Nausica, Via Milano 24, tel: 0924-33030. Open summertime only.

Campobello di Mazara
Sombrero, Lido di Tre Fontane, tel: 0924-80300.

Castelvetrano
Lido Hawai, Loc. Triscina, tel: 0924-84101.

Marsala
Villa del Sole, Lungomare Mediterraneo, 57, tel: 0923-952911. Open summertime only.

San Vito lo Capo
El Bahira, Loc. Salinella, tel: 0923-972577. The office is situated at Via La Malfa 68 in Palermo, tel: 091-322696. Open April to October.
La Fata, Via Piersanti Martarella 78, tel: 0923-972133. Open all year.
Soleado, Via della Secca, tel: 0923-972688.

EGADI ISLANDS

Favignana
Egadi, Contrada Arena, tel: 0923-921555. Open all year.
Miramare, Loc. Marasolo, tel: 0923-921330. Bungalows available. Open all year.
Quattro Rose, Contrada Mulino a Vento, tel: 0923-921223. Open all year.

AGRIGENTO PROVINCE

Agrigento
Campeggio Internazionale, San Leone, tel: 0922-416121. Open all year.
Nettuno, San Leone, tel: 0922-416268. Open all year.

Eraclea Minoa
Eraclea Camping, tel: 0922-846023. Open April–September. 3-star. Camp site by the beach below the ruins of a Greek theatre. No hotels and few houses. In good weather, the remains of Minoa are visible in the sea.

Lampedusa (Pelagie Islands)
La Roccia, Loc. Cala Greca, tel: 0922-970964. Open all year.

Menfi
Le Palme, Contrada Lido Fiori, tel: 0925-78392. Open all year.

SIRACUSA

Augusta
La Baia del Silenzio, Loc. Campolato, tel: 0931-981881. Open all year.

Avola
Sabbia d'Oro, Contrada Chiusa di Carlo, tel: 0931-822415. Open all year.

Melilli
Happy Holiday, SS.114, Contrada Campane, tel: 0931-914082. Open May to October.

Portopalo di Capo Passero
Campeggio Captain, Contrada Capo Isola delle Correnti, tel: 0931-842595. Open June to October

Siracusa
Campeggio Fontane Bianche, Loc. Fontane Bianche, tel: 0931-790333. Open 1 May to 30 September.

CATANIA PROVINCE

Acireale
Panorama, Via S. Caterina, 65, tel: 095-763 4124. Open all year.

Calatabiano
Castello di San Marco, San Marco, tel: 095-641181. Open all year.

Catania
Europeo, Viale Kennedy 91, tel: 095-591026. Open all year.

Riposto
Praioia, Loc. Carruba, tel: 095-964366. Open April to September.

ETNA ENVIRONS

Linguaglossa
Clan dei Ragazzi, Pineta di Ragabo, tel: 095-643611. Open all year.

Taormina
Camping S. Leo, Capo Taormina, Via Nazionale, tel: 0942-24658. All year.

Letojanni
Camping Euro Marmaruca, Via IV Novembre, tel: 0942-36676.
Camping Paradise International, SS 114, tel: 0942-36306. Open April to September.

MESSINA PROVINCE

Forza d'Agro
Forza d'Agro Mare, tel: 0942-751158. Open July and August.

Capo d'Orlando
Camping S. Rosa, Via Trazzera Marina, tel: 0941-901723. Open 15 June to 15 September.

Furnari
Camping Bazia, Contrada Bazia, tel: 0941-800130. Open summertime only.

Gioiosa Marea
Camping Gioiosa, Contrada Capo Calavà, tel: 0941-301523. Open April to September.
Camping Residence Cicero, Via Cicero S. Giorgio, tel: 0941-39554. Open summertime only.
Camping Tirreno, Contrada Calavà, tel: 0941-301028. Open 1 June to 30 September.

Oliveri
Camping Baia del Principe, Via Lungomare 11, tel: 0941-313817. Open summertime only.

Tusa
Camping lo Scoglio, SS 113, tel: 0921-334345. Open summer only.

AEOLIAN ISLANDS

Lipari
Camping Baia Unci, Via Marina Garibaldi Canneto, tel: 090-981 1909. Open Easter to end of October.

Vulcano
Camping Togo, Via Porto Levante, tel: 090-985 2303. Open April to September.

Eating Out

What to Eat

Forget the diet while in Sicily. Refusing to try the many specialities would be sacrilege. Sicilian cooking is simpler than that of many Italian regions. Fresh vegetables, fish and fruit play an important part. The fresh herbs of the island are also very important in the flavours of its cooking. Inland, dishes are made from traditional sheep and horse cheese (*caciocavallo*). Tomatoes, parsley, lemons, together with the various sea food influences are predominant.

In the west of the island, the Moorish influence is still felt in dishes made with pine nuts and raisins, or in Trapani's couscous.

Sicilian cakes, biscuits and desserts, often made with almonds, range from the sweet to the extremely sweet. Sicilians eat them in quantity. Try them with a dry white wine. Fruit is also widely used in desserts, as are ricotta cheese and honey. Pistachio nuts are used to flavour both cakes and ice-creams. Each province has its own specialities.

Order as the Sicilians would, beginning with *antipasti* (hors d'oeuvres). Vegetables claim major roles: *melanzane* (aubergine/eggplant) – grilled, marinated, fried or baked. *Caponata* is a mix of fried aubergines, tomatoes, celery, carrots and capers. But, keeping in mind that this is only the start of the meal, try the *insalata di mare*, seafood with oil, lemon and herbs, or the *pesce spada affumicato* (smoked swordfish).

Next comes pasta, in all shapes and flavours, mixed with tomatoes and vegetables or seafood. For the main dish try *sarde a beccafico*, fresh filleted sardines stuffed with bread crumbs, pine nuts, raisins and capers, then baked. Mussels are very good in Sicily, as is fish. For simpler tastes, try a steak of grilled swordfish or tuna. Meat courses are often veal cooked in various sauces or fillet steak. Sicilian sausages made with chopped pork and fennel are also tasty. After a substantial Sicilian meal, you may be content with fresh fruit or ice-cream for dessert, but if you can manage it, try the *cassata*, a sponge cake with a filling of ricotta cheese and candied fruits, or *cannoli*, brandy biscuits, filled with ricotta cheese, candied fruits and small chocolate chips.

Although Sicilians normally eat at least three courses, they have become accustomed to the eccentricity of tourists, who sometimes choose to order only one course.

Where to Eat

There are various types of places to eat and drink:
Bar/Caffè: all types of beverages; also, they usually serve sandwiches and snacks.
Locanda, Osteria, Rosticceria, Trattoria: offer simple local dishes.
Ristorante: offers more elaborate and expensive menus.
Pizzeria: serves pizza and sometimes pasta dishes.
Gelateria: ice-cream parlour.
Tavola Calda: serves hot, inexpensive food. Usually self-service. You may be expected to eat standing up at the counter.

Most restaurants display a menu outside, and some offer a *menù turistico*: a fixed-price three-course meal. This is usually uninspired but good value.

All bars and restaurants must by law issue a receipt (*ricevuta fiscale*). Depending on the local level of activity by the *Guardia della Finanza*, you may find this pressed upon you, or not. Take it with you when you leave: the restaurant (and you) are liable to a fine if you don't.

Restaurant Menus

The menu, please/*il menù, per favore*
The bill, please/*il conto, per favore*
Thank you, that was a very good meal./*Grazie. Abbiamo mangiato molto bene.*

Starters (Antipasti)
aubergine in tomato sauce/*melanzane in parmigiana*
aubergine, olives and tomato/*caponata*
ham/*prosciutto*
mixed cold starters/*antipasti misti*
peppers in oil/*peperonata*
seafood salad/*insalata di mare*
stuffed tomatoes/*pomodori ripieni*

First Course (Il Primo)
clear soup/*il brodo*
light soup/*la minestrina*
mixed/green salad/*un'insalata mista/verde*
egg/*un'uova*
pasta dishes: including *pasta fagioli* (pasta soup with beans); *pasta al forno* (baked, stuffed pasta); *penne; ravioli; rigatoni; spaghetti; tagliatelle; tortellini; cannelloni* and *vermicelli.*

Second Course (Il Secondo)
meat/*la carne*
fish/*il pesce*
What kind of fish do you have?/*Che pesce ha?*
anchovies/*le accuighe*
beef/*il manzo*
chicken/*il pollo*
chickens' livers/*i fegatini di pollo*
clams/*le vongole*
crab/*il granchio*
dried salted cod/*baccalà*
eel/*l'anguilla*
lamb/*l'agnello*
liver/*il fegato*
lobster/*l'aragosta*
mackerel/*lo sgombro*
meatballs/*le polpette*
meat slices (rolled & stuffed)/*gli involtini*
mullet/*il cefalo*
mussels/*le cozze*
octopus/*il polipo*
oysters/*le ostriche*
prawns/*i gamberi*
pork/*il maiale*

rabbit/*il coniglio*
red mullet/*la triglia*
salami/*salame*
  (including mortadella)
sardines/*le sarde*
sausage/*la salsiccia*
shrimps/*i gamberetti*
squid/*i calamari*
steak/*la bistecca*
swordfish/*il pesce spada*
tripe/*la trippa*
trout/*la trota*
tuna/*il tonno*
veal/*il vitello*

Price Guide

Prices given are for a three-course meal for one, with half a bottle of house wine:
$$$ = Expensive
(L50,000–L70,000)
$$ = Moderate
(L35,000–L50,000)
$ = Inexpensive
(L20,000–35,000)

Vegetables

artichokes/*i carciofi*
asparagus/*gli asparagi*
aubergine (eggplant)/*le melanzane*
basil/*il basilico*
beans/*i fagioli*
courgettes/*gli zucchini*
fennel/*i finocchi*
garlic/*l'aglio*
green beans/*i fagiolini*
green vegetables/*la verdura*
mushrooms/*i funghi*
onion/*la cipolla*
peas/*i piselli*
peppers/*i peperoni*
potatoes/*le patate*
spinach/*gli spinaci*
tomato/*il pomodoro*
vegetables (side dishes)/*i contorni*

Fruit, Nuts, Cheese & Desserts

almonds/*le mandorle*
apple/*la mela*
cheese/*il formaggio*
cherries/*le ciliege*
figs/*i fichi*
fruit/*la frutta*
fruit salad/*la macedonia*
grapes/*le uva*
ice cream/*il gelato* (best is *cassata*)

macaroons/*amaretti*
medlar/*la nespola*
melon/*il melone*
Parmesan/*il parmigiano*
peach/*la pesca*
pear/*la pera*
persimmons/*i cachi*
pineapple/*l'ananas*
prickly pears/*i fichi d'india*
strawberries/*le fragole*
sweets/*i dolci*
tart or cake/*la torta*
watermelon/*il cocomero*

Regional Specialities

The following describes the regional specialities, province by province, beginning with the provincial capitals in all cases. (Also consult the chapter entitled *Food*). The provinces are listed in the order in which they appear in the *Places* section of the book. If the word *contrada* appears in the address, it means that the restaurant is outside the town, probably in a rural area.

Also under each section is mention of noteworthy places to eat ice creams and *pasta reale* (marzipan).

PALERMO

The most famous Palermitan dish is *pasta con le sarde* (also known as *pasta alla palermitana*), pasta with a sauce of fresh sardines, tomato sauce, pine nuts and raisins. *Incasciata* is made with broccoli, sausage, raisins, garlic and pine nuts. *Pasta con le seppie* is pasta with a black sauce made from cuttle fish or octopus. Fish is important in Palermitan cooking.

Il braciolone are thick slices of meat filled with boiled eggs, parsley, cheese and pork lard. *Pupi di zucchero* are sugar statues made for special occasions.

Snacks: Street stands in Palermo, instead of hot dogs, sell *stigghiola*, goat intestines filled with onions, cheese and parsley and then grilled. *Frittelle* are corn mealpancakes served with various fillings. *Panelle*, fried chick pea squares, are common street food.

Palermo City

Palermo's top hotels also have renowned restaurants. In particular, consider dining at Villa Igiea, the Excelsior Palace and Albergo delle Palme (*see Where to Stay, Palermo, page 329*.)

L'Abbuffata, Via Messina Marina 442, tel: 091-474685. Hearty portions at moderate prices. **$$**

Acanto Blu, Via Guardinone 19, tel: 091-326258. Reservations essential. No credit cards. Closed lunchtime, Sunday and September. **$$**

Ali Baba, Piazza San Francesco da Paola (near the Politeama and Palazzo di Giustizia). Sicilian food with the Moorish influence common to the west of the island. **$**

Antica Focacceria San Francesco, 58 Via A Paternostro, tel: 091-320264. This institution is not to everyone's taste but deserves a visit. It is quaint, hectic, always open, and rough and ready. The place for innards, *arancini* and *panini di panelle*. **$**

Cafe Quattro Canti, Corso Vittorio Emanuele 315. Good for snacks like *crostini*; eat in the tea room.

Cappuccio, Via Villareale 20. A *tavola calda*/bar selling snacks like stuffed sardines, quiches and salami.

La Carbonella, Via delle Madonie, 39 Traversa Regione Siciliana, tel: 091-513161. Out of the centre location. Pizza in the evenings; plus an outside dining area. Closed Monday and August. **$$**

Charleston, Piazzale Ungheria 30, tel: 091-321366. Top quality Sicilian cuisine, arguably Sicily's best. Dress elegantly, especially in the evenings (no shorts). Reservations required. Closed Sunday. From 1 June to early October the restaurant moves to Mondello, inside the Stabilimento Balneare (a private beach), tel: 091-450171. **$$$**

Cucina Papoff, Via La Lumia, 29/b, tel: 091-325355. Refined yet imaginative Sicilian cuisine in an Art Nouveau setting. Friendly atmosphere. Try the *u maccu*, broad beans in fennel. Closed Sunday and August. **$$**

Galileo, Via Galileo Galilei 49, tel: 091-681 9812. **$$**

Gigi Mangia, Via Principe di Belmonte 104/D, tel: 091-587651. Delicious vegetarian appetisers. Try the *Il Colonnello Va A Favignana*, a pasta dish with tomatoes, herbs and *bottarga*. Closed Sunday. **$$**

Gourmand's, Viale della Libertà 37, tel: 091-323431. Restaurant in sophisticated ultra-modern style. The dishes are light and delicate, including *antipasti* and *spada affumicato*. Smoked tuna and swordfish are homemade specialities. Closed Sunday and August. **$$$**

Osteria da Ciccio, Via Firenze 6, tel: 091-329143. Offers peperoni (peppers) and swordfish in garlic and herbs. Closed Sunday. **$$**

Da Peppino, Piazza Sferracavallo 78, tel: 091-532934. Fish dishes only. Closed Thursday. **$$**

Pizzeria Bellini, Piazza Bellini. A bustling pizzeria in a lovely location, suitable after a visit to La Martorana church. Marlon Brando praises it in the Bellini's autograph book. It is open until 2am in summer so makes an attractive spot from which to view the illuminated churches. **$$**

Ristorante la Botte, Contrada Lenzitti 20, Circonvallazione Monreale, tel: 091-414051. Out of the centre location. Normally open only Friday and Saturday, but can accommodate groups during the week upon booking. Closed August. **$$**

Roney's, Viale della Libertà 13. Chic terrace bar for superior people-watching. Snacks and light food, from *calamari fritti* and *arancini* to ice cream. **$$**

La Scuderia, Viale del Fante 9, tel: 091-520323. Excellent Sicilian cuisine. Closed Sunday and for two weeks in August. **$$$**

Self Service, Piazza Politeama (near tourist office). Sicilian food to eat on the premises or to take away. **$**

Shanghai, Vicolo dei Mezzani 34, tel: 091-589702. The food is cheap; the house is crumbling. This is definitely not the smartest place in Palermo, but it is on everybody's list. The den views the chaotic Vucciria market, from which the food is hauled up in wicker baskets. Food may be cooked in front of you. There is also an outside dining area. No credit cards. Closed Sunday and February. **$**

Trattoria al Buco, Via Granatelli 33, tel: 091-323661. Sound cuisine served in an attractive modern decor. Closed Monday. **$$**

Trattoria il Vespro, Via B. d'Acquisto 9, tel: 091-589932. Closed Monday, except summer, and for one week in August. **$$**

Trattoria Stella (Albergo Patria), Via Alloro 104, tel: 091-616 1136. This snug neighbourhood restaurant is in the courtyard of a ruined palazzo. Its hearty cuisine makes it popular with locals. In summertime open Monday, closed Sunday. Closed Monday (rest of year) and for 2 weeks in August. **$$**

Mondello

Mondello continues to be a fashionable summer dining place. Many *trattorie* have outdoor terraces and sea views.

Chamade Kuletto's Amare, Via Regina Elena 45/47, tel: 091-450512. Great selection of appetisers and delicious pizzas. Terrace. Open daily. **$$**

Charleston le Terrazze, Via Regina Elena, tel: 091-450171. On the jetty off the bay. Summer residence of the Charleston, the famous Palermo restaurant. Quality and price match the city branch. Dress code enforced for dinner (no shorts). Closed October to May. **$$$**

Ristorante Totuccio, Via Torre 26/a, tel: 091-450151. A restaurant/piano bar located on the first floor, with good shellfish and a wide selection of *antipasti*. Try the *zuppa di vongole* (clam soup). Pizza served evenings only. Closed Wednesday and January. **$$$**

At the other end of the market, one can snack cheaply from the stalls. *Pasta alle sarde*, deep fried fish, whitebait, shrimps, vegetables, mussels, couscous and *frittelle* are all available – and the sea view is free.

PALERMO PROVINCE

The province of Palermo, with the exception of Palermo and Cefalù, have unexceptional *ristoranti*. Try *locande, osterie* or *trattorie* instead. Many of these open and close as the mood takes them; many remain shut throughout the winter.

Monreale

With the advent of mass tourism, prices in Monreale have risen out of all proportion to the quality of the cuisine and service.

Osteria delle Lumache, Via San Castrense 50. This is an unpretentious place for standard Sicilian fare. **$**

Alternatively try the *focacceria* (bakery) next door for typical snacks. But the best way to eat in Monreale is to go to a well-stocked grocery and have a *panino* made up to taste.

Riccardo III, C. da Grotte-Monreale, tel: 091-414237. This interesting restaurant is situated inside an old stable with a fireplace. No credit cards. Open weekends only, closed August. **$$**

Cefalù

Eating out can be expensive in the height of the season. However, many of the *trattorie* on the seafront (*Lungomare*) do *antipasto al buffet*, self-service starters at low prices.

Hosteria del Duomo, Via del Seminario 5, tel: 0921-421838. Lovely open-air location overlooking the cathedral. Authentic *caponata* and *penne* and *carpaccio di pesce*, thin slices of raw fish in a light marinade. Closed Monday, except summer, and December. **$$$**

Kentia, Via Nicola Botta 15, tel: 0921-423801. Renowned for its charm, good cuisine and garden. Sample the *scaloppine ai funghi* and *panzerotti di magro* (cannelloni). There is reasonably priced Sicilian set menu. Closed Monday, except summer, and for 3–4 weeks in November. **$$$**

Da Nino Alla Brace, Lungomare 11, tel: 0921-422582. Recommended for French/Sicilian cuisine in a

garden setting. Young locals also congregate here to eat pizzas – served only in the evenings. Exceptional fish. Closed Tuesday, except summer, and November. **$$**
Osteria Magno, Via Belvedere 3, tel: 0921-423679. Restaurant and *pizzeria* (served evenings only) with seafood specialities. Closed Tuesday, except summer, and several weeks in winter. **$$$**
Lo Scoglio Ubriaco, Via Corso di Bordonaro 2, tel: 0921-423370. A terrace overlooking the harbour: watch the fishing boats whilst enjoying *spaghetti al cartoccio* (baked spaghetti). Closed Tuesday and two weeks in November. Open daily from 15 June to 15 September. **$$**

Terrasini
Caffè del Duomo, Piazza Duomo. This is the place for snacks, ice-creams and cakes.
L'Orlando Furioso, Viale Rimembranze 1, tel: 091-868 2553. Good spaghetti with lobster and grilled fish. Outside dining area. Closed Tuesday, except summer. **$$**

Ustica Island
There are a few *trattorie* around the port, all about the same in standard and price.

TRAPANI PROVINCE
Il cuscus, a variation of Arab couscous, is the most famous speciality and is flavoured with fresh rock fish soup. Vegetable couscous is also available. *Tonno alla marinara*, fresh tuna, caught locally, stuffed courgettes and aubergines (eggplant) are also common. Desserts include *le mostacciole* from Erice, and *le paste vergini* from Alcamo.

Trapani
Casablanca, Via San Francesco d'Assisi 69. Moderate, specialising in couscous, crêpes and fish.
Colicchia, corner of Via delle Belle Arti and Via Carosio (near Via Torrearsa), tel: 0923 547612. The place for *granita* or ice cream in the summer. *Cannoli* available. Closed Monday, except summer.

Gino, Piazza Garibaldi. Another place for ice cream.
Da Peppe, Via Spalti 50, tel: 0923-28246. Tuna specialities from May to early July, fish dishes all year. Closed Saturday, except in summertime. **$$$**
P & G Ristorante, Via Spalti 1 (by the Villa Margerita park and the station), tel: 0923-547701. This casual seafood place serves *neonata* (new-born sardines), *risotto marinara* (seafood risotto) and, Friday only, couscous. Closed Sunday and August. **$$**
I Trabinis, Circolo Arcigola, Largo Porta Galli, tel: 0923-24462. Reservations essential. No credit cards. Closed Wednesday and Christmas. **$$**
Trattoria Safino, Piazza Umberto I (opposite the railway station). Huge portions at low prices. **$**

Price Guide

Prices given are for a three-course meal for one, with half a bottle of house wine:
$$$ = Expensive (L50,000–L70,000)
$$ = Moderate (L35,000–L50,000)
$ = Inexpensive (L20,000–35,000)

Erice
Erice's quaint streets are overflowing with bars and restaurants so visitors are spoilt for choice. Consult the chapter on *Trapani Province* for Erice and descriptions of many of the local pastry shops.
Al Ciclope, Viale Nasi 45, tel: 0923-869183. Prices range from inexpensive to very expensive depending on your choice of menu. Closed Tuesday, except in summertime.
Taverna di Re Aceste, Via Conte Pepoli, tel: 0923-869084. Authentic tavern famous for couscous and its tasty pesto sauces. **$$**
Ulisse, Via Chiaramonte 45, tel: 0923-869333. Closed Thursday. **$$**

Marsala
Marsala abounds in lively seafood restaurants along the Lungomare. Combine it with a wine-tasting at any one of 300 establishments. (*See Wine section below.*)
Al Baglio Oneto, C da Baronazzo Amafi 55, tel: 0923-996963. The house specialities, including *Sarde a beccafico, cuscus*, and *cassata Siciliana*, are definitely worth sampling. Closed Wednesday, except summer. **$$–$$$**
Caffe Kalos, Piazza della Vittoria (outside Porta Nuova). Pizza, *antipasti*; snacks of pastries and *arancini*.
Enzo e Nino, Via Favorita 26, tel: 0923 989180. Fish and cousous specialities. **$$**
Ristorante Marsa-Allah, Lungomare Boeo 50, tel: 0923-715234. Seafood dishes and charcoal roasts. **$$**

Mazara del Vallo
La Barchessa, Lungomare Mazzini. This old *baglio* (winery or warehouse) is now an outdoor *pizzeria*. **$**
Odeon, on the junction of Via Crispi and Corso Umberto. This bar is the place for breakfast or snacks.
Ristorante Baby Luna, Via Punica 1, tel: 0923-948622. Fish specialities. Closed Monday and two weeks between October and Christmas. **$$**
Ristorante del Pescatore, Via Castelvetrano 191, tel: 0923-947580. Swordfish and spicy pasta dishes. Closed Monday. **$$–$$$**

San Vito lo Capo
Antica Trattoria Cusenza, Via Savoia 24, tel: 0923-972768. Fish dishes. **$$**
Ristorante Riviera, Via Lungomare, tel: 0923-972480. An unpretentious *trattoria* in a small but lively resort. Closed Monday, November and part of December. Open Monday from 15 June to 15 September. **$$**

Selinunte
Lido Azzurro, Via Marco Polo 51, Marinella di Selinunte (on the sea front), tel: 0924-46211. Fresh fish

dishes. Closed late October to late February. **$–$$**
Ristorante Pierrot, Via Marco Polo. Old-established fish restaurant with good *antipasti di mare*. **$$**

EGADI ISLANDS

Tuna fish is the speciality and there are a number of good restaurants on the islands of Levanzo and especially Favignana. Ask for the *tonno all'araba*, Arab-style tuna, cooked in oil and wine with peppers and capers.

Favignana Island

Egadi, Via Cristoforo Colombo 17, (Porto), tel: 0923-921232. Michelin starred restaurant renowned for its fish, including tuna. No credit cards. Closed Wednesday, except summer, and several weeks in the winter. **$$$**
El Pescador, Piazza Europa 38 (Porto), tel: 0923-921035. Run by a fishing family. The house speciality is spaghetti with fresh tuna and capers (*spaghetti della casa*). The restaurant can be relied on to take the pick of the fresh catch. Closed Wednesday, except summer, and several weeks in winter. **$$–$$$**
Ristorante il Nautilus, Via Amendola 5 (Porto; beside the old *tonnara*, the tunnery), tel: 0923-921671. Excellent *carpaccio di tonno* and *spaghetti con tonno e gamberi* (with tuna and prawns). An inexpensive set menu includes spaghetti with shrimps, capers and tomatoes. No credit cards. Closed Tuesday, except summer. **$$**
La Tavernetta del Porto, Contrada del Porto, Portopalo, tel: 0923-842494. This restaurant is not far from a small fishing village. **$$**

AGRIGENTO PROVINCE

Specialities: *Coniglio all'agrodolce*: rabbit cooked with aubergines, capers, olives, celery, sugar and wine. Fresh grilled fish, particularly in the coastal areas such as Sciacca, Porto Empedocle and Lampedusa. *La 'mpignulata*: a dessert, prepared with almonds and sugar. *Cucchiteddu* is also a dessert: a cake filled with pumpkin

preserve. Try *cuscusu*, an almond and pistachio sweet, from the Santo Spirito convent in Agrigento.

Agrigento

Le Caprice, Strada Panoramica 51, tel: 0922-26469. Sicilian specialities and sea views. One of Sicily's best restaurants. Amazing array of *antipasti* and shellfish; tasty swordfish, shrimps and mussels; well worth the expense. Closed Friday and first half of July. **$$$**

La Corte degli Sfizi, Via Atenea 4, Cortile Contarini, tel: 0922-595520. This is a trendy and fairly inexpensive restaurant/*pizzeria*. Several set menus at differing prices. Pizza available at lunchtime. Closed Wednesday, except summer, and November. **$$**
Taverna Mosè, Contrada San Biagio, Mosè, tel: 0922-26778. Situated 1 km (¾ mile) along Caltanissetta road. Although overrated, the *pasta alla norma*, sole and *scaloppine alla pirandello* (scallops with fresh vegetables) are good and the terrace offers a cool retreat. An atmospheric spot with a view of the temples. Closed Monday and August. **$$$**
Del Vigneto, Cavalieri Magazzeni 11, tel: 0922-414319. Set outside town on the Gela road (follow the signs). Authentic cuisine in rustic setting, overlooking vineyards. Closed Tuesday and November. **$$**
Villa Athena, Via Passeggiate Archeologiche 33, tel: 0922-596288. This lovely hotel-restaurant scores highly on atmosphere and views across the Valley of the Temples. Service can

be surly. Reservations are recommended. **$$$**
For a change, have a picnic in the temples. Provisions can be purchased from the **Alimentari** (grocery store) at Via Goeni 23, Piazza Moro.

Caltabellotta

Trattoria La Ferla, Via Colonnello Vita, tel: 0925-951444. A lovely restaurant with authentic, moderately-priced rural cuisine in a scenic village in the mountains. No credit cards. Closed Monday and for two weeks which vary every year. **$$**

Sciacca

The best fish restaurants are in the lower town, near the port and are mostly inexpensive.
Hostaria del Vicolo, 10 Vicolo Sammaritano, tel: 0925-23071. Unpretentious pasta and seafood. Closed Sunday and Monday evening, and 15–31 October. **$$$**

CALTANISSETTA PROVINCE

Specialities include: *minestra di verdura* (minestrone); *caponata* with onions and olives; fried ricotta; *ravioli*. But Caltanissetta is one of the provinces least well-served by restaurants. Home cuisine is good but provincial restaurants are few and far between and bars are generally depressing or intimidating, a result of the province's rural nature and its unfamiliarity with tourism. None of the restaurants selected below approaches the standard of other provinces. In most of the inland towns there will be little choice of restaurant anyway.

Caltanissetta (City)

The city is not a gastronomic centre.
Cortese, Corso Sicilia 166, tel: 0934-591686. The restaurant offers Sicilian specialities at moderate prices. Visa only accepted. Closed Monday and two weeks in August. **$$**
Il Gattopardo, Via Pacini, 20, tel: 0934-598384. This is both a

restaurant and pizzeria but it is open for dinner only. No credit cards. Closed lunchtime, Monday and one week in August. **$**

Butera
Lido degli Angeli, Contrada Falconara, (turn left after castle on the road from Licata), tel: 0934-349054. Restaurant is always open. No credit cards. **$$**

Gela
Centrale Toto, Via Generale Cascini 99, tel: 0933-913104. Simple regional cuisine. Useful if stuck in dreaded Gela. Visa only accepted. Closed Sunday. **$$**

Mazzarino
Alessi, Via Caltanissetta 20, tel: 0934-381549. Restaurant and pizzeria. Pizza only for dinner. Open daily. **$$**

Mussomeli
La Baracca, Via Dogliotti, tel: 0934-952190. Sandwiches and drinks only. No credit cards. Closed Friday and two weeks in August. **$**

ENNA PROVINCE
Specialities are: *La frascatola*: a soup made from milk and flour. *Maccheroni a tre dita*: an egg and flour pasta with a sauce made from cheese, sugar and cinnamon. *Le sfingi*: a rice flour doughnut with honey. And the famous *pasta reale*, marzipan fruits.

Enna
Restaurants in Enna city are far more authentic and welcoming than those around the lakeside resort of Lago Pergusa. From many of Pergusa's *pizzerie*, you can watch the motor racing or boating.
Ariston, Via Roma 353, tel: 0935-26038. An established restaurant serving typical regional dishes. Closed Sunday and two weeks in August. **$$**
Centrale, Via VI Dicembre 9 (off Via Roma), tel: 0935-500963. This established restaurant offers particularly good vegetable pasta dishes. Outside dining area. Closed Saturday except summer. **$$**

La Fontana, Via Volturo 6, tel: 0935 25465. Simple family-run *trattoria*. **$$**
La Griglia, Via Falantano 19. A *caratteristica trattoria* with tasty *bruschetta* and *macheroni alla norma* (with fennel). **$**
Hostaria Impero, Via Reepentite 17, tel: 0935-26018. No credit cards. Closed Sunday. **$**

Piazza Armerina
Mosaici, Contrada Paratore 11, tel: 0935-685453. Reservations essential in the summer. No credit cards. **$$**
La Ruota di Pioni Fiorella, Contrada Paratore Casale (near Roman Villa, Casale), tel: 0935-680542. This is a good *trattoria*, specialising in home made pasta. Try the *maccheroni*, fresh tomato pasta and pickled aubergines. **$$**
La Tavernetta, Via Cavour 14 (near the Dumo), tel: 0935-685883. This town *trattoria* serves pasta with aubergine and wild herbs. Fish specialities. No credit cards. Closed Sunday, but call ahead.**$$–$$$**

RAGUSA PROVINCE
Dishes from Ragusa tend to be rich and highly flavoured, due to the variety of vegetables, cheese and meat available. *Impanata* is a type of pie containing goat or lamb in a sauce of parsley and garlic. *Trippa* in *tegame* is tripe cooked with fried aubergines, cheese, walnuts, almonds, sugar and cinnamon. *La pasta 'ncasciata* is home-made pasta with a sauce made from ricotta, meat, tomatoes and eggs. Desserts: *sospiri di monaca* (nun's sighs) are made from egg yolks, almonds and sugar. The *pecorino* and *caciocavallo* cheeses from Ragusa are justly famed.

Ragusa
Fumia, Via dei Cappuccini 23, tel: 0932-621463. No credit cards. Closed Monday. **$$**
Osteria del Braciere, Contrada San Giacomo Bellocozzo, tel: 0932-231224. An authentic rural *trattoria* just northeast of Ragusa. No credit cards. Closed lunchtime, Monday and 15 July to 15 August. **$$**

U Sarucinu, Via Convento 9, Ibla, tel: 0932-246976. Facing San Giorgio, serving rustic dishes in a vaulted cellar. Set menu available. Closed Wednesday. **$–$$**
Villa Fortugno, 4 km (3 miles) along the Strada Provinciale to Marina di Ragusa, tel: 0932-28656/667134. Country house cuisine with Sicilian sausages and pork stews. Closed Monday and for ten days in August. **$$**

Modica
Trattoria La Rusticana, Viale Medaglie d'Oro 34, tel: 0932-942950. No credit cards. Closed Sunday in July and August, Sunday evening from September to June. **$$**
Trattoria delle Torri, Via Nativo 30–32, tel: 0932-751286. Reservations essential. Located in Costa, the charming Arab quarter, this *trattoria* serves wonderful traditional fare. American Express only. Closed Monday and for a few weeks during the year. **$$**

SIRACUSA PROVINCE
Swordfish is a local speciality, as are locally caught oysters and shrimps. Apart from fish and seafood dishes, the province has few specialities to offer that are not easily found elsewhere on the island. Two exceptions are: *pasta fritta* (sweet balls of honey-coated pasta); *tonno alla marinara* (tuna with onions and spices and stuffed artichokes).

Siracusa
The better restaurants are on the island of Ortygia, where Siracusani beat a retreat at night (*see Nightlife, page 360*).
Archimede, Via Gemmellaro 8, tel: 0931-69701. Arguably the best, or at least the most authentic restaurant on Ortygia. Service is friendly; the food is varied but seafood predominates, with an array of subtle (and fishy) *antipasti*. Closed Sunday, except summer. **$$**
Capriccio, Contrada Canalicchio (2 km/1¼ mile from the Greek Theatre, following the SS. 124 road), tel: 0931-69885. This

boisterous restaurant, *pizzeria* and piano bar is suited to convivial groups. Large choice of *antipasti*. Al fresco dining. Pizza served only for dinner. **$**

Darsena, Riva Garibaldi 6, tel: 0931-66104. With a view overlooking the bridge and inner harbour, this bold, bright *trattoria* serves barely dead shrimps and fish. Closed Wednesday and for several weeks in September or October. **$$**

La Foglia, Via Capodieci 29, Ortygia, (close to the Arethusa fountain), tel: 0931-66233. Vegetarian soups, salads and fish dishes. Fourteenth-century-style glasses and plates, hand embroidered tablecloths. Closed Tuesday, except December and summertime. **$$**

Fratelli Bandieri, Via Trieste 42, tel: 0931-65021. Once Siracusa's best restaurant, it still serves an incredible range of dishes. No credit cards. Closed Monday. **$**

Porticciolo, Via Trento, tel: 0931-61914. Near the market. Offers delicious mixed fish grills or fresh lobster. Closed Monday and for ten days in November. **$$**

Ristorante Minerva, Piazza Duomo 20, tel: 0931-69404. This is conveniently placed for lunch after visiting the magnificent Cathedral. No credit cards. Closed Monday. **$–$$**

La Scaletta, Largo Porto Marina 1, tel: 0931-24727. In Ortygia, in a picturesque spot overlooking the sea. Rustic, quaint, good value, but crowded. The menu features *cucina casalinga*, including spaghetti and seafood dishes. American Express only. **$$**

If you fancy a picnic in the archaeological zone, pick up provisions from **Gastronomia**, Via Teocrito 127.

Noto

Trattoria del Carmine, Via Ducezio 9, tel: 0931 838705. Home cooking and local specialities in a baroque town not known for its cuisine. No credit cards. Closed Monday, except summer. **$$**

CATANIA PROVINCE

Specialities: *pasta alla norma*, one of Sicily's most famous dishes and now served all over the island, originates in Catania. The simple but delicious sauce is made from tomatoes, aubergines and salted ricotta cheese. The taste may vary considerably according to the cook's private recipe, and it is worth trying the dish more than once. *Lo zuzo* is pork marinated in lemon. Desserts and sweets: *torrone* (nougat) is traditional, and *pasta di mandorle*, small almond cakes come from Acireale. The large fish market in Catania, near Piazza Duomo, is well-worth a visit.

Catania

Catania is renowned for its excellent and diverse restaurants. They display eastern Sicilian dishes, such as *agnello alla menta* (lamb with bacon, mint and garlic). It is best to book if dining in expensive restaurants.

La Cantinaccia e le Sue 4 Stagioni, Via Calatafimi 1/A, tel: 095-382009. This upmarket but intimate restaurant is designed in rustic style. Cuisine is international and Sicilian with pizza served in the evening. Closed Wednesday and August. **$$$**

Enzo, Via Malta 26, tel: 095-384884. A welcoming and inexpensive *pizzeria*. Try the *porcina pizza* with sausage and mushrooms. **$**

Il Giardino d'Inverno, summer: San Giovanni la Punta (10 km/6 miles from Catania); winter: Via Asilo S Agata 34, tel: 095-532853. This patrician villa is designed in Art Nouveau style. Dishes include *crêpes con spinaci* (spinach pancakes) and *trancio di salmone* (salmon in herbs). Pizza served evenings. There is also an elegant tea room on the premises. Closed Monday. **$$$**

Hostaria la Zagara, SS. 114 road in the Vaccarizzo area, tel: 095-295020. Renowned for its mixed grills of meat or fresh fish. No credit cards. Closed Tuesday. **$$**

La Siciliana, Viale Marco Polo 52,

tel: 095-370003. Considered Catania's best restaurant. Not cheap, but worth it. Specialities include roast lamb, breaded cutlets, seafood, imaginative vegetable dishes and good Cerasuolo wine. Closed Sunday evening, Monday and one week in August. **$$$**

Spinella and **Savia**, Via Etnea. Catania's best place for hot snacks, pastries and ice-cream. Both opposite the entrance to Villa Bellini.

Catania Coast (North)

Barbarossa, Strada Provinciale, Aci Castello, SS. 114 road to Aci Castello, tel: 095 295539. Seafood as well as stuffed pancakes and notable wines. Closed Monday. **$$–$$$**

Holiday Club, Via dei Malavoglia 10, Aci Trezza, tel: 095-277575. Set in spacious grounds with fine sea views. Dishes include tasty risotto, and seasonal vegetables such as asparagus, chicory (endive) and mushrooms. **$$$**

Selene, Via Mollica 24, tel: 095-494444. This restaurant is set on a rocky spur on the seafront between Ognina and Aci Castello. There are excellent views from the terrace. Delicacies include spaghetti with clams or shrimps. Closed Tuesday and August. **$$$**

Il Timo Ristorante, Sheraton Hotel, Via A. da Messina 45, 95020 Cannizzaro, tel: 095-271557. (It lies along the Lungomare Catania-Acireale, near Aci Castello.) This luxurious spot is renowned for its grilled swordfish and fishy *antipasti*. **$$$**

Acireale

Nino Castorina, Corso Savoia 109, tel: 095-601547. (Closed Monday.) Also at Corso Umberto 63, tel: 095-601546. (Closed Tuesday.) Not restaurants but the place for ice cream, *pasta reale* (marzipan) and pastries.

Panoramico, Viale Ionico 12 Litoranea, tel: 095-885291. A panoramic restaurant with a *pizzeria* and a piano bar. Seafood in the restaurant. **$$**

ETNA ENVIRONS

Delicacies include wonderful vegetables gathered from Etna's fertile slopes and woodlands. Wild mushrooms, asparagus, honey, nuts and fruit are of a high standard. Wild boar (*cinghiale*) and rabbit (*coniglio*) available in season.

Belpasso

La Cantina, Strada Provinciale Nicolosi-Belpasso, tel: 095-912992. A rustic restaurant and pizzeria offering different menus. The star is asparagus or asparagus risotto. No credit cards. Closed Monday and three weeks in November. **$$**

Mount Etna

At Rifugio Sapienza there are mediocre restaurants and snack bars. The best of a poor choice is **La Cantoniera**, which was destroyed in the lava flow of 1982 and then rebuilt.

Nicolosi

Al Bongustaio, Via Etnea 105 F. A typical restaurant with tasty homemade *antipasti*, many made with mushrooms. **$$**
Etna, Via Etnea 93, tel: 095-911937. Traditional Etna cuisine in a post-modern restaurant and *pizzeria*. Specialities include mushroom risotto; *cinghiale alla griglia* (grilled wild boar); and *insalata di funghi crudi* (raw mushroom salad). Pizza only in the evening. Closed Monday and for 2–3 weeks in February or March. **$$**

Pedara

La Bussola, Parco Comunale, Pedara, tel: 095-780 0250. Designed in heavy Spanish style, the restaurant concentrates on Etna dishes, from roasts to game and mushroom delicacies. Also bar and pizza in the evening. Closed Monday. **$$**

Randazzo

Da Veneziana Alfio, Via dei Romano 8, tel: 095-7991353. A restaurant with tasty regional dishes. Closed Sunday evening and Monday. **$$**

Trecastagni

Al Mulino, Via Mulino al Vento 48, tel: 095-780 6634. Set in a grand villa overlooking an old windmill. Specialities include pasta with mushrooms and sausage with herbs. Closed Monday. **$$–$$$**

Zafferana Etnea

Al Parco dei Principi, Via delle Ginestre 1, tel: 095-708 2335. Interesting regional cuisine, with Etna produce. Closed Tuesday. **$$–$$$**

TAORMINA

Taormina has a huge choice of eating places to suit all pockets and tastes, from international style to regional specialities. However, many hotels insist on half-board arrangements so you may be obliged to restrict restaurant sampling to lunch. The hill-top village of Castelmola offers inexpensive alternatives to dining in Taormina itself while, at the foot of the cliffs, the coastal area of Mazzarò has lively and inexpensive *trattorie* and lovely sea views.

Taormina (Town)

Try to avoid most restaurants in Corso Umberto which cater to indiscriminate tourists and tend to be bland and expensive. In general, dining in Taormina is more elegant and select than eating out in Mazzarò or Castelmola.
L'Angolo, Via Damiano Rosso 17, tel: 0942-625202. Pizzeria near the cathedral. Closed Wednesday and January. **$$–$$$**
Gambero Rosso, Via Naumachia 11, tel: 0942-23011. This is family-run, welcoming, with good Sicilian cuisine. **$$**
Il Giardino, Via Bagnoli Croci 84 (near the park gates), tel: 0942-23453. Very friendly, family-run restaurant. With gentle persuasion, the cook will play his guitar and sing Sicilian folk songs. **$$**
Granduca, Corso Umberto 170/172, tel: 0942-24420. This chic, old-fashioned and rather grand restaurant offers lovely views over the bay. The price covers the view as much as the food. **$$**

Da Lorenzo, Via Roma 4, tel: 0942-23480. Prohibitive prices but a glorious setting. Closed Wednesday and for 15 days in December. **$$$**
Oasy Due, Via Apollo Arcageta 9 (near the Post Office), tel: 0942-24771. The food is exceptional. **$**

Taormina/Mazzaro

The coast is reached by a cable car (*funivia*) from Taormina.
La Conchiglia, Piazzale Funivia (near the cable car), tel: 0942-24739. Serves very good pizza at weekends in the low season and all week summer. Moderate prices. Closed Tuesday and for 15–20 days in October or November. **$**
Da Giorgio, Vico Sant' Andrea 7, tel: 0942-625502. On the beach of Isola Bella. Excellent for fish. **$$**

Prices given are for a three-course meal for one, with half a bottle of house wine:
$$$ = Expensive
(L50,000–L70,000)
$$ = Moderate
(L35,000–L50,000)
$ = Inexpensive
(L20,000–35,000)

Oliviero, Via Nazionale 137, tel: 0942-23125. At Mazzarò beach. Excellent restaurant. It also has a piano bar. **$$-$$$**

Castelmola

In season, this tiny village above Taormina represents a boisterous alternative to the town – and the steep climb is one way of working up an appetite. The village specialises in inexpensive bars and *paninoteche* (sandwich places) which are popular with younger visitors – and with heavy drinking German and Scandinavian visitors.
Bar Turrisi, tel: 0942-28181. Toasted sandwiches and mini-pizzas. Interesting exhibit of curios.
Ciccino's, Piazza Duomo, tel: 0942-28081. A rustic *pizzeria* near the cathedral, excellent for thin pizza cooked in a wood-fired oven (*forno a legno*). **$**

MESSINA PROVINCE

Tuna, swordfish, shellfish and lobster, together with the more expensive fish, form the base of this province's cooking. Famous for the *ghiotta* (fish soup), which may contain small rock fish, swordfish or dried cod, prepared with tomatoes, onions, celery, capers, olives and olive oil. *Fritto misto* will contain small fish, prawns and squid, fried in batter. *La pignolata* is a dessert consisting of an almond and sugar base covered in chocolate or icing sugar. *Cannoli*, filled with ricotta cheese, are also traditional.

Messina

Most of the better restaurants lie along Viale San Martino and in or around Via Santa Cecilia. For fish dishes it is best to leave the town centre and go to the Gazzira lake district.
Donna Giovanna, Via Risorgimento 16, tel: 090-718503. Traditional Sicilian cuisine; always crowded.
No. 1, Via Risorgimento 192, tel: 090-717411. Good pizzas – evenings only. Closed lunchtime, Tuesday and 1 June to 31 August. **$**

AEOLIAN ISLANDS

Fish plays a starring role, particularly in *ghiotto* sauce, a blend of capers, oil, tomatoes, garlic and basil. Black rice is popular, coloured by seppia (fish-ink). Octopus, cuttlefish and swordfish are also popular.

Alicudi

Ericusa, Via Perciato, tel: 090-988 9902. This is the only place to stay on the island and offers a reasonable restaurant too. (This is best organised on a full-board arrangement.) No credit cards. Closed October to May. **$$**

Lipari

The various *trattorie* around the harbour are mostly open-air, good, and fairly expensive. The exorbitant local service charge will add 20 percent to the menu prices. The local "tourist menus" should be avoided.

Filippino, Piazza Municipio, tel: 090-981 1002. This is a favourite with the islanders themselves. It is exclusive, pricey but good. Delicacies include fish risotto and complicated main courses. Reservation recommended. Closed Monday, except summertime, and November. **$$$**

Price Guide

Prices given are for a three-course meal for one, with half a bottle of house wine:
$$$ = Expensive (L50,000–L70,000)
$$ = Moderate (L35,000–L50,000)
$ = Inexpensive (L20,000–35,000)

Panarea

Restaurants are expensive in this wealthy island ghetto – wine and fish cost more here than in most Sicilian establishments.

Salina

The better bars and *trattorie* are in the Santa Marina area facing the shore of Lipari. Many dishes contain the tasty local capers. Try Salina's excellent *malvasia* wine.

Stromboli

The best restaurants are in Stromboli town (San Vincenzo) but there are also several good *trattorie* in Ginostra.
Villa Petrusa, Via Soldato Panettieri 4, tel: 090-986045. This restaurant in the main street offers reasonable food. No credit cards. Closed November to mid-March. **$$**

Vulcano

Lanterna Blu, Via Lentía 58, tel: 090-985 2178. Locals flock to this restaurant for its tasty fish dishes. In winter call ahead for opening times. **$$**

Drinking Notes

Wine

Travelling along some roads, you could be excused for thinking that the vine had little significance to modern Sicilian agriculture. Certainly, there are sizeable parts of the island, notably in the areas given over to the other bastions of the Mediterranean triumvirate of staples – grain and the olive – or in the barren central uplands where practically nothing grows at all, where vineyards are scarce. Nevertheless, it is difficult to spend more than a day or so in Sicily without coming across either huge seas or little puddles of vineyards and without being confronted by numerous bottles of their produce.

Grapes and wine have always formed a major part of the Sicilian economy. In the more recent past they had little more than commodity value, being despatched up the strength and colour of insipid offerings from further north: traditional, low, bush-trained vines can develop prodigious amounts of sugar under Sicily's powerful sun. In the past couple of decades, though, there has been a full scale return to producing wines for drinking, not blending, and to harnessing native grape varieties to that end.

The Sicilians have been aided in this by two factors, one man-made, one natural: these last twenty years have seen the rapid growth of the understanding of the 'hows' and 'whys' of good wine together with the technology to control and assist winemaking; and the indigenous grape varieties are ideally suited to the island's climate, particularly when grown at altitude on Sicily's innumerable hill slopes.

Surprisingly, it is the white wines that have taken the lead. From grapes wire-trained not too close to the heat-reflecting soil, astutely pruned, harvested before their acidity drops too low, then carefully fermented at cool temperatures to conserve their aromas, light, dry, delicately floral white wines emerge that can rival some better known names of the wine world as well as being ideal for drinking with Sicilian dishes in a Sicilian climate.

White Western Wines
A market leader is **Terre di Ginestra**, from its high (900 metres/2,900 ft) vineyards above San Cipirello, behind Palermo. The grapes are grown on north-facing slopes to avoid excess sun and handled with extreme skill to produce excellent crisp whites.

The locals cannot agree as to whether **Catarratto** or **Inzolia**, the other popular indigenous grape, makes superior wine.

Tenuta di Donnafugata has chosen Inzolia. *Donnafugata*, meaning Woman who Fled, was an obvious title for an estate with vineyards around Santa Margherita Belice. Not only was this village the refuge of the consort of the Bourbon King Ferdinando IV, who had to flee Palermo in 1812, and who was dubbed Donnafugata as a result but Giuseppe Tommasi di Lampedusa set his magnificent novel *The Leopard* there, evoking the consort's sojourn by using the fictional name Donnafugata for the palace.

Try the standard white, Donnafugata Bianco (based on a Catarratto-Inzolia blend) or Vigna di Gabbri (a refined white made from Inzolia grapes).

Duca di Salaparuta, also keen on Inzolia, produces wine under the Corvo label (*corvo* means crow). It is based at Casteldaccia, just east along the coast from Palermo. It buys grapes from numbers of small growers.

A basic but good drinking wine is Corvo Bianco. But the star is the premium Colomba Platino (meaning platinum dove). Even finer is the oak-matured Bianca di Valguarnera, produced from Inzolia.

Further west, behind the town of Alcamo, lie huge wine estates under the name of Alcamo, a controlled *Denominazione di Origine Controllata* (DOC) area. Try any wines under the Rapitalà estate label.

Wines on Pantelleria
De Bartoli also works on the island of Pantelleria. The Bukkuram (Father of the Vine) estate is named after the zone where the grapes grow. The grapes used are the **Moscato** variety, locally called **Zibibbo**, which are trained as low, individual bushes against the incessant winds.

Try his delicate but sweet Moscato di Pantelleria or the classic, rich Moscato Passito di Pantelleria, from grapes that have been left to dry and concentrate rapidly in the sun after picking.

Wines on the Aeolian islands
The island of Salina has a similar tradition but with **Malvasia** rather than Moscato vines. Sample the wines from the estates of Carlo Hauner; Caravaglio and Cantine Colosi.

Etna Wines
Wines from the slopes of Etna tend to have a heavier and fruitier flavour than those from other parts of the island. In theory, Etna should produce Sicily's best red wines but the expertise in the west of the island is often lacking in the east. An exception should be made for the white and red Murgo wines from the estate of Barone Scammacca.

Wines from Vittoria
Cerasuolo di Vittoria (*cerasuolo* means cherry-coloured) is found in the south-east around Vittoria. The wine is another of Sicily's scarce DOCs, made from a blend of the red variety, **Nero d'Avola**, and the best local variety, **Frappato**.

Rosé Wines
It would also be a mistake to overlook Sicily's rosés. Made predominantly from **Nerello Mascalese**, a light-coloured red grape ideally suited to making delicately fruity pinks, they are often the ideal accompaniment to many of Sicily's classic dishes.

There are numerous other wines of interest: Settesoli's Feudi dei Fiori (white) and Bonera (red), the range of wines from Fattorie dei

Marchesi Platamone, Cellaro (red, white and rosé), Principe di Corleone (red and white), Avide's Cerasuolo di Vittoria, Murana's Moscato di Pantelleria and Moscato Passito di Pantelleria, all of these and more are worthy of attention. New wines are popping up all the time and others get better every year. The moral is therefore clear: if in doubt, try.

Regaleali: The Count's Wines
The Regaleali estate deep in the Sicilian interior is fascinating, both for its wines and as an insight into local wine-growing traditions. The estate is owned by the Conte Tasca d'Almerita, one of the Sicilian aristocrats who has best used the wine trade to adapt itself to the modern world.

Regaleali, the name of the locality and the Count's estate, is near Vallelunga, and is reached from the Palermo-Agrigento artery by tortuous winding roads that slow the pace of all but the most suicidal of drivers. Its vineyards lie between 450 and 650 metres (1,500–2,100 ft), which together with the strong, cooling breezes they attract and their distance from the sea, give very cool nights to balance warm days – almost ideal conditions for vine growing.

The estate has been in the hands of the Conte Tasca family since 1834. Originally extending over more than 1,200 hectares (2,965 acres), it was reduced to less than 200 hectares (500 acres) after World War II by the Marshall Plan, a fact that still seems to rankle with the present incumbents. It was also planted mainly with grain. The changeover to vines has been slow and steady, and is still going on. There are also bees for honey, sheep for cheese, olive trees for oil, and other crops; indeed the estate is well-nigh self sufficient.

The centre of the estate, the family home and cellars, are reached by long sweeping drives through the vineyards. From the entrance to the villa the view is of the family's land for as far as the eye can see. It is the sense of calm

Marsala Wine

All wines so far mentioned have come from the western side of the island. This is not surprising as not only is the west usually reckoned to have better conditions for white winemaking but it also seems to be more go-ahead than the east. This may be an effect of the fame of Marsala and its commercial infrastructure. Whatever the reason, Marsala is the island's focus. Produced in a large area in the extreme west, around the port of Marsala, at its best it rivals the top sherries, madeiras and ports with which it competes.

Marsala is the best-known of all Sicilian wines, originally made famous by the English Woodhouse family. Essentially marsala is made by strengthening (fortifying) a base wine with grape brandy and ageing the resulting liquid.

Marsala is struggling hard to shrug off a negative image: the name has long been associated with cheap, sickly-sweet liqueurs. However, the best estates are largely succeeding in producing fine wines. Take the chance to try some Florio or Pellegrino marsalas: you will discover excellent, dry, smooth sherry-like wines. The best ones of all are labelled *Vergine* or *Riserva*.

While most of the marsala companies have impressive cellars in town, the architect of marsala's revival stays firmly by his vineyards. Marco De Bartoli, an explosively talented individual, driven by a deep fury at the scant regard of his neighbours for their heritage, he has been perfecting a series of marsalas that show just what rich gems the British might have discovered two centuries ago when one Mr Woodhouse arrived in Marsala and started the wine's trade.

De Bartoli's wide range of wines spans sweet and dry, ultra-long-aged and youthful; all of them are based on the **Inzolia** and **Grillo** grapes, the latter being the perfect grape for marsala.

and quiet, though, that gives the estate its particular feel: the hurly-burly of modern-day Sicily seems miles away. Through the main gateway to the villa lies a secluded courtyard where one or more relaxing Tascas often rock languidly backwards and forwards on a shaded garden swing.

The current Count is now in his eighties and has officially passed the running of the estate to the next generation. There is little doubt, however, that his influence remains strong: the Count has real presence and naturally instils deference, if not awe, in all who encounter him.

All this would be of little more than passing interest, of course, were the wines not so fine. It was, however, Regaleali that led the way back to quality winemaking in the quantity-dominated post-war years and the wines are still among Sicily's leaders.

Straight Regaleali white, red and rosé are not to be sneezed at; there's also a pair of elegant sparkling wines and a clutch of wines from fashionable, imported grape varieties. The estate's reputation, though, hangs on two others. Nozze d'Oro, meaning Golden Wedding, is a white, first made in 1985 to celebrate the Count's 50th wedding anniversary.

Now produced in years when weather conditions are particularly favourable, it is refined, rounded, herby, buttery and long-ageing. The Count's favourite, however, is "his" red, Rosso del Conte, made from the grape varieties **Nero d'Avola** and **Perricone**. Intense, full and powerful, it too ages slowly and while examples from the early 1980s are still giving pleasure, those from 1988 onwards, are really exciting.

Buying Wine Direct

Wine growing has a long tradition in Sicily. It is possible to visit the following wine growers and to buy directly from them. It is the rule rather than the exception for producers to make wines of different qualities (and prices), the best coming from particularly favoured vineyards or tight selections of the best grapes. This is not an exhaustive list but all of these vineyards are known to produce good quality wines. Not all of the growers speak a foreign language, but where they do, it is noted below. Do telephone beforehand.

Az. Agr. Vecchio Samperi, Marco De Bartoli, C/da Fornara Samperi 292, 91025 Marsala (TP), tel: 0923 962093. Speaks French.

Cantine Piero Colosi, Via Militare Ritiro 23, 98152 Messina, tel: 090 53852.

Carlo Hauner, Tamara Thorgevsky, Lingua di Salina, 98050 S. Marina Salina (ME), tel: 090 9843392. Speaks English.

Casa Vin. Duca di Salaparuta, Livia Astuni, Via Nazionale SS 113, 90014 Casteldaccia (PA), tel: 091 953988.

Contrada Rapitala, Camporeale, tel: 0924 36115.

cos, Giusto Occhipinti, Piazza del Popolo 34, 97019 Vittoria (RG), tel: 0932 864042. Speaks French.

Loc. Malfa, 98050 Isola di Salina (Messina province).

Regaleali, Distributed by: MD Distribuzione, Via Denti di Piraino 7, 90142 Palermo, tel: 091-6371266; Fax: 091-363198.

Tenuta di Donnafugata, Gabriella Anca Ralla, Loc. Marzaporro, 90030 Contessa Entellina (PA), tel: 0923 999555. Speaks English.

Tenuta San Michele, Barone Scammacca, Barone Scammacca del Murgo, Via Bongiardo (CA), tel: 095-953613.

Terre di Ginestra, Maurizio Miccichè, Piano Piraino, 90040 San Cipirello (PA), tel: 091 8576767. English spoken.

Marsala (various producers)

In Marsala are found the cellars of Florio, Lombardo, Vito Curatolo Arini, Rallo, Pellegrino, C.S. Marsala.

Florio (now owned by Martini) and Pellegrino lead the market in terms of sales. Wine-tasting (including a film and a short guided tour of the cellars) is possible at the bigger producers (*stabilmenti*).

De Bartoli Marco (at Fornara Samperi address above).

Pellegrino, 39 Via Fante, Marsala, tel: 0923-951177.

Stabilmento Florio, V. Vincenzo Florio 1, tel: 0923 781111. The Florio cellars are particularly amenable to visits and offer an interesting and enjoyable tour of the cellars. The *Vergine* marsala is best. Closed Friday pm.

Cookery School

Regaleali, the wine growers, also run a traditional cookery school on their wine estate near Vallelunga. The short courses are led by the family chef. Guests stay on the estate, living with members of Conte Tasca d'Almerita's family. Courses are taught in English or Italian but, if there is the demand, other languages may be considered.

For details, contact Anna Tasca Lanza at:

Regaleali Cookery School, Viale Principessa Giovanna 9, 9139 Palermo (Mondello), Sicily, tel: 091-450727; fax: 091-542783.

Culture

Sicily Sights

Sicily's sights are listed under the chapter headings used in the *Places* section of the book.

The opening times of most monuments are:

Churches and cathedrals: 8.30am–noon and 4–7.30pm.

Archaeological sites: 9am to one hour before sunset.

Museums, galleries and monuments: 8.30am–2pm.

Most museums and archaeological sites close one day a week, usually on Monday. Opening times vary according to the season and are usually shorter in winter, on Sundays and on holidays. Many archaeological sites base their closing time on sunset.

Most museums, galleries and archaeological sites charge a small amount for admission. Reductions are available for children, students and senior citizens on production of a valid form of identification.

In museums and archaeological sites, be prepared for the civil service homeward rush: the staff will begin shepherding visitors, none too politely, towards the exit about 20 minutes before closing. Many archaeological sites are guarded at night, so resist the temptation to climb the fence and watch the sunrise.

Churches, and sometimes museums, may appear permanently closed: there is almost always a *custode* (custodian) or *sacristano* (sacrist) somewhere nearby with a key. Enquire in a bar or of passing locals. In the middle of the countryside, try knocking at the door of the nearest farm. It is usual to give a tip to the custodian.

By doing the same thing, you may sometimes obtain entrance on days when a building is officially closed to the public, or to places closed for restoration. The discouraging, and sometimes disgraceful, sign "*chiuso per restauri*" graces a distressingly large number of monuments. The Italian Government may be praised for its investment in the Sicilian cultural heritage. But the effect on the monument does not always equal Rome's investment and the time between start and completion of work is exceptionally long. A few notorious sites have been *sotto restauro* for the past 25 years, and have barely been open to the public in living memory.

PALERMO CITY

Sadly, some of Palermo's most impressive buildings, including the churches, are rarely open to the public nowadays. Many are nevertheless still worth visiting just to see the exterior. Given that some of the city sights have unreliable opening times, visitors pressed for time may like to consider a guided tour of the city booked with the Palermo Tourist Office, Piazza Castelnuovo 35, tel: 091-583847. Ideally request Pilar Visconti, a highly recommended guide.

For information on the Vucciria Market, *see Shopping page 365.*

Churches

Casa Professa (also known as *Il Gesù*), Piazza Casa Professa. First Jesuits' church in Sicily. Lovely Baroque building. Open daily 7.30–11am.

Cattedrale (Duomo), Corso Vittorio Emanuele. Norman Cathedral containing Royal tombs and small museum. Cathedral is open daily 7am–noon and 4–7pm. Museum open 9.30–11.30am and 4–5.30pm daily.

La Magione, Via Magione. Fine Cistercian foundation in a rather run down area. Open daily 8–11.30am and 3–6.30pm. Also open for Sunday service.

La Martorana (Santa Maria dell'Ammiraglio). Dreamlike Arab-Norman church with Byzantine mosaics. Open daily 9.30am–1pm and 3.30–5.30pm. In winter, closes at 5.50pm and on Sunday afternoons.

Oratorio del Rosario, Via dei Bambinai 2. Near Vucciria market. Grandiose baroque. Serpotta masterpiece. Open daily 9am–1pm and 3–5.30pm

Oratorio di San Lorenzo, Via dell'Immacolatella 5 (left of San Francesco church). It has been recently restored. Caravaggio's Nativity was stolen from here in 1669 so it's been deliberately made hard to see the oratory as a result.

Oratorio di Santa Cita, Via Valverde 3. Serpotta masterpiece. Open 8.30am–12pm.

Sant' Agostino, Via Sant'Agostino. 13th century, interior redecorated in 1671 by Serpotta. Beautiful rose window and portal. Open daily 7am–noon and 4–5.30pm.

San Cataldo, Piazza Bellini. Key available from custodian of La Martorana.

San Domenico, Piazza San Domenico (near the Vucciria Market). Baroque monastic church. Open Tuesday to Saturday 9.30am–12.30pm and 4–6pm; closed Saturday afternoon.

San Francesco d'Assisi, Piazza di San Francesco d'Assisi. Gothic church with Renaissance arch. Open daily 8.30am–12.30pm and 4–6.30pm. (Opposite is a typical place for eating spleen, lungs and other innards.)

San Giovanni degli Eremiti (St John of the Hermits), Via dei Benedettini. Byzantine style church with five domes set in a garden rich with exotic plants. Remains of a mosque visible in the church. Lovely cloisters. Modern "Arab-style" lavatory: a welcome relief. Open daily 9am–1pm and Monday, Tuesday and Thursday 3–5.30pm.

San Giovanni dei Lebbrosi (St John of the Lepers), Via Cappello, 38. Near Corso dei Mille. The oldest church in Palermo (1076). Open daily 4–5.15pm.

Also see Ponte dell' Ammiraglio, the Norman bridge (built 1113) in Corso dei Mille nearby.

San Giuseppe Teatini, Corso Vittorio Emanuele/Piazza Pretoria (Piazza Vigliena). Grand baroque interior. Open daily 7.15am–noon and 6–8pm.

San Ignazio all'Olivella, Piazza Olivella. Baroque; frescoes by Novelli. Classical oratory next-door. Open 9am–4.30pm.

Santa Caterina, Piazza Bellini. Baroque Dominican foundation. Open daily 8am–noon.

Oratorio di Santa Caterina d'Alessandria, Via Monteleone. A Procopio Serpotta masterpiece.

Santa Maria di Porto Salvo, Via Porto Salvo. 16th-century with Catalan-Gothic elements inside.

Santa Maria della Catena, Piazza delle Dogane (off Piazza Marina). Catalan-Gothic with austere interior. Open daily 8.30am–12.30pm.

Santa Maria della Gancia, Via Alloro. Late Gothic frescoed church. Open daily 9am–5pm.

Santa Maria in Valverde, Piazza Valverde. A Carmelite church; splendid multi-coloured marble nave by Amato. Open daily 9am–1pm and 3–5.30pm.

Santa Cita, Corner of Via Valverde and Squiarcialupo. 16th-century church with works by Gagini. (Overlooks Oratorio di Santa Zita). Open daily 9am–1pm and 3–5.30pm.

Santo Spirito (also known as *dei Vespri*), Via dei Vespri. Norman church. The revolt known as the Sicilian Vespers broke out here on 31 March 1282 at the hour of Vespers. Open daily 8am–2pm.

Santa Teresa della Kalsa, Piazza Kalsa, Corso Vittorio Emanuele. Baroque church built for the Barefoot Carmelites; now linked to Mother Teresa. Open daily 7am–7pm.

Museums & Art Galleries

Museo Archeologico Regionale, Piazza Olivella, tel: 091-611 6805. Includes great Classical finds from all over Sicily. One of the richest archaeological collections in Italy and well-worth the visit. Open daily 9am–1.30pm. Tuesday, Wednesday and Friday 9am–1.30pm and 3–6.30pm holidays 9am–1pm.

Museo delle Marionette (International puppet museum), Via Butera 1, tel: 091-328060. Large collection from all over the world, particularly of Sicilian puppets. Fascinating overcrowded storerooms downstairs. Puppet shows are also held here. Open Monday to Friday 9am–1pm and 4–7pm. Closed on Saturday afternoon and holidays.

Museo Etnografico "G. Pitre", Via Duca degli Abruzzi (by Parco della Favorita), tel: 091-740 4885. Large collection of Sicilian folklore and customs, including painted carts. Open daily 8.30am–1pm and 3.30–6.30pm. Closed on Friday and holidays.

Museo Risorgimentale, Piazza San Domenico 1 (near Vucciria), tel: 091-582774. A collection of Garibaldi portraits, medals and sculptures. Open Monday, Wednesday and Friday 9am–1pm. Entrance free.

Palazzo Abatellis, Via Alloro 4. The palace dates from 1490 and now houses the **Galleria Regionale della Sicilia**, tel: 091-616 4317. This art museum includes medieval and Moorish works as well as Renaissance paintings by Antonello da Messina (The Annunciation, Three Saints). There is also a bust of Eleonora of Aragon by Francesco Laurana on display. Open daily 9am–1.30pm and 3–7.30pm; holidays 9am–12.30pm.

Palazzo Mirto, Via Merlo 2, tel: 091-616 4751. 16th-century palace, lived in until relatively recently and furnished as an aristocratic home. Open daily 9am–1pm and 3–6.30pm; Saturday 9am–1pm.

Notable Buildings

Chiosco Ribaudo and **Chiosco Ribaudo**, Piazza Massimo. Two Art Nouveau kiosks in florid, filigree style.

Convento dei Cappuccini, Via Cappuccini, tel: 091-212117. Gruesome catacombs contain 8,000 mummified Palermitans. Mummification continued until 1881. Open 9am–noon and 3–5pm. (Take bus 5 or 27.)

La Cuba, Caserma Tukory, Corso Calatafimi, 100. Moorish pleasure pavilion set in army barracks. Open daily 9am–1pm. Monday, Tuesday and Thursday 9am–1pm and 3–5.30pm. Sundays 9am–noon (check with the guardroom). Outside these times, an enquiry to a soldier often works wonders.

La Cubola, Corso Calatafimi 575. Tiny Moorish pavilion set in grounds of Villa Napoli. Ask the custodian at Villa Napoli or see the exterior only.

La Zisa, Piazza Guglielmo II Buono, tel: 091-652 0269. Built under the Normans but in Arab style. Contains a museum of Arab art. Open daily 9am–1pm and 3–6.30pm.

Palazzina Cinese, Piazza Niscemi. Set in Parco della Favorita. Built in 1799. Exotic chinoiserie fantasy, "closed for restoration"; consult the tourist office to protest. Worth seeing from outside.

Palazzo Aiutamicristo, Via Garibaldi. Catalan-Gothic palace. Walk through the gateway at No. 22 and you can see the lovely arcaded courtyard and delicate loggias.

Palazzo Chiaramonte (or Steri), Piazza Marina 61. Formerly the headquarters of the Inquisition, now houses the University rectorate. Officially closed to the public. With a bit of bravado and a manufactured excuse, it's worth walking into the courtyard and pleading to see the Sala Magna, the fine interior with its mudejar (coffered) Moorish ceiling.

Palazzo Lampedusa, Via Lampedusa. Bombed rubble remaining from Lampedusa's Palermitan home.

Palazzo Pretorio (delle Aquile), Piazza Pretorio. The former Senate, now the Town Hall. Exterior only.

Palazzo dei Normanni, Piazza Indipendenza, tel: 091-705 4749; fax: 091-656 1737. The palace houses: the Sicilian Parliament; the Royal Apartments; Sala di Re Ruggero (King Roger's Room); and the Cappella Palatina (Palatine Chapel) with Byzantine and Arab-Norman mosaics. You must make a written request in advance.

Palazzo Sclafani, Piazzetta S Giovanni Decollato. Noble palace built in 1330. See facade, arches and doorway.

Politeama, Piazza Politeama. Elegant neoclassical theatre in Pompeiian style. Opera and ballet venue.

Porta Nuova, Corso Calatafimi. A grand Spanish gateway decorated with statues of eight great Moors.

Santuario di Santa Rosalia, on Monte Pellegrino, tel: 091-540326. Sanctuary of Palermo's patron saint. Views of the city and the bay. Open: Monday to Saturday 7am–12.30pm and 2–7.30pm, Sunday 7am–8pm. Ring for entrance. Free. Bus 812 from Palermo.

Teatro Massimo, Piazza Verdi. A neoclassical theatre started by Filippo Basile and completed by Ernesto Basile. It is one of the largest opera houses in Europe.

Villa Igiea, Salita Belmonte. Built as a villa by the Florio family in the 19th century. Decorated in Art Nouveau style. Now a luxury hotel: the public rooms can be seen for the cost of a drink at the bar.

Villa Malfitano, Via Dante. Mansion and walled park. Open daily 9am–1pm, closed Sunday. (Also open for concerts.)

Villa Niscemi (next-door to Palazzina Cinese). Lovely villa currently being restored. Request to see it at the Palermo tourist office.

Parks
Orto Botanico (Botanical Gardens), Via Lincoln, tel: 091-616 2472. Not a building, but maybe more welcome. Tropical plants. Open weekdays 9am–5pm; Saturday and Sunday 8.30am–1.30pm.

Parco della Favorita, Viale Diana, set on the slopes of Monte Pellegrino. Lovely park laid out by the Bourbons.

Parco d'Orleans, behind Palazzo dei Normanni. Well-maintained park, officially part of the President's domain.

Piazza Marina. Compact but endearing park with hanging banyan trees, set within an historic square.

Villa Bonanno, Piazza della Vittoria. Tatty public gardens with the remains of Roman villas.

Villa Giulia, Via Lincoln. Italianate gardens with fountains, statues, parterres, pavilions and a sundial. Closed for restoration.

MONDELLO
Grotte dell'Addaura, Monte Pellegrino, tel: 091-696 1319; fax: 091-670 2078. Prehistoric caves with palaeolithic rock drawings. For information, contact the Palermo Sovrintendenza Archeologica. Closed for restoration.

PALERMO PROVINCE
Bagheria
Villa Cattolica, a modern art gallery in a traditional summer villa. Closed for restoration. The tomb of painter Renato Guttuso is in the grounds.

Villa Palagonia, this most bizarre villa is open to the public daily 9am–12.30pm and 3–7pm.

Villa Valguarnera, Piazza Garibaldi. A private residence so only visible from beyond the walls.

Baida
Saracen village church. Contains a statue of John the Baptist by Gagini. Key from the custodian.

Caccamo
Castello, Via Termitana 6. To visit this magnificent castle by request, ring for entrance (La Rosa).

Cefalà Diana
Terme Arabe, Palermo-Agrigento road. Moorish baths. Exterior only viewable.

Cefalù
Tempio di Diana. Built in the 4th–2nd centuries BC. Open to the skies. Makes a good morning or evening stroll, visiting the battered Roman remains and Saracen fortifications. A steepish climb but lovely views.

Duomo. Massively imposing Norman Cathedral with Byzantine mosaics. Open daily 8am–noon and 4–6pm.

Museo Mandralisca, Via Mandralisca. A jumble of archaeological finds and treasures. Paintings include Antonello da Messina's enigmatic Ritratto di un

Ignoto (Portrait of an Unknown Man). Open daily 9am–12.30pm and 3.30–6pm.

Termini Imerese
Himera, Contrada Buonfornello. Set along the SS 113, tel: 091-814 0128. By request only.

Monreale
Duomo. Cathedral combining Norman, Saracen and Byzantine architecture in one harmonious whole. One of the most beautiful buildings on the island. The entire ceiling is spectacularly decorated with Byzantine mosaics. Open daily 8am–noon and 3.30–6pm.
Chiostro (Norman cloisters), next door to the Cathedral. Graceful and harmonious. Saracen-style fountain in the southwest corner. Open daily 9am–1pm; Monday, Tuesday and Thursday 9am–1pm and 3–6pm.

San Martino delle Scale
Abbazia di San Martino. Benedictine Abbey, tel: 091-418104. Church 16th century, monastery mainly 17th. Home to a collection of interesting baroque paintings. Open Monday to Saturday 4.30–7pm; Sunday 9am–1pm and 5–7pm.

Solunto
A Phoenician and Roman trading post. The scenic ruins are open Monday to Saturday 9am–6pm, Sunday 9am–12.30pm.

TRAPANI PROVINCE
Trapani
The town was important in the past as a port, and is still the departure point for ferries to the Egadi Islands, to Pantelleria and to North Africa. Situated on the edge of the salt beds stretching away towards Mozia and Marsala, the old town is compact and can best be visited on foot.

Check with the efficient Trapani provincial tourist office, Via Sorba 15, tel: 0923-27273 or 27077 for futher details and information on ferry sailings.
Fontana di Saturno, Piazza Saturno. Fountain.

Museo Nazionale Pepoli, Via Agostino Pepoli 200, tel: 0923-531242. In the former Carmelite monastery. Collection includes works by Antonello Gagini and by Titian. Archaeological collection includes objects from Lilibeo, Erice and Selinunte. Open daily 9am–1.30pm, except Tuesday and Thursday 9am–1.30pm and 3–6.30pm.
Museo delle Saline (Salt Museum), Salina Culcasi, Nubia. Set in an old mill on the coast 5 km (3 miles) from Trapani. (Call the tourist office for opening times: tel: 0923-27273.)
Museo Trapanese di Preistoria, Torre di Lugny, tel: 0923 223668. A simple prehistory museum in a coastal Spanish tower. Open 9.30am–12.30pm and 4.30–7pm.
Palazzo della Giudecca (Palazzo Ciambra), Via della Giudecca. Impressive 16th-century palace in former Jewish quarter. Worth viewing the exterior.
Santuario dell' Annunziata, Via A. Pepoli, tel: 0923-531242. Rococo interior. The star church in Trapani. Virgin's chapel contains 14th-century sculpture, Madonna di Trapani. Bus 1, 10 or 11 from Piazza Matteuitti. Open daily 7am–noon and 4–7pm.
Sant' Agostino, Piazza Saturno. Gothic church.
Santa Maria del Gesù, Via Sant' Agostino. Gothic and Renaissance facade. Works by della Robbia and Gagini.

Erice
Castello Pepoli, Viale Conte Pepoli. Exterior only.
Castello di Venere. Medieval (13th-century) castle built on the site of the sanctuary to Venus Erycina. Open Saturday to Thursday 10am–1pm and 3–5pm.
Chiesa Madre, Via V. Carvini. Built between the 14th and 16th centuries.
Elymi, **Carthaginian** and **Norman** walls. New walls were set into the previous ones. Can be freely visited.
Museo Civico, Piazza Umberto, tel: 0923-869258. Small museum with

Roman and Punic finds. Open daily 8.30am–1.30pm.

Marsala
Duomo, Piazza della Repubblica. 18th-century cathedral dedicated to St Thomas of Canterbury.
Insula Romana, Viale Vittorio Veneto. Remains of a 3rd-century Roman house. Open 9am–12.30pm. Free.
Museo degli Arazzi, Via Garraffa 57, tel: 0923-712903. Museum of Flemish tapestries. Open 9am–1pm and 4–6pm. Closed Monday.
Museo Nazionale Lilibeo, Lungomare Florio 30, tel: 0923-952535. Contains exhibits from Mozia and a reconstructed Punic fighting ship. Open Monday, Tuesday, Thursday and Friday 9am–1.30pm; Wednesday, Saturday and Sunday 9am–1.30pm and 4–7pm.
San Giovanni, off Viale Sauro (seafront). Church over the Sybil's grotto. Currently closed but check with tourist office.
Stabilimento Florio, Lungomare Florio, tel: 0923 781111. One of the traditional marsala producers. Tours and tastings. Open Monday–Friday 8.30am–1.30pm.

Mazara del Vallo
Duomo, Piazza della Repubblica, tel: 941919. Open daily 8am–8pm. Sunday 9am–noon.
Museo Civico, Collegio dei Gesuiti, Piazza Plebescito, tel: 0923-940266. Roman finds. Open daily 8.30am–2pm. Closed Sunday.

Mozia (Motya)
Site of **Carthaginian City**. On an island in the Stagnone lagoons. Parts of the old walls, gate, submerged causeway, necropoli, dry dock. Fascinating. Boats run 9.30am–1pm and 3–6pm.
Museo Whittaker. Named after the marsala wine family who own Mozia island, the small museum contains some of the artefacts found on the island. Open daily 9am–1pm and 3–6.30pm.

Segesta
Temple and **theatre** in wonderful rural setting. Open 9am to 1 hour before sunset. In theory it is free but unless you want a 20-minute walk to the theatre, take the paying tourist shuttle from the site car park.

Selinunte
Temples, and much of what was once a great Greek city. Open 9am to 1 hour before sunset. A new entrance and museum now open. **Cave di Cusa**, Classical quarries situated 3 km (2 miles) from Campobello; 13 km (8 miles) from Selinunte; open permanently. **SS Trinita di Delia**, in the countryside 3 km (2 miles) west of Selinunte, tel: 0924 82209. An Arab-Byzantine church. Ring the bell at the adjoining farm to see if it is convenient to visit.

EGADI ISLANDS
The Egadi offer natural sites rather than churches and museums. However, to check temporary sites or activities contact the Pro Loco (tourist office), Piazza Madrice 7, tel: 0923-921647. Open Monday to Saturday 9am–1pm.

Levanzo Island
Grotta del Genovese. A cave of prehistoric paintings. You need an appointment so contact the custodian, Signor Giuseppe Castiglione, at Via Calvario 11 (near hydrofoil quay), tel: 0923-921704.

AGRIGENTO PROVINCE
Agrigento & Valley of the Temples
Casa di Pirandello, Frazione Villaseta, Contrada Caos, tel: 0922-511102. Pirandello museum in the playwright's home in a village outside Agrigento.
Museo Regionale Archeologico S. Nicola. Classical museum in the Valle dei Templi, tel: 0922-401565. It contains much that has been found on the site, including the *telamone* (gigantic statues); a model reconstruction of the site; and interesting collection of vases and sculpture. Labels in Italian only;

no written guide to exhibits. Free. Open daily 9am–1.30pm; Wednesday, Thursday, Friday and Saturday 9am–1.30pm and 2–6pm.
Valle dei Templi. The site of Greek Akragas and Roman Agrigentum. Temples of Hera (*Giunone*), Ercole, Concordia, Zeus (*Giove Olimpico*). Beautifully lit up at night.

Eraclea Minoa
Eraclea Minoa. Greek theatre in a setting above the sea. Open 9am to 1 hour before sunset. Rural setting overlooking the clean beach below, 30 minutes by car on the road to Sciacca.

Sciacca
Castello Incantanto Filippo Bentivegna, Via E Ghezzi, tel: 0925-993044. Open daily 10.30am–1.30pm and 4–7.30pm (out of season, open mornings only).
Pinacoteca e Museo Scaglione, Casa Scaglione, Piazza Duomo, tel: 0925 83089. Open Tuesday, Thursday and Friday 8am–1pm and 3–7pm.
Stufe di Monte Cronio, Localita di Monte Kronio, tel: 0925-26153. Vaporous thermal treatment around a mountain cave with small antiquarium attached. Usually open 8am–1pm but check.

CALTANISSETTA PROVINCE
Although the province is lovely from the point of rugged mountain scenery, it has minimal tourist infrastructure and the fewest number of museums and organised sites of any province.

Caltanissetta
Despite being the capital, there are no "must see" sights. However, the following offer fleeting interest.
Castello di Pietrarossa, western end of town. A ruin. Visible from exterior.
Museo Civico, Via Colajanni, 3. Bronzes and early sculptures. Open daily 9am–1pm and 3.30pm to one hour before sunset. Closed Sunday. Free.
Museo del Folclore, Via N Colajanni, tel: 0934-21013.

Museo Mineralogico, Viale della Regione 7, tel: 0934-591280. Minerals museum. Open daily 9am–1pm.
Palazzo Moncada, off Corso Umberto, tel: 0934-74111. Feudal mansion which houses city offices.

Gela
Capo Soprano fortifications. (Take Via Manzoni to the sea.) Huge Greek walls. Open 9am to one hour before sunset.
Museo Archeologico Regionale, Corso Vittorio Emanuele 2, tel: 0933-912626. Classical archaeological museum being refurbished. Open daily 9am–1pm and 3–6pm.

Mussomeli
Castello Manfredonico. Fabulous brooding castle with fine fortifications. To check opening times call the Biblioteca Comunale (informazione turistiche), tel: 0934-991495.

ENNA PROVINCE
Enna
Castello di Lombardia, tel: 0935-500962. Perched above the town, the medieval castle still looks unassailable. Open daily 9am–1pm and 3pm till one hour before sunset. Closed for restoration.
Duomo. Piazza del Duomo. A mixture of styles, the cathedral contains a beautiful wooden ceiling and various works of art. Open daily 9am–1pm and 4–7pm.
Museo Alessi, tel: 0935-24072. Small, well-designed museum of sacred art. Open daily 9am–1pm and 4–7pm. Closed Monday.
Torre di Federico II, Giardino Pubblico. A medieval tower and fine views. Closed for restoration.

Piazza Armerina
Duomo. 17th-century church built over the 15th century original. 15th-century Crucifix by the Master of the Cross of Piazza Armerina.
Villa del Casale (Roman Villa), tel: 0935-680036. 3rd–4th century villa famous for its mosaics and its completeness. Free. Open daily 9am–1pm and 3–5.30pm.

Aidone

Morgantina. Rural archaeological site dating from the Bronze Age. Greek agora, luxury houses, theatre, granary and temples. Open daily 9am–1pm and 3pm to one hour before sunset.
Museo Archeologico, tel: 0935-87307. The museum contains artefacts from the site at Morgantina. Open Monday to Saturday 9am–1pm and 3–7pm.

RAGUSA PROVINCE

Ragusa City is more a place for wandering around at a leisurely pace than for visiting specific sights.

Ragusa

Basilica di San Giorgio, Piazza del Duomo, Ragusa Ibla.
Duomo, Piazza San Giovanni, Ragusa Alta.
San Giorgio Vecchio, Piazza Odierna, Ragusa Ibla.
San Giuseppe, Piazza Porta Pola, Ragusa Ibla.
Santa Maria delle Scale, Via XXIV Maggio. The Gothic church links Ragusa Alta and Ragusa Ibla.
These churches are in theory open between 9am–1pm but in practice tend to open and close at unpredictable times.
Giardino Ibleo, Ragusa Ibla. Peaceful park with three churches.
Museo Archeologico, Palazzo Mediterraneo, Via Natalelli. Archaeological collection under Hotel Mediterraneo. Bronze Age burial objects, Hellenistic and Roman pottery. Open daily 9am–1.30pm and 4–7.30pm.

Camarina

Prehistoric and Classical archaeological site on the coast, west of Marina di Ragusa; 34 km (21 miles) south-west of Ragusa. Small museum open daily 9am–2pm and 3.30–6.30pm. Ruins open 9am–6pm, tel: 932-826004.

Castello di Donnafugata

The Moorish-style castle is situated 20 km (13 miles) from Ragusa, direction Santa Croce Camarina. At Donnafugata railway station, take a turning to the right off the main road. Closed for restoration.

Cava D'Ispica

The prehistoric quarries (cave) and tombs occupy a long valley 8 miles (13 km) and are situated near Modica. Cava d'Ispica is well-signposted east of Mòdica: follow signs to *scavi* (archaeological excavations), tel: 0932-951133. Temporarily closed.

Mòdica

Museo Civico, Palazzo dei Mercedari, Via Merce. Open daily 9am–1pm. Free.
Museo Ibleo delle Arte e Tradizioni artigianali, Palazzo dei Mercedari. Folk museum. Open daily 10am–1pm and 3.30–7.30pm.

SIRACUSA PROVINCE

Siracusa's man-made sights tend to be located in the provincial capital. Some may be under restoration, so check with the city tourist office in Via Maestranza 33, tel: 66932.

Siracusa

Basilica di San Giovanni. Cripta di San Marziano, tel: 0931-721665. Open 9am–12.30pm and 2.30–4.30pm in summer, closed Tuesday.
Castello Euriolo. Eurialo Castle, 10 km (6 miles) from Siracusa, on the Ciane river. Dionysius' 4th-century BC defensive system. In winter, open daily 9am–3pm. In summer, open daily 9am–6pm, tel: 0931-711973.
Catacombe di San Giovanni. Via San Giovanni, tel: 0931-721665. 4th-century San Giovanni Catacombs. Currently the only catacombs open. Guided tours only. Closed Tuesday.
Duomo. Incorporates part of the original 5th-century BC temple to Athena. Became a church in 7th century AD. Open daily 8am–12.45pm and 4–7pm.
Galleria Regionale, Palazzo Bellomo, Via Capodieci, tel: 0931-69511. Mixed collection of Sicilian art housed in a 13th to 15th-century Gothic palace. Closed for repairs at time of writing. Check

locally for re-opening. Opening times: 9am–1pm.
Ginnasio Romano. Roman Gymnasium, Via Elorina, tel: 0931 481111. Open 9am–1pm. Free.
Museo Archeologico Paolo Orsi, Villa Landolina, Viale Teocrito, tel: 0931-464022. Well-organised, extensive museum containing finds dating from pre-historic to Roman times. Open Tuesday to Saturday 9am–1pm. Arguably the best Classical museum in Sicily.
Parco Archeologico della Neapolis. Archaeological Park, tel: 0931-66206. Contains Greek Theatre, Roman Amphitheatre, the Orecchio di Dionisio (Dionysus ear), San Nicolo church, Roman baths, the Latomia del Paradiso (Paradise quarries). In winter open 9am–3pm, in summer open 9am–6pm.

Fonte Ciane

This mythical spring is where papyrus flourishes. Take a lovely boat trip through the papyrus. The round trip takes 4 hours. Alternatively, go by road: take Viale Ermocrate or Viale Orsi towards Floridia, then turn right at Via Necropoli del Fusco, direction Canicattini Bagni. Make an appointment with the boat guide, Sig. Bella, tel: 0931-69076.

Megara Hyblaea

One of the earliest Greek colonies in Sicily, tel: 0931-512364. From Siracusa, take Corso Gelone towards Catania. After 20 km (12 miles), a road on the right leads to the Classical site in the shadow of industrial clouds. Open 9am–2 hours before sunset.

Noto

Noto is a museum in itself: a baroque city in which most buildings have equal value.
Duomo, Piazza Municipio, tel: 0931-512364. 18th-century cathedral built after the earthquake; the attractiveness of the building lies partly in the harmony of the square. The interior is under long-term restoration, the facade has been completed. Open 9am–2 hours before sunset.

Palazzo Municipale, Palazzo Vescovile, Palazzo Sant'Alfano – Piazza Municipio. The buildings around the square complement each other. The yellow stone and the elegance of proportions produce a sense of harmony and tranquillity. However, this did not prevent the last earthquake shaking some foundations.

Palazzolo Acreide
Zona Archeologica Akrai. A Greek theatre and carvings dedicated to the goddess Cybele date back to the 3rd century BC. Christian places of worship and necropoli also existed in old stone quarries during the Byzantine period. Open daily 9am to one hour before sunset. Also insist on seeing the Santoni (strange sculptures of Cybele). These are at a site down the hill and visitors need to be supervised.

CATANIA PROVINCE
Outside Catania City, the sights are few in this dullish province, the best relate to Etna. (See *Etna Environs, page 267*.)

Catania
The city sights embrace baroque and Roman. Some buildings are dilapidated but worth seeing, as are the intimate museums. Many Roman sites are visible from different angles so it is not always necessary to enter the site.
Anfiteatro Romano, Piazza Stesicoro. Open Monday to Saturday 9am–1pm.
Casa Museo G. Verga, Via S. Anna 8, tel: 095 715 0598. Verga's house. Open daily 9am–1pm and 3–6.30pm.
Duomo, Piazza del Duomo. Originally medieval Cathedral, but altered. Most of present building dates from 18th century. Open 9am–12.30pm.
Monastero dei Benedettini. Open 9am–12.30pm. Closed Sunday.
Museo Belliniano, Piazza San Francesco 3, tel: 095-715 0535. Bellini's house. Open Monday to Saturday 9am–1.30pm, Sunday 9am–12.30pm.

Museo Civico del Castello Ursino, Piazza Federico di Svevia, tel: 095-345830. Catania's best historical collection of sculpture and paintings set in a Hohenstaufen dynastic fortress. Open daily 8.30am–1pm Free.
Orto Botanico dell'Universita, Via Antonino Longo 19, tel: 095-430901 for opening times of the botanical gardens. Open Monday to Saturday 9am–1pm. Free.
Palazzo Biscari, Via Museo Biscari. Ornate baroque mansion. View the exterior only.
Porta di Carlo V, Piazza Pardo. Spanish gateway.
Porta Garibaldi. Grand lava-stone gateway.
Teatro Bellini, Piazza Bellini. Newly-restored theatre.
Le Terme di Santa Maria della Rotonda, Via SM della Rotonda. Open daily 9am–1pm. (Please note that you have to book the visit in advance.)
Teatro Greco, Via Vittorio Emanuele 266, tel: 095-715 0508. Open Monday to Saturday 9am–2 hours before sunset; Sunday 9am–2pm. Closed for restoration.
Via Crociferi. A street of fine baroque palazzi.
Villa Bellini. Charming gardens to the north of town.

Caltagirone
Museo della Ceramica, Via Roma, tel: 0933-21680. Ceramics in the public gardens. Open daily 9am–6.30pm.
Museo Civico, Carcere Borbonico, tel: 0933-41315. Small town museum in ex-Bourbon prison. Historical objects and ceramics. Open Tuesday, Thursday, Friday, Saturday and Sunday 9.30am–1.30pm and 4–7pm; Monday and Wednesday 9.30am–1.30pm. Free.

ETNA ENVIRONS
Obviously an ascent of Mount Etna is the prime activity or a train or car trip around the base. (*See Excursions page 360, Etna Environs, page 267*.) Nicolosi is "the Gateway to Etna" and makes a good starting point.

Adrano
Ponte Saraceno. Charming medieval Saracen bridge.
Museo Archeologico Normanno, Piazza Umberto, tel: 095-7692660. Eclectic historical collection in a Norman castle. Open Monday to Saturday 8.30am–1.30pm; Sunday 9am–noon. Free.

Bronte
Castello e Abbazia di Maniace, near Bronte, tel: 095-6900018. 13th-century abbey belonged to Admiral Nelson. Open Monday to Saturday 8.30am–1.30pm; Sunday 9am–noon.
Museo dell'Antica Civiltà Locale alla Masseria Lombardo, tel: 095-691635. Rural life museum. Open daily 9am–1pm.

Linguaglossa
Museo Etnografico, Pro Loco, Piazza Annunziata 5, tel: 095-643094. Collection of Etna flora and fauna in local tourist office. Open Monday to Saturday 9am–12.30pm and 4–7pm; Sunday 10am–12.30pm.

Nicolosi
Parco dell'Etna, Viale della Regione, tel: 095-914588. Worth calling and dropping in for information before setting out on a walk through the Etna Natural Park or a climb of Mount Etna's slopes. Also contact Nicolosi tourist office.

Paternò
Castello, Collina Turistica. Medieval castle. Open daily 9am–12.30pm.

Randazzo
Chiesa di San Martino. 14th century. Bell tower is built of a mixture of lava and limestone.
Chiesa di Santa Maria, Piazza Santa Maria. Norman Hohenstaufen dynastic church with Catalan additions. Telephone 095-921204 for the opening times of church and treasury.

TAORMINA
Badia Vecchia, Via Circonvallazione. 14th-century abbey. View exterior only.

Duomo, Piazza del Duomo. 16th-century exterior. Open daily 9am–1pm and 4–7pm.

Odeon, Via Teatrino Romano. Small Roman theatre. View over the railings. Open daily 9am–noon.

Naumachia, Via Naumachia. Possibly a gymnasium in ancient times. Free access.

Palazzo Corvaja, Piazza Vittorio Emanuele. 15th-century palace, now houses the tourist office and various temporary exhibitions. Open daily 8am–2pm and 4–9pm.

Palazzo dei Duchi di San Stefano. 14th-century palace now containing sculpture museum. Open daily 9am–noon and 3–6pm.

Palazzo Ciampoli, Corso Umberto. 15th-century palace with mullioned windows. Closed to the public.

San Agostino, Piazza 9 Aprile. 15th-century Gothic church, now a library.

San Domenico, Piazzale San Domenico. Formerly a monastery, now a five star hotel. Paying guests only.

San Pancrazio. Built on the site of a Greek temple.

For all current church opening times, see the tourist office in Palazzo Corvajo, tel: 23243.

Teatro Greco, Via Teatro Greco, tel: 0942-23220. The Greek theatre in one of the world's most perfect natural settings. Open 9am–sunset. On-site museum currently closed.

MESSINA ENVIRONS
Messina

Much was destroyed in the 1908 earthquake but the historic centre and harbour are worth a half-day visit. Ferries leave regularly for the mainland and the Aeolian Islands.

Cimitero, Via Catania (entrance Via Piazza Dante). The city cemetery south of Messina. One of the most picturesque in Southern Italy. Fine views of Calabria.

Duomo, Piazza del Duomo. The Cathedral is a superb fake with some original elements. See the clockwork cherubs on the neo-Gothic campanile strike the hours at midday. The Cathedral is closed noon–4pm. Closed Monday.

Museo Regionale, Via della Libertà, tel: 090-358716. See Antonello da Messina's Madonna polyptich, and works by Caravaggio. Open Monday, Wednesday and Friday 9am–1.30pm; Tuesday, Thursday and Saturday 9am–1.30pm and 3–5.30pm; Sunday 9am–12.30pm. It's 3 km (2 miles) from the centre, along Via della Libertà (take bus 8 or 27).

Santissima Annunziata dei Catalani, Piazza Catalani. One of the few 13th-century buildings in the city to have survived earthquakes. Delicately beautiful. University chapel. Occasionally open for services.

Giardini Naxos

Scavi (excavations) and **Naxos Museo Archeologico**, Capo Schisò, tel: 0942-51001. The remains of the oldest Greek settlement in Sicily. Open daily 9am–6pm.

Milazzo

Most visitors see it before sailing off to the Aeolian Islands as this is the main port of embarkation.

Castello, tel: 090-922 1291. Impressive fortifications dating in part from the Hohenstaufen dynastic building of the 13th century and in part from the Spanish of the 15th. Open Tuesday to Saturday 9am–7pm; Sunday 9am–1pm. Free.

Faro, Capo Milazzo. Milazzo lighthouse, sited on a cape at the end of a panoramic drive. Fine views of the Aeolian Islands. View from exterior only.

Patti

Villa Romana, Zona Archeologica, Frazione Tindari, tel: 0941-361593. Excavations on the Roman Villa continue. Open 9am to one hour before sunset.

Tindari

Santuario, Piazza Belvedere, tel: 0941-369026. Sanctuary of the Black Madonna. Adjoining the ruins is the kitsch church housing the *madonna nera*, the prized icon. Open daily 8.45am–12.30pm and 2.30–5pm.

Tyndaris, Capo Tindari. Site of the original Greek city. Open daily 9am to one hour before sunset. The museum is open daily 9am–2pm.

AEOLIAN ISLANDS

Apart from on Lipari Island, man-made sights, such as churches and museums, are of only passing interest. It is the natural volcanic sights that command the attention.

Long hikes, climbing volcanoes and leisurely boat trips are recommended on all the islands. There is a volcano to suit everyone but the temperature, height and strenuousness of the climb should be checked below before embarking on any trip. Boat trips are highly recommended and can be readily booked at the islands' main ports.

Filicudi Island

Grotta del Bue Marino: mysterious caves sited an hour's boat trip from the island. These are generally seen as part of a complete boat trip around the island. Also ask to see La Canna, huge rock obelisks. In a late afternoon light, the caves and rocks take on a surreal glow. The trip is booked through fishermen at Filicudi Porto.

Lipari Island

Castello (Castle). The citadel is set on a steep lava rock.

Duomo. The Norman Cathedral was rebuilt in the 13th century and has a baroque facade.

Museo Eoliano, located in several buildings around the Cathedral, tel: 090-988 0174. The best museum on any of the offshore islands. It houses finds from the Neolithic era and Bronze Age necropoli; also Greek pottery and terracotta masks. Open daily 8.30am–2pm and 4–7.30pm.

Obsidian and pumice fields, Canneto. Take a bus from Via Vittorio Emanuele in Lipari Town to Canneto. If driving, take the road through Monte Rosa tunnel on the outward journey. Follow the signs to Forgia Vecchi and Pierra to look at the obsidian fields, created by old lava flows. These are the only obsidian deposits known in Europe.

Parco Archeologico. It stretches out in front of the Duomo and includes 6 BC tombs in the so-called Site of Diana. Open Monday to Saturday 9am–2pm. Free.

Live Arts

There is a wealth of artistic activity in Sicily. Most of the provincial capitals have their own theatre or opera house. Catania and Palermo have their own companies, and stage complete seasons of musical and theatrical events. In summer virtually every province stages some form of cultural event, from film festivals to opera, ballet, classical music to theatre and art exhibitions. Many include internationally known companies and artistes.

The following Arts Diary lists a few of the largest and best known, but expect Palermo, Catania, Siracusa and numerous other cities to stage their own festivals. Details are available through tourist offices, the local press, or the magazine, *Ciao Sicilia*.

PALERMO
Venues
Teatro Biondo, Via Roma, tel: 091-582364/743 4341. Drama.
Al Convento, Via Castellana Bandiera 66, tel: 091-637 6336. Cabaret.
Teatro Franco Zappalá, Via Autonomia Siciliana, tel: 091-543380/362764. Dialect theatre.
Teatro Golden, Via Terrasanta 60, tel: 091-300609. Classical music.
Al Massimo, Piazza Verdi 9, tel: 091-589575/589070. Drama, music hall.
Teatro Metropolitan, Viale Strasburgo 356, tel: 091-688 6532. Drama, ballet, classical music.

Cabaret
Al Convento, Via C. Bandiera, 66.
Anthony, Via Don Orione, 16, tel: 544766.
Cafè Chantant, Via Stabile, 136, tel: 586394.
Teatro Madison, Piazza Don Bosco, 13, tel: 543740.

CATANIA
Teatro Massimo Bellini, Piazza Teatro Massimo, tel: 095-312020. For opera, classical music and ballet.
Teatro Metropolitana, Via S Euplio, tel: 322323. For drama, opera, classical music and jazz.
Winter concert season from November to June.
Villa Bellini: concerts and other open-air events in the gardens.

ERICE
Erice stages the summer **Settimana di Musica Medievale e Rinascimentale** (Medieval and Renaissance music festival) in its lovely churches. To find out details, contact Erice tourist office, Via C. A. Pepoli, tel: 0923-869388.

SIRACUSA
Siracusa is home to the **Istituto Nazionale del Drama Antico** (Institute of Classical Drama) so has home-grown talent to display in the great Greek tragedies. In 1991 German director Jean-Marie Straub filmed Antigone in the Greek theatre.

Classical Greek Drama

As in Siracusa, Sicily's Classical theatres often return to the original function, as great settings for Greek drama. The season usually lasts from May to July, with different dramatic cycles performed in the traditional Greek theatres.
Segesta: Every second year, alternating with Siracusa.
Taormina: Variable, alternating with opera, dance, music. Siracusa and Taormina theatres are also used for ballet and opera. There are plans to continue the lapsed practice of holding a major ballet festival in the Selinunte temples.

Sicilian Puppet Theatre

Plays performed by puppets can still be seen in Acireale, Catania, Palermo and Siracusa.
Associazione Figli d'Arte Cuticchio, Via Bara all'Olivella 95, Palermo, tel: 323400. The latest and perhaps last generation of old family puppeteers. They put on modernised, shortened versions of traditional puppet theatre. Mimmo Cuticchio is one of the few remaining amazing recitors of the *cuntastorie*.

Recommended venues for Puppet Shows are:
Acireale: Cooperativa E. Macri, Corso Umberto 179, tel: 095-604521 or 606272. (Also in Via Alessi, Acireale.)
Monreale: Munna, Cortile Manin, Monreale (near Palermo).
Palermo: Opera dei Pupi, Vicolo Ragusi, tel: 091-329194. Teatro Bradamante, Via Lombardia, 25, tel: 091-6259223. It puts on a free show at 9.30pm most summer evenings.
Siracusa: Opera dei Pupi, Via Nizza 14. In summer, there are usually performances on Tuesday, Thursday and Saturday at 9.30pm. Check times with Siracusa tourist office.

Outdoor Activities

Nature Reserves

This is a summary of the best. Consult the relevant tourist offices for regulations, a complete list of reserves, with maps and suggested routes through them.

Bosco della Ficuzza and Rocca Busambre. This reserve covers the area around Corleone, Godrano and Mezzojuso.

Palermo Province. From Palermo tourist office get the booklet on nature reserves and protected areas entitled 14 *aree di interesse naturalistico*. The maps are helpful even for non-Italian speakers.

Parco dell'Etna, Via della Regione, 25, Nicolosi, tel: 095-914588. Information on the Etna protected area.

Parco delle Madonie. Also request Madonie–Carta dei Sentieri, a map and leaflet on mountain walks from Palermo tourist office.

Riserva Naturale Marina, Ustica, Palermo Province. Contact Municipio di Ustica (Ustica Town Hall), tel: 8449045.

Riserva dello Zingaro, Castellammare del Golfo and San Vito Lo Capo. There are three main entrances to the park. This well-designed reserve is closed to traffic and contains observation points, footpaths, caves and a visitors' centre.

Excursions

MOUNT ETNA

How you see Mount Etna will depend on the season, your finances, your transport and time, as well as Etna's current volcanic activity. However, for those on a limited budget but with a day to spare, the rail route around Etna is recommended. If there is any sort of volcanic activity, an organised tour is recommended from your resort. Independent travellers will prefer to drive to Etna and take the cable car to the top. If you can afford it, and should Etna's activity merit it, consider hiring a guide. The guides will tell you honestly what you should be able to see on any particular day. In winter it is not possible to reach the summit.

Ferrovia Circumetnea (Etna Railway): tel: 095-374842. This circular rail route runs from Catania to Giarre-Riposto (114 km/71 miles). It skirts Etna's foothills and the volcanic towns of Adrano, Bronte, Linguaglossa, Maletto, Paternò and Randazzo. It is possible to go round the volcano in a day since the journey takes from four to five and a half hours. Book at the Circumetnea office in Catania (Corso delle Province 13). As there is little accommodation in the area, book ahead for an overnight stop. *See Sports, page 365 for skiing on Etna.*

Advice on Ascent: The usual approach is by car, public bus or coach to the Rifugio Sapienza. From there, take the cable car to the summit and explore (with a pre-booked official guide).

Organised Excursions: Etna is accessible on a day trip from Taormina or Catania. But if planning to climb Etna, allow for an early start. It is easiest to book an organised excursion with a local operator (e.g. Sun Services at Taormina). Allow at least a morning for the ascent, with an early start. A full day excursion is more usual, particularly if you want time to explore the Etna foothills.

Independent Excursions: If you wish to travel independently, it is best to book a guide to ensure that you will see volcanic activity in safety. Book an official Italian Alpine Guide from Rifugio Sapienza the day before (*see below*). Check conditions prior to setting out and plan to be at the refuge early.

Qualified guides are available for hire at Rifugio Sapienza but negotiate on price and discuss what you want to see. Also decide which time of day is best, according to season, weather, and the type of volcanic activity you want to see. Overnight, dawn, early morning and sunset are the best times to see the different aspects of Etna.

Guides: For an official guide at Rifugio Sapienza, tel: 095-914141.

For last minute trips, an official guide, Nino Longo, may be contacted at the centre (during the day) or at home (evenings, tel: 095-7914304). The guide may well speak very limited English. To ensure that there is no linguistic misunderstanding, check which of the following can be seen and agree on a "menu" and fixed price. "Menu": A pit of molten lava (*un pozzo di lava*); small, secondary but active cone (*piccolo cono erruttivo*); the lava front (*la fronte lavica*); secondary craters (*crateri secondari*).

Costs: The price of a standard organised coach tour of Etna, including a trip to the summit varies greatly. The cost of the cable car (funivia) from Rifugio Sapienza to the summit is about 30,000 lire. A personal guide from the Rifugio Sapienza will cost anything from 50,000 lire to 150,000 lire, depending on the duration and complexity of the visit. The cost of the cable car is not included.

Clothing: Protective clothing is advisable for an ascent up Etna, including glasses to protect against sun and volcanic ash, sturdy walking shoes or mountain boots (or skis). Cold mountain temperatures (20°C/68°F lower than in Catania) mean that warm clothing is required. Organised Etna excursions often provide protective clothing but check. The summit will be snowy from November to March.

EGADI ISLANDS

Lévanzo, Grotta delle Genovese (prehistoric paintings): Necessary to telephone in advance for an appointment with Mr Castiglione, the custodian of the Grotto, tel: 0923-924032. He will guide those who wish to make the trip by land or advise on boats for those who wish to reach the cave by sea.

Favignana: The famous, if horrific, seasonal spectacle is *La Mattanza*, the ritual slaughter of tuna. (For details, and to see whether you can stomach it, first read *The Great Tuna Massacre* box story in *The Egadi Islands* chapter, *page 169*.)

To follow the *Mattanza* by boat, try to find a willing fisherman at the docks in Favignana.

The bicycle is the usual means of transport here and can be rented cheaply at the port.

ALCÁNTARA GORGE

The **Alcántara Gorge** consists of rock formed from lava. The rock is black and has formed fascinating and strange crystalline shapes. The river runs for several miles through a deep cut in the ground. (*See Etna Environs, page 267.*)

The place has become a tourist magnet, with coach trips, quite unnecessary lifts down to the river and wellington boots on loan. Nevertheless it is well worth visiting. Both river and rock deserve to be explored and there is an ordinary bar-restaurant on hand for snacks afterwards. It can be reached by car, or by bus from Taormina or Messina.

AEOLIAN ISLANDS

Panarea Island

Calcara, San Pietro quay. Mud-bathing in a pool with a hot spring (122°F/50°C). Views of fumaroles and small geysers.

Salina Island

Monte Fossa delle Felci. The ascent up this extinct volcano (962 metres/3,150 ft) begins at Santa Marina, the port on the east coast of the island.

Stromboli Island

Serra Vancura and **Sciara del Fuoco**. The climb to the top of the volcano (3,040 ft/926 metres) overlooks Stromboli's active crater. There is a choice between a hectic organised hike to the top and a leisurely night viewing of the volcano from a boat at the foot of

Sciara del Fuoco. From the boat, at best you will see fireworks and fiery pieces rolling down into the sea. **Warning!** A climb up this volcano is only now permitted in the company of an official guide (Club Alpino Italiano, tel: 986093, April to October). Check the current situation at the tourist office in Ficogrande. Sturdy shoes, warm clothes, water, a snack and a flashlight are required, not to mention considerable stamina. At the pace the guides choose to set, it is an arduous climb for all but the fittest. Before agreeing to a trip, consult with the bookers and only accept if the guides agree to a reasonable pace, the speed requested by the majority of participants. At present, the group is harried up the volcano with little rest. At the top, only about an hour is allowed before the return run down the volcano. Volcanic activity is very unpredictable and it is possible to see anything from showers of sparks to virtually nothing.

Strombolicchio. A boat trip visits this stunning sheer rock a mile offshore. From afar, it looks like a castle.

Vulcano Island

Fossa di Vulcano. A climb up a crater from Porto Levante. This is the star attraction on the island. The climb should take a couple of hours (293 metres/952 ft) and is fine if you are reasonably fit and have sturdy shoes, a water bottle and some sort of protective clothes.

Porto di Levante. This beach includes a yellowish natural pool where visitors wallow in mud and "take the waters". Test the temperature with your hand before going in. Parts of the pool can be scalding. Temperatures can reach 212°F (100°C). After rinsing off in the cool sea, see the underwater fumaroles, holes spurting volcanic gases.

Vulcanello. A 30-minute climb to the top of the extinct volcano (124 metres/406 ft). From the summit is a view of Lipari and Vulcano.

Beaches

As an island, Sicily offers a vast range of beaches, from volcanic rocks to golden sands. Most beaches in the main resorts are paying, in subtle gradations to suit most people's pockets. The beaches on the offshore islands tend to be free, with the notable exception of Panarea and the Chicer islands. Out of season, many of the beaches are used as rubbish tips and are therefore best seen from a distance.

The tourist season, and the beaches, begin opening in April and the seas are delightful from May until October, with only the tricky month of August to be dealt with.

The "beach season" begins in August, when beaches become phenomenally crowded in Cefalù, Taormina coast and Mondello, near Palermo. Some public (free) beaches suffer from itinerant traders peddling undesirable junk jewellery and fake Lacoste T-shirts. Also in August, normally pleasant bays, like Castellammare del Golfo (west of Palermo) are taken over by motor launches. Then rages a battle between the sun-worshippers and the speed-freaks.

However, there are compensations in people-watching and in the sophisticated nightlife that spills onto the beaches. Beaches in Mondello are well-equipped with showers, bars and games. Even in August, there are retreats from the crowds. For instance, there are always clean, tranquil beaches in the Riserva dello Zingaro, the nature reserve west of Palermo.

Recommended beaches: All the offshore islands have lovely, often volcanic, beaches, from which boat trips can easily be arranged. Ustica, the Egadi Islands and the Aeolian Islands are ever-popular with Sicilians and visitors. For swimming, all islands are to be recommended with the exception of the Stagnone Islands, stagnant waters near Mozia. Beaches at Cefalù, Mondello, Taormina are kept extremely clean in season. Beaches south of Siracusa are beautifully unspoilt and even wild near Capo Passero. Beaches between Catania and Taormina, especially those around Aci Trezza and Aci Castello, tend to be rocky, exciting and often well-equipped.

Beaches to avoid: It is easier to say which stretches of coastline to avoid than which to head for. The polluted coast around the so-called Gela Riviera should be avoided at all costs (apart from visiting the impressive Greek walls nearby). The beaches around Porto Empedocle, Agrigento, are also polluted. The beaches north of Siracusa should be treated with caution. Although a cleaning programme is underway, many still suffer from chemical effluents. Avoid the beaches around the ports of Augusta, Messina, Milazzo and Palermo.

Sailing

Palermo province has lovely beaches not too far from Palermo City. Many have exclusive yacht clubs and a sophisticated nightlife. West of Palermo, the stretch of coast from Mondello and Capo Gallo to Isole delle Femmine is a standard yacht excursion. Equally well, east of Palermo, from Romagnolo to Capo Zafferano makes a pleasant boat trip.

The wild stretch of northern coastline from Capo d'Orlando to Cefalù is one of the loveliest in Sicily, particularly near the lagoons below Tindari.

Thermal Spas

Many islands and resorts offer the chance to wallow in mud baths or take water cures. These are available at Sciacca (Agrigento Province); Castellammare del Golfo (Trapani Province); or on the Egadi and Aeolian Islands. Italians and Germans take the therapeutic effects of such water cures very seriously.

Nightlife

Compared with much of Italy, Sicilian nightlife is more introverted, centred on restaurants and private parties rather than mass discos. Even so, the advent of tourism has led to an explosion of bars and clubs on the coastal resorts. Cefalù and Taormina are the main centres for civilised nightlife, revolving around piano bars and the more sophisticated nightclubs.

It may seem surprising that two such small places monopolise the high life of Sicily to such a degree. After all, Palermo, Catania or Siracusa might seem more natural candidates. But this has a lot to do with the special status that Cefalù and Taormina have. For nightlife to come alive, there must be a certain level of security, and Cefalù and Taormina offer this. In these two havens of tranquillity, the *scippi* (bag-snatchers) and petty criminals that plague the cities and discourage people from venturing out in the evenings, barely exist. In many ways this is good news for foreigners. It is far easier to join a scene as open as that of a holiday resort than that of a big city.

In the summer, even city slicker Sicilians come out of their shells a little way. But they do it in the coastal resorts of Sferracavallo, Mondello or Sant'Agata, rather than back home. Summer nightlife consists of hanging out around the harbour in whichever bar is this year's in-place to be. The music may be loud but the ambience seems fairly relaxed.

Another factor affected Sicily's night life in 1992–93. A security blitz caught bars, restaurants and nightclubs without their documents in order. The Italian government decided to crack down on the black

economy and effectively sent in the paratroops to do it. One result was the disappearance of many clubs and bars which had been running for years. So far, nothing has come along to take their place. That does not mean there is nothing left to do: plenty still survive. So if you do wish to try out the disco scene, one of the following may suit you.

Evening Entertainment

For a totally different type of nightlife, see the section on *Live Arts, page 357.* Sicily can offer a wide range: from avant-garde films to traditional puppet shows. Although there are no major rock venues, open-air concerts take place in Catania and other cities. Evening entertainment often ties in with the local festivities (*see The Festive Calendar, page 362*).

Young Nightlife

The small coastal resorts in Palermo and Messina provinces abound in discos catering to the young. Rough and ready video bars and short-lived clubs pop up in Giardini-Naxos (near Taormina) and on most of the north coast resorts. In most towns, the neighbourhood pizzeria or gelateria are the focus of attention – and a moped-riding crowd.

Sophisticated Nightlife

For more sophistication, try piano bars in all the main resorts. In order to fit in, it is best to dress elegantly. Even here, there is a wide range of wealth amd style. The resort of Mondello, and particularly the Aeolian island of Panarea, offer spots for the ostentatious jet set. The discreet rich prefer to retreat to the remote island of Pantelleria.

Gay Nightlife

Taormina is still the focus for the native and foreign gay community. At any time, it should have several gay clubs and bars. Le Perroquet (Piazza San Domenico, tel: 24462) is currently popular. However, the 1992 blitz means that clubs may have changed name or address, so check locally. There is little of an organised gay scene in Sicily but attitudes towards homosexuality are relatively relaxed. Contact Arci-Gay, a gay organisation in Palermo, tel: 091-324917/8.

The Passeggiata

The *passeggiata* (stroll) is an Italian institution that finds favour in Sicily. Mondello is the place to see a nightly parade of Milanese fashion. On summer nights, the offshore islands come alive. In particular, Ustica, the Egadi Islands (especially Lévanzo) and the Aeolian Islands (particularly Lipari) are awash with strollers admiring one another.

City Nightspots

Catania
Catanese nightlife is fairly diverse, revolving around gelaterie, bars, discos and clubs. Popular young locations are: **Gelaterie del Duomo**, Piazza del Duomo; **Bar Centrale**, Via Etnea 121; and **Pasticceria Caprice**, Via Etnea 30. These are the places for *gelati* (ice creams) *arancini* (typical snacks) and *granite* (sorbets).
Discotheques:
Divina, Via Carnazza 53, tel: 095-399631.
Empire, Via Milazzo, tel: 095-375684.
Il Banacher, Via Vampolleri 66 (on the SS 114 near Aci Castello). One of the best-known open-air discos.
    Check out the newest ones locally.

Cefalù
Like Taormina, Cefalu's clubs need to be checked on the spot. Piano bars like **Kentia** are popular (Via Nicola Botta 4, tel: 0921-20008).

Erice
Erice, like Cefalù and Taormina, is another safe pocket. Despite its tiny size, Erice boasts a number of piano bars and night clubs. **Blu Notte**, in Via San Rocco is a piano bar and nightclub. **Boccaccio**, in Via dei Misteri, is more of a discotheque.

Mondello
Some socialising is a question of private parties in summer villas. However, **Villa Boscogrande** (Via Tommaso Natale, 91, tel: 091-241179) is public, a club set in a dreamy *palazzo* where Visconti filmed scenes for *The Leopard*. Mondello can also be an inexpensive youth hang-out.
Piano bars:
Mondello Palace, Viale Principe di Scalea 2.
Thula Club, Viale M di Savoia 102.
Villa Verde, Via Piano Gallo 36.

Palermo
Palermitan high society in particular is relatively closed. Much socialising takes place at private functions, often taking over a nightclub or restaurant for the night. Nevertheless, in the early evening, the upmarket quarter around Viale della Libertà witnesses a *passeggiata* and chic cafés like Roneys are busy. City bars, however, tend to close early and the crowds head to Mondello and the coast. By 10pm the city seems dead.
Bars and ice cream parlours:
The bars and *pasticcerie* on the pedestrianised Principe di Belmonte are the focus of early evening gatherings. Outside this area, jazzy or simple ice cream parlours prevail.
Gelateria Ilardo, Foro Italico.
Al Gelato, Viale Strasburgo.
Gelato, Piazza Europa 2.

Discotheques and nightclubs:
Several discos are in Viale Strasburgo, a residential middle class quarter. Check local discos and nightclubs with your hotel.
Brasil Club, Via P Bonanno 69 (Monte Pellegrino).
Il Cerchio, Viale Strasburgo 312 (Suburban Palermo).

Metropolis, Piazza Marina 50 (Historic city centre).
Piano bars:
Drive Bar, Via del Bersagliere 70.
Grand Hotel des Palmes, Via Roma 396 (city centre).
Mazzara Escargot, Via Generale Magliocco 15.
Villa Florio, Discesa Tonnara 4 (Arenella, on the coast).
Villa Igiea, Salita Belmonte 43/b (out of town; the undoubted star).

Siracusa
Much of Siracusa's nightlife is really café life on the island of Ortygia. Most cafés are on Fontana Aretusa, Porta Marina and around the Duomo. Lungomare Alfeo has some lively bars. The **Malibu** disco attracts 3,000 for '70s pop parties and is great fun. For magical live entertainment, the **Greek theatre** is the stage for Classical drama. Contact the tourist office for information.

Taormina
A sophisticated evening is guaranteed in the bars and restaurants of Taormina's hotels. (*See Where To Stay* and *Eating Out pages 328* and *338.*) Check the latest clubs locally; clubs change locations and hands at an amazing rate.
Discotheques and nightclubs:
Bella Blu, Via Guardida Vecchia, tel: 24239.
Septimo, Via San Pancrazio, 50, tel: 625522.
L'Ombrello, Piazza Duomo, tel. 23733. Music club.

Festivals

The Festive Calendar

Every day of the year somewhere in Sicily a town or village celebrates a religious or cultural festival. At Easter, in particular, virtually every village has its own traditional celebration. Ferragosto (15 August) is also a traditional festival almost everywhere. Other major religious feasts such as All Saints and Christmas produce another crop of celebrations, as does carnival time.

See also references to province by province festivities within the *Places* section.

January

There are Epiphany (6 January) festivals all over Sicily.
Caltanissetta: Epiphany pageant evoking the Three Kings.
Mezzojuso: Byzantine procession called A Vulata d'A Palumma.
Piana degli Albanesi: Greek Orthodox rites celebrate Christ's baptism. The women wear traditional dress.

February

Agrigento: the first week of February. The almond blossom and folklore festival, held in the Valley of the Temples.
Catania: 1–5 February. Celebration in honour of the city's patron, St Agata. Giant candles (*ceri*) are carried through the streets. High points are a procession of 17th-century carriages and another in which the saints' relics are towed by citizens dressed in traditional white gowns.
Sciacca: Carnival, one of the best on the island.
Taormina: Popular Carnival with locals.

March

Acireale: week before Lent. The most famous carnival on the island. A huge procession closes the town centre to traffic, and outdoor concerts and dances take place in the main square.

April/Easter

Holy Week (Settimana Santa) is the major religious festival, celebrated all over the island. Virtually every village and town has processions on Palm Sunday, Maundy Thursday and Good Friday. The most interesting are held at Enna, Caltanissetta, Marsala, Prizzi, San Fratello and Trapani.
Aidone: Easter Sunday pantomime meeting between Christ and his mother.
Barrafranca: Another meeting between Christ and his mother.
Caltanissetta: Palm Sunday Mass. Maundy Thursday procession of the guilds (*Reale Maestranza*) with the Mysteries (*I Misteri*).
Enna: Holy Week is magnificent; the highlight is the Good Friday processions parading the "urn of the dead Christ".
Gangi: Palm Sunday and Good Friday processions with statues borne aloft by the confraternities.
Marsala: Maundy Thursday. The Mysteries re-enacted by locals in costume.
Mezzojuso: Greek Orthodox celebrations, traditional processions and costumes.
Noto: Good Friday procession called *Santa Spina*.
Palermo: Greek Orthodox celebrations in La Martorana church. Plaited palm branches hung over the doors of churches. Christ's "dead body" paraded by liveried young men.
Petralia Sottana: Palm Sunday "reunion" of Christ and his Madonna.
Piana degli Albanesi: Easter according to the Byzantine rite. Palm Sunday procession with the bishop on a donkey. 23 April. Costume procession for St George's day.
Prizzi: Easter Sunday Dance of the Devils and Death.

Ragusa: The Mysteries (*I Misteri*) statues in procession.
San Fratello: Good Friday Festival of the Jews.
Trapani: The Mysteries (*I Misteri*). Friday and Saturday recreation of the Passion. Mournful dirges but moving event.

May–July

Agrigento: 1st and 2nd Sundays in June. San Calogero harvest thanksgiving. Rolls shaped like saints are tossed at crowds.
Caltagirone: 24–25 July. *Festa di San Giacomo.* The 142 steps of Maria del Monte are covered in candles.
Palazzolo Acreide: 29 June. Festival of San Paolo.
Palermo: 10–15 July. *U Fistinu.* Mountain procession. Celebration of Santa Rosalia, the city's patron saint.
Messina: *La Varetta.* June procession with relics.
Siracusa: July festival of the sea.
Siracusa: First Sunday in May. Festival of Santa Lucia of the Quails (*delle quaglie*). Commemorating the miracle of 1646 when the city was saved from starvation by the arrival of quails (or wheat, depending which version you believe). A type of wheat porridge (*cuccia*) is eaten.
Taormina: End of May. Display of Sicilian carts and folklore.
Trecastagni: 12 May. Garlic fair and a religious festival; barefoot penitents.

August

Caccamo: 1–15 August. Historical castle pageant.
Gangi: 5th. *Festa della Spiga.* Floats, street parties and fireworks.
Messina: 14th. Parade of the Giants, the mythical city founders; followed by barefoot penitents.
Piazza Armerina: 13th–14th. *Palio dei Normanni.* Jousting tournament and processions in medieval costumes celebrates the victory of the Normans over the Arabs.
Ragusa: 29th. Festival of St John the Baptist.

September

Caccamo: *Lu Tirunfo di la Manna.* Festival celebrates manna.

Calascibetta: 1st–3rd. *Sagra di Buon Riposo,* a folk and food festival, with a livestock market, a race (*Corsa dei Berberi*) and much sausage eating.

Camastra: 9th. San Biagio. Blessing of the harvest. Costumes representing the four seasons. Blessing of candles; breaking of bread. Parade of floats.

Catania: 8th. Festival of Maria SS Bambina. Fisherman's festival with a procession of boats.

Palermo: 4th. Pilgrimage to the Grotto of Santa Rosalia, Palermo's patron saint, on Monte Pellegrino.

Tindari: 8th. Birth of the Virgin, a festival celebrated all over Sicily, especially on the coast.

October–December

Petralia Sottana. 6 October. *Sagra delle Castagne.* Celebrates chestnuts and other produce. Procession of floats.

Zafferana Etnea. All October. *Ottobrata Zafferanese.* Gastronomic feast celebrating local produce: grapes, mushrooms, mustard, honey and wine.

Ognissanti (All Saints Day). 1st November celebration everywhere. Presents given to the dead. A strong tradition in Palermo Province.

Il Giorno dei Morti (Day of the Dead). 2nd November visits to family graves at cemeteries or catacombs. Picnics.

Siracusa, 13 and 20 December, Festival of Santa Lucia, the city's patron saint. Bare foot procession and a borrowed Swedish girl, "Lucia of Sweden".

Natale (Christmas). Cribs (*presepi*) decorated in churches, particularly in Acireale, Palermo Province, Trapani and Ragusa.

Exhibitions & Fairs

January/February

Agrigento: Almond Fair; it runs January to March.

Agrigento: International Folklore Festival (February).

Palermo: Symphony Season continues, Teatro Politeama.

March/April

Catania: Etna Bicycle Race (April).

Catania: Drama, Classical and Jazz season continues.

Palermo: Drama, Opera and Classical season continues.

May

Caltanissetta: Livestock and Crafts Fair.

Catania: Sicilian Theatre in the World.

Palermo: Panormus Veteran Car Rally

Palermo: Trade Fair (held between May and June)

Siracusa and **Segesta:** Classical comedies and tragedies in the Greek theatres. The season runs from May to June. Held in Siracusa in even years and in Segesta in odd years.

Taormina: Folk festival and display of Sicilian carts.

June

Catania: *Musica Estate.* Concert, dance and theatre season lasts until October.

Erice: *Estate Ericina.* Summer season, including competitions for the most flowery courtyards.

Siracusa and **Segesta:** Classical comedies and tragedies in Greek theatres.

Taormina: June to mid-September. *Taormina Arte:* Festival of cinema, music, opera, ballet and theatre held in the Greek theatre.

July

Agrigento: *Settimana Pirandelliana.* A week celebrating Pirandello's plays in drama, film and academic debate.

Cefalù: *Estate Cefaludese.* Music and summer puppet shows for everyone.

Enna: *Estate Ennese.* Summer in Enna, including recitals and concerts in the city castle. Also the *Grand Prix del Mediterraneo* at Lake Pergusa.

Erice: Festival of Medieval Music, held in town churches.

Palermo: *Targa Florio,* International Sicily Rally.

Siracusa: Summer Season; opera, music and ballet.

Taormina: International Film Festival. A prestigious event that is popular and widely reported.

August

Agrigento: Persephone Festival.

Enna: *Estate Ennese.* Summer in Enna festival continues.

Segesta or **Siracusa:** Classical festival continues.

Siracusa: Summer Season continues, with music and ballet.

Taormina: *Taormina Arte* continues.

September

Catania: Bellini International Music Prize.

Millo: Table grapes and Etna Wine Fair.

Palermo: Sicily International Tennis Championships.

Taormina: the last month of *Taormina Arte* season.

October/November

Catania: Concert season starts in the Teatro Massimo Bellini.

Catania: Classical concert seasons of the "Associazione Musicale Etnea" and "Lyceum Club" start, run till June.

Catania: Jazz concert season of *Associazione Catania Jazz e del Brass* starts, runs till June.

Catania: Theatre season opens in the Teatro G. Verga, Teatro A. Musco and in the Metropolitan, Ambasciatori, Piccolo Teatro, and Nuovo Teatro.

Monreale: Sacred (organ) music in the Cathedral.

December

Caltagirone: Biennale of Sicilian Ceramics.

Palermo: *Fiera del Mediterraneo* (Trade Fair).

Palermo: Opera season (Teatro Massimo) begins and runs until May.

Zafferana Etnea: Award of the Brancati literature prize.

Sport

Participant Sports

Diving

Sicily's coasts are rich in flora and fauna. Both snorkelling and scuba diving are popular. The island of Ustica is the haunt of sub-aqua fans. Its coastline is protected and offers spectacular diving in deep water. There are the remains of a wreck visible in one place. The area around Isola Bella, Taormina, is popular with snorkellers. The Egadi islands, particularly Marettimo, are also a favourite with divers: crystal clear, deep water. Tanks can be filled on most islands, and several, including Ustica, also have decompression chambers.

Snorkelling can be enjoyed by anyone who can swim, and it is well worth mastering the art since along Sicily's coasts it gives instant access to an exciting and different world. It is particularly worthwhile on the rocky shorelines of the north and the islands.

Hiking

Walks range from peaceful coastal strolls through the nature reserve of Lo Zingaro on San Vito Lo Capo (Palermo Province) to hikes in the Nebrodi and Madonie mountains. Walks through Sicily's volcanic landscapes are ever-popular. In particular, the Aeolian Islands offer magnificent unspoilt coastal walks. The excitement of walking on Etna exerts an obvious pull. It is not wise to walk on Etna without a guide: please see *Excursions* information on guides, page 359. Etna Trekking (Via Roma 334, Linguaglossa, tel: 095-647592) is an agency that organises hikes. Call the information office in Linguaglossa, tel: 095 643094.

Riding

Riding is not really a traditional sport in Sicily: mules rather than horses have been used to carry loads across the mountains. Nevertheless, riding is catching on, and there are more and more stables available from which horses can be hired. Particularly in the Nebrodi and Madonie, trekking over longer distances has begun to gain in popularity. The following are some of the stables in Palermo province.

Balestrate: Fattoria Manostalla, C. da Manostalla, tel: 091-8787033.
Castelbuono: Ranch San Guglielmo, loc. San Guglielmo, tel: 092-71150.
Cefalù: Villagrande Ranch, C. da Vallegrande, tel: 0921-420286.
Gratteri: Fattoria Pianetti, C. da Pianetti, tel: 0921-421890.
Montelepre: Don Vito, Piano Aranci, tel: 091-8784111.

Skiing

Ski on black snow with a view of orange trees? Not quite. You would need a very strong telescope to see the orange trees, but they are there. Etna is frequently snow-capped all summer, and the skiing season normally runs from December to April. The snow really is black, at least in patches, where ash, dust and lava from minor eruptions have blown across it. In places, "hot" rocks, those which are still cooling, melt the snow and then stand out through it like lumps of coal.

The views really are spectacular, and perhaps there is an element of bravado in the idea of skiing on a live volcano. Caution: every now and then, Etna really does come to life again, and the skiing areas have to close because of danger from ash or lava flows.

Main Ski Resorts

Linguaglossa is on the northern side of Etna. Autobus della neve (snow bus) runs every Sunday between January and April from Piano Provenzano, organised by the Ferrovia Circumetnea (*see Excursions, page 359*). General information from the Pro Loco,

Piazza Annunziata, tel: 095-643094.
Nicolosi (Rifugio Sapienza) is on the southern side of Etna, above Zafferana Etnea. For information on the pistes, tel: 095-914141.

Swimming

It is not a problem to find somewhere to swim, whether in the sea, lakes or rivers. The smaller islands offer the cleanest and clearest water (*see Diving, abpve*). There may be plenty of sea but patches of it are severely polluted (the coasts around Augusta, Gela, Termini Imerese are nobody's choice). For detailed advice on the choicest swimming locations, *see Beaches, page 360*.

Windsurfing

Surf boards can be hired locally. The south coast is the best place for surfing because of the strong dry wind.

Spectator Sports

Cycling

The round Etna bicycle race is held in April. It is an interesting event to take part in, but perhaps more fun is to be standing on the sidelines watching and enjoying the scenery.

Motor Racing

If you like racing cars, then investigate Lago Pergusa at Enna. It does not hold Formula One, but events are normally held there at least once a month.

Shopping

Shopping Hours

Normal shopping hours during weekdays are 9am–1pm and 4–7.30pm. All shops except those selling food are normally also closed on Monday mornings. Food shops close on Wednesday afternoons. In many tourist resorts, the shops are open 7 days a week.

Where to Buy

For fashionable clothes, the best bets are Viale della Libertà in Palermo, Via Etnea in Catania and Corso Umberto in Taormina. Here you will find designer clothes from Valentino, Coveri, Gucci and Armani. For cheaper shopping try Via Maqueda (the continuation of Viale della Libertà) in Palermo and the side streets off Via Etnea in Catania.

For everyday items, the upmarket chain stores are Coin and Rinascente. Upim and Standa aim at the lower end of the market.

Markets

Markets make a change from the round of museums and churches. Observing what is sold and how gives some insight into the life of the less wealthy part of society, and also shows the riches of Sicily's soil.

Catania
Pescheria fish market, mornings only, in the Via Dusmet and Porta Uzeda quarter (watch your wallet).
Carlo Alberto market. Between Via Pacini, Piazza Stesicoro and Piazza Carlo Alberto. Fruit, vegetables and flea market.

Palermo
Vucciria Market, in and around Piazza Caracciolo, near the junction of Via Roma and Corso Vittorio Emanuele. Palermo's oldest market: fish, meat, vegetables and almost anything else. Beware of pickpockets. Daily from 8.30am.
Mercato del Capo, around Sant' Agostini, Beati Paoli and Via Porta Carini, behind Teatro Massimo. Second-hand clothes.
Mercato di Ballarò, Via Ballaro, just off Piazza del Carmine. Fruit and vegetables, together with a market selling fabrics and household goods.
Mercato dei Lattarini, Via Calderai, near La Martorana between Via Maqueda and Via Roma. Mixed household market.
Mercato di Via Sant' Agostino, Via Banderia. In a street which runs from Piazza San Domenico to Via Maqueda. Flea market and second-hand clothes.
Mercato delle Pulci, Piazza Peranni, near the Cathedral and behind the San Giacomo barracks. Antiques, junk, furniture, paintings and furnishings.

Taormina
Weekly market, Parcheggio Von Gloeden. Held every Wednesday 8am–12.30pm.

Antiques

Siracusa is renowned for its reproductions of Classical Greek coins. Palermo has a daily antiques market near the Cappucini Catacombs. There are some real treasures here, but also plenty of fakes and rubbish. A Sicilian saying has it that if you arrive here early enough in the morning you can buy back what was stolen from you the night before. The customs frown on exporting stolen goods, so be wary in your purchases. The market is unfortunately also a haunt of bag-snatchers, so guard your wallet in every possible sense.

Antique Shops
Catania: Bottega Antica, Via XX Settembre 50, tel: 095-501190.

Enna: L'Antiquario, Sant'Agata 100, tel: 0935-500377.
Palermo: Hera, Viale della Libertà 39, tel: 091-322280.

A number of shops around Corso Umberto sell a mixture of antiques and bric-a-brac. You will need some expertise to pick up anything but junk, but browsing is enjoyable.

Art

Most art galleries are concentrated in Catania, Palermo and Siracusa, with a sprinkling in Cefalù and Taormina.
Egadi Islands: Bottega d'Arte, Via Marzamemi 7, Favignana, tel: 0923-921696. Gianni Matto sells his naive fishing paintings from this workshop.

Bookshops

Books are one of Sicily's happier but lesser-known exports. Bookshops abound in Palermo, Catania and Siracusa. For second-hand books (including lavish books on art and history), try the Quattro Canti area in Palermo, especially the university quarter and Via Roma. Sellerio, one home-grown publisher, deserve support for their beautiful books on the island's culture, literature, history and art. Books are available from Libreria Sellerio di Sellerio Olivia, Via La Farina 10, Palermo, tel: 091-6254476. Novecento, another respected Palermitan publisher, is based at Via Siracusa 7/a, tel: 6256814.

Jewellery

Coral and gold jewellery is made and sold on the island. The best is from jewellers in Palermo, Catania or Taormina's main shopping areas. Fairly expensive craft jewellery is sold in Cefalù, in shops off Corso Ruggero. Cheaper coral pieces can be bought from tourist shops and stalls in resorts. Traditionally, Trapani was the centre for coral but although the fantastic coral in the city museum is local, the coral in the shops is imported.

Catania jewellers

Cartier, Corso Italia 67, tel: 095-376736.
Fallico, Via Etnea 250, tel: 095-312128.

Around Etna

Necklaces made from lava make a very interesting and novel present for friends back home. At various other volcanoes, sulphur crystals are sold as souvenirs. Jewellery is sold in Erice, along with other crafts, from woodwork to pottery.

Traditional Crafts

Pottery, puppets and papyrus represent the best of traditional Sicilian handicrafts. They make excellent gifts or souvenirs. Sadly, painted carts, Sicily's other great glory, are harder to transport home.

Lace & Embroidery

This is best bought from a tiny boutique in the interior, or from an old lady selling it from her home. Elsewhere, in the resorts, it tends to be over-priced and of poor quality.
Catania: Ricamificio Ionio, Viale A Alagona, 37, tel: 095-712 3970.
Palermo: S.A.R.A.M. Di Brancato Gandolfo, Viale Libertà, 230/b, tel: 091-6254152.

Santo Stefano Ceramics

Santo Stefano di Camastra comes into sight behind a jumble of crockery on the Messina–Palermo road. Tiers of dishes, soup tureens and fruit bowls rise at ever increasing heights on each bend in the road, while cracked platters along the hard shoulder testify to cars that have come a cropper among the cauldrons and cake stands.

High quality local clay, an excellent position, good workmanship and beautiful pottery have ensured the town's fame. Styles are very mixed but the authentic ware has a rustic look and feel and favour fish designs. Look out, too, for lovely wall tiles decorated with smiling suns and local saints.

Caltagirone Ceramics

Caltagirone ceramics have always been famous for their instantly recognisable animal and floral designs in sky blue and copper green with touches of yellow. Look out for the tall alberelli, jars with nipped-in waists once used for storing dry drugs. Also consider acquiring painted tiles, sturdy vases, chunky little stoups and indefinable groups of figurines.

Some of the newer and more individualistic styles are also highly attractive. If you can manage to carry the weight, pottery is an ideal gift to take home. In Palermo, buy from De Simone, Via Stabile 133. In Monreale buy from Elisa Messina, Piazza Guglielmo A. Belvedere.

Painted Carts

Models of traditional Sicilian carts can now be found all over the island, but especially in Bagheria and Palermo province generally. In Aci Sant'Antonio (Catania Province) craftsmen make carts to commission. (The finest are in the local museum.) If you are lucky, you may pick up a painted panel of a cart in a Palermo antique shop but expect to pay a fortune for such painstaking craft work.

Pottery

Pottery, one of Sicily's glories, has been around for a long time. When Agatocles, Tyrant of Siracusa, was asked in 3rd century BC why he preferred earthenware crockery in his dining halls, he replied that he was "born of a father potter". Kilns from the period have been found around Gela, Siracusa and Catania as well as on Mozia. A Graeco-Roman kiln has survived at Morgantina, complete with brick cladding and double firing door.

When the Arabs arrived in Sicily in 827, they introduced the glazing techniques used in Persia, Syria and Egypt. Tin-glazed pottery or majolica, appeared in the Trapani area in 1309. An example of this type of Palermitan tiled floor is visible (with difficulty) in the

Papyrus Paper

This is a traditional craft centred around Siracusa, made from the papyrus which has been grown since Classical times. To see the plant in its natural habitat, visit Fonte Aretusa spring on Ortygia or the river Ciane just outside Siracusa. Stalls and shops all over the city sell inexpensive examples. These range from copies of Egyptian designs to portraits of your family while you wait.

The Centro Paparius (Papyrus Institute) on Viale Teocrito (near the San Giovanni catacombs) also gives demonstrations of how the crafted paper is made. For more information tel: 22100.

Rugs

Erice has a tradition of hand-woven rugs which can be bought in many of the shops there.

Straw & Cane

Monreale produces traditional straw and cane goods which can be bought directly from the artisans.

Puppets (Pupi)

Puppetry's main traditions are in Palermo and some of the best models are still made there.

church of San Benedetto in Caccamo. The 1693 earthquake destroyed much of eastern Sicily as well as razing the ceramics workshops of Caltagirone to the ground. As market demands still had to be satisfied, quality gave way to quantity.

At the end of the 19th century the market, led by the Bourbons, became flooded with imported Neapolitan wares. To stem the flow, a pottery factory was set up in San Stefano di Camastra. This was so successful that the town has since become the best-known ceramics centre in Sicily. The local college produces designers and craftsman by the family; indeed, half the town is now involved in the pottery business.

Last of the puppet makers
Vincenzo Argento, Corso Vittorio Emanuele 445, Palermo, tel: 091-611 3680, ends a 160 year-old family tradition. He will make you a *paladino* (paladin or knight) to order in his tiny workshop. After carving the wooden body, he solders on the copper armour and creates the costume with the help of his wife. Open 7.30am–8pm

In Taormina, **Francesco and Sabatino del Popolo Lampuri**, Via Luigi Pirandello, 51, tel: 0942-626043. The shop sells inexpensive puppets, with finishing touches added by the family.

Language

Conversation

The language spoken is Italian, supplemented by Sicilian dialects. Dialects may differ enormously within a few villages, and are an essential part of Sicilian culture. A few examples of Sicilian dialect:

Sicilian	Italian	English
Viene ca	Vieni qui	Come here
iddu	lui	him
idda	lei	her
cane	qui	here
dane	la	there

In large cities and tourist centres you will find many people who speak English, French or German. In fact, due to the massive emigration over the last 100 years, you may encounter fluent speakers of these languages, often with a New York, Melbourne, Brussels or Bavarian accent. Its owner may have spent years working abroad.

One dialect with a difference is that of Piana degli Albanesi in Palermo province: here Albanian is spoken. The population is descended from Albanians who arrived in the 15th century.

Sicilians are deeply hospitable. You will certainly manage without Italian, but learning a little will enhance your enjoyment enormously.

Pronunciation is claimed by all Italians to be simple: you pronounce as you read. This is approximately true. A couple of important rules for English speakers: **c** before **e** or **i** is pronounced **ch** e.g. ciao, mi dispiace, la coincidenza. **Ch** before **i** or **e** is pronounced as **k** e.g. la chiesa.

Nouns are either masculine (**il**, plural **i**) or feminine (**la**, plural **le**).

Plurals of nouns are most often formed by changing an **o** to an **i** and an **a** to an **e** e.g. *il panino*: *i panini*; *la chiesa*: *le chiese*.

There is, of course, rather more to the language than that, but you can get a surprisingly long way in making friends with a mastery of a few basic phrases.

It is worth buying a good phrase book or dictionary, but the following basics will help you get started.

Questions & Answers

I'd like .../*Vorrei ...*
I'd like that one, please./*Vorrei quello lì, per favore*
Is there ...?/*C'è (un) ...?*
Do you have ...?/*Avete ...?*
Yes, of course./*Si, certo*
No, we don't./*No, non c'è*
(Also used to mean: s/he is not here)

Basics

Hello (Good day)/*Buon giorno*
Good evening/*Buona sera*
Good night/*Buona notte*
Goodbye/*Arrivederci*
Hi/Goodbye (familiar)/*Ciao*
Yes/*Sì*
No/*No*
Thank you/*Grazie*
You're welcome/*Prego*
Alright, OK/*Va bene*
Please/*Per favore or per piacere*
Excuse me (get attention)/*Scusi* (singular)/*Scusate* (plural)
Excuse me (in a crowd)/*Permesso*
Can you show me/*Puo indicarmi...?*
Can you help me/*Puo aiutarmi, per piacere?*
I'm lost/*Mi sono perso*
Sorry/*Mi dispiace*
I don't understand/*Non capisco*
I am English/American/*Sono inglese/americano*
Irish/Canadian/*irlandese/canadese*
Do you speak English?/*Parla inglese?*
Le piace la Sicilia?/Do you like Sicily? (Question asked by all new acquaintances.)
Mi piace moltissimo/I love it (correct answer).
E`meravigliosa/It's wonderful.

E`avolosa: the alternative answer when asked what you think of Sicily: it's wonderful.
Both of these last phrases can equally be applied to food, beaches, the view etc.

Practical Necessities

Where is the lavatory?/*Dov'è il bagno?*
Gentlemen/*Signori/Uomini*
Ladies/*Signore/Donne*

Transport

airport/*l'aeroporto*
aeroplane/*l'aereo*
arrivals/*arrivi*
boat/*la barca*
bus/*il autobus*
bus station/*autostazione*
connection/*la coincidenza*
departures/*le partenze*
ferry/*il traghetto*
ferry terminal/*stazione marittima*
flight/*il volo*
hydrofoil/*l'aliscafo*
left luggage/*il deposito bagagli*
No smoking/*vietato fumare*
platform/*il binario*
port/*il porto*
railway station/*stazione ferrovia*
return ticket/*un biglietto di andata e ritorno*
single ticket/*un biglietto di andata sola*
sleeping car/*la carrozza letti*
station/*la stazione*
stop/*la fermata*
taxi/*il taxi*
train/*il treno*
What time does the train leave?
Quando parte il treno?
What time does the train arrive?
Quando arriva il treno?
What time does the bus leave for Monreale?/*Quando parte l'autobus per Monreale?*
How long will it take to get there?
Quanto tempo ci vuole per arrivare?
You need to change at Palermo.
Bisogna cambiare a Palermo
Can you tell me when to get off?
Mi può dire scendere alla fermata giusta?
The train is late/*Il treno è in ritardo*

Directions

right/*a destra*
left/*a sinistra*
straight on/*sempre diritto*
far away/*lontano*
nearby/*vicino*
opposite/*di fronte*
next to/*accanto a*
traffic lights/*il semaforo*
junction/*l'incrocio, il bivio*
building/*il palazzo*
Turn left/*Gira a sinistra*
Where is ...?/*Dov'è ...?*
Where are ...?/*Dove sono...?*
Where is the nearest bank/petrol station/bus stop/hotel/garage?
Dov'è la banca/il benzinaio/la fermata di autobus/ l'albergo/ l'officina più vicino?
Can you show me where I am on the map?
Può indicarmi sulla cartina dove mi trovo?
How do I get there?/*Come si può andare?*
You're on the wrong road/*E sulla strada sbagliata*

Road Signs

Alt/Stop
Attenzione/Caution
Caduta massi/Danger of falling rocks
Deviazione/Deviation
Divieto di campeggio/No camping allowed
Divieto di passaggio/No entry
Divieto di sosta/Sosta vietata
No parking
Galleria/Tunnel
Incrocio/Crossroads
Limite di velocità/Speed limit
Passaggio a livello/Railway crossing
Parcheggio/Parking
Pericolo/Danger
Pericolo di incendio/Danger of fire
Rallentare/Slow down
Rimozione forzata/Parked cars will be towed away
Semaforo/Traffic lights
Senso unico/One way street
Sentiero/Footpath
Strada interrotta/Road blocked
Strada senza uscita/Dead end
Vietato il sorpasso/No overtaking

Numbers

1	*Uno*
2	*Due*
3	*Tre*
4	*Quattro*
5	*Cinque*
6	*Sei*
7	*Sette*
8	*Otto*
9	*Nove*
10	*Dieci*
11	*Undici*
12	*Dodici*
13	*Tredici*
14	*Quattordici*
15	*Quindici*
16	*Sedici*
17	*Diciassette*
18	*Diciotto*
19	*Diciannove*
20	*Venti*
30	*Trenta*
40	*Quaranta*
50	*Cinquanta*
60	*Sessanta*
70	*Settanta*
80	*Ottanta*
90	*Novanta*
100	*Cento*
1,000	*Mille*
Million	*Milione*

Shopping

How much does it cost?/*Quanto costa?*
(half) a kilo/*un (mezzo) kilo*
100 grams/*un etto*
200 grams/*due etti*
a little/*un pochino*
Give me some of those/*Mi dia alcuni di quelli lì*
That's enough/*Basta cosi*
That's too expensive/*E troppo caro*
It's too small/*E troppo piccolo*
It's too big/*E troppo grande*
I like it/*Mi piace*
I don't like it/*Non mi piace*
I'll take it/*Lo prendo*

Hotel

I'd like/*Vorrei*
a single/double room/*una camera singola/doppia (matrimoniale)*
with bath/shower/*con bagno/doccia*
for one night/*per una notte*

How much is it?/*Quanto costa?*
Is breakfast included?/*E compresa la colazione?*
half/full board/*mezza pensione/pensione completa*
key/*la chiave*
towel/*un asciugamano*
toilet paper/*la carta igienica*
Do you have a room with a balcony/view of the sea?
C'è una camera con balcone/una vista del mare?
Can I see the room?/*Posso vedere la camera?*
Is it a quiet room?/*E una stanza tranquilla?*
We have one with a double bed
Ne abbiamo una matrimoniale
Can I have the bill, please?
Posso avere il conto, per favore?

Bar Snacks & Drinks

For specialities and menu *see Eating Out, page 338.*

coffee/*un caffè*
espresso (small, strong and black);
un cappuccino (with hot, frothy milk); *un corretto* (with alcohol)
tea/*un thè*
lemon tea/*un thè con limone*
fresh orange/*una spremuta di arancia*
lemon juice/*una spremuta di limone*
(mineral) water/*acqua (minerale)*
ice/*ghiaccio*
red/white wine/*vino rosso/bianco*
beer/*una birra*
milk/*latte*
bottle/*una bottiglia*
ice-cream/*un gelato*
cone/*un cono*
pastry/*una pasta*
sandwich/*un tramezzino*

Bar Notices

Prezzo in terrazza
Terrace price, often double what you pay standing at the bar
Si prende lo scontrino alla cassa
Pay at the cash desk, then take the receipt to the bar to be served

Finding the Sights

Custode/Custodian
Sacristano/Sacristan
Suonare il campanello/Ring the bell
Abbazia/Abbey
Aperto/Open
Chiuso/Closed
Chiesa/Church
Entrata/Entrance
Monastero/Monastery
Museo/Museum
Ruderi/Ruins
Scavi/Excavations/archaeological site
Spiaggia/Beach
Tempio/Temple

Is it possible to see the church?
E possibile visitare la chiesa?
Where can I find the custodian/sacristan/key?
Dovè posso trovare il custode/il sacristano/la chiave?
We have come a long way just to see ...
Siamo venuti da lontano proprio per visitare ...
It is really a pity it is closed
E veramente peccato che sia chiuso
(The last two should be tried if entry seems a problem!)

Further Reading

Literature

Bufalino, Gesualdo. **Argo il Cieco (Blind Argus)** Sellerio, Palermo. **Blind Argus** and **Night's Lies**. Harvill.
Cardella, Lara. **Volevo i Pantaloni**. Mondadori. A bizarre account of a young girl's struggles with rural prejudice.
Consolo, Vincenzo. **Le Pietre di Pantalica**.
Gilmour, David. **The Last Leopard: A Life of Giuseppe di Lampedusa**. Quartet.
Lawrence D.H. **Sicilian Carousel**.
Maraini, Dacia. **Bagheria and The Silent Duchess**.
Pirandello, Luigi. **Six Characters in Search of an Author**. Methuen.
Renault, Mary. **The Mask of Apollo**. A novel set in ancient Siracusa.
Sciascia, Leonardo. **Sicilian Uncles**. Carcanet.
Sciascia, Leonardo. **The Wine-Dark Sea**. Paladin.
Sciascia, Leonardo. **The Day of the Owl**. Paladin.
Sciascia, Leonardo. **La Sicilia Come Metafora**. Saggi.
Tomasi di Lampedusa, Giuseppe. **The Leopard**. Collins.
Verga, Giovanni. **I Malavoglia, House by the Medlar Tree**. Dedalus.
Vittorini, Elio. **Conversation in Sicily**. Quartet.

History & Culture

Barzini, Luigi. **The Italians**. Penguin.
Bonomo, Giuseppe. **Pitrè la Sicilia e i Siciliani**. Sellerio, Palermo. Academic study of Sicilian folklore.
Buttitta, Antonino. **Easter in Sicily**. Sicilian Tourist Service, Palermo. An introduction to Sicilian festivals.
Finley and Mack Smith. **History of Sicily**. Chatto and Windus. The best overall Sicilian history.
Marks, Gay. **Le Mie Isole**. Edizioni

La Ziza, Palermo. Personal account.
Muccioli, Nino. **Leggende e Racconti Popolari della Sicilia**. Newton Compton, Rome. Legends and festivals.
Norwich, John Julius. **Kingdom in the South**. The Norman period (out of print, available through libraries).
Regione Sicilia. **Archaeology in Sicily**. D'Agostini, Italy.

Crime & Society

Arlacchi, Pino. **Gli Uomini del Disonore**. Mondadori. An account of the Mafia through the eyes of Antonino Calderone, a recent *pentito* from Catania.
Blok, Anton. **The Mafia of a Sicilian Village**. Harper and Row.
Dolci, Danilo. **Sicilian Lives**. Writers and Readers.
Falcone, Giovanni. **Cose di Cose Nostra**. Rizzoli, Italy (published as **Men of Honour** in English.) Judge Falcone's testament.
Haycraft, John. **Italian Labyrinth, Italy in the 80s**. It includes sections on the church, corruption and Mafia.
Lewis, Norman. **The Honoured Society**. Eland Press. A colourful if exaggerated account of the wartime Mafia.
Lodato, Saverio. **Potenti**. Garzanti, Italy. An analysis of the Mafia's curent support within Sicily's institutions.
Maxwell, Gavin. **Ten Pains of Death**. Alan Sutton. An account of the people the author met while living in Scopello in the 1950s.
Maxwell, Gavin. **God Protect me from my Friends** (out of print but available through libraries). A biography of the legendary bandit, Salvatore Guiliano.
Puzo, Mario. **The Godfather**. Pan (UK) or Putnam (US).
Puzo, Mario. **The Sicilian**. Bantam Books.
Servadio, Gaia. **To a Different World**. Hamish Hamilton.
Shawcross, Tim and Young, Martin. **Mafia Wars**. The Sicilian and US Mafia's role in the drug trade.
Sterling, Clare. **The Mafia**. Grafton. An excellent analysis of the Mafia, particularly the "Pizza Connection".

Travel & General

Bellafiore, Giuseppe. **Palermo**. Bess, Palermo.
Cronin, Vincent. **The Golden Honeycomb**. Granada.
Duncan, Paul. **Sicily**. John Murray.
Fava, Giuseppe. **I Siciliani**. Cappelli Editore.
Fernandez, Dominique. **Le Radeau de la Gorgone**. Grasset, France. Personal account of architecture and people.
Goethe, J.W. **Italian Journey 1786–1788**. Penguin, London.
Maupassant, Guy de. **Voyage en Sicile**. Edrisi, Palermo.
Pitt-Kethley, Fiona. **Journeys to the Underworld**. Abacus. Bawdy and patchily funny account of her island adventures.
Simeti, Mary Taylor. **On Persephone's Island**. Penguin.
Simeti, Mary Taylor. **Sicilian Food**. Random Century (first published as *Pomp and Sustenance*).

Other Insight Guides

There are some two dozen titles in Apa's Italy series. *Insight Guides* include titles on Italy, Naples, Corsica, Sardinia, Rome, Venice, Tuscany and Umbria. *Insight Pocket Guides*, take the short-stay traveller to Rome, Florence, Milan, Venice and Tuscany. *Insight Compact Guides*, mini encyclopedias, feature Florence, Rome, Venice, Tuscany, Milan, the Italian Riviera and the Italian Lakes.

ART & PHOTO CREDITS

All photography by
Lyle Lawson except:

Magnum 93, 94, 95

Maps Berndtson and Berndtson
© 1999 Apa Publications GmbH & Co.
Verlag KG (Singapore branch)

Index

The Insight Approach

The book you are holding is part of the world's largest range of guidebooks. Its purpose is to help you have the most valuable travel experience possible, and we try to achieve this by providing not only information about countries, regions and cities but also genuine insight into their history, culture, institutions and people.

Since the first Insight Guide – to Bali – was published in 1970, the series has been dedicated to the proposition that, with insight into a country's people and culture, visitors can both enhance their own experience and be accepted more easily by their hosts. Now, in a world where ethnic hostilities and nationalist conflicts are all too common, such attempts to increase understanding between peoples are more important than ever.

Insight Guides:
Essentials for understanding

Because a nation's past holds the key to its present, each Insight Guide kicks off with lively history chapters. These are followed by magazine-style essays on culture and daily life. This essential background information gives readers the necessary context for using the main Places section, with its comprehensive run-down on things worth seeing and doing.

Finally, a listings section contains all the information you'll need on travel, hotels, restaurants and opening times.

As far as possible, we rely on local writers and specialists to ensure that information is authoritative. The pictures, for which Insight Guides have become so celebrated, are just as important. Our photojournalistic approach aims not only to illustrate a destination but also to communicate visually and directly to readers life as it is lived by the locals. The series has grown to almost 200 titles.

Compact Guides:
The "great little guides"

As invaluable as such background information is, it isn't always fun to carry an Insight Guide through a crowded souk or up a church tower. Could we, readers asked, distil the key reference material into a slim volume for on-the-spot use?

Our response was to design Compact Guides as an entirely new series, with original text carefully cross-referenced to detailed maps and more than 200 photographs. In essence, they're miniature encyclopedias, concise and comprehensive, displaying reliable and up-to-date information in an accessible way. There are almost 100 titles.

Pocket Guides:
A local host in book form

However wide-ranging the information in a book, human beings still value the personal touch. Our editors are often asked the same questions. Where do *you* go to eat? What do *you* think is the best beach? What would *you* recommend if I have only three days? We invited our local correspondents to act as "substitute hosts" by revealing their preferred walks and trips, listing the restaurants they go to and structuring a visit into a series of timed itineraries.

The result: our Pocket Guides, complete with full-size fold-out maps. These 100-plus titles help readers plan a trip precisely, particularly if their time is short.

Exploring with Insight:
A valuable travel experience

In conjunction with co-publishers all over the world, we print in up to 10 languages, from German to Chinese, from Danish to Russian. But our aim remains simple: to enhance your travel experience by combining our expertise in guidebook publishing with the on-the-spot knowledge of our correspondents.

" I was first drawn to the Insight Guides by the excellent "Nepal" volume. I can think of no book which so effectively captures the essence of a country. Out of these pages leaped the Nepal I know – the captivating charm of a people and their culture. I've since discovered and enjoyed the entire Insight Guide series. Each volume deals with a country in the same sensitive depth, which is nowhere more evident than in the superb photography. "

Sir Edmund Hillary

The World of Insight Guides

400 books in three complementary series cover every major destination in every continent.

Insight Guides

Alaska
Alsace
Amazon Wildlife
American Southwest
Amsterdam
Argentina
Atlanta
Athens
Australia
Austria
Bahamas
Bali
Baltic States
Bangkok
Barbados
Barcelona
Bay of Naples
Beijing
Belgium
Belize
Berlin
Bermuda
Boston
Brazil
Brittany
Brussels
Budapest
Buenos Aires
Burgundy
Burma (Myanmar)
Cairo
Calcutta
California
Canada
Caribbean
Catalonia
Channel Islands
Chicago
Chile
China
Cologne
Continental Europe
Corsica
Costa Rica
Crete
Crossing America
Cuba
Cyprus
Czech & Slovak Republics
Delhi, Jaipur, Agra
Denmark
Dresden
Dublin
Düsseldorf
East African Wildlife
East Asia
Eastern Europe
Ecuador
Edinburgh
Egypt
Finland
Florence
Florida
France
Frankfurt
French Riviera
Gambia & Senegal
Germany
Glasgow

Gran Canaria
Great Barrier Reef
Great Britain
Greece
Greek Islands
Hamburg
Hawaii
Hong Kong
Hungary
Iceland
India
India's Western Himalaya
Indian Wildlife
Indonesia
Ireland
Israel
Istanbul
Italy
Jamaica
Japan
Java
Jerusalem
Jordan
Kathmandu
Kenya
Korea
Lisbon
Loire Valley
London
Los Angeles
Madeira
Madrid
Malaysia
Mallorca & Ibiza
Malta
Marine Life in the South
    China Sea
Melbourne
Mexico
Mexico City
Miami
Montreal
Morocco
Moscow
Munich
Namibia
Native America
Nepal
Netherlands
New England
New Orleans
New York City
New York State
New Zealand
Nile
Normandy
Northern California
Northern Spain
Norway
Oman & the UAE
Oxford
Old South
Pacific Northwest
Pakistan
Paris
Peru
Philadelphia
Philippines
Poland
Portugal
Prague

Provence
Puerto Rico
Rajasthan
Rhine
Rio de Janeiro
Rockies
Rome
Russia
St Petersburg
San Francisco
Sardinia
Scotland
Seattle
Sicily
Singapore
South Africa
South America
South Asia
South India
South Tyrol
Southeast Asia
Southeast Asia Wildlife
Southern California
Southern Spain
Spain
Sri Lanka
Sweden
Switzerland
Sydney
Taiwan
Tenerife
Texas
Thailand
Tokyo
Trinidad & Tobago
Tunisia
Turkey
Turkish Coast
Tuscany
Umbria
US National Parks East
US National Parks West
Vancouver
Venezuela
Venice
Vietnam
Wales
Washington DC
Waterways of Europe
Wild West
Yemen

Bermuda★
Bhutan★
Boston★
British Columbia★
Brittany★
Brussels★
Budapest &
    Surroundings★
Canton★
Chiang Mai★
Chicago★
Corsica★
Costa Blanca★
Costa Brava★
Costa del Sol/Marbella★
Costa Rica★
Crete★
Denmark★
Fiji★
Florence★
Florida★
Florida Keys★
French Riviera★
Gran Canaria★
Hawaii★
Hong Kong★
Hungary
Ibiza★
Ireland★
Ireland's Southwest★
Israel★
Istanbul★
Jakarta★
Jamaica★
Kathmandu Bikes &
    Hikes★
Kenya★
Kuala Lumpur★
Lisbon★
Loire Valley★
London★
Macau
Madrid★
Malacca
Maldives
Mallorca★
Malta★
Mexico City★
Miami★
Milan★
Montreal★
Morocco★
Moscow
Munich★
Nepal★
New Delhi
New Orleans★
New York City★
New Zealand★
Northern California★
Oslo/Bergen★
Paris★
Penang★
Phuket★
Prague★
Provence★
Puerto Rico★
Quebec★
Rhodes★
Rome★
Sabah★

St Petersburg★
San Francisco★
Sardinia
Scotland★
Seville★
Seychelles★
Sicily★
Sikkim
Singapore★
Southeast England
Southern California★
Southern Spain★
Sri Lanka★
Sydney★
Tenerife★
Thailand★
Tibet★
Toronto★
Tunisia★
Turkish Coast★
Tuscany★
Venice★
Vienna★
Vietnam★
Yogyakarta
Yucatan Peninsula★

★ = Insight Pocket Guides
with Pull out Maps

Insight Compact Guides

Algarve
Amsterdam
Bahamas
Bali
Bangkok
Barbados
Barcelona
Beijing
Belgium
Berlin
Brittany
Brussels
Budapest
Burgundy
Copenhagen
Costa Brava
Costa Rica
Crete
Cyprus
Czech Republic
Denmark
Dominican Republic
Dublin
Egypt
Finland
Florence
Gran Canaria
Greece
Holland
Hong Kong
Ireland
Israel
Italian Lakes
Italian Riviera
Jamaica
Jerusalem
Lisbon
Madeira
Mallorca
Malta

Milan
Moscow
Munich
Normandy
Norway
Paris
Poland
Portugal
Prague
Provence
Rhodes
Rome
St Petersburg
Salzburg
Singapore
Switzerland
Sydney
Tenerife
Thailand
Turkey
Turkish Coast
Tuscany
UK regional titles:
    Bath & Surroundings
    Cambridge & East
        Anglia
    Cornwall
    Cotswolds
    Devon & Exmoor
    Edinburgh
    Lake District
    London
    New Forest
    North York Moors
    Northumbria
    Oxford
    Peak District
    Scotland
    Scottish Highlands
    Shakespeare Country
    Snowdonia
    South Downs
    York
    Yorkshire Dales
USA regional titles:
    Boston
    Cape Cod
    Chicago
    Florida
    Florida Keys
    Hawaii: Maui
    Hawaii: Oahu
    Las Vegas
    Los Angeles
    Martha's Vineyard &
        Nantucket
    New York
    San Francisco
    Washington D.C.
    Venice
    Vienna
    West of Ireland